MINORITIES' CLAIMS: FROM AUTONOMY TO SECESSION

Minorities' Claims: From Autonomy to Secession

International law and state practice

GNANAPALA WELHENGAMA

Ashgate

Aldershot • Burlington USA • Singapore • Sydney

Published by
Ashgate Publishing Limited
Gower House
Croft Road
Aldershot
Hampshire GU11 3HR
England

Ashgate Publishing Company
131 Main Street
Burlington
Vermont 05401
USA

Ashgate website: http://www.ashgate.com

British Library Cataloguing in Publication Data
Welhengama, Gnanapala
 Minorities' claims : from autonomy to secession :
 international law and state practice. - (Interdisciplinary
 research series in ethnic, gender and class relations)
 1.Minorities - Legal status, laws, etc. 2.Autonomy
 3.Secession
 I. Title
 341.4'81

Library of Congress Control Number: 00-132638

ISBN 0 7546 1077 2 ✓

Printed and bound by Athenaeum Press, Ltd.,
Gateshead, Tyne & Wear.

Contents

Acknowledgements   xi
Abbreviations   xiii
List of Cases   xvi
List of Statutes and Constitutions   xix
List of Conventions, Treaties and Declarations   xxi
Preface   xxiv
Series Editor's Preface   xxvi
Foreword by Richard Jones   xxviii

1   *Claims From Autonomy to Secession: Introduction*

1.1   Objectives   1
1.2   Minorities?: "Cat Owners and Bald Peoples   2
      do not Fit the Standard Picture of Minority
      Groups"?

The Minority Issue and Ethnic Conflicts

1.3   The Minority Issue and the League of Nations: 3
      "It Drags Out All Our Dirty Linen and Washes
      it Publicly"
1.4   The Minority Issue and the UN: "If the Peoples   10
      of the Earth Are Fighting and Dying to Preserve and
      to Secure the Liberty of Individuals Under the
      Law..."
1.5   Beyond Traditionally Identified Limited   23
      Rights
1.6   Conflict Scenario: Being Caught Up In a Wasp's   25
      Nest
1.7   The UN's Concerns: "Conflicts Within States Are   29
      Proving as Bloody as Conflicts Between States in
      the Past"
1.8   Ethnic Conflicts and Ethnic Cleansing   31

2   *Minorities?*

        Introduction   46
2.1   The Dilemma of Defining *'Minority'*: "Controversial   47
        and, as yet, Unfruitful"
2.2   Reluctance: "In Law All Definitions are   51
        Dangerous"?
2.3   States' Attitudes: "The Game is Not Worth the   57
        Candle"
2.4   European Response   60
2.5   From Racial Minorities to National Minorities?   63
        Conclusion   67

3   *Peoples, All Peoples, Nations and Minorities*

        Introduction   76
3.1   Peoples and Nations' Right to Self-Determination: 77
        Who are the Right Holders?
3.2   No Ethnic Connotations Were Meant in the   80
        Charter by 'Peoples' and 'All Peoples'
3.3   'All Peoples' Instead of 'Peoples' and 'Nations'   83
        in the Covenants
3.4   Peoples in the 'Declaration on Friendly Relations'   86
        (GA Res. 2625 (xxv) 1970)
        Conclusion   89

4   *Claims for Autonomy With Shared-Sovereignty*

        Introduction   96
4.1   Autonomy   97
4.2   Autonomy Means Self-government?   100
4.3   Categories of Autonomous Models   102
4.4   Variations of Autonomous Models: "From a   106
        Classic Federation to Various Forms of Cultural
        Home Rule"
4.5   Autonomy with 'Shared' or 'Divided Sovereignty'   108
4.6   Autonomy Within a Federal Structure   112

4.7	Autonomy is Non-derogable?	114
	Conclusion	117

5   *Claims For Autonomy Through the Right to Self-determination?*

	Introduction	125
5.1	Autonomy as a Part of Self-determination?	125
5.2	The Right to Autonomy Under International Law: "Artificial Concept of Dubious Legal Consequence"?	132
5.3	Indigenous Peoples' Right to Autonomy: "We are not Looking to Dismember Your States and You Know It"	134
5.4	Maximum Right: "Only Self-Government Through Internal Self-determination"?	140
5.5	Human Rights Committee and the Claim of the Right to Self-determination by Indigenous Peoples: "Article 1 (ICCPR) Is Our Goal, Our Vision"	145
5.5.1	AD, The Grand Captain of Mikmaq Tribal Society v Canada	146
5.5.2	Bernard Ominayak, Chief of the Lubicon Lake Band v Canada	147
5.5.3	Ivan Kitok v Sweden	149
	Conclusion	150

6   *Models of Autonomy and Movements for Autonomy*

	Introduction	159
6.1	Autonomy as a Strategy: "First Equality, Then to Priority and in Extreme Cases to Exclusivity"?	161
6.2	Reasons Behind the Emergence of Movements for Autonomy	165
6.3	Self-government through Autonomy Depends on the Good Will of the Empowering State?	167
	Conclusion	171

7   *Claims for Autonomy: The Concerns of States*

       Introduction   179
7.1   Autonomy for Minorities: "An Entrance on a   180
       Dangerous Path Leading Towards Secession"?
7.2   Claims for Autonomy: Endless Process?   183
7.3   Attitudes of the States: "Technically Difficult   185
       or Politically Sensitive or Both"
7.4   Developments in Europe: "Like Throwing a Bone   192
       to the Yapping Dogs"?
7.5   Indigenous Peoples and Autonomy: "They are   195
       Assumed to Remain Within Existing Sovereign States"?
7.6   Future Directions?   198

8   *Secessionist Movements*

       Introduction   206
8.1   Ethnic Revivalism as a Prelude to Secession   206
8.2   The Post-modern Tribal-state Scenario   207
8.3   Separatism, Irredentism and Secession   212
8.3.1 Irredentism   212
8.3.2 Secession   214
8.4   Secession: "Pregnant With Such Unutterable   216
       Calamities"?
8.5   The Ubiquitous Nature of Secessionist   220
       Movements: "Locked in a Life-or-Death Struggle"?

9   *The Right to Secession: The Views of Jurists*

       Introduction   231
9.1   Self-determination? : "For Which Poets Have   233
       Sung and Patriots Have Laid Down Their Lives"
9.2   Emergence From a Principle to a Legal Right   235
       "With all its Contradictory, Subversive and
       Threatening Nature"
9.3   The Right to Secession: "An Ultimate Remedy   236
       for Trapped Minorities"?
9.4   Qualified or Limited Right to Secession?   241

9.5   Secession by Consensus?   243
9.6   "Recognition of Secession Will Inaugurate   244
       Anarchy in International Life"?
       Conclusions   247

10   *The Right to Secession: International Law*
       and UN Practice

       Introduction   255
10.1   There is no Right to Secession Explicitly or   257
       Implicitly in the UN Charter
10.2   A Right to Secession is not in the   259
       Colonial Declaration: "If Care is not Taken, the
       Other Very Important Principle, the Territorial
       Integrity of the State Will be in Jeopardy"
10.3   A Right to Secession is Not in the Declaration   262
       on Friendly Relations (GA Res. 2625, 24 October 1970)
10.4   Can the Legitimacy of Secession be Discerned   265
       in Paragraph 7 of the Declaration on Friendly
       Relations?
10.5   There is No Right to Secession Explicitly or   268
       Implicitly Provided For in Article 27 of the ICCPR
10.6   The UN Declaration on Minorities Does Not   272
       Explicitly or Implicitly Provide for a Right to
       Secession
10.7   "Frontiers Can Only be Changed by Peaceful   273
       Means and by Common Agreements"
10.8   European Concerns: "Secessionist Activities   275
       Bring Shame, Bloodshed and Suffering to Our Continent"
10.9   From the Helsinki Final Act to the Badinter   277
       Committee: "Any Right to Engage in Activity or
       Perform any Action in Contravention of the
       Purposes and Principles of…"
       Conclusions   280

11   *Secessionist Attempts: Case Studies*

       Introduction   289

11.1	Katanga 1960-1963: "The UN's First Face-to-Face Confrontation with the Spectre of Secession"?	289
11.2	Biafra 1967-1970	290
11.3	Bangladesh, 1971: Self-determination through Gun-Barrels?	291
11.4	The Republic of Kosovo?	293
11.5	An Independent Republika Srpska Krajina and Republika Srpska of Bosnian Serbs	297
11.6	Nagorny Karabakh	299
11.7	Abkhazian Secession: "Secessionist Goals Through Sophistries and the Rape of International Law"?	299
11.8	Secessionist Struggles in Chechnya, Tartastan, Tajikistan and Cyprus	300
	Conclusion	302

12 *The Right to Secession Through the Right to Self-determination? Attitudes of States*

	Introduction	308
12.1	The Right to Self-determination Does not Entail a Right to Secession	313
12.2	Secession is Illegal, and it is Not a Positive Rule in International Law	314
12.3	Secession is Valid only if it is Achieved through Peaceful and Democratic Means	315
12.4	The Right to Create an Independent State Applies Only to Peoples under Colonialism or Other Form of Foreign Domination?	316
12.5	An Acknowledgement of Secession Will Entail a Danger of Anarchy and Untold Human Suffering?	317
12.6	Frontiers Inherited From the Colonial Era Should be Maintained: "Even the Slightest Recognition Would be Unwise"?	319
12.7	Future Directions?	320
Conclusions		328
Index		335

Acknowledgements

My enthusiasm for human rights increased when I was studying human rights at the London School of Economics in 1992-1993 under Rosalyn Higgins (then former Professor of Public International Law at LSE, now an honourable judge in the ICJ at the Hague), and during my studies at the School of Oriental and African Studies, in particular Ethnic Minorities and the Law with Dr. Menski. This placed me in an ideal position to examine closer issues relating to minorities.

This book is largely based on my Ph.D thesis. New materials, in particular, chapters 2 and 9 are included while most other chapters have been significantly revised.

I completed my Ph.D thesis under the supervision of Professor Dominic McGoldrick of the University of Liverpool. His expertise, advice and critical comments on many issues raised in my thesis have helped me enormously to analyse and present arguments objectively. Above all his guidance led me to come to conclusions on many contentious issues in very positive and constructive ways. I am grateful to Professor McGoldrick for agreeing to supervise me even though he was extremely busy as the Director of the International and European Law Unit.

Helpful comments made by Mr. David Turns, Lecturer in Law at the Faculty of Law, University of Liverpool and Professor Malcolm Evans at the Faculty of Law, University of Bristol, on many issues were instrumental in improving this work. Professor Nanette Neuwahl should be specially mentioned for her encouragement. Dr. Menski, Senior Lecturer in Law at the University of London, agreed to read the whole manuscript without any hesitance and made many useful suggestions. His comments and suggestions have undoubtedly contributed to the improvement of many chapters. However, I, alone, am responsible for any misinterpretation of law and facts and any other omissions or errors in this book.

A great number of my former colleagues at the School of Law at the John Moores University encouraged me in many ways. Of these, former Director of the School of Law, Social Work and Social Policy, Professor Penelope Pearce, Bill Douglas (former Deputy Director), Richard Jones (Reader in Law), Stephan Jones (former Senior Lecturer in Law and now

District Chairman of the Appeal Service, Social Security), and Simon Rahilly (Senior Lecturer in Social Work and Social Policy) should be mentioned with affection for their understanding and continuing friendship during difficult times. I also owe my gratitude to Robert Meanders and Elizabeth Douglas for their generosity and continuing support for my work.

John Backwell, former Senior Lecturer in Social Work and Social Policy at JMU, took great care in reading my whole manuscript. He spent many evenings commenting on my work or discussing and expressing his concerns about current ethnic conflicts. He and his wife, Gwen Backwell, are some of the most wonderful friends I have come across in this country.

My special thanks go to my son Chamene Welhengama and my wife Sandaseeli Welhengama for providing an environment in which I have been able to carry out my research. My son helped me on many occasions when my computer created problems. I am deeply grateful to both of them.

Finally my thanks should go to Mr. Stephen Cooper, Information Technology Manager, and Mr. Philip Gray, Faculty Administrator, both at the Liverpool Law School at the University of Liverpool for their assistance. They have always been prepared to help me whenever I needed it. I am also grateful to Chief Ben Agwuna, Director, Ms. Julie Smith, Mrs Gloria Hill Andre, Mr. Tony and Mr. Francis Odita of Charles Wootton College for helping me in various ways in my professional work. Also my gratitude goes to the staff of the Library of the Liverpool Law School, in particular, Mrs. Wendy Spalton, Mrs. Wendy Neale and Mrs. Chris Bennett, and the staff of the Liverpool City Library in helping me to find materials in completing this work. I would also like to acknowledge the supportive role of the staff at Ashgate Publishing Limited in the efficient production of this book.

Dr. G. Welhengama, Ph.D (Liverpool); LL.M (London); LL.B; BA (Sri Lanka); Attorney-at-Law of the Supreme Court of Sri Lanka; Formerly Research Fellow in Law and Head of the Institute of Minorities, School of Law, Social Work and Social Policy at the Liverpool John Moores University (1991-1997); for sometimes Tutor in Law, Sri Lanka Law College (1984).

January, 2000
Liverpool, UK

Abbreviations

A/C.3/SR	Summary Reports of the 3rd Committee of the General Assembly
AJCIL	African Journal of Comparative International Law
AJIL	American Journal of International Law
ASIL	Proceedings of American Society of International Law
Bull. EC	Bulletin of the European Communities (now EU)
BYIL	British Year Book of International Law
Case W.Res.J.Int.L	Case Western Reserve Journal of International Law
CJIL	Colombia Journal of International Law
CSCE	Conference on Security and Co-operation in Europe
CYIL	Canadian Year Book of International Law
ECHR	European Convention on Human Rights
ECOSOC	Economic and Social Council
EJIL	European Journal of International Law
ESCOR	Official Reports of the Economic and Social Council
Eur.Ct. HR	European Court of Human Rights
FRY	Federal Republic of Yugoslavia
GA Res.	General Assembly Resolutions
GAOR	Official Records of the General Assembly
HRC	Human Rights Committee
HRLJ	Human Rights Law Journal
HRQ	Human Rights Quarterly
ICCPR	International Covenant on Civil and Political Rights
ICESCR	International Covenant on Economic, Social and Cultural Rights
ICJ Reports	Reports of International Court of Justice
ICLQ	International and Comparative Law Quarterly

ICTY	International Criminal Tribunal for the former Yugoslavia
IHRR	International Human Rights Reports
IJIL	Indian Journal of International Law
ILM	International Legal Materials
ILO	International Labour Organization
ILR	Israel Law Review
IYHR	Israel Year Book on Human Rights
IYIL	Italian Year Book of International Law
JAS	Journal of Asian Studies
KLA	Kosovo Liberation Army
LJIL	Leiden Journal of International Law
LNOJ	Official Journal of the League of Nations
LNTS	League of Nations' Treaty Series
LTTE	Liberation Tigers of Tamil Eelam
MAS	Modern Asian Studies
MLR	Modern Law Review
MSOP	Movement for the Survival of the Ogoni People
NILR	Netherlands International Law Review
Nord, Jint.L	Nordic Journal of International Law
Notre Dame LR	Notre Dame Law Review
NQHR	Netherlands Quarterly of Human Rights
NYIL	Netherlands Year Book of International Law
OAS	Organisation of American States
OAU	Organisation of African Unity
OSCE	Organisation for Security and Co-operation in Europe
PCIJ	Permanent Court of International Justice
SC. Res.	Security Council Resolutions
SFRY	Socialist Federal Republic of Yugoslavia

SPLM	Sudan Peoples' Liberation Movement
UBC Law Review	University of British Colombia Law Review
UDHR	Universal Declaration of Human Rights
UN	The United Nations
UN Doc.	Documents of the United Nations
UNTS	United Nations Treaty Series
UNYHR	United Nations Year Book of Human Rights
Va. J. IL	Virginia Journal of International Law
YBUN	Year Book of the United Nations
Yale J. Int'l. L	Yale Journal of International Law
WIGP	Working Group of Indigenous Peoples

List of Cases

AB et al v Italy, 1990, Communication no. 413/1990 (HRC)

Acquisition of Polish Nationality (advisory opinion), Series B/7, 15, 1923

Calder v British Colombia (AG) (1973) 34 DLR (3rd) 145 SCC

Case Concerning East Timor (Portugal v Australia) 1995 ICJ Reports 90

Case Concerning the Temple of Preah Vihear, Cambodia v Thailand (Merits) 1962, ICJ Reports, 6

Casimel v Insurance Corporation of British Colombia 106 DLR (4th) 720 (BCCA), (1993), 728

Cayuga Indians (Gr. Britain) v US 6 RIAA 173, 1926

Chechnya Case, the judgment delivered by the Constitutional Court of the Russian Federation, 31 July 1995

Cherokee Nation and Mabo (No. 2) 1992, 175 CLR 1

Chief Ominayak and the Lubicon Lake Band v Canada, Communication no.167/1984 (HRC)

Dagi v BHP (No. 10) (1995) VIC LEXIS 1182 (Australia)

Dagi v BHP (No. 2) (1997) IVR 428 (Dagi v Australia)

Delgamuukw v British Colombia, 104 DLR (4th) BCCA (1993)

Demir and Others v Turkey, 23 September 1998 (Eur.Ct.HR)

Domininque Guesdon v France, UN Doc. A/45/40, 1990, Annex IX, G

Frontier Dispute Case (Burkina Faso v Republic of Mali) ICJ Reports 1986, 554

GB v France, 347/1988 (HRC), UN Doc. A/47/40, 1992, Annex XG

Greco-Bulgarian Communities Case (1930), PCIJ, Series B, No. 17

Guerin v The Queen (1984) 2 SCR 335

Guerin v The Queen (1984) 13 DLR (4th), 321

Guinea-Guinea-Bissau Maritime Delimitation Case, 77 ILR 1988, 636

Harvey v New Brunswick (AG) (1996) 2 SCR 876

Hospital Products Ltd v US Surgical Corporation (1984) 156 CLR 41

Ivon Kitok v Sweden, Communication no. 197/1985, UN Doc. A/43/40 (HRC)

Kasivarsi Reindeer Herders' Cooperative v Ministry of Trade and Industry Sup. Admin. Ct. Fin. 15 May 1996
Kayano and Kaizawa v Government of Japan, Hanrei Jiho, no. 1598, Sapporo Dist. Ct. 27 March 1997

Light Houses Case, AB/62 (1934), 3 World Court Reports, Hudson ed. 1938
Light Houses in Crete and Samos Case, AB/71 (1937), 4 World Court Reports, Hudson (ed), 1943

Mabo (No. 2) (1992) 175 CLRI
Mamel Case, AB/49 (1932), 3 World Court Reports, 35 Hudson ed. 1938
Mikmaq Tribal Society v Canada, Communication no.78/1980 (HRC)
Minority Schools in Albania (Advisory Opinion), Ser.A/B 64, 1935 PCIJ Reports 17
MK v France, Communication no. 222/1987 (HRC)

Namibia Case, Advisory Opinion, 1971 ICJ Reports 16
National Coalition of Union of Burma v Unocal 176 FRD 329, CD. Cal. 1997
Nicaragua Case, Merits, (Military and Paramilitary Activities in and against Nicaragua, Nicaragua v US) 1986 ICJ Reports, 14

Prosecutor v Anto Furundzija, JL- PIU-372- E, 10 December 1998 (International Criminal Tribunal for Former Yugoslavia)
Prosecutor v Dazen Erdemovic, no. IT-96-22-T, 29 November 1996 (International Criminal Tribunal for Former Yugoslavia)
Prosecutor vs Dusko Tadic a/k/a, case no. IT-94-1-T, 7 May 1997 (International Criminal Tribunal for Former Yugoslavia)

Radislav v Krstic, 1998, JL/PIU/368-E (International Criminal Tribunal for Former Yugoslavia)
Rann of Kutch Case (award) 7 ILM 633, 1968
R v Gladstone (1996) 2 SCR 723
R v Oaks (1986) ISCR 103
R v Provincial Electoral Boundaries (Sask) (1991) 2 SCR 158

R v Public Service Employee Relations Act (1987) ISCR 313
R v Sparrow (1990) I SCR 1075
Re. Secession of Quebec (1998) 2 SCR 217
R v Van der Peet (1996) 2 SCR 507
RL et al v Canada, Communication no. 358/1989

San Andres v Colombia, 1990, Communication no.318/1988 (HRC)
Sandra Lovelace v Canada, Final Views of the HRC, Communication no. 24/1977, UN Doc. A/36/40 (HRC)
Slaight Communications Inc v Davinson (1989) I SCR 1038

Tekin v Turkey, 9 January 1998 (Eur.Ct.HR)
TK v France, Communication No. 220/1987 (HRC), UN Doc. A/45/40, Annex XA, 1990
Tom Beanal v Freeport-Mcmoran (1997) WL 178, 10 April 1997

Western Sahara Case (Advisory Opinion), 1975, ICJ Reports 12
Whispering Pines Indian Band, 1991, Communication no.358/1989 (HRC)
Wik Peoples v States of Queensland (1996) 141 ALR 129
Worcester v The State of Georgia 31 US 350, 6 Pet 515 (1832)

Yasa v Turkey, 2 September 1998 (Eur.Ct.HR)
Yosofa Alomang v Freeport- McMoran (1996) US Dist. LEXIS 15, 908, 17 October 1996

List of Statutes and Constitutions

Act no. 670 Concerning the Autonomy of the Aaland Islands, 1951
Act no.1144, Autonomy of Aaland, 1991
Act on Cultural Autonomy for National Minorities, 1993 (Estonia)
Act on Self-Governing National Entities, 1994 (Slovenia)
Act on Unrestricted Development and Right to Cultural Autonomy,
    1948 (in respect of South Tyrol / Alto Adige)

Canadian Constitution Act, 1982
Charter for the Kingdom of the Netherlands, 1954
Constitutional Act of Finland, 1994
Constitutional Act of Human Rights and Freedoms of National and Ethnic
    Communities or Minorities in the Republic of Croatia, 1992
Constitution of Bosnia and Herzegovina, 1996
Constitution of Iraq, 1970
Constitution of the Russian Federation, 1993
Constitution of Spain, 1978
Constitution of Sri Lanka, 1978

Eritrean Constitution, 1952
Eritrean Federal Act, 1952

Faeroe Islands Home Rule Act, 1948

Greenland Home Rule Act, no. 577, 1978
Guarantee Law (Finland), 1921

Indian Self-determination and Educational Assistance Act, 1975 (the USA)
Indigenous Peoples Rights Act, 1997 (the Philippines)

Law of Autonomy in the Region of Kurdistan, Act no.33, 1974,as amended
    in 1983)
Law on Cultural Autonomy for National Minorities (Estonia), 1993

Law on the Free Development of National and Ethnic Groups of Latvia and
    Their Right to Central Autonomy, 1991
Law on National Cultural Autonomy (Russian Federation), 1996
Law on Self-Managing Ethnic Communities (Slovenia), 1994
New Autonomy Statute, 1972 (in respect of South Tyrol)

Republic of China, Decree no. 26, 1990

Southern Provinces Regional Self-Government Act 1972 (in respect of
    south Sudan)
Statute of Autonomy of the Basque Country, Organic Law, 1979
Ukrainian Act on National Minorities, 1992

List of Conventions, Treaties and Declarations

African Charter on Human and Peoples' Rights, 1991
Alma Ata Declaration, 1991
Anandpur Sahib Resolution, 1973

Bangkok Declaration (Final Declaration of the Regional Meeting for Asia of the World Conference on Human Rights), 1993

Charter of Paris for a New Europe, 1990
Council of Europe Framework Convention for the Protection of National Minorities, 1994
CSCE Document of the Copenhagen Meeting of Conference on the Human Dimension, 1990
CSCE Document of the Moscow Meeting of the Conference on the Human Dimension of the CSCE, 1992

Declaration of Principles on Interim Self-Government Arrangements Concerning Gaza and Jericho, 13 September 1993
Declaration on the Granting of Independence to Colonial Countries and Peoples, 1960
Declaration on Principles of International Law Concerning Friendly Relations and Coorperation among States in Accordance with the Charter of the United Nations, 1970

EC's Declaration on the Guidance on the Recognition of New States in Eastern Europe and in the Soviet Union, 1991
European Charter for Regional or Minority Languages (Council of Europe), 1992
European Charter of Local Self-Government, 1985
European Convention for the Protection of Human Rights and Fundamental Freedoms, 1950

Final Declaration of the Conference on the European Charter on Local Self-Government at Barcelona, 1992

Framework Convention for the Protection of National Minorities, 1995

General Framework Agreement for Peace in Bosnia and Herzegovina, 1995

German -Polish Convention relating to Upper Silesia, 1922

Helsinki Final Act (Final Act of the Conference on Security and Co-operation in Europe), 1975

Hungary-Romania Treaty on Understanding, Co-operation and Good Neighbourliness, 1996

ILO Convention Concerning Indigenous and Tribal Peoples in Independent Countries, 1989

Indo-Sri Lanka Accord, 1987

International Convention on the Prevention and Punishment of the Crime of Genocide, 1948

International Covenant on Civil and Political Rights, 1966

International Covenant on Economic, Social and Cultural Rights, 1966

Lebed - Maskhadow Peace Agreement, 1996 (in respect of Chechnya)

Paris Agreement, 5 September 1946 (between Austria, Italy in respect of South Tyrol/Alto Adige)

Proposal for an Additional Protocol to the European Convention on Human Rights Concerning Persons Belonging to National Minorities, 1993

Recommendation 1201 on an Additional Protocol on the Rights of Minorities to the European Convention on Human Rights, 1993

Resolutions of the First Assembly of the Heads of State and Government of the Organization of African Unity, 1964

The Establishment of the International Tribunal to Prosecute Persons Responsible for Serious Violations of International Humanitarian Law Committed in the Territory of the former Yugoslavia Since 1991, SC Res. 808/1993 and 827/1993

Treaty of Neuilly-sur-Seine, 1919

Treaty of Paris, 1919Treaty of Saint-Germain-en-Laye, 1919
Treaty of Sevres, 1920
Treaty on Social Accord, 1994 (Russian Federation)
Treaty of Versailles, 1919

UN Declaration on the Rights of Persons Belonging to National or
    Ethnic, Religious and Linguistic Minorities, 1992
UN Draft Declaration on the Rights of Indigenous Peoples, 1994
United Nations Charter, 1945
Universal Declaration of Human Rights, 1948

Preface

The issues arising from claims for autonomy and secession by minorities have been chosen for this thesis for their contemporary relevance. Ongoing conflicts in many parts of the world are largely ethnic in character, and there seems to be no end to such conflicts. This has generated an unprecedented interest in issues concerning minorities in recent times. Issues such as *autonomy* and *secessionist rights* of minorities have thus become a focus of debates amongst scholars, politicians and minority rights campaigners. Most prominently, some human rights campaigners and scholars have been expressing comments about the entitlement of minorities to secession by virtue of the right to self-determination. Such developments could not only give false hopes to many minority groups but also give rise to tensions between minorities and nation-States and often create clandestine secessionist movements, armed insurrections and sporadic outbreaks of violence. Encouraged by such unexpected assistance, some minorities are now campaigning for the right to autonomy and in extreme cases, the most contentious and ambitious claim, the right to break away from an existing State and to set-up their own State on ethnic, religious and linguistic grounds.

Most States continue to believe that such claims are hazardous to the very foundation of the nation-State system and international peace. Therefore, it is not advisable, from their perspective, to deviate from the current position of international law on minorities' claims. Contemporary international law appears to be struggling to cope with these new developments. As Sigler (1983: 19) says, "there seems to be no coherent theory to account for these claims". There are conflicting legal and political arguments as to the validity of such demands. Although there is much research in this area, it is apparent that jurists and publicists are not in agreement as to the scope of application and legal validity of claims for autonomy or secession. Not many commentators seem to have grasped the position of international law about such claims.

The focus of the present study is an examination of the validity of claims for autonomy and secession by minority groups. This will also analyse the scenario of clashes resulting from minorities' claims from *autonomy* to *secession* and States' refusal to respond to such claims in a constructive manner. Claims, refusals and rivalries between minorities and States, and how these clashes may result in the continuation of conflicts in contemporary polities are discussed. Attention is especially paid to UN and States' practice in dealing with claims for autonomy and secession.

Chapter One discusses the scope and objectives of the thesis, and how deep ethnic conflicts affect contemporary multiethnic polities. The failure to provide a definition of *minority* and reasons given for it by both States and jurists are investigated in *Chapter Two*. *Chapter Three* examines in brief the conceptual dimension of *peoples* in terms of the peoples' right to self-determination and discusses whether *minorities* are covered by it. *Chapter Four* examines the conceptual basis of autonomy. The validity of the claim that autonomy emanates from and gains its legitimacy through the right to self-determination is examined in *Chapter Five*. Movements for autonomy and models of autonomy are discussed in *Chapter Six*. States' attitudes towards claims of autonomy by minorities are examined in *Chapter Seven*. *Chapter Eight* analyses the conceptual basis of *secession*, and its kindred concepts, *irredentism and separatism*. The views of jurists on secession are analysed in *Chapter Nine*. *Chapter Ten* discusses the legitimacy of secession by examining international law and the practice of the United Nations and other regional bodies. Secessionist attempts, based on selected case studies, are examined in *Chapter Eleven*. How States generally respond to secessionist claims is analysed in *Chapter Twelve*. *Chapter Thirteen* summarises the main points raised in the previous chapters and comes to a conclusion on whether autonomy and secession can provide a meaningful answer to current ethnic conflicts and minorities' grievances.

Finally, the author has used *Claims of Minorities* instead of 'Rights of Minorities', because autonomy and secession have not recognised as legal rights in international law. Heyking (1928: 47) once wrote: "A right necessarily implies the possibility of claiming it. The notion of right is a conception of law, not of politics".

References

Heyking, B. (1928), 'The International Protection of Minorities: The Achilles' Heel of the League of Nations', 13 *Problems of Peace and War*, pp. 31- 51.
Sigler, J. A. (1983), *Minority Rights: A Comparative Analysis*, Greenwood Press: Westport, Connecticut and London.

Series Editor's Preface

I am pleased to write the preface to Dr Gnanapala Welhengama's important work on how minority claims for autonomy easily escalate to struggles for outright secession. I first met Dr Welhengama in 1994 when I was beginning a lectureship job in Liverpool and at the same time pursuing a claim for racially discriminatory selection practices against another university. Among my colleagues at that time, he was the most supportive perhaps because of his specialist knowledge of minority claims against discrimination. He wrote a very critical review for a modern law journal of the Industrial Tribunal ruling that although the university in question did not follow proper procedure, there was no proof that the improper procedure was racially motivated. Soon afterwards, funding for the Institute of Minorities that he ran single-handedly disappeared and he was forced to teach part-time elsewhere while completing this interesting study.

The scenario that Dr Welhengama outlines in the book – that of increasing ethnic violence that leads to increasing demands for autonomy or secession and consequent civil wars between ethnic nationalities and nation States around the world – is something that both he and I experienced first hand. I was six years old when the Igbo and other Easterners were being massacred in tens of thousands in different parts of Nigeria, leading to demands for autonomy as a guarantee of safety for the Igbo and other Easterners in their enclave but when the military government rejected the call for autonomy, a sovereign state of Biafra was declared and the three-year war of secession cost about three million lives. In the case of Dr Welhengama, he was a successful practicing attorney in Sri Lanka when the struggle for Tamil autonomy quickly escalated to a war of secession that is still on-going, forcing him to flee into exile as a refugee. Given this personal interest and the many years of meticulous research, teaching and post-graduate scholarship in the field, no one is better qualified to write a book like this than Dr Welhengama.

It is hoped that the international community in general, and scholars who specialise in international law in particular, will learn one or two things from this book about how to explain and hopefully prevent the discriminatory practices that lead to ethnic protest and demand for autonomy, how to guarantee democratic space to allow individual and group autonomy within civil society, and how to prevent the war of secession from becoming inevitable when democratic processes of negotiation could yield better results with broader international support under the postmodern conditions of regional unity and cooperation in which nation States are becoming increasingly outmoded and irrelevant.

The book focuses on the post World War II conflicts such as those in Bangladesh, Biafra, the Balkans, Caucasus and other secessionist conflicts. Such a broad coverage makes the book relevant to most parts of the world and even those conflicts not mentioned specifically and those parts of the world not yet embroiled in conflict could benefit from the historical lessons analysed here by the author.

Dr Biko Agozino
Associate Professor
Indiana University of Pennsylvania

Foreword

The School of Law and Applied Social Studies at the Liverpool John Moores University established in 1991 the *Institute of Minorities*, with the aim of developing a centre for researching into the issues concerning minorities and their rights. The Institutes' first appointment was Dr. Welhengama as a research fellow. The Institute began a close co-operation with the school's courses on Welfare, Law and Social Policy offering courses at both undergraduate and postgraduate levels. The Institute developed as its main research themes the personal laws of ethnic minorities and their position in international and human rights law. The Institute has born many fruits including a joint text between Dr. Welhengama and myself on 'Ethnic Minorities in English Law'.

I am honoured to introduce this new book based on Dr. Welhengama's Ph.D studies on minorities' claims for autonomy and secession. It is evident throughout the text that the author has been able to analyse some of the most controversial issues in international and human rights law in a constructive way. The ubiquitous nature of ethnic clashes in contemporary multiethnic polities provides significant legal and social challenges. I am sure this book will contribute to a more fully understanding of these problems and help shed light on possible solutions.

Richard Jones, LL.B (London); MA (Nottingham)
Reader in Law
School of Law and Applied Social Studies
Liverpool John Moores University
Liverpool, UK

January, 2000.

1 Claims From Autonomy to Secession: Introduction

Part I

1.1 *Objectives*

The following issues are investigated, assessed and critically analysed:

a) Ethnic violence has been on the increase for a considerable time in almost all parts of the world, and has engulfed the current political debate both at international and domestic levels;

b) Most minority groups are either fighting for greater political power through greater autonomy or in extreme cases engaged in the building of ethno-nation-States challenging the contemporary understanding of the right to self-determination and or justifying their struggles in terms of the right to secession by virtue of the right to self-determination;

c) Ethnic clashes involving minority groups and nation-States are forcing the United Nations and other international bodies to modify existing laws and or to create new sets of laws to cater for the claims of minorities.

This book also:

a) identifies and examines the extent to which contemporary international law and the international community are prepared to accommodate the concerns of 'minorities';

b) analyses how the claims of minorities for political rights beyond traditionally understood limited rights clash with the concerns of nation-States and the norms of contemporary international law; and

c) identifies the extent to which clashes between minorities and nation-States develop in post-modern plural societies. The clashes scenario will be examined by referring to sample cases in various parts of the world.

These will be confined to post World War II conflicts such as Bangladesh, Biafra and the most recent cases such as Kosovo and other secessionist movements in the Balkans and Caucasus.

Analyses of the issues raised in this work are principally confined to the period from 1945. However, references are made in brief to the pre-World War II period, in particular to the League of Nations.

1.2 *Minorities?: "Cat Owners and Bald Peoples do not Fit the Standard Picture of Minority Groups"?*

This book limits its focus to *minorities* as identified in article 27 of the International Covenant on Civil and Political Rights, 1966 (ICCPR),[1] and the Declaration on the Rights of Persons Belonging to National or Ethnic, Religious and Linguistic Minorities, 1992[2] (Declaration on Minorities, 1992) who are non-dominant and numerically inferior in comparison with the dominant group. Ethnic, national, religious and linguistic minority groups are referred to in this work as *ethnic minorities* or *minorities*, because the author is of the opinion that religions, languages and cultures are salient defining characteristics of ethnic groups. Other vulnerable social and cultural groups such as women, homosexuals, and the disabled are excluded.

There are conflicting views amongst some scholars about whether social and cultural groups should be covered by the term *minority*. Humphrey (1989: 50) argued that even though such disadvantaged groups may have some of the characteristics of real minorities, it would be better if another term could be found to describe them. Such groups, as Sanders (1991:370) noted, in particular those "suffering from discrimination, have a tendency to assert a collective character, simply as part of the struggle" (see also Nowak, 1993:491). By way of an example, he refers to the homosexual community in the USA who identify themselves as the *Queer nation*. Referring to women and homosexuals, Special Rapporteur Deschenes questioned how it could be possible to identify them as minorities in terms of international law.[3] Therefore, minority groups who identify themselves with ideological opinions associated with age, disability, or sexual orientation are outside the terms of minorities of this study (see also Zayas, 1993). "Bald people, cat owners, and members of armed forces do not fit the standard picture of a minority group" either (Gilbert, 1992:69-70). As is evident from present UN practice, international law does not accept all groups, which want to be protected and identified as *minorities*. Sigler (1983:4-5) argues that international law regards many sub-groups as social groups rather than minorities. As Thornberry writes (1991a:16), international law is not concerned with "every conceivable classification of minority" (see also Ramcharan, 1989:201).

Another term, which is frequently used in this book, *plural society/ies,* is used to identify deeply divided contemporary multiethnic, multireligious and multilingual societies. The author has followed the description of the term *plural societies* provided by Professor Arend Lijphart. Most contemporary societies, according to Lijphart (1995:276), are "sharply divided along religious, ideological, linguistic, cultural, ethnic, or racial lines into virtually separate subsocieties with their own political parties, interest groups, and media of communications. The most common of these distinctive features is *ethnicity*, but the different categories overlap considerably".

Part II: The Minority Issue and Ethnic Conflicts

1.3 The Minority Issue and the League of Nations: "It Drags Out All Our Dirty Linen and Washes it Publicly"

The minority issue is not a new phenomenon. Where there is a minority there is always a possibility of clashes between it and the majority community. Moreover, minorities are vulnerable to assimilation, segregation and fusion. The latter is akin to the policy of Romanisation practised in the old Roman Empire (Macartney, 1934:27-29). In extreme cases, they are subjected to oppression and persecution at the hands of State machinery and or majority groups. This often results in conflicts, involving basically a minority and the dominant majority groups, culminating in the involvement of the State. These conflicts often spill across the boundaries of many States, giving an international dimension to many ethnic conflicts. For centuries, therefore, particularly in Europe and the Middle East, there have been experiments made with a view to finding ways and means not only to keep minorities under control but also to find reasonable solutions to minority problems. It is believed that the first such initiative took the form of the *millet* system introduced in the Ottoman Empire during the 15th century by Sultan Mehmet II to guarantee certain rights for non-Muslim religious and ethnic minorities. The main objective was to ensure that its various ethnic and religious groups received protection within the Empire. Sigler (1983:70) states that the *millet* system was "something akin to modern minority group rights" because it was based on the recognition of groups and their institutions. It was also international in character, because it was operated across national boundaries in large parts of Europe and Asia. Subsequently, the welfare of religious and national minority groups have become legitimate concerns of the European powers. The Treaty of Vienna, 1606 (between Hungary and Transylvania), the Treaty of Olivia, 1660 (between Sweden and Poland), the Treaty of Westphalia, 1648 (France and the Holy Roman Empire and their Allies), the Treaty of Nijmegen, 1678 (between France and Holland), the Treaty of Ryswick, 1697 (between France and Holland), the Treaty of Paris, 1763 (between France, Spain and Great Britain), the Congress of Vienna, 1815 (between France, Great Britain, Portugal, Prussia, Russia and Sweden), the Treaty of Berlin, 1878 (between Germany, Austria, Hungary, France, Great Britain, Italy, Russia and Turkey), the International Convention of Constantinople, 1881 (between Germany, Austria, Hungary, France, Great Britain, Italy, Russia, and Turkey) are worthy of mention (see details Sigler, 1983:68-69; Capotorti report, 1979:1-2).

Throughout the 16th, 17th and 18th century conflicts were largely religious in character. Ethnic minorities, however, became a political issue during the 19th century with the rise of nationalism in Southern, Eastern and Central Europe. Certain States were compelled to introduce laws in their domestic legal system to protect minorities. For instance, the Austrian Constitutional Law, 1867 had taken a significant step in addressing legitimate concerns of ethnic minority groups. It recognised that "all the ethnic minorities of the States shall enjoy the same rights and, in particular, have an absolute right to maintain and develop their nationality and their language". This was considered a significant step in minority protection (see Capotorti report, 1979:3). Similarly, the Polish Constitution 1815, Hungary's Act XLIV, 1868, and the Constitution of the Swiss Confederation 1874 are other notable instances where certain constitutional guarantees were introduced to protect minorities and to address their concerns.

Minority consciousness vis-à-vis the emergence of nationalism gradually laid the foundation for future ethnic conflicts which later spread to other parts of the globe. Referring to these developments Sigler (1983:72) wrote that "nationalism was the seedbed of modern minority rights, and minority discontent was one of the most unsettling forces in international relations". With the fall of the 20th century, solutions to this new conflict scenario were sought through various bi-lateral and multilateral treaties and declarations.

The first modern international experiment with the minority issue was made by the League of Nations[4] which, according to Robinson (1971:62), "constitutes an unsurpassed high point in a centuries old tradition" (see details in Jones, 1949; Capotorti report, 1979:4). Yet the Covenant of the League of Nations did not contain any provision for the protection of minority rights (Azcarate, 1945:92). This was due to conflicting views amongst the leaders who played a major role in the process of drafting the League Covenant at the Paris Peace Summit. Some attempts were made, notably by the former US President Wilson, to include such a clause. He urged:

> The League of Nations shall require all new States to bind themselves as a condition precedent to their recognition as independent or autonomous States to accord to all racial or national minorities within their several jurisdictions exactly the same treatment and security, both in law and in fact, that is accorded to the racial or national majority of their people.

Later, Wilson proposed an additional article:

> Recognising religious persecution and intolerance as fertile sources of war, the Powers signatory hereto agree, and the League of Nations shall exact from all new States and all States seeking admission to it the promise, that they will make no law prohibiting or interfering with the free exercise of religion, and that they will in no way discriminate, either in law or in fact, against those who practice any particular creed, religion or belief whose practices are not inconsistent with public order or public morals (see Azcarate, 1945:168; and also see Miller, 1928:91).

These proposals were rejected by a majority of States and subsequently abandoned by the US delegate. Such a move was considered by many as undesirable or impossible to implement (Jones, 1949:604-605). Nonetheless, it was believed by the leading players of the League of Nations that the ultimate goal, that is international peace, would be achievable only through an effective mechanism capable of protecting minorities (Macartney, 1934:274). Minority issues were, however, left for States to deal with in what were subsequently popularly known as 'minorities treaties' and 'declarations'. Of these the Polish Treaty, 1919 (between Poland the Principle Powers and its Allies) became a standard formula for subsequent treaties, such as the Treaties of Saint-Germain-en-Laye, 1919, Neuilly-sur-Seine, 1919, Trianon, 1921 and Lausanne, 1920 (Azcarate, 1945:92 and 169; Robinson, 1971:63-64). Amongst declarations, the Declaration by Albania, October 2, 1921, the Declaration by Estonia, September 17, 1923, the Declaration by Finland, June 27, 1921, the Declaration by Latvia, July 7, 1923 and the Declaration by Lithuania, May 12, 1922 should in particular be mentioned.

In addition, some special measures were taken to address individual cases, such as the Jewish minorities in Greece, Poland, Rumania, Lithuania; the Valachs of Pindus in Greece, the Ruthanians in the Carpathian Mountains, the non-Greek monastic communities of Mount Athos in Greece; the Moslem minorities in Albania, Greece, and the Kingdom of the Serbs, Croats and Slovenians; the Czecklers and Saxons in Transylvania; the non-Moslems in Iraq; and the Kurds' linguistic rights in Iraq (see Robinson, 1971:68; Jones, 1949:607; Heyking, 1928:607).

Thus, signatory parties undertook to assure full and complete protection of life and liberty to all inhabitants in their countries without distinction of birth, nationality, language, race or religion. They also promised to accord equality of treatment before the law and security in law and in fact irrespective of ethnic or racial background (Azacarte, 1945:172-173; see also Macartney, 1934:212-286). However, these treaties, as emphasised by Clemenceau in his famous letter to M. Paderewski, "did not constitute any fresh departure" in respect of minority protection (see Robinson, 1943:166). The rights guaranteed were inherently limited. Baron Heyking (1928) points out that most minority treaties did not even specifically mention the right to private property of a minority although indirectly measures were taken to regulate property belonging to individuals of a minority population. The League of Nations was of the opinion that the right to property was not a legal right that can be claimed by minorities as such (Heyking, 1928:37).

It should, however, be mentioned that the Minorities Section (a branch formed under the Secretariat) operating under the Council of the League of Nations adopted procedures necessary to ensure that the guarantees included in the minorities treaties would be effectively implemented. For the first time in the history of minority rights, minorities or States which were concerned about the violation or danger of violation of minority rights guaranteed in minorities treaties were given the right to petition to an international institution, that is the League Council, even though it was not to the satisfaction of minority groups (see Azcarate, 1945:102-123).

As stated in *Minority Schools in Albania*,[5] one of the main objectives was to ensure that the nationals belonging to racial, religious or linguistic minorities should in every respect be treated equally with the other nationals of the State. In addition, it was also held that the intention of the League was to eliminate a dangerous source of opposition, recrimination and dispute arising from racial and religious hatred. The principal 'political objectives' of the League system were: a) to avert inter-State wars arising out of ethnic conflicts, and b) to prevent national minorities from disturbing peaceful inter-state relations, and c) to prevent oppression and persecution of national minorities. As Azcarate (1945:14-15), the former Director of the Minorities Section of the League of Nations, remarked, "only then would it be possible, they thought, to prevent states from interfering in questions concerning national minorities in other states, or at the very least to mitigate the dangers of interference by requiring interceding states to act through the League of Nations and the institutions especially created by the latter to that end, thus avoiding direct and dangerous discussions on delicate questions between governments".

As these developments were being progressed within the institutions of the League of Nations, some States began to question the desirability and consequences of establishing a strong international mechanism guaranteeing preferential treatment or special protective measures for a segment of a population of independent States. In fact, it gradually became clear that some States wanted to see a gradual and painless assimilation of minorities with the majority groups in the countries in which they lived. This was subsequently known as the 'Mello-Franco thesis'. During the debate at the assembly of the League of Nations, one delegate, Mr. Briand, argued:

The real problem is, while ensuring that the minorities shall preserve their language, culture, religion and traditions, *to keep them as a kind of small family within the larger family*, not with the objective of weakening the larger family, but with the object of harmonizing all its constituent elements with those of the country as a whole. The process at which we should aim is not the disappearance of the minorities, but a kind of assimilation which will increase the greatness of the nation as a whole without in any way diminishing the importance of the smaller family (emphasis added, cited in Macartney, 1934:276).

Later, indirectly criticising the minority regime, he added:

No movement must be allowed to persist which, under cover of unexceptional sentiments, would lead to widespread unrest in the world or breed fresh insecurity. However worthy of respect certain doctrines and propaganda may be, one thing stands before them all- peace. No special circumstances, no individual aspirations, however justifiable, can be allowed to transcend the interests of peace. Peace must prevail, must come before all. If any act of justice were proposed which would disturb world peace and renew the terrible disasters of yesterday, I should be the first to call upon those promoting it to stop, to abandon it in the supreme interest of peace.

In February 1926, Mr. de Mello-Franco, the delegate of Brazil on the Council, and a special rapporteur to minority issues, stressed:

It seems to me obvious that those who conceived this system of protection did not dream of creating within certain States a group of inhabitants who would regard themselves as permanently foreign to the general organization of the country. On the contrary, they wished the elements of the population contained in such a group to enjoy a status of legal protection which might ensure respect for the inviolability of the person in all its aspects and which might gradually prepare the way for the conditions necessary for the establishment of a complete national unity (Macartney, 1934:277).

The Mello-Franco thesis was supported by Great Britain, Czechoslavakia, and Belgium, and appeared to be the collective opinion of the Council of the League (Heyking, 1928:40). The British delegate, Sir Austin Chamberlain, pointed out in 1929:

The object of the Minorities Treaties, and for the Council in discharging its duties under them was, as M. de. Mello-Franco has said, to secure for the minorities that measure of protection and justice which would gradually prepare them to be merged in the national community to which they belong (Macartney, 1934:277).

The League of Nations had been concerned only with the protection of certain minority groups in selected States in Eastern and Central Europe (defeated States and newly formed or enlarged States), such as Austria, Hungary, Bulgaria, Turkey, Poland, Greece, Czechoslovakia, Rumania, and Yugoslavia. Later, Albania, Lithuania, Latvia, Estonia and Iraq joined the system by making Declarations (Sigler, 1983:73; see further Macartney, 1934). Although some States, notably Lithuania, and subsequently Finland and Lettland tried to make minority regime applicable to all members of the League of Nations their motions to the League Assembly never succeeded due to differences of opinion amongst members (Heyking, 1928:40). The delegate of South Africa, Professor Gilbert Murray, was of the opinion that "the States which are not bound by any legal obligation to the League with respect to minorities will, nevertheless, observe in the treatment of their own racial, religious, or linguistic minorities, at least as high a standard of justice and toleration as is required by any of the treaties" (see details in Heyking, 1928:42). But they failed to pursuade other States. It is not surprising therefore that the League of Nations was unsuccessful in creating a universal system in protection of minorities. Moreover, the system was politically motivated, and minority treaties and declarations were not primarily based on humanitarian concerns" (Macartney, 1934:273; Jones, 1949:609).

Furthermore, the minority regime was not eagerly supported by minorities nor did the Treaties guarantee minority rights even though the States concerned undertook to implement them in good faith. In particular, the system was subjected to severe criticism by the Congress of Minorities, which acted as a representative of minority groups in Europe, for lack of coherent and effective implementation procedures. On the other hand minorities themselves complained that the system created by the League was not effective enough to protect them and their traditional institutions against existing State structures. It is of importance to note that the minorities were not parties to the so-called minorities treaties nor were they given *locus standi* in any proceedings against State parties alleged to have violated provisions of minorities treaties. Therefore, as correctly argued by Heyking (1928:47), minorities treaties did not give the minority any legal foundation for establishing their claims before the League or the Permanent Court of International Justice (see also Azcarate, 1945:104-105). In particular, the method adopted by the League, i.e. "compromise, adjustments, friendly pressure and persuasion" to implement treaty obligations was criticised by minority groups (Azcarate, 1945:131). It should be remembered that the Congress was alleged to have been in collaboration with and to have been supported by both politically and financially interested third parties (Azcarate, 1945:131).

Some States complained that the minority regime operated by the League of Nations "is intolerably wounding to our susceptibilities. It allows insidious propaganda to be directed against us; it allows any one who cares to send in a 'petition' to attack our good name publicly, it drags out all our dirty linen and washes it publicly, and puts us in the odious position of having to appear in a public court as defendants against our own citizens" (details in Macartney, 1934:371). They also complained that the system impeded the development of national unity and weakened the unity of the States by encouraging a segment of the population to look for a third party to protect them against the States within which they lived. It was further pointed out that "minorities were asking not for rights but for privileges, and they should be refused as being in contradiction with the equality principle" (see details in Robinson, 1971:69-70).

It was also alleged that the system operated under the League of Nations did not encourage minorities to show their loyalty to the States in which they lived. This subsequently resulted in the adoption of two resolutions by the League of Nations Assembly in 1922, which emphasised the obligation of minorities to their respective States. The resolution reads:

> While the Assembly recognises the primary right of the Minorities to be protected by the League from oppression, it also emphasises the duty incumbent upon persons belonging to racial, religious or linguistic minorities to cooperate as loyal fellow-citizens with the nations to which they now belong.[6]

This loyalty requirement has been criticised by some commentators as "negative loyalty", that is, minority groups were required to abstain from hostile, clandestine and irredentist activities against the States of which they formed a part (Azcarate, 1945:91). It is therefore not surprising that, after 20 years of experiment, minority regimes operating under the League system gradually collapsed with the outbreak of World War II. States such as Poland openly declared that they would no longer be bound by minority treaties. The Minority Section was dissolved in 1939. By then it had become clear to anyone who felt genuine concern about minority issues, that the system could no longer command any reasonable support. On the other hand, countries such as Germany did their best to bring down the minority regime altogether.

Consequently, minority treaties and 'minority regimes' operated under the League of Nations were considered non-operative due to desuetude or by operation of the *clausula rebus sic stantibus*.

1.4 *The Minority Issue and the UN: "If the Peoples of the Earth Are Fighting and Dying to Preserve and to Secure the Liberty of Individuals Under the Law…"*

For a long time, the rights of minorities were a less focused issue in the post World War II period. Mainstream politicians and statesmen and the United Nations followed a very cautious approach whenever a minority issue was raised. The concept of minority protection similar to that of the 'minority regime' operated under the League Council was rejected by the new system. The prevalent opinion in the post-League system seems to have been that issues relating to minorities should be left to the States to deal with individually on a case by case basis. Minority issues, in the view of the majority of States, could be dealt with effectively by unilateral, bilateral or multilateral treaties thus encouraging States to find solutions to minority problems without internationalising them. Most States that had experienced the League's minority regime no longer wanted to see internationalisation of minority rights (Sigler, 1983:76) as will be further shown below. Thus, there were many treaties, in particular involving eastern and central European States, to address minority issues. Amongst these, the Austrian State Treaty for the Re-establishment of Independent and Democratic Austria, 1955 (to protect Slovenian and Croatian minority groups in Austrian Carinthia, Burgenland and Styria), Annex II of the Memorandum of Understanding on the Free Territory of Trieste between Italy, USA, UK and Yugoslavia, 1954 (concerning Slovenians in the area of Trieste in Italy, and Italians in Slovenia), the Treaty between Italy and Austria, 1946, also called the 'Gruber-de Gasperi agreement (on the special status of Trentino province and Alto Adige/South Tyrol and in respect of the rights of German speaking peoples in these provinces), the declaration of the Federal Republic of Germany, 1955 (in respect of the status of the Danish minority) and the Declaration of Denmark in 1955 (on the general rights of persons belonging to the German minority in Southern Jutland), the Polish-Czechoslovakia Treaty, 1947 (concerning the protection of Poles, Czechs and Slovaks), the Treaty between the UK and Singapore in 1957 (concerning among others the protection of Malays) the Treaty of Friendship and Mutual Aid between Poland and Czechoslovakia in 1947, and the Treaty between India and Pakistan in 1950 (concerning the Hindu and Muslim minorities in each country) are worthy of mention (see McKean, 1985:47-50; Nova, 1965; Robinson, 1971; Kertesz, 1949).

The new system, which was referred to as "a general international organization for the maintenance of international peace and security" (Goodrich, 1961; Green, 1956), was built up after World War II and has, as far as rights are concerned, centred on individuals' rights. The eventual objectives of all its functions and activities, as stated by the former Secretary General U Thant, was to be the wellbeing of individual men and women.[7] Thus, the post World-War II trend was not so sympathetic to minorities nor were they reflected in any serious discussions amongst new world leaders leading up to both the UN Charter, 1945 and the Universal Declaration of Human Rights, 1948. The leaders of 'the Grand Alliance' wanted, by the 1941 Atlantic Charter, to create a stable global system able to stand against future aggressors. Subsequent meetings at the Quebec Conference (August, 1943), the Moscow Conference (1943), the Teheran

Conference (November, 1943), the Dumbarton Oaks Conference (August, 1944), and finally at San Francisco (August, 1945) carried out further necessary groundwork for a new international organisation of which the main concerns were to be:

a) the pacific settlement of disputes between States; and
b) the adoption of suitable measures to prevent threats to the peace or breaches of peace (see details in Luard, 1982:27).

It was assumed that the main areas of future disputes might be between States. It seems that, first, the so-called 'Big-Four' (the USA, the Soviet Union, the UK, and China) and then the 'Big Five' (the USA, the Soviet Union, the UK, China, and France) had not contemplated a future scenario of major disputes involving ethnic groups in the same territory causing severe problems for international peace and security.

At Hot Springs in Virginia (from May 18 to June 3, 1943) the basic concerns were about food and agriculture. However, as pointed out by P. C. Jessup (1944:367), this was "a genuine United Nations meeting" although wider issues such as security, peace and human rights were not on its agenda. At Dumbarton Oaks the theme of the conference was widened. A proposal submitted by the US delegate for the promotion and observance of human rights initiated a controversy among the members of the 'Big Four'. Both the Soviet Union and UK delegates opposed such a move arguing that it would give licence to third parties to intervene in the domestic affairs of independent States. Moreover, it was argued that human rights of citizens were purely domestic matters, which should not be interfered with. Later, an amended resolution was adopted at the insistence of the US delegate which required member States to show respect for human rights and fundamental freedoms (see Luard, 1982:32). Yet any reference to human rights was restricted to only one provision (McKean, 1985:53). Minority issues were not mentioned at all. Unsurprisingly, the Dumbarton Oaks proposal focused, as Goodrich (1961:245) points out, on winning the war and creating an effective and strong international organisation which could secure international peace and security in the aftermath of the war (see also Armstrong, 1949:1-16).

It was widely known that the atmosphere at the San Francisco Conference was extremely negative towards minority rights (McKean, 1985:59; Goodrich, 1961:244). In fact, there was an intense debate within official circles and lobbying groups as to whether provisions guaranteeing minority rights should be included in the final communiqué at all. It was commonly agreed by leaders of the 'Big Five' and their advisers that a continuation of the minority regime prevalent under the League of Nations or a similar one under the new system would not be advisable (Capotorti report, 1979:26), because it was widely held that such a system, conferring preferential treatment for a selected segment of a population in a State, would in effect contradict the universal character of a new world organisation. Furthermore, the leaders were concerned about the possibility that interested parties would exploit such a special minority regime when and where they wished to do so. The use of the German minority in the Sudetenland as a Trojan horse by Hitler to expand the Nazi State prior to World War II caused concerns (Sigler, 1983:4). The final communiqué issued by the San Francisco Conference, however, placed more emphasis on human rights than Dumbarton Oaks, because the 'sponsoring Big Four Powers' came under enormous pressure from lobbying groups to ensure that the new organisation should at least promote and encourage respect for human rights and for the fundamental rights of individuals (Robinson, 1971:79). Yet there was no mention in the final communiqué about minority rights. It focused on fundamental human rights, that is the equal rights of men and women in individualistic terms. The new world organisation was not so enthusiastic about the promotion of human rights (Goodrich, 1961; Russel, 1958), nor did it show any interest in minority rights. The prevailing attitude was demonstrated by Sumner Wells, the American Under Secretary in 1943:

> Finally, in the kind of world for which we fight, there must cease to exist any need for the use of that accursed term 'racial or religious minority'. If the peoples of the Earth are fighting and dying to preserve and to secure the liberty of the individual under law, is it conceivable that the peoples of the United Nations can consent to the reestablishment of any system where human beings will still be regarded as belonging to such minorities? (US Department of State, Bulletin, June 5, 1943:482, cited in Sigler, 1983: 482).

Some politicians who were aggrieved by campaigns by minorities against their States even suggested the creation of 'ethnically cleansed States' after post-World War II. Eduard Benes, then Chairman of the Czechoslovak National Council-in-Exile in 1941, emphatically stated this:

> It will be necessary after this war to carry out a transfer of population, on a very much larger scale than after the last war. This must be done in as humane a manner as possible, internationally organized and internationally financed. The protection of minorities in the future should consist primarily in the defence of

human democratic rights and not of national rights. Minorities in individual states must never again be given the character of internationally recognized political and legal units, with the possibility of again becoming sources of disturbances (cited in Robinson, 1971: 77).

Similarly, the Polish Government-in-exile stressed on 24th February 1942 that any protection for minorities should be given only to those minorities who were fulfilling their civil duties towards the State (cited in Robinson, 1971:77). Lord Metson, a British politician, was cautious. He argued that "the rights of minorities may be grossly exaggerated, just as they are sometimes grievously violated, and the abundant experience which has now accumulated should offer some guidance as to their proper scope and their reasonable limitations" (Times, 21 December 1940, cited in Robinson, 1971:78). Rev. Gregory Feige, on behalf of the European Federation, demanded in 1941 that minorities should stop all activities against the States in which they live. He emphasised:

> The cessation of all irredentist movements. Repudiation of the maxim that loyalty to race (or language-group etc) supersedes loyalty to the national State. Allegiance to the European Federation and the member State within whose borders the minority may happen to live. The European Federation at the same time guarantees to every minority, including the Jews (inasfar as Jews wish to be considered so and not merely a religious group) protection against persecution or discrimination. Full cultural autonomy, on the basis of the above mentioned principles of allegiance and cooperation with the minority group... (America's Peace Aims, pamphlet, no. 28, cited in Robinson, 1971: 79).

Moreover, Jacob Robinson's personal experience summarises the anti-minority feelings prevalent amongst major powers during the early 1940s. He writes:

> To complete the picture of the state of opinion on protection of minorities by an international organization, I shall describe two personal experiences of my own. During the last year of the War, the US State Department's section dealing with problems of an international organization was greatly expanded. Distinguished scholars were called upon, among them Clyde Eagleton of New York University. I maintained constant contact with him and used to go to Washington D.C. frequently, for this purpose. In one of our early conversations it was made clear to me that the United Nations would not be a continuation of the League (in which the US did not participate), and the errors of the Covenant (guaranteeing the territorial integrity of its members or protection of minorities) would be avoided. A second involved the representatives of Serbia-Croatia-

Slovenia in Washington D.C. After the publication of the book *Were the Minorities Treaties a Failure?* he came to me on behalf of his Government to inquire as to whether we pleaded the resurrection of the minorities systems. My reply that it was an analysis of a past phenomenon without any legal-political postulates for the future calmed his apprehensions (Robinson, 1971:80).

The new political leadership thus focused on issues in a wider framework whilst refusing to promote minority rights simply based on colour, race, ethnicity, language or religious differences etc. As McKean (1985:53) points out, any minority protection that existed under the League of Nations was considered "outmoded and unsuccessful".

Interrelated themes such as the protection of succeeding generations from the scourge of war, the promotion of social progress and better standards of living, greater freedom, tolerance and co-existing peacefully together with one another as good neighbours were the main objectives of the new world order. Above all, the post-war leaders were of the view that these new values would strengthen international peace and security. Therefore, member States were urged to take joint and separate action in co-operation with the new organization to achieve these goals. Accordingly, the new UN regime has more or less been based on two pillars, the United Nations Charter, 1945 and the Universal Declaration of Human Rights, 1948.[8]

The broad theme of the new system was, as enumerated in article 1 (i) of the UN Charter, "to maintain international peace and security, and to that end, to take effective collective measures for the prevention and removal of threats to the peace, and for the suppression of acts of aggression or other breaches of the peace, and to bring about by peaceful means, and in conformity with the principles of justice and international law, adjustment or settlement of international disputes or situations which might lead to a breach of the peace" (see further Hudson, 1945:75). The protection and promotion of human rights was lower in the priority list of the Charter. However, as mentioned in the preamble and articles 1 (3), 13, 55 (c), 56, and 76 (c) of the Charter, the Charter also reaffirmed "faith in fundamental human rights and in the equal rights of men and women" without distinction as to race, sex, language, or religion (see further Bowen, 1979:121). As mentioned in the Charter in article 1 (3), its other goals, *inter alia*, were to solve international problems of an economic, social and cultural or humanitarian character, and to promote and encourage respect for human rights and fundamental freedoms for all.

It is worthy of mention that there are references to the rights of *peoples* and *inhabitants* in the Charter, i.e. to the self-determination of peoples (articles 1 (2) and 55); the culture of peoples (article 73 (a); political aspirations of the people (article 73 (b), and inhabitants of the trust territories (article 76 (b). As will be shown in chapter 3, *minorities* are not, however, identified with *peoples* and *inhabitants*. Any reference to minorities *per se* was purposefully omitted.

The UDHR[9] is principally a statement of the civil rights of individuals on a universal basis (see articles 2-21), although it enumerated social and economic rights in articles 22-27. It was meant to be "short, simple, easy to understand and expressive", and above all "acceptable to all members of the United Nations" (Moller, 1992:1). However, the minority issue achieved the attention of the drafting committee during the preparation of the UDHR especially in the 3rd committee and in plenary sessions. The inclusion of a provision for the protection of minorities was proposed by Denmark, the former Yugoslavia and the USSR.[10] Both this and a separate proposal submitted by the USSR were rejected.[11] The latter proposed, "Every people and every nationality within a State shall enjoy equal rights. State laws shall not permit any discrimination whatsoever in this regard. National minorities shall be guaranteed the right to use their native language and to possess their own national schools, libraries, museums and other cultural and educational institutions". This was however rejected because the majority was of the opinion that such initiatives might create incentives for separatist movements. Most importantly a special provision drafted by the Sub-Commission on the Prevention of Discrimination and the Protection of Minorities was also not included due to a lack of support from the Commission on Human Rights and the Third Committee (see Capotorti, 1979:11).

On the other hand, one of the most influential members of the Drafting Committee, Mrs Eleanor Roosevelt, opposed the inclusion of a provision on minority rights in the human rights document despite its claim to be a universal declaration.[12] Consequently, the UDHR failed to include a provision on minority rights. However, the General Assembly declared, after the adoption of the UDHR that the United Nations could not remain indifferent to the fate of minorities.[13] It was further said:

   a) It was difficult to adopt a uniform solution for this complex and delicate question, which has special aspects in each State for which it arises;
   b) Concerning the universal character of the UDHR it is not appropriate to include a specific provision on the question of minorities in the text; and

c) Before taking any effective measures for the protection of racial, national, religious or linguistic minorities, it is necessary to make a thorough study of the problem of minorities.

The above resolution concluded with a request to the Economic and Social Council, "to ask the Commission on Human Rights and the Sub-Commission on the Prevention of Discrimination and the Protection of Minorities to make a thorough study of the problem of minorities in order that the United Nations may be able to take effective measures for the protection of racial, national, religious or linguistic minorities".

However, for various reasons both the Sub-Commission and other organs of the UN failed substantially to implement the measures envisaged in the above resolution. According to John P. Humphrey (1968:870), the UN had no interest in the creation of a machinery for the promotion of minority rights due to pressure from, in particular, the European and Latin American countries. The latter especially "were not very inclined to protect the minorities they wanted to assimilate".[14] Claude (1955:168) points out that in the embryonic stage of the UN "there has been a general tendency in the United Nations debates for speakers to state bluntly that the minority problem does not exist in their own countries..." (see also Sigler, 1983:67; Laponce, 1960). Thus, as Goodrich (1961:244) points out opposition to minority rights was largely based on the following grounds:

a) it encourages minorities to resist any integration with the dominant culture and other ethnic groups;
b) such measures will strengthen ethnic consciousness and ethnic differences;
c) it encourages minority groups not to work in coorperation with the State in which they live;
d) it might create an environment, which encourages minorities to maintain their resistance to political integration and to remain rebellious and discontented;
e) it might lead to irredentist and secessionist movements.

In addition to the above reasons, Hurst Hannum (1989:14) identifies some 'socio-political realities' which obstruct any wider recognition of minority rights in the UN system. Foremost amongst these is the view that, "the existence of 'minorities' does not fit easily within the theoretical paradigm of the State". Both Marxist regimes and Western democracy see a minority as an anomaly and an obstruction that contradicts the fundamental structure of the contemporary polities. It is also argued by some that any international recognition of minority rights would undermine national unity and the requirement of national development.

The strongest point against minority rights was that the very process of singling out a minority for special treatment was detrimental to the stability of the nation-State system. It was thought likely to create invidious distinctions between citizen, and that the accommodation of minority rights might lead to the creation of privileged classes. Thus the minority issue was no longer considered a universal political problem, and was taken off the agenda of the Political Committee (Capotorti report, 1979:28).

Some commentators have severely criticised the stance adopted by the UN in its formative stages regarding minority rights in the post-war era. Humphrey (1968:870) sees this as a case of abandoning its responsibilities. It was also pointed out by others that the relegation of the minority issue to a mere Sub-Committee, which was not composed of State representatives, and entrusted with two opposite jobs, i.e. the prevention of discrimination and the protection of minorities, proves that the UN did not take the minority issue seriously in its formative years. Moreover, the Sub-Commission was not given sufficient encouragement or even allowed to embark upon its agenda by the Commission on Human Rights and the Economic and Social Council as will be shown further in chapter 2. Consequently, the Sub-Commission did not engage in any action designed to protect and promote minority rights in the period between 1955 and 1971 (Capotorti report, 1979:28). According to Jacob Robinson (1971:90), minorities may, under these circumstances, be vulnerable to a less sympathetic state structure. First, they may face discriminatory treatment because of their ethnic, religious or linguistic characteristics, second, gradual weakening of their position may result in a loss of their identity as a cultural, ethnic or religious group.

Thus, Minorities were seen as a question (see details in Azcarate, 1945; Leff, 1999:205-235), a source of dissension,[15] a problem,[16] the seeds of war, or an Achilles' heel.[17] They were even identified with fifth columns or regarded as the enemy within. Claims of minorities were rightly or wrongly viewed with suspicion. Even today, writes Sohn (1981:270), "they lead to friction between States, intervention by one State in another, or to an appeal to the United Nations for international intervention". Briefly, the general perception of minorities was extremely negative. Similar attitudes prevailed within the Council of Europe. It decided that the discussion of minority rights in public would "do more harm than good".[18]

Thus, neither the majority of States nor the UN generally enthuses about minority rights. States were concerned about their sovereignty, territorial integrity and the sanctity of their boundaries. The new UN regime heavily invested in such selected principles as:

a) the fundamental rights of individuals;
b) non-discrimination; and
c) equal rights and equality before the law (see further Eide, 1991:1311-1346).

In particular, by guaranteeing the rights specified in *b* and *c*, it was believed by many that individuals belonging to a minority could be protected without having an elaborated system of group rights (see details in Capotorti report, 1979:27). This resulted in the adoption of a number of conventions and declarations by the UN and international organisations. In fact the origin of this approach can be seen in the UN Charter itself. Articles 1 (3), 13 (1) b, and 55 (c) all deal with non-discrimination. But it can be argued that this is an attempt at the promotion of the universal human rights of individuals rather than the promotion and protection of minority rights (De Nova, 1965:275 cited by Capotorti, 1979:4). Unlike the League of Nations, these provisions and the Charter in general, as mentioned above, did not provide any institutional mechanism to deal with the protection of minority rights nor did it create any legal obligations to preserve minorities' institutions, culture or ethnic or racial peculiarities, traditions and their national characteristics.

The UDHR further expanded the concept of the principle of non-discrimination and made it its central theme. It proclaims in article 2, "Everyone is entitled to all the rights and freedoms set forth in this Declaration, without distinction of any kind, such as race, colour, sex, language, religion, political or other opinion, national or social origin, property, birth or other status". It further states, "No distinction shall be made on the basis of jurisdictional, political, or international status of the country or territory to which a person belongs, whether it be independent, trust, non-self-governing or under any other limitation of sovereignty". Thus, the thrust of this article is to promote and assert the principle of equality without which, it was assumed, the basic rights enumerated in the Declaration cannot be attained. The idea of non-discrimination and equality has been given more prominence than other rights in the UDHR

(Greenberg, 1984:309; see also Skogly, 1992:57-71). They run through the fabric of whole documents like a golden thread which not only illuminates the whole Declaration but also provides a solid foundation for other rights as well (see also articles, 4, 7, 10, and 23 (2).[19]

The ILO's Discrimination (Employment and Occupation) Convention, 1958, ILO's Equality of Treatment (Social Security) Convention, 1962; the UNESCO Convention against Discrimination in Education, 1960, the Convention on the Elimination of All Forms of Racial Discrimination, 1966, the Convention on the Elimination of All Forms of Discrimination against Women, 1979, the Declaration on the Elimination of All Forms of Intolerance and of Discrimination based on Religion or Belief, 1981, and the Declaration on the Elimination of Intolerance and Discrimination, 1982, are other major international documents dealing with non-discrimination and measures aimed at the elimination of inequality. These Conventions, in the view of Capotorti (1979:7), provide equality "in more than formal terms; to this end they make provision for special measures benefiting under-privileged groups." In particular, the UNESCO Convention mentioned above "reflects a fairly advanced conception of the cultural rights of minorities in the educational field" (Capotorti, 1979:8). Above all it aims at preventing discrimination against groups, not merely persons belonging to racial, ethnic or religious groups. The Convention on the Elimination of All Forms of Racial Discrimination, 1966 is the most advanced international Convention adopted in this area. It (by article 1) prohibits any distinction, exclusion, restriction or preference based on race, colour, descent, or national or ethnic origin. This also imposes obligations upon States to take all necessary actions to prevent discrimination against racial or ethnic groups.

The continuation of this trend can be seen in the International Covenant on Civil and Political Rights, 1966 (see articles 2 (1),[20] and 26)[21] and the International Covenant on Economic, Social and Cultural Rights, 1966 (article 2 (2). The non-discrimination provisions of both these Covenants, as contended by Capotorti (1979:5-6), made significant and far reaching progress in comparison with the treaty provisions operated under the League of Nations, considering the fact that the latter system provided protection against discrimination only for those minorities living in certain States in Central and Eastern Europe. On the other hand, the Covenants' provisions on non-discrimination had a universal basis, which in the end helped to create non-discrimination as a normative principle in international law.

Can minorities be protected from discrimination and persecution under these non-discrimination provisions? Can States be compelled to observe the principle of non-discrimination enunciated in the foregoing documents by conferring on minorities equal treatment in fact and in law? These are complex issues. Nevertheless, post-World War II experiments clearly indicate that the application of non-discrimination or equality before the law in member States of the UN has not often been successful. Nonetheless, some States, in particular the countries belonging to the Council of Europe, have applied these principles to a certain extent successfully in their respective countries more so than any other States in other parts of the globe. The European Convention on Human Rights and Fundamental Freedoms, 1950 has been remarkably successful in promulgating provisions on anti-discrimination and equality both before the law and in fact. Article 14 states that "The enjoyment of the rights and freedoms set forth in this Convention shall be secured without discrimination on any ground such as sex, race, colour, language, religion, political or other opinion, national or social origin, associated with a national minority, property, birth or other status". Any individuals belonging to a minority can complain to the European Court of Human Rights in the event that they are subjected to discrimination within the meaning of article 14 in addition to their rights being violated in contravention of rights guaranteed in the Convention. But it is to be noted that only a few States in Europe have subscribed to the Convention's principles. Minorities' rights are still violated on a large scale whilst minorities continue to be hounded and persecuted simply because they do not belong to a dominant majority or subscribe to its beliefs.

The strategy of non-discrimination did not work under the League of Nations, which, as has been seen earlier, applied a very rigid anti-discriminatory regime, and the principle of 'equality' was used as "a cornerstone of the protection of minorities" (see Azcarate, 1945:20-27). Simply by the application of these principles, the experts and authorities of the League of Nations perceived that minority issues could be solved. Nonetheless, this strategy failed, producing a disastrous outcome in the period between 1920-1939.

There are two main issues of concern. First, unless, as Azcarate (1945:21), correctly points out "a regime of real and effective equality is established within the State between the majority and minority", non-discriminatory measures and equality before the law and in fact cannot be effectively implemented to the satisfaction of minorities. Even the most sophisticated European human rights system has not been successful in eliminating discrimination, despite being armed with a Court and a Commission, due to a lack of resources and complexities of the issues concerned. Second, non-discrimination or equality in law would not suffice to appease minorities. They are only minimum rights in the catalogue of their rights. As history proves repeatedly, and as we are witnessing now in the Balkans, the Caucasus, South-East Asia and in many other places, the ultimate goal of most ethnic groups is to achieve their own nation-States consisting of their own ethnic, religious, cultural, juridical and social institutions. Ultimately, everything comes down to boundaries. Minorities' concerns have always been with the reconstruction of existing boundaries, because most minority groups think either that they are on the wrong side of the boundaries or that the territories inhabited by the minority groups are not properly recognised in terms of the ethnic or national origin of their population. The common perception amongst minority groups appears to be that the frontiers should be flexible and changes should be made to existing borders taking into account ethnic, racial and other differences in contemporary multiethnic polities.

The system created by the UN has not found any other magic formulae to address minorities' concerns. In fact, as Azacarte (1945:26) argued, any universal system for preventing discrimination against minorities may not be a successful one in the majority of States because minority issues differ from country to country and require different solutions. The adoption of a more comprehensive universal system with a view to accommodating preferential treatment for minorities has been resisted by many States although the application of such measures on a temporary basis was found justified by a few States. This is attributable to a widely held view that such a system creates privilege groups to the disadvantage of the majority and contradicts the rationale of equality. It may even not find many advocates in western liberal democracies. Moreover, the very idea of equality amongst individuals will be violated by the application of any preferential treatment based simply on race, colour, ethnic or national origin, or the religious, linguistic or cultural characteristics of a group of citizen in a given State. Furthermore, even States that have experimented with such innovative mechanisms as affirmative or positive discrimination have not been able to implement them successfully. In fact some countries, notably the US, have been rethinking the practicability and justification of such policies in recent times, because preferential treatment for minority groups often gives rise to a backlash amongst the majority group.

Consequently, minority rights have been kept in the grey area of human rights, or as Capotorti (1979:3) noted, remained 'a neglected question' for long. In this hazardous process minorities have lost their bargaining power in almost all fields within the modern nation-State system. It is not surprising, therefore, that it is minorities who are increasingly marginalised, disadvantaged or otherwise the object of prejudice and discrimination.

1.5 *Beyond Traditionally Identified Limited Rights*

There has been an apparent reluctance by States to experiment with minority rights beyond traditional limits. The opinion of the international community is divided on this. A majority of States is opposed to any extension of minority rights beyond those rights enshrined in article 27 of the International Covenant on Civil and Political Rights, 1966 (ICCPR).

States' reluctance to consider minorities' rights as a different category of human rights was vividly demonstrated during the debate on article 27 of the ICCPR, 1966. It states:

> In those states in which ethnic, religious or linguistic minorities exist, persons belonging to such minorities shall not be denied the right, in community with the other members of their group, to enjoy their own culture, to profess and practise their own religion, or to use their own language.

The inclusion in the ICCPR of an article on minorities thereby recognising their identity as a separate group does represent an advance over the UDHR, which is silent on the identity and rights of minorities (Salzberg, 1973:164). Nonetheless, article 27 does contain certain weaknesses. The right-holders were not defined, as will be further discussed in chapter 3.

In the original draft of the UN Sub-Commission on the Prevention of Discrimination and Protection of Minorities (Sub-Committee) the phrase "ethnic, religious and linguistic minorities' was used. During the discussion on this draft resolution it was suggested that the word *minorities* should be replaced by the phrase "persons belonging to minorities", because *minorities* as such were not subjects of law (see Thornberry, 1991b:149), whereas 'persons belonging to minorities', it was argued, could easily be defined in legal terms. To maintain the idea of a group or community it was also suggested that the phrase "in community with the other members of their group" should be inserted after the words "shall not be denied the right".

This was later adopted by the Sub-Committee (see details Capotorti Report, 1979:32).

Most States did not want to see an effective article on minorities in the ICCPR. Amongst them, the Latin American countries played a decisive role in ensuring that the proposed article 27 (originally it was article 25) would not be obligatory. They were of the view that any article effectively guaranteeing and protecting minorities' rights would awaken ethnic consciousness and might subsequently cause problems for national unity (Capotorti Report, 1979:65). Their common stance was that in the Americas minority problems similar to those of Europe and Asia did not exist. Therefore, acting in conjunction, the Latin American countries used every possible tactic to weaken the structure of article 27 (see Thornberry, 1991b:154-155).

This article has generated heated debate about its exact meaning and its implications for minority groups. Many scholars are of the view that the 'article holders' are at the mercy of the modern nation-State system. There are also various interpretations offered by scholars as to how the article might be applied. As Nowak (1993:485 and 497-505) points out, article 27 is formulated in an extremely cautious and vague manner even though it has some collective elements. It thus leaves many questions open. This "modest and rather negative" article, in the view of Shaw (1997:485), is centred on persons belonging to minorities rather than on minorities as such. According to Thornberry (1991b: 173), article 27 rights are a "hybrid between individual and collective rights because of the community requirement". Capotorti has cautiously and carefully tried to interpret article 27 by giving the benefit of the doubt to minorities. He states that minorities can enjoy these rights collectively because they are the ultimate beneficiaries (Capotorti report, 1979:206-210 and 217). According to Special Rapporteur Eide, article 27 constitutes only a 'minimum' right.[22] Eide (1991:1320) further said, "it is essentially a clarification of the application of the individual human rights to members of minority groups". Dinstein (1976:111-118) is positive. He states that these rights are conferred on minorities on a group basis and can therefore be exercised by minorities as such. Ermacora's view (1983:274) is that article 27 contains both an individualistic and a collective element- the position also adopted by the Human Rights Committee.[23]

The majority of States' opposition to the granting of greater political powers to minorities was evident during the UN debate on the Liechtenstein proposal that autonomy at a regional level as an *optional mechanism* be granted as a solution to minorities' problems.[24] This proposal was criticised by many Asian and African States as a ploy to extend the scope of the principle of self-determination at the expense of the territorial integrity and sovereignty of States. These States were not convinced of the practicability of treading such a delicate path. Greater political power at regional level is regarded as a recipe for disaster by many States who argue that the erosion of the power of the State may encourage secessionist movements.

1.6 *Conflict Scenario: Being Caught Up In a Wasp's Nest*

Half-a-century ago, Gaetano Salvemini (1946:341) said of discussions about 'ethnic factors' that they were like "putting one's fingers into a wasp's nest". This is equally applicable to the scenario of contemporary ethnic conflicts. In fact living in contemporary multiethnic polities is like being trapped in a wasp's nest. There seems to be no exit for individuals caught up in such conflicts which are spreading alarmingly across many parts of the world. At both the national and international levels, fundamental forces are at work reshaping patterns of social organization and spreading fear. As mentioned by the former Secretary-General Ghali, (1996:4), ethnic conflicts[25] have suddenly resurfaced "giving rise to fierce claims of subnational identity based on ethnicity, religion, culture and language, which often resulted in armed conflicts." One of the main reasons for this has been the democratisation and liberalisation which have swept through Central and Eastern Europe and also through some African States. Even though ethnic revival has been prominent since the 1960s, this process intensified, in particular in Europe, with the fall of the Berlin Wall and the dismemberment of the former USSR, thereby giving rise to new issues arising from violent ethnocentric campaigns. Within 18 months, from June 1991 to December 1992, the former Yugoslavia, the USSR and Czechoslovakia disintegrated, creating ethnically and politically unstable States. Politically and ethnically motivated minority groups have emerged and or been rejuvenated despite being suppressed since World War II. The new political environment, as argued by Leff (1999:206), "opened the window of opportunity to renegotiate the constitutional framework for ethnonational relations". Suddenly, most minority groups began to question the legitimacy and justification of existing boundaries of States thus exposing their lack of obedience to political entities to which they belong. This creates an environment, in which ethnonational groups and States become embroiled in most virulent and destructive conflicts as is apparent in the current ethnic conflicts in the Balkans, Caucasus, and South East Asia in post-world wars. This raises serious questions about the stability of modern nation-States, which are moulded in the Westphalian nation-State system.

In the recent past, ethnic consciousness has been rekindled and ethnic revivalism has emerged, threatening the stability of the nation-State system by "brutal ethnic, religious, social, cultural or linguistic strife" (Ghali, 1995:6). In many parts of the world, the resurgence of ethno-populist movements is now visible.[26] Neighbours become enemies, mistrust between minority groups and majority populations has alarmingly widened. Thus the phenomenon of ethnic revivalism "came as one of the surprises of the last thirty years" (Sanders, 1991:372), threatening the nation-State system and exposing its limitations and inadequacies in accommodating the interests of ethno-national groups. Most minorities are now well organised, politically as well as militarily. In extreme cases, they have been "developing into popular guerrilla movements, international coalitions and networks" (Rupasinghe, 1992:38-39). Popular myths, historical achievements, and generation-old animosities are contributing to the "exhumation of buried antagonism" between the dominant majority and the minority in many contemporary polities (Thornberry, 1993:11). These new ethnic movements differ from national liberation movements which were prominent during the 1950s and 1960s, and class-based proletarian militant organisations which can normally be seen active in western industrial cities (see details Glazer, 1982:47-56). They are also significantly different in terms of organisational structure, political aims and in their national and international impact.

It is not now uncommon for even small minority groups to be engaged in clandestine and often destructive and violent activities with a view to achieving greater autonomy or post-modern tribal States with new frontiers severing all political connection for good with majority communities (Mullerson, 1993:793-811; Lawson, 1996:153; see also Bremmer and Taras, 1993). Hannum (1990:6) argues that many ethnic groups use violence as a "convenient vehicle for channelling political dissatisfaction into political organisation". Separatist ethnic movements believe that the time has come, "now or never" (Mullerson, 1994:19). Nakhichevan, Nagorny Karabakh, Chechnya, Tatarstan, Kosovo, Aceh, and Jaffna, most of them previously unheard of names in international politics, are emerging out of obscurity as new candidates for post-modern tribal-States. It has been said that more than half of all major armed hostilities in multiethnic polities between 1989-1995 were conflicts involving minority groups (Nordqist, 1998:60: see also Lawson, 1996:153-175). A major research study identified that 233 "politicised communal groups" have been active world-wide during the period 1945-1989 (Gurr, 1993:5-7). Another researcher found that in 1988, 99 out of 111 armed conflicts were ethnic conflicts involving autonomy or secession (Stavenhagen, 1996:154). These developments have shattered the conventional belief that the UN system would eventually be able to achieve peace in the post-war era by respecting and guaranteeing individual rights on a universal basis.

Even politicians in Western countries have been taken by surprise. Former US President George Bush, addressing the UN General Assembly stated, "revival of ethnicity ushers in a new era teeming with opportunities and perils".[27] The major milestone of this new era, in the view of Franck (1993), can be seen since 1990, or perhaps, as Mullerson (1994) suggests with the fall of the Berlin Wall in Autumn 1989 (see further Kymlicka, 1995:1).

Conflicts are more or less centred on religious, ethnic, racial and nationalist identities. They are, as was revealed in *Prosecutor* v *Dazen Erdemovic,* often exploited for political ends.[28] Most minority groups are extremely concerned about maintaining their identity and the differences between themselves and others, and are prepared to compete as such. As Granoff says (1993:24), with the demise of the Cold War "these differences are becoming increasingly pronounced and wars continue to be fought over these identities". In addition, claims to lands, water, air space, natural resources, language policies, national anthems, national symbols, flags, public holidays etc., are increasingly becoming contentious issues which often give rise to modern tribal-wars. The conflicts between Christians and Muslims in the Spice Islands (Ambon, Hulmahern, Ternate, Ceram and Buru) are mainly due to conflicting claims about the ownership of lands and other natural resources. It is alleged by Muslim tribal leaders that Christians have been making attempts to capture the Spice Islands. Militant Muslim fighters have already declared a *jihad* (holy war) against Christians. The main slogan appears to be "blood must be paid for with blood". This has already cost the lives of more than 1,500 civilians on both sides (see *Independent*, January 8, 2000). Recently, for example, a dispute about the national ownership of a long-haired sheep dog in Rumania led to confrontation between Rumanians and Rumanian Hungarians. When the Rumanians tried to register the sheep dog as their national symbol with the International Canine Association the Hungarian minority groups opposed it, arguing that it was their national symbol too. The most recent fighting between the Yoruba and Hausa Fulani in Nigeria broke-out in July and later in November 1999 due to disagreement about the ownership of the discarded oil pipelines and which ethnic group should control the food-market in the suburb of Ketu.[29] Sri Lankan Tamils are still complaining half a century later that their national and religious symbol, the bull, was not included in the Sri Lankan national flag which depicted only a 'lion', the symbol of the Sinhalese (see Ponnambalam, 1983).

The perceived wisdom seemed to be that only in the third world and in under-developed countries do such movements emerge. Such notions no longer have any credibility as Moynihan (1994:21) correctly pointed out. Franck (1993:3) writes that ethnic conflicts are now "openly flaunted everywhere, unapologically, with zealously raised arms and firearms". The most poignant contemporary case is that of the Yugoslav crisis. However, these conflicts are not confined to the Balkans, they continue to become a world-wide phenomenon. Minority groups are no longer deprived of weapons which have become the bargaining method of negotiation between the participants involved in those conflicts. It has been explained that (McLellan and Richmond, 1994:670):

> Nation-states no longer have a monopoly over so-called conventional weapons. Proliferation in the global arms-bazaar is available to dissident minorities and terrorists as long as they have the money to pay for them or can persuade dealers to give them credit. The result is a proliferation of devastating civil wars that reduce once visible states and communities to near anarchy.

Some scholars blame minority groups for "lacking the craft of mastering the art of living in harmony with communities different to themselves" (see Jackson, 1994:66). Sigler (1983:9) writes: "minorities are conflict groups. They are sources of unrest and social dissatisfaction. Unless suppressed or discouraged, they help precipitate social change. Minorities often form their own political parties or join dissident factions of a ruling party. They hope to improve their lot by agitating from within the government, when permitted, or against the government, if need be". It is often assumed that minorities are disruptive, a threat to the integrity of the State, and unwilling to accept the society in which they live" (see details McGoldrick, 1993:156). Another political commentator alleged that minorities dissatisfied with existing power arrangements, particularly in the developing world, are challenging the political structures of the global State system thus turning volatile Latin America, Eastern and Central Europe, Africa and Asia into a gigantic laboratory in which contemporary and future ethnic politics will be tested day in and day out (Parkinson, 1995:336-340). It is no surprise, therefore, that the term "'balkanized' has become synonymous with recurrent instability rooted in ethnicity"

(Jackson, 1994:66). Internal stability prevails whilst the State and ethnic communities co-exist harmoniously and with proper understanding. When this collapses, tension is "liable to arise leaving scars" (Caenegem, 1995:13; see also Soyinka, 1996).

1.7 *The UN's Concerns: "Conflicts Within States Are Proving as Bloody as Conflicts Between States in the Past"*

The UN is now deeply concerned about the growing frequency and severity of contemporary tribal-wars,[30] because these disputes have often had a spill-over effect in international relations (see Said and Simmons eds. 1976). Former UN Secretary-General Ghali warned, "armed conflicts today, as they have through history, continue to bring fear and horror to humanity."[31] He noted:

> New assertions of nationalism and sovereignty spring up, and the cohesion of states is threatened by brutal ethnic, religious, social, cultural and linguistic strife. Social peace is challenged on the one hand by new assertions of discrimination and exclusion and, on the other, by acts of terrorism seeking to undermine evolution and change.[32]

The UN has been aware of the fact that threats of fragmentation and assertions of difference are on the rise, with horrific violence engulfing many regions of the world. The break-up of multiethnic *plural societies* spreads as many continue to suffer from instability.[33] Conflicts within States, says the United Nations High Commissioner for Human Rights, "are proving as bloody as conflicts between States in the past".[34] In 1975, Isaacs (1975:3) stated that ethnic violence, since World War II, had claimed more than ten million lives (see further Lemarchand, 1994). Since then, this number has continually increased as ethnic clashes have flared up in many parts of the world. It is reported by the UN that in the first half of the 1990s, nearly 5 million peoples died world wide as a result of wars and armed conflicts. Of this, according to the UN Commissioner for Refugees Ms Sadako Ogata, in Africa alone, at least 3.5 million people died and 5.3 million Africans became refugees[35] as a consequence of ethnic conflicts and tribal wars.[36] In fighting in Bosnia, as estimated by UN experts, 200,000 people were killed.[37] In ethnic conflicts in Rwanda, it is estimated, between 500,000 and 1 million people were slaughtered,[38] the second largest genocide after Cambodia since World War II. The Pol Pot government of Democratic Kampuchea (DK) was responsible for killing 1 million civilians.[39] In fighting in Kosovo in 1999 many Kosovar Albanians, Gypsies and Serbs were killed, and the massacres are still on the increase. Tribal fighting in Somalia claimed the lives of 300,000 civilians.[40] The Middle East, Tajikistan,[41] Abkhazia,[42] Sudan,[43] the Central Africa,[44] and Afghanistan[45] are other notorious places where tribal wars claimed many thousands of civilians, simply because their ethnic or religious identities. With border clashes along the Badme Front (1,000 kilometres long) the Eritreans and Ethiopians have returned once again to their violent past.[46] Tens of thousands of both civilians and militia have already been killed in this tribal war in which the World War I tactics as well as most modern weaponaries such as Mig 29s and Sukhoi 27s are used. The revenge attack by the anti-independence militia with the collaboration of the Indonesian army against the civilian population of East Timor and the Russians' onslaught on the Chechens are the latest brutal violence reported. The sole purpose appeared to be inflicting maximum damage to the enemy. At the end of 1995, there were 35-40 million internally displaced persons due to world-wide conflicts (Ghali, 1996:4). Thus, the most significant violence after 1945 has found its *"casus belli* in ethnic, tribal, and racial groups." (Said and Simmons, 1976:16; see also Cohen and Deng, 1998:12-16).

This is increasingly causing concerns to many member States of the UN, because, "the cohesion of societies is being increasingly threatened and, in some cases, destroyed by ethnic or religious strife".[47] In practice this has "often led to the establishment of dictatorship and (been) accompanied by bloodshed and violations of the rights of individuals".[48] As some States admit, present ethnic conflicts often lead to instability in many areas of the world, notably in the multiethnic polities in the developing countries.[49] In fact, many States such as Rwanda, Somalia, Liberia, the former Yugoslavia and the former USSR collapsed, whilst others survived but as failed States or as Jackson (1994:29) describes them 'quasi States'. Conflicts caused by ethnic and religious groups, however exaggerated and illogical, have been equated with the "threat of nuclear weapon".[50] This may be largely due, *inter alia,* to:

a) exploitation of unsuspecting masses against other sectors of the population by xenophobic movements;[51]
b) "frustration of groups within societies";[52]
c) a lack of respect for the principle of self-determination and non-interference in the internal affairs of States particularly by powerful States which encourage secessionist movements for their own purposes;[53]

d) provocation of racial hatred[54] and religious and ethnic intolerance;[55]

e) fear of diversity;[56] and

f) most importantly, confusion in the appreciation of the actual dimension of the right to internal self-determination as opposed to the right to external self-determination.[57]

In addition, scarcity of resources and the deterioration of socio-economic conditions have contributed to the growth of ethnic conflicts.[58] Negative perceptions of minorities have no doubt played a significant role in this conflict process too.

On the other hand persecution of minorities is a continuing phenomenon. Minorities are "increasingly marginalised, disadvantaged or otherwise the object of prejudice and discrimination" (Monshipouri, 1994:580). Even some States now admit that "acts of terrorism against minorities" are perpetrated in some parts of the world.[59] A survey in 1989 concluded that out of 126 larger countries, 261 minority groups or 913,812,000 minority individuals are at risk. Analysing these figures, Roth (1992:87) says that the actual figures should be more than that since the survey did not include blacks in South Africa, Palestinians in Israeli-occupied territories or the Baltic people in the USSR. These numbers indicate how far minority groups are vulnerable in many contemporary States.

1.8 *Ethnic Conflicts and Ethnic Cleansing*

The ubiquitous nature of ethnic conflicts, according to Albania, has now become a threat.[60] As the Senegal representative to the UN stated conflicts between ethnic groups caused serious problems to the stability and security of various parts of the world,[61] and to the territorial integrity of newly independent States (see also Manning, 1989). They often "lead to enormous suffering and grief".[62] The ideology of 'ethnocentrism' is the driving force behind the sudden escalation of ethnic conflicts and ethnic cleansing. Levine and Campbell (1971:8) suggest William Graham Sumner as far back as 1906 introduced this much abused word to modern social science. It is still a good basis for a comprehensive analysis of modern ethnocentric claims and resulting clashes. According to Sumner (1906:12-13), the basic ideologies of ethnocentrism are:

Loyalty to the group, sacrifice for it, hatred and contempt for outsiders, brotherhood within, warlikeliness without...all group together, common products of the same situation...It is sanctified by connection with religion. Men of other groups are outsiders with whose ancestors the ancestors of the we-group waged war. The ghosts of the latter will see with pleasure their descendants keep up the fight, and will help them. Virtues consist in killing, plundering, and enslaving outsiders. Ethnocentrism is the technical name of this view of things in which one's own group is the center of everything...Each group nourishes its own pride and vanity, boasts itself superior, exalts its own divinities, and looks with contempt on outsiders.

Ethnocentrism has found its natural partner, "the shameful phenomenon of ethnic cleansing",[63] the notorious catchword of our time. This most inhuman, gruesome and horrendous experiment has recently been and is being carried out in Eastern Europe and in many States of Asia and Africa. People are being "murdered, tortured, not because of what they do but because they belong to one ethnic group or another"[64] and to get rid of undesirable ethnic elements. Notorious examples are nowadays provided by majority and minority groups alike. For example, the Chechens against the Russians in Chechnya, the Croats against the Serbs in Croatia, the Tamils against the Sinhalese and the Muslims in the Northern and Eastern provinces of Sri Lanka; in Bosnia-Herzegovina, the Serbs against the Muslims and Croats; under the former (now disposed) military regime in Rwanda, the minority Hutu against the Tutsi. This strategy is normally used by the majority community against minorities, for example, the persecution of the Kurds in Turkey, Iraq and Iran; the Indonesians against the East Timor Catholic population, the Muslims against the Hindus in Kashmir, the Hindus against the Muslims and the Sikhs in India. It happened in Kampuchea when the Polpot regime started to annihilate Vietnamese ethnic groups in that country.

The term 'ethnic cleansing' is relatively new, although the practice is not a new phenomenon (see details Preece, 1998:817-842; Bell-Fialkoff, 1993:110-121). Ethnic cleansing of Indians in North America is a well-known instance. In fact from the first decade of the twentieth century, this notorious practice of forced migration and population exchange had been experimented with by many States in Europe. One of the the pioneers of this brutal practice in the 20th century was Turkey which carried out ethnic cleansing against non-Muslims such as the Armenians and Greeks, and subsequently against the Kurds. Later, the League of Nations also gave its seal of approval for population transfers in the belief that homogenous polities would result in the ending of ethnic conflicts. Many States eagerly participate in the programmes of population transfers and forced migration schemes. Amongst them, Greece, Turkey,[65] Germany[66], the Soviet Union,[67]

Rumania, Bulgaria,[68] Yugoslavia,[69] and Poland[70] played a significant role. Amongst politicians who encouraged and experimented with this practice, Stalin, Hitler, and Mussolini[71] were prominent political figures in the 1930s and early 1940s (see details in Robinson, 1971:71-81; Macartney, 1934: 430-449; see also Ladas, 1932). Of course it was the Nazis who brought this practice to its peak during the World War II by carrying out genocide against the Jews and other racial groups. With the ending of World War II other prominent political powers of the day such as the USSR, the USA and Britain also took part in this process (by the Potsdam Agreement of 2 August 1945) by expelling over 12 million Germans from Eastern Europe (Bell-Fialkoff, 1993:110). This time it was done in the name of international peace and justice. However, the practice of ethnic cleansing was rejuvenated in recent history with the commencement of brutal ethnic war in Bosnia-Herzegovina and Croatia (Petrovic, 1994:343).

The UN General Assembly concluded in resolution 47/80, 16 December 1992 that ethnic cleansing is "totally incompatible with universally recognized human rights and fundamental freedoms",[72] international humanitarian law, and with other major human rights treaties and declarations.[73] Policies and ideologies of ethnic cleansing promote racial hatred in the belief that one racial, ethnic, or religious group is superior to others. This will inevitably be an obstacle to friendly and peaceful relations among nations whilst seriously undermining peace and security among peoples living side by side within the same State.[74] Its ultimate object is, as stated by UN Special Rapporteur Tadeusz Mazowieck, to exert control over a given territory by terminating or expelling members of other ethnic groups.[75] Cassese, distinguished jurist and a Judge of the International Criminal Tribunal for the former Yugoslavia (ICTY), points out that ethnic cleansing is "a pinnacle of human criminality".[76] It involves killings, torture, beatings, systematic rape, arbitrary searches, disappearances, destruction of houses and property, threats of violence aimed at forcing individuals to leave their homes and mass expulsions of defenseless civilians from their homes. In addition, systematic destruction and profanation of mosques, churches and other places of worship,[77] as well as other places of cultural heritages,[78] the torturing of leading citizens such as religious and political leaders and intellectuals belonging to the 'enemy ethnic group', etc., are vital elements of ethnic cleansing. Violent as well as non-violent methods are used to achieve ethnically pure, homogenous territory consisting of individuals belonging to only one ethnic group (Petrovic, 1994).

Are ethnic cleansing and genocide two different concepts, as some States seem to think? [79] Or is the term 'ethnic cleansing' complementary to genocide? The prohibited acts which constitute genocide as mentioned in the Convention on the Prevention and Punishment of the Crime of Genocide, 1948[80] are identical to the crimes recognised by the UN resolutions on ethnic cleansing (Stavenhagen, 1996:195). Ethnic cleansing may therefore violate, *inter alia*, the provisions of the Genocide Convention. Individuals or groups responsible for committing ethnic cleansing can be prosecuted under the Genocide Convention in conjunction with a crime against humanity, and a violation of the laws or customs of war, as stated in *Prosecutor* v *Anto Furundzija* and *Radislav Krstic* before the ICTY.[81] The General Assembly resolutions 47/147, December 18, 1992, 47/121, December 18, 1992, and 49/196, December 23, 1994 recognised the "abhorrent policy of ethnic cleansing" as "a form of genocide".[82] However, ethnic cleansing, unlike genocide, involves both physical and non-physical destruction of peoples and properties. A far greater range of activities is covered by ethnic cleansing than by genocide. For example, as mentioned in GA Res. 49/205, December 23, 1994, the systematic rape of women and forced pregnancies are some of the practices used as "weapons of war and instruments of ethnic cleansing".[83] Charges of rape have been made in *Furundzija* against some of the accused on the grounds that they had violated the laws or customs of war, and committed outrages upon personal dignity.[84] On the other hand, the ultimate goal in ethnic cleansing appears to be the military occupation and conquest of a territory with a view to achieving ethnically pure territory. The main political objective of ethnic cleansing is to defend one's own ethnic group against another ethnic, racial or religious group or groups.[85]

Ethnic conflicts demonstrate that attempts to suppress minorities can be an illusion and may end in failure. It seems that ethnic conflicts and ethno-nationalism do not disappear for ever,[86] at the most they may fade for a while, only to be reborn on a later occasion (Malinverni, 1991:265). Ours is an era in which ethnic consciousness are the determining factors in deciding whether and with whom we should go to war or make peace. There is no doubt that we are at a turning point in this new postmodernism where things seem increasingly to be judged in ethnic, religious and linguistic terms. The process of dismantling what we have achieved during the past few decades since World War II is unfolding with unprecedented haste. Peretz (1992:65), perhaps with a little exaggeration, says:

What we are experiencing ...is not the shaping of new coherence but the world breaking into its bits and pieces, bursting like big and little stars from exploding galaxies...each one straining to hold its own small separate pieces from spinning off in their turn.

What are the underlying reasons for these new developments in the 1990s? Is it wrong for minorities to seek their own nation-States based on ethnic, religious and linguistic identities and go their own ways? To what extent are the claims of minorities compatible with the norms of contemporary international law? Need such claims necessarily contribute to the escalation of ethnic conflicts in modern societies? Above all, what are the implications for international peace and security? Can the UN or the international community accommodate another 5000-6000 new nation-States?

Notes

[1] GA Res. 2200 A (XXI) Annex, 16 December 1966.
[2] GA. Res. 47/135, 18 December 1992.
[3] UN Doc. E/CN.4/Sub.2/1985/31, para. 20, p.5. See further Ramaga, P.V. (1993), 'The Group Concept in Minority Protection', 15 (3) *HRQ*, p. 58.
[4] See details on minority regime under the League of Nations, Robinson, J. (1943); Azcarate, P. De. (1945); Heyking, B. (1928), see details below; See also Macartney, C. A. (1934), *National States and National Minorities*, OUP: London; Roucek, S. (1929), *The Working of the Minorities System Under the League of Nations*, Orbis: Prague; Janowski, O. I. (1945), *Nationalities and National Minorities*, The Macmillan Group: New York. The main characteristics of minority regime were examined in the following cases: *Minority Schools in Albania*, Series AB/64, 17, Hudson ed. (1934- 35), *World Court Reports*; *The German Settlers in Poland*, Advisory Opinion, Series B/6, 1923, Hudson ed. (1934- 35), *World Court Report*, p. 207.
[5] See *Minority Schools in Albania*, Series AB/64, 17, Hudson ed. 1934-1935, *World Court Reports*.
[6] *LNOJ*, Special Supplement, no. 9, October 1922, p. 35.
[7] See Human Rights Day Message of the former Secretary General U Thant in 1965, *UN Press Release*, SG/SM/393, 15 November 1965.
[8] GA Res. 217, UN Doc. A/810, 71 (1948).
[9] See generally, Humphrey, J. P. (1994), *Human Rights and the United Nations: A Great Adventure*, Transnational Publishers: New York; the same author (1979), 'The Universal Declaration of Human Rights: Its History, Impact and Juridical Character', in Ramcharan, B.G. ed. *Human Rights: Thirty Years After the Universal Declaration*, Martinus Nijhoff.
[10] A/C.3/307/Rev. 2.
[11] GAOR, 3rd session, part I, Annexes, Agenda Item 58, UN Doc. A/784.
[12] UN Doc. E/CN.4/SR. 73, p. 5.

[13] GA Res. 217 C (III), 1948.

[14] See further, The Centre for Human Rights (1994), *The United Nations Actions in the Field of Human Rights*, UN Publication: New York and Geneva, para. 1629.

[15] See German delegate's comment, A/C.3/SR.1103, 14 November 1961, para. 52, p. 216.

[16] A/C.3/SR.1103, 14 November 1961, para. 15, p. 214 (the UK).

[17] See details Heyking, below, pp. 31-51.

[18] See Resolution 136/1975 of the Council of Europe, cited in McKeen (1985: 2), as below.

[19] See generally, Eide, A. Alfredsson, G. Melander, G. Rehof, L. A. and Rosas, A. eds. (1992), *The Universal Declaration of Human Rights: A Commentary*, Scandinavian University Press: Oslo.

[20] It states, "Each State Party to the present Covenant undertake to respect and to ensure to all individuals within its territory and subject to its jurisdiction the rights recognised in the present Covenant, without distinction of any kind, such as race, colour, sex, language, religion, political or other opinion, national or social origin, property, birth or other status".

[21] Article 26 states, "All persons are equal before the law and are entitled without any discrimination to the equal protection of the law. In this respect, the law shall prohibit any discrimination and guarantee to all persons equal and effective protection against discrimination on any ground such as race, colour, sex, language, religion, political or other opinion, national or social origin, property, birth or other status".

[22] UN Doc. E/CN.4/Sub.2/1990/46, 20 July 1990, *Possible Ways and Means of Facilitating the Peaceful and Constructive Solution to the Problems Involving Minorities*, para. 17, p. 5 and para. 24, p. 7.

[23] See *Sandra Loveless* v *Canada*, Final Views of the HRC, Communication no. 24/1977, UN Doc. A/36/40; *Ivon Kitok* v *Sweden*, HRC, Communication no. 197/1985, UN Doc. A/43/40.

[24] UN Doc. A/Res/48/147/ Add. 1, 1991.

[25] See generally Horowitz, D. L. (1995), *Ethnic Groups in Conflict*, University of California Press: California; Gurr, T. R. (1993) *Minorities at Risk: A Global View of Ethnopolitical Conflict*, Institute of Peace Press: Washington; Moynihan, D. P. (1994), *Pandaemonium: Ethnicity in International Politics*, Oxford UP: Oxford; James, A. and Jackson, R. H. eds. (1995), *States in a Changing World: A Contemporary Analysis*, Clarendon Press: Oxford; Gottlieb, G. (1993), *Nation Against State: A New Approach to Ethnic Conflicts and the Decline of Sovereignty*, Council of Foreign Relations Press: New York; Gurr, T. R. and Harff, B. (1994), *Ethnic Conflict in World Politics*, Westview Press: Boulder; Olzak, S. (1992), *The Dynamics of Ethnic Competition and Conflict*, Stanford UP: Stanford; Silva, K. M. De. and May, R. eds. (1991), *Internationalization of Ethnic Conflict*, Frances Printer: London; Stephen, R. (1990), *Ethnic Conflict and International Relations*, Dartmouth Publishers: Brookfield; Stevenhagen, R. (1990), *The Ethnic Question, Conflicts, Developments and Human Rights*, UN UP: Tokyo.

[26] See A/R/Pub/91/3, *Report of the Seminar on the Political, Historical, Economic, Social and Cultural Factors Contributing to Racism, Racial Discrimination and Apartheid,* UN: New York 1991, para. 97, pp. 19-20.

[27] 'The Revival of History Poses a Great Challenge', in *The Independent,* 24 September, 1991.

[28] *Prosecutor* v *Dazen Erdemovic,* No. IT -96-22-T, 29 November 1996. In this case a soldier of Croat ethnic origin having being recruited by the Serb militia was then forced to kill hundreds of Muslims civilians. See on this Turns, D. (1998), 'The International Criminal Tribunal For the Former Yugoslavia: The Erdemovic Case', 47 (2) *ICLQ,* pp. 461-474. See also the statement issued by the UN High Commissioner for Human Rights, 'On the Eve of the Twenty-First Century', The Paris Meeting, 7 December 1998, http://www.europa.eu.int.

[29] See Wallis, W. 'Forty Killed in Ethnic Clashes in Nigeria', *Financial Times,* 27 and 28 November 1999.

[30] Preamble in GA Res. 52/109, 12 December 1997 ('Measures to Combat Contemporary forms of Racism, Racial Discrimination, Xenophobia and related Intolerance'); See also GA Res. 52/132,12 December 1997 ('Human rights and mass exodus').

[31] *An Agenda for Peace: Preventive Diplomacy, Peace Making and Keeping,* UN Doc. A/47/277, 17 June 1992, para. 13.

[32] *Ibid.* para. 11.

[33] The report of the Secretary-General on the work of the organization, GAOR, 52nd session, suppl. para. 1, p. 1, 1997.

[34] Statement issued by the Commissioner on Human Rights on the Eve of the twenty-first Century, The Paris Meeting, 7 December 1998. See http://www. Europe. eu.int. 8 December 1998.

[35] Statement made by The UN High Commissioner for Refugees, Sadako Ogata, see details Smith, A. D. 'Out of Sight: Five Millions are Refugees', *The Independent,* 22 June 1999.

[36] United Nations Standing Advisory Committee on Security Questions in Central Africa (1997), *United Nations' Concern for Peace and Security in Central Africa: Reference Document,* UN: New York, p. 1.

[37] See details *The United Nations and the Situations in the Former Yugoslavia,* UN publication, New York, DPI/1312/Rev.4, July 1995.

[38] See *The United Nations and the Situations in Rwanda,* UN, New York, UN publication, DPI/1484 /Rev.1, April 1995, p. 21.

[39] 'United Nations Advance Mission in Cambodia', in the *Blue Helmets: A Review of United Nations Peace Keeping,* 3rd ed. UN: New York, 1996, p. 449.

[40] See *The United Nations and the Situations in Somalia,* UN publication, DPI/1312/Rev.4, New York, May 1995, p. 1.

[41] *The United Nations and the Situations in Tajikistan,* New York, DPI/1685, April. 1995.

[42] See also chapter 26, 'United Nations Observer Mission in Georgia', in the *Blue Helmets,* above, p. 571.

[43] GA Res. 52/140, 12 December 1997. *The report of the Special Rapporteur of the Commission on Human Rights on the situation of human rights in the Sudan,* Fifth Interim Report, UN Doc. A/52/510, see A/C.3/52/SR.34, 17 February 1998, para. 12-16, pp. 3-4.

[44] *The report of the Secretary-General,* A/52/PV.5, 22 September 1997, pp. 2-3.

[45] UN News NS/8/98, Sept. 1998. UN Doc. A/52/493, 1998, the report of the High Commissioner for Human Rights, and A/C.3/52/SR.33, 18 February 1998, pp.5-6 (the number of displaced persons due to tribal conflicts are estimated at 1.2 million).

[46] See Gilkes, P. 'The Biggest Conflict in the World', *The Independent,* 22 June 1999.

[47] A/C.3/48/SR.22, 30 November 1993, para.18, p.5 (Sri Lanka). See also A/C.3/49/SR.6, 31 October 1994, para. 54, p. 10 (Albania).

[48] A/C.3/49/SR.8, 25 October 1994, para. 9, p. 4 (Russian Federation).

[49] A/50/PV.18, 4 October 1995, p. 8 (Nigeria).

[50] A/C.3/49/SR.6/31, October 1994, para. 30, p. 6 (Russian Federation).

[51] A/C.3/50/SR.5, 27 October 1995, para. 9, p. 4 (Mauritania).

[52] A/C.3/48/SR.21, 26 November 1993, para. 16, p. 5 (Equador).

[53] A/C.3/49/SR.6, 31 October 1994, para 8, p. 3 (Libyan Arab Jamahiriya).

[54] A/C.3/49/SR.6, 31 October 1994, para. 57, p. 10 (Turkey).

[55] A/C.3/47/SR.6. 21 October 1992, para. 18, p. 6 (Malaysia). A/C.3/51/SR.26, 18 September 1997, para. 2, p. 2 (Nepal).

[56] A/C.3/51/SR 28, 19 September 1997, para.2, p.2 (Slovenia).

[57] A/C.3/48/SR.21, 26 November 1993, para. 14, pp. 4-5 (the Philippines).

[58] A/C.3/50/SR.5/ 27 October 1995, para.1, p.2 (Mauritania).

[59] A/C.3/50/SR.8, 30 October 1995, para. 9, p.4 (Libyan Arab Jamahiriya).

[60] A/C.3/49/SR.6, 31 October 1994, para.54, p.10 (Albania).

[61] A/C.3/49/SR. 4, 26 October 1994, para.16, p. 4.

[62] A/C.3/52/SR.37, 3 December 1997, para. 44, p.5 (Azerbaijan).

[63] A/C.3/49/SR.6, 31 October 1994, para.54, p.10 (Albania). A/C.3/51 SR.28, 19 September 1997, para.17, p.5 (Guyana); A/C.3/50/SR.6, 20 October 1995, para.1, p.2 (Malaysia). A/C.3/50/ SR.7, 30 October 1995, para.9, p.4 (Japan).

[64] *Chicago Tribune,* 24 May 1992, cited in Moynihan, above, p.18.

[65] An exchange of population of both nationals (550,000) was agreed by the Greek and Turkish Treaty, 7 November 1919.

[66] Under the German-Rumanian Treaty, 22 October 1940, 15,000 Germans were removed from Dobrudja and 55,000 from Southern Bukovina.

[67] 128,000 Germans in Volhynia, Eastern Galicia and the Narew areas in Poland were expelled by the occupied Soviet forces on 3 Nov. 1939. When the USSR annexed the Baltic States, 67,000 Germans from Lithuania, Latvia, and Estonia were forced to leave on 10, January 1941.

[68] According to the Bulgarian and Rumanian Treaty of 7 September 1940, both parties agreed to a reciprocal repatriation under which 63,000 Bulgarians and 11,000 Rumanians were exchanged.

[69] The Treaty between Poland and Yugoslavia (1946) agreed reciprocal population transfers.

[70] In the treaty between Poland and the Soviet Union in 1944 it was agreed that the Poles and Jews living in the USSR should return to Poland whilst the Russians, Ukrainians, Byelorussians, Ruthenians and Lithuanians living in Poland should be taken by the USSR.

[71] By the Hitler-Mussolini Convention, 23 June 1939 it was agreed that the Germans living in Italy should be returned to German. At least 75,000 Germans left for Germany.

[72] GA Res. 47/80, 16 December 1992, para.3 ('Ethnic Cleansing and Racial Hatred'). See also GA Res. 46/242, 25 August 1992.

[73] Ethnic cleansing violates the principles embodied in the UN Charter, the Universal Declaration of Human Rights (UDHR); the International Convention on Civil and Political Rights (ICCPR), Res. 2100 A (XXI) Annex; the International Convention on the Elimination of All Forms of Racial Discrimination, Res. 2106 A (XX) Annex; the Convention against Torture and other Cruel, Inhuman or Degrading Treatment or Punishments, Res. 39/46; International humanitarian law, including the Geneva Convention of 12 August 1949 (UN Treaty Series, vol. 75, nos. 970-973) and the Additional Protocol thereto of 1977 (UN Treaty Series, vol.1125, nos. 17512 and 17513).

[74] GA Res. 47/80, 16 December 1992 ('Ethnic Cleansing and Racial Hatred').

[75] UN Special Rapporteur Tadeusz Mazowieck, *The report of the situation of human rights in the territory of the former Yugoslavia*, SC Res. 24809/ 1992.

[76] On behalf of the International Tribunal for the prosecution of persons responsible for serious violation of international humanitarian law committed in the territory of former Yugoslavia since 1991, A/52/PV.44, 4 November 1997, p.2.

[77] GA Res. 49/196, 23 December 1994, para.6 ('Situation of human rights in the Republic of Bosnia and Herzegovina, the Republic of Croatia and the Federal Republic of Yugoslavia'). See also GA Res. 47/147, 18 December 1992, p. 3.

[78] GA Res. 49/196, 23 December 1994, preamble.

[79] A/C.3/50/SR.6, 20 October 1995, para. 1, p. 2 (Malaysia).

[80] Genocide is a crime under international law. According to Article II of the Convention on the Prevention and Punishment of the Crime of Genocide 1948, genocide means any of the following acts committed with intent to destroy, in whole or in part, a national, ethnical, racial or religious group, as such:

> Killing members of the group, causing serious bodily or mental harm to members of the group, deliberately inflicting on the group conditions of life calculated to bring about its physical destruction in whole or in part, imposing measures intended to prevent births within the group, forcibly transferring children of the group to another group.

[81] The Trial Chamber, Press release, JL-PIU-372-E, The Hague, 10 December 1998. Similar charges were levelled against *Radislav* v *Krstic*, see Office of the Prosecutor, Press release, JL/PIU/368-E, The Hague, 2 December 1998, the statement by the Prosecutor regarding the detention of Radislav Krstic.

[82] GA Res. 47/147, 18 December 1992, para. 3; GA Res. 47/121, 18 December 1992 ("The Situation of Human Rights in the Territory of the former

Yugoslavia"); GA Res. 49/196, 23 December 1994 ('Situation of human right in the Republic of Bosnia and Herzegovina, the Republic of Croatia and the Federal Republic of Yugoslavia').

[83] GA Res. 49/205, 23 December 1994, para. 2 ('Rape and abuse of women in the areas of armed conflict in the former Yugoslavia').

[84] *Anto Furundzija* v *Prosecutor*, The Trial Chambers, Press Release, JL-PIU - 372-E, The Hague, 10 December 1998.

[85] A/C.3/48/SR.9, 16 November 1993, para. 61, p. 13 (Japan).

[86] Smith and Hutchinson expressed rather optimistic view on this. They write, "ethnic conflicts and nationalism are becoming a secondary concern and increasingly irrelevant. They may trouble the surface of world developments for a time, but they will soon disappear as people come to appreciate the massive problems of planetary survival". See Smith, A. D. and Hutchinson, J. eds. (1994), *Nationalism,* Oxford UP: Oxford, p.11.

References

Armstrong, H. F. (1949), 'Coalition for Peace', 27 (1) *Foreign Affairs: An American Quarterly Review*, pp. 1-16.

Azcarate, P. De. (1945), *The League of Nations and National Minorities: An Experiment*, Carnagie Endowment for International Peace: Washington.

Bell-Fialkoff, (1993), 'Brief History of Ethnic Cleansing', 72 *Foreign Affairs,* pp. 110-121.

Boven, T. van. (1979), 'United Nations and Human Rights: A Critical Appraisal' in Cassese, A. ed. *UN Law, Fundamental Rights: Two Topics in International Law*, Alphenaan den Rijn: Sijthoff, p. 121.

Bremmer, I. and Taras, T. eds. (1993), *Nations and Politics in the Soviet Successor States*, Cambridge UP: Cambridge.

Caenegem, R. C. Van. (1995), *An Historical Introduction to Western Constitutional Law*, Cambridge UP: Cambridge.

Campbell, D. T. (1971), *Ethnocentrism: Theories of Conflict, Ethnic Attitudes and Group Behaviour*, John Wiley and Sons: New York.

Capotorti, F. (1976), 'The Protection of Minorities: Under Multilateral Agreements on Human Rights', 2 *IYIL*, pp. 3-32.

Caportorti, F. (1979), *Study of the Rights of Persons Belonging to Ethnic, Religious and Linguistic Minorities*, UN Doc. E/CN. 4/Sub.2/384.

Claude, I. L. (1955), *National Minorities: International Problem*, Mass: Harvard University Press.

Cohen, R. and Deng, F. M. (1998), 'Exodus Within Borders: The Uprooted Who Never Left Home', 77 (4) *Foreign Affairs*, pp. 12-16.

Dinstein, Y. (1967), 'Collective Human Rights of Peoples and Minorities', 25 *ICLQ*, pp.111-118.

Eddison, E. (1993), *The Protection of Minorities at the Conference on Security and Co-operation in Europe*, in *Papers in the Theory and Practice of Human Rights*, no.5, Human Rights Centre: University of Essex.

Eide, A. (1991), 'Importance and Ambiguity of Minority Issues', 66 *Notre Dame LR*, pp. 1311-1353.

Eide, A. et al (1992), *The Universal Declaration of Human Rights: A Commentary*, Scandinavian University Press: Oslo.

Ermacora, F. (1983), 'The Protection of Minorities before the United Nations', 182 *Receil Des Cours*, pp. 251-370.

Franck, T. M. (1993), 'Postmodern Tribalism and the Right to Secession', in C. Brolmann,. R. Lefeber, and M. Zieck (eds), *Peoples and Minorities in International Law*, Martinus Nijhoff: Dordrecht /Boston/London, pp. 3- 27.

Gahali, B. B. (1995), *Confronting New Challenges: Annual Report on the Work of the Organisation*, UN: New York.

Ghali, B. B, (1996), 'Overview', in *The United Nations and the Independence of Eritrea*, Department of Public Information, UN: New York, pp. 3-37.

Gilbert, G. (1992), 'The Legal Protection Accorded to Minority Groups in Europe', 23 *NYIL*, pp. 67- 104.

Glazer, N. (1982), 'From Class-Based to Ethnic Based Politics', in J. E. Daniel (ed), *Governing Peoples and Territories*, Institute for the Study of Human Issues: Philadelphia, pp.47-56.

Goodrich, L. M. (1961), *The United Nations*, Stevens and Sons Ltd: London.

Grannoff, J. (1993), 'A Unity Beyond Religious and Ethnic Conflicts', in *New Realities: Disarmament, Peace Building and Global Security*, UN Publication: New York, pp. 23- 25.

Green, J. F. (1956), *The United Nations and Human Rights*, The Brooking Institution: Washington.

Greenberg, J. (1984), 'Race, Sex and Religious Discrimination', in T. Meron (ed), *Human Rights in International Law: Legal Policy Issues*, Clarendon Press: Oxford, pp. 309.

Gurr, T. R. (1993), *Minorities at Risk: A Global View of Ethnopolitical Conflict*, Institute of Peace Press: Washington.

Hannum, H. (1989), 'The Limits of Sovereignty and Minority Rule: Minorities, Indigenous Peoples, and the Right to Autonomy', in E. L. Lutz, H. Hannum, and K. J. Burke (eds), *New Direction of Human Rights*, University of Pennsylvania Press: Philadelphia, pp. 1-24.

Hannum, H. (1990), *Autonomy, Sovereignty and Self-Determination*, University of Pennsylvania Press: Philadelphia.

Hannum, H. (1991), 'Contemporary Developments in the International Protection of the Rights of Minorities', 66 *Notre Dame LR*, pp. 1431- 1448.

Heyking, B. (1928), 'The International Protection of Minorities: The Achilles' Heel of the League of Nations', in 13 *Problems of Peace and War*, Grotius Society Publication, London, pp. 31- 51.

Hudson, M. O. (1945), 'The New World Court', 24 (1) *Foreign Affairs: An American Quarterly Review*, pp. 75-84.

Humphrey, J. P. (1968), 'The United Nations Sub-Commission on the Prevention of Discrimination and Protection of Minorities', 62 *AJIL*, pp. 869-888.

Humphrey, J. P. (1979), 'The Universal Declaration of Human Rights: Its History, Impact and Juridical Character', in B. G. Ramcharan (ed), *Human Rights: Thirty Years After the Universal Declaration*, Martinus Nijhoff, pp. 21-37.

Humphrey, J. P. (1989), *No Distant Millennium: The International Law of Human Rights*, UNESCO: New York.

Humphrey, J. P. (1994), *Human Rights and the United Nations: A Great Adventure*, Transnational Publishers INC: New York.

Isaacs, H. R. (1975), *Idols of the Tribes*, Hamper and Row: New York.

Jackson, R. H. (1994), *Quasi-States: Sovereignty, International Relations and the Third World*, Cambridge University Press: Cambridge.

Jessup, P. C. (1944), 'UNRRA: Sample of the World Organization', *Foreign Affairs: An American Quarterly Review*, pp. 362-373.

Jones, M. G. (1949), 'National Minorities: A Case Study in International Protection', 14 *Law and Contemporary Problems,* pp. 599-626.

Kertesz, S. D. (1949), 'Human Rights in the Peace Treaties', 14 *Law and Contemporary Problems*, pp. 627- 635.

Kunz, J. L. (1954), 'The Present Status of the International Law for the Protection of Minorities', 48 *AJIL,* pp. 282-287.

Kymlicka, W. (1995), *The Rights of Minority Cultures*, Oxford UP: Oxford.

Ladas, S. R. (1932), *The Exchange of Minorities: Bulgaria, Greece and Turkey*, New York.

Laponce, J. C. (1960), *The Protection of Minorities*, University of California Press: Berkeley and Los Angeles.

Lauterpacht, H. ed. (1912), *Oppenheim's International Law*, vol. 1, Peace, 8th ed. Longman: London.

Lawson. S. (1996), 'Self-Determination as Ethnocracy: Perspectives from the South Pacific', in M. Sellers (ed), *World Order, Sovereignty, Human Rights and the Self-Determination of Peoples*, BERG: Oxford/Washington, pp. 153-175.

Leff, C. S. (1999), 'Democratization and Disintegration in Multinational States: The Breakup of the Communist Federations', 51 (2) *World Politics,* pp. 205-235.

Lemarchand, R. (1994), *Burundi: Ethnocide as Discourse and Practice*, Woodraw Wilson Centre, Cambridge UP: Cambridge.

Levin, R. A. and D. T. Campbell (1971), *Ethnocentrism, Theories of Conflict: Ethnic Attitudes and Group Behaviour*, John Wiley and Sons: New York.

Lijphart, A. (1995), 'Self-Determination Versus Pre-Determination of Ethnic Minorities in Power-Sharing Systems', in W. Kymlicka (ed), *The Rights of Minority Cultures*, Oxford UP: Oxford, pp. 275- 287.

Luard, E. (1982), *A History of the United Nations: The Year of Western Domination, 1945-1955*, vol. 1, Macmillan: London.

Macartney, C. A. (1934), *National States and National Minorities*, Oxford UP: London.

Malinverni, G. (1991), 'The Draft Convention for the Protection of Minorities', 12 (6/7) *HRLJ*, pp. 265- 269.

Manning, N. (1989), *The Cauldron of Ethnicity in the Modern World*, Chicago UP: Chicago.

McGoldrick, D. (1993), 'The Development of the Conference on Security and Coorperation in Europe', in B. S. Jackson and D. McGoldrick (eds), *Legal Visions of the New Europe*, Graham and Trotman/Martinus Nijhoff: London, pp. 135- 182.

McKean, W. (1985), *Equality and Discrimination Under International Law*, Clarendon Press: Oxford.

McLellan, J. and Richmond, H. A. (1994), 'Multiculturalism in Crisis: A Postmodern Perspective on Canada' 17 (4) *Ethnic and Racial Studies*, pp. 663- 683.

Miller, D. H. (1928), *The Drafting of the Covenant*, vol. II, G. P. Putnam's Sons: New York.

Moller, J. (1992), 'Article 7', in Eide, A. et al, *The Universal Declaration of Human Rights: A Commentary*, Scandinavian University Press: Oslo, pp. 115-142.

Monshipouri, M. (1994), 'Comments on Minorities at Risk', 16 *HRQ*, pp. 580- 584.

Moynihan, D. P. (1994), *Pandaemonium: Ethnicity in International Politics*, Oxford UP: Oxford.

Mullerson, R. (1993), 'Minorities in Eastern Europe and the Former USSR: Problems, Tendencies and Protection', 56 *MLR*, pp. 793-811.

Mullerson, R. (1994), *International Law, Rights and Politics: Developments in Eastern Europe and the CIS*, LSE and Routledge: London.

Nordquist, Kjell-Ake, (1998), 'Autonomy as a Conflict-Solving Mechanism: An Overview', in M. Suksi (ed), *Autonomy: Applications and Implications*, Kluwer Law International: The Hague/London/Boston, pp. 59- 74.

Nowa, R. de. (1965), 'The International Protection of National Minorities and Human Rights', 11 *Howard LJ*, pp. 275- 286.

Nowak, M. (1993), *UN Covenant on Civil and Political Rights: CPPR Commentary*, N. P. Engel: Strasbourg.

Parkinson, F. (1995), 'Ethnicity and Independent Statehood', in Jackson and James eds. (1995), above, pp.336-340.

Peretz, M. (1992), *New Republic*, cited in Moynihan (1994), as above.

Petrovic, D. (1994), 'Ethnic Cleansing: An Attempt at Methodology', 5 *EJIL*, pp. 342- 359.

Ponnambalam, S. (1983), *Sri Lanka: The National Question and the Tamil Liberation Struggle*, Tamil Information Centre with Zed Books: London.

Preece, J. J. (1998), 'Ethnic Cleansing as an Instrument of Nation-State Creation: Changing State Practices and Evolving Legal Norms', 20 (4) *HRQ*, pp.817-842.

Ramcharan, B.G. (1989), *The Concept of Present Status of the International Protection of Human Rights: Forty Years After the Universal Declaration*, Martinus Nijhoff: Dordrecht/Boston/London.

Robinson, J. (1943), *Were the Minorities Treaties Failure?* Institute of Jewish Affairs: New York.

Robinson, J. (1946), *Human Rights and Fundamental Freedoms in the Charter of the United Nations*, Institute of Jewish Affairs: New York.

Robinson, J. (1971), 'International Protection of Minorities: A Global View', *IYHR*, pp. 61-91.

Roth, S. J. (1992), 'Towards a Minority Convention: Its Need and Content', in Y. Dinstein, and M. Tabory (eds), *The Protection of Minorities and Human Rights*, Kluwer: Dordrecht, pp. 83-117.

Rupasinghe, K. (1992), 'Democratization Process and Their Implications For International Security', in *Peace and Conflict Issues After the Cold War*, UNESCO, pp. 25- 44.

Rusel, R. B. (1958), *A History of the United Nations Charter*, The Brookings Institution: Washington.

Said, A. A. and Simmons, L. R. eds. (1976), *Ethnicity in an International Context*, New Jersey.

Salvemini, G. (1946), 'The Italio-Jugoslav Frontier', 24 (2) *Foreign Affairs: An American Quarterly Review,* pp. 341-346.

Salzberg, J. (1973), *The United Nations Sub-Commission: A Fundamental Analysis*, University Microfilms International: Ann Arbor.

Sanders, D. (1991), 'Collective Rights', 13 *HRQ*, pp. 369-386.

Shaw, M. N. (1997), 'Peoples, Territorialisms and Boundaries', 3 *EJIL*, pp. 478-507.

Sigler, J. A. (1983), *Minority Rights: A Comparative Analysis*, Greenwood Press: London.

Skogly, S. (1992), 'Article 2', in Eide *et al* ed. above , pp. 57-71.

Smith, A. D. and Hutchinson, J. eds. (1994), *Nationalism*, Oxford UP: Oxford.

Sohn, L. B. (1981), 'The Rights of Minorities', in Henkin, L. ed. *The International Bill of Rights: The Covenant on Civil and Political Rights*, Colombia UP: New York, pp. 270-289.

Soyinka, W. (1996), *The Open Space of a Continent,* Oxford UP: Oxford.

Stavenhagen, R. (1996), *Ethnic Conflicts and the Nation-States*, Macmillan: London.

Sumner, W. G. (1906), *Folkways*, Ginn: New York cited in R. A. Levine, and D. T. Campbell, *Ethnocentrism: Theories of Ethnic Conflict: Ethnic Attitudes and Group Behaviour*, John Wiley and Sons: New York.

Symonides, J. (1991), 'Collective Rights of Minorities in Europe', in R. Lefeber, M. Fitzmourice, and E. W. Vierdag (eds), *The Changing Political Structure of Europe: Aspects of International Law*, Nijhoff: Dordrecht, Boston and London, pp. 107- 125.

The United Nations (1996), *The Blue Helmets: A Review of United Nations Peace Keeping*, 3rd ed. UN: New York.

Thornberry, P. (1991a), *Minorities and Human Rights Law*, Minority Rights Group: London.

Thornberry, P. (1991b), *International Law and the Rights of Minorities*, Oxford UP: Oxford.

Thornberry, P. (1993), 'The UN Declaration on the Rights of Persons Belonging To National or Ethnic, Religious and Linguistic Minorities: Background, Analysis and Observations', in A. Phillips, and A. Rosas, (eds), *The UN Minority Rights Declaration*, Turku/Abo: London, pp. 11- 72.

Thornberry, P. (1993), 'The Democratic or Internal Aspects of Self-Determination with Some Remarks on Federalism', in C. Tomuschat (ed), *Modern Law of Self-Determination*, Martinus Nijhoff: Dordrecht/Boston and London, pp.101-138.

Zayas, M. D. (1993), 'The International Judicial Protection of Peoples and Minorities', in C. Brolmann, R. Lefeber, and M. Zieck (eds), *Peoples and Minorities in International Law*, Martnus Nijhoff: Dordrecht/Boston/London, pp. 253-287.

2 Minorities?

Introduction

Minority is not legally defined. No one knows precisely what a *minority* is although it is generally accepted that "such groups exist in nearly every country". As many States recognised, a majority of States are now ethnically diverse.[1] According to Roth (1992) contemporary polities are a mosaic of distinct peoples. According to some reports, there are about, 5,000 'distinct communities' world-wide (Gurr and Scarritt, 1989). Special rapporteur Eide noted that "nearly all States are pluri-ethnic or pluri-religious and will remain so. If anything, national societies will become more, not less".[2]

The dictionary meaning of the term *minority* is "the condition or fact of being small, inferior, or subordinate". This term was in use in religious literature as far back as 1533. In 1646 Sir T. Brown used it to indicate 'smallness' ("There may, I confess, from this narrow time of gestation ensue a minority, or smallness in the exclusion").[3] In the political sense it is said to have been used first by Edmund Burke in 1790 ("In a democracy, the majority of the citizens are capable of exercising the most cruel oppression upon the minority") although in 1736 *minority* was used by Ainsworth to indicate 'a lesser number' (Ermacora, 1983:287).

Yet, in terms of general international law there is no precise definition of *minority* (Capotorti Report,[4] 1979:5; Shaw, 1991; Hannum, 1991:1431; Gilbert, 1992:70). Special Rapporteur Capotorti remarked (at 5), "The preparation of a definition capable of being universally accepted has always proved a task of such difficulty and complexity that neither the experts in this field nor the organs of the international agencies have been able to accomplish it to date". Uncertainty about the precise definition has created confusion and ambiguity, and the concept of *minority* has become a controversial subject amongst international jurists and States. Without knowing who minorities are it is difficult to accommodate specific rights (Packer, 1993:26) because minority rights are different from general human rights. Consequently the rights and claims of minorities may be obstructed when they try to assert legal claims based on group identity before international tribunals. It is not necessary to emphasise that the identity of a person with a group is associated with his or her rights. How international

46

law has so far failed to identify and define a *minority* in specific legal terms
and why States have been reluctant to do so is the focus of this chapter. Non-
recognition of minority rights has also been instrumental in the escalation of
tension between minorities and States.

2.1 *The Dilemma of Defining 'a Minority': "Controversial and, as yet, Unfruitful"*

States generally seem to be reluctant to agree a precise definition of
minorities. Special Rapporteur Capotorti reported (1979: 95):

> When it comes to determining what groups constitute minorities, all kinds of
> difficulties arise. We have seen that, religious minorities apart, relatively few
> States expressly recognize the existence in their populations of groups described
> as 'ethnic or linguistic minorities' and that, while a considerable number of States
> have introduced measures granting special rights to various ethnic and linguistic
> groups, the majority prefer not to apply the term 'minority' to them.

Eddison (1993:3) referred to the difficulties which States face in the search
for an internationally acceptable definition of minority, as "a fundamental
paradox of human rights discourses", "definitional vacuum", and
"conceptual imprecision". She says that such attempts "have been notably
controversial and, as yet, unfruitful" (Eddison, 1993:3). One possible reason
given by Wright (1996:195) is that international law has consistently resisted
attempts to arrive at a precise definition (see further Bagley, 1950). Is it due
to the fact, as argued by Andrysek (1989:13 cited in Packer, 1993), that the
concept of *minority* is so "complex, vague and imprecise"? However, as
Ramaga (1992:409) states, the dilemma of defining the term *minority* is not a
new phenomenon. This is, in his view, due to "historical vagaries of
terminology" (see also Nowak, 1993:487). Other possible reasons are also
discussed, e.g. a) the system has been operating with ambiguities"; and b) the
concept of minorities lies upon the fault line of international personality
(Thornberry, 1991a:6), and it occupies an "indeterminate space along the
uneasy and volatile spectrum that ranges from the State itself at one end to
the individual at the other" (Shaw, 1991:14). Therefore the omission of a
definition of minority, as pointed out by Thornberry (1991b), is "not a great
surprise to international lawyers". This situation has become so confused and
uncertain that many scholars simply prefer to ignore it (Packer, 1993:24).
Rodley (1995:6) for example, seems not to want even to "revisit the

vexatious problem of the definition of a minority," because it is impossible "to identify the persons that would be the group rights holders."

It seems that there are two schools of thought on the desirability of having a precise definition of the concept of *minority*. One view appears to be that it is not imperative to have a definition of what constitutes a *minority* to take measures to promote the rights of minorities within the nation-State system. Capotorti, Thornberry, Hannum, Malinverni and Alfredsson and Zayas, to cite a few, support this theory. For instance, Alfredsson and Zayas (1993:3) argue that a lack of definition does not necessarily prevent the adoption of meaningful measures for the protection and promotion of the rights of minorities. According to Hannum (1991:1431), even without a definition, the term *minority* can be understood using common sense. Thornberry (1991b: 164) is of the view that for the sake of clarity it may be useful to have a definition, but, "the lack of a universal definition does not, however, prevent a description of what is and has been understood by the terms, including contradictory understandings and possible future interpretations". Malinverni (1991:267) argues that a definition is not indispensable or necessary for the protection of minorities. Many of these arguments are in agreement with the former Special Rapporteur to the Sub-Commission, Capotorti, who considered that a precise definition would no doubt "be of a great value" to the protection of minorities' rights, but pointed out that a definition should not be a "precondition" for the application of minority rights agreed by international treaties (Capotorti report, 1979:95). He pointed out (at 95):

> At the present stage, it would be illusory to suppose that a definition likely to command general approval could be achieved. In the view of the Special Rapporteur, such a definition would certainly be of great value on the doctrinal plane, but it should not be considered a pre-condition for the application of the principles set forth in article 27 of the Covenant. There are other examples of the occasional application of a rule in positive law without general agreement having being reached on the precise meaning of its terms. It should be noted in this connexion that the Commission on Human Rights did not consider it necessary to define the term 'minority' before setting up the Sub-Commission on Prevention and Protection of Minorities. It will also be recalled that the General Assembly of the United Nations did not wait for an exhaustive and universal definition of the notion of the 'right of peoples to self-determination' before proclaiming the application of the principle.

He continues (at 95):

The problem of defining the term 'minority' has never been an obstacle to the drawing-up of the numerous international instruments containing provisions on the rights of certain groups of the population to preserve their culture and use their own language. The terminology used to refer to such groups varies from one instrument to another. We have seen, for example, that the UNESCO Convention against Discrimination in Education mentions 'national minorities', while the expression 'national, ethnical, racial or religious group' is used in the Convention on the Prevention and Punishment of the Crime of Genocide and 'racial or ethnic group' in the International Convention on the Elimination of All Forms of Racial Discrimination. Further examples are the fact that the agreement signed in 1946 between the Italian and Austrian Governments speaks of the 'German-speaking inhabitants' of Bolzano Province and some communes of Trento Province; that the agreement between Pakistan and Indian refers to 'minorities'; that the 1954 memorandum of understanding on the status of Trieste refers to Italian and Yugoslav 'ethnic groups'; and that the 1955 Austrian State Treaty speaks of the 'Slovenian and Croat minorities.

Moreover, this is generally how most legal systems work. Many terms lack precise definition whether they are in the international or domestic arenas (Packer, 1993:23). Of course many international treaties regulating minority rights have prevailed without a precise definition since the 17th century (Capotorti report, 1979:1; Thornberry, 1991b:10), not to mention the great experiment of minority regime under the League of Nations. Max van der Stoel, the OSCE High Commissioner on National Minorities (1993:22), also sees difficulties to be overcome in finding a definition. He stated (at 22):

What is a minority? I do not pretend to improve on the work of many experts who over the years have not been able to agree on a definition, so I won't offer you one of my own. I would note, however, that the existence of a minority is a question of fact and not of definition...Even though, I may not have a definition of what constitutes a minority, I would dare to say that I know a minority when I see one (see further Lerner, 1991:10).

There is an element of truth in this assertion. "Most of the time", writes Alfredsson (1992:93), "it is rather self-evident which groups constitute minorities". He further argues that with a few exclusions definitional issue can be resolved. However, a weakness of this argument is his belief that the unresolved areas could be left to the States and international organs to deal with. As will be shown below, this has never worked as far as the issue of definition is concerned.

Ermacora (1983), Sohn (1981), Eide (1991), Gilbert (1996) and Packer (1993) dispute the practicability of such views mentioned above. It can be argued, as pointed out by these eminent scholars, that without finding a meaningful and commonly agreed definition, the claims of minorities may not properly be arbitrated or identified within the meaning of public international law since there are provisions regulating the rights of minorities and their protection particularly in UN treaties, resolutions and declarations. Ermacora (1983:270), for example, is of the view that minority protection is only possible if there is a clarity about the term *minority*. He states (at 287):

> In certain situations it might even not be necessary for the purpose of United Nations work to define the said notions. However, for the legislative policy of the United Nations, for the consideration of State reports in proceedings before the Human Rights Committee, the Committee on Racial Questions, for solving State disputes, for considering situations of massive and gross violation of human rights or for deciding about individual cases it is necessary to know what the expression minority or group will mean.

Having agreed with such views, Sohn (1981:280) emphasised that it is not only a question of theoretical importance, but also a practical one to have a precise definition. In terms of article 27 of the ICCPR, argues Sohn, lack of a definition gives rise to many legal complexities (see further Pejic, 1997:675). Eide (1991) has also repeatedly emphasised the usefulness of developing guidelines, which help understand the nature of such groups and the basis for group membership. He stressed that the definition of a minority is one of the substantial issues to which the international community has to find a positive answer (Eide, 1991:1347; see also Packer, 1993:24-26). Such arguments do have a strong basis. For the purpose of legal requirements, and above all for the identification of rights holders, argued Packer (at 26), there should be a definition (see further Dyke, 1995:31-56). In agreeing with Packer, Gilbert (1996:162) also points out that rights cannot be accorded to a "wholly nebulous concept"; it is therefore necessary to have a precise definition. In the view of Sigler (1983), this is not an impossible task either if there is a will on the part of the international community. He points out (at 4-5) that "however vague and imprecise the meaning of the term 'minority', it is possible to strive for a common sense definition that meets the ordinary expectations of ordinary people". Without clear-cut conceptual guidelines, as some critics say, the system of minority protection is open to manipulation, thereby allowing unwilling States to abuse the system (Nowak, 1993:487). Any attempt to confer rights without identifying the right holders is comparable to putting the cart before the horse (Packer, 1993:50).

2.2 *Reluctance: "In Law All Definitions are Dangerous"?*

For a long time, specifically since the regime of the League of Nations, minorities have been defined and identified by reference to religion, language, culture, ethnicity, nationality and race (Ramaga, 1992: 410) or by their historical country of origin: for instance, the 'German speaking inhabitants', 'German speaking citizens', and 'German speaking elements'[5] or simply, 'minority elements'.[6]

Some notable attempts were made by the Permanent Court of International Justice in 1923, 1930 and 1935 respectively in the *Advisory Opinion on the Acquisition of Polish Nationality* (Series B/7, 1923) the *Greeko-Bulgarian Communities* Case (PCIJ, Series B/17, 1930) and *Minority Schools in Albania* Case (Series AB/64/17, 1935). In the *Greeko-Bulgarian Communities* case it was held:

> By tradition...the 'community' is a group of persons living in a given country or locality, having a race, religion, language and traditions of their own and united by this identity of race, religion, language and traditions in a sentiment of solidarity, with a view to preserving their traditions, maintaining their form of worship, ensuring the instruction and upbringing of their children in accordance with the spirit and traditions of their race and rendering mutual assistance to each other.

In the *Minority Schools in Albania* case the PCIJ held:

> The idea underlining the treaties for the protection of minorities is to secure for certain elements incorporated in a State, the population of which differs from them in race, language, or religion, the possibility of living peaceably alongside that population, and co-operating amicably with it, while at the same time preserving the characteristics which distinguish them from the majority, and satisfying the ensuing special needs.

It is clearly evident that rather than providing a definition in legal terms in both these cases the PCIJ tried to find certain characteristics which distinguish the minority from the majority population. It also placed emphasis on subjective factors. Any subsequent investigation into the definition of *minority* could have been initiated using these judgments as a foundation. Yet there is no evidence that the Economic and Social Council or the Commission on Human Rights tried to do so.

In 1947, by Res. 9 (ii) of 1946, the Economic and Social Council empowered the Commission on Human Rights to find a definition and to produce a draft containing the measures necessary for the protection of minorities. Consequently, a Sub-Commission on the Prevention of Discrimination and Protection of Minorities (Sub-Commission)[7] was created by the Commission on Human Rights, of which the original terms of references were; "In the first instance, to examine what provisions should be adopted in the definition of the principles which are to be applied in the field of the prevention of discrimination on grounds of race, sex, language or religion, and in the field of the protection of minorities, and to make recommendations to the Commission on urgent problems in these fields." This provision was, however, later revised as follows: "To undertake studies, particularly in the light of the Universal Declaration of Human Rights; and to make recommendations to the Commission on Human Rights concerning the prevention of discrimination of any kind relating to human rights and fundamental freedoms and the protection of racial, national, religious and linguistic minorities".

The Sub-Commission was in fact very zealous in fulfilling its obligations and in particular in its desire to find a definition of minorities in order to protect them and promote their rights. In its first session it identified some basic characteristics of a minority:

> A minority is a non-dominant group, while wishing in general for equality of treatment with the majority, wish for a measure of differential treatment in order to preserve basic characteristics which they possess and which distinguish them from the majority of the population.... The characteristics meriting such protection are race, religion, and language. In order to qualify for protection a minority must owe individual allegiance to the government of the State in which it lives. Its members must also be nationals of that State.[8]

In its second session the Sub-Commission placed on its agenda the "Definition and Clarification of Minorities"[9] which was prepared by the Secretary General. It contained 'principle elements' which were to be taken into account in any future attempts at a definition.[10] At its third, fourth and fifth sessions, the Sub-Commission suggested that the Commission on Human Rights should adopt a draft resolution containing a definition of minorities.[11] In 1951 the Sub-Commission at its third session submitted to the Commission on Human Rights a draft resolution[12] containing a definition of minorities. Its main recommendations were:

> a) The term minority includes only those non-dominant groups in a population which possess and wish to preserve stable ethnic, religious

or linguistic traditions or characteristics markedly different from those of the rest of the populations;

b) Such minorities should properly include a number of persons sufficient by themselves to preserve such traditions or characteristics;

c) Such minorities must be loyal to the State of which they are nationals.[13]

Although the Commission on Human Rights examined this proposal the Sub-Commission was not offered any significant encouragement to proceed with the task of finalising a definition. In fact, on each occasion, the reports sent by the Sub-Commission to the Commission on Human Rights were sent back for further consideration. Several studies carried out by the Sub-Commission during the period 1947-1954 were not successful due to the non-cooperation of both the Commission on Human Rights and the Economic and Social Council, and to the realpolitik of State representatives (Humphrey, 1968:877; Salzberg, 1973:140-46; Ermacora, 1983:270). In 1951 the Economic and Social Council even attempted to discontinue the work of the Sub-Commission,[14] the move that did not succeed due to the intervention of the UN General Assembly. Subsequently, the Sub-Commission decided in 1954 at its 7th session not to proceed with the task of drafting a definition.[15]

The prevailing view amongst State representatives was that all definitions are hazardous (*omni definitio periculosa*) (see Rosenne, 1993:515). Some are still of the view that it is extremely difficult to find a definition[16] free from political bias (Ermacora, 1983:269) and acceptable to the international community due to chameleon-like attributes of minorities.[17] Although the concept of minority has certainly been 'one of the most discussed issues'[18] especially in the Sub-Commission, in its early years even the top ranking officials of the Sub-Commission expressed their doubts about the usefulness of having a definition, on the grounds, *inter alia*, that the definition of minorities would be purely academic.[19] More significantly, as pointed out by the first Secretary General of the UN in 1950, the definition of a *minority* is particularly difficult because of the fact that "minorities are social realities which are dynamic rather than static, and which change under the influence of varying circumstances".[20] It was further said that the term *minority* could not for practical purposes be defined simply by interpreting the word in its literal sense. If this were the case, "nearly all the communities existing within a State would be styled *minorities*, including families, social classes, cultural groups, speakers of dialects etc. Such a definition would be useless."[21]

This issue aroused some interest again in the 1960s. There was much argument for and against a definition of a minority during the period leading up to 1965. This debate influenced the Sub-Commission to proceed with its initial work on a definition. Yet the decisive moment came in 1966 with the completion of the ICCPR. Since then, the definitional issue has taken a new direction and momentum. Article 27 of the ICCPR recognises three categories of minority groups, i.e. ethnic, religious and linguistic minorities. Capotorti writes (at 35):

> Although the expression 'rights of minorities' is used in common parlance, it is persons belonging to minorities, in community with the other members of their group, who are regarded in article 27 as having the right to enjoy their own culture, to practise their own religion and to use their own language.

However, there is still no definition provided in this article, so leaving the matter open for experts to deal with it in the future. Therefore the Sub-Commission decided in 1967 to include in its programme and future tasks an undertaking to study "the notion of minority, taking into account ethnic, religious and linguistic factors in multi-national societies" (Resolution 9 (xx) 1967), as soon as possible.[22] In 1969 ECOSOC mandated the Sub-Commission to undertake the envisaged study. To fulfil this task, the Sub-Commission appointed Francisco Capotorti in 1971.

The appointment of Capotorti as a Special Rapporteur is one of the best steps the UN has taken in this field. But he had to overcome enormous difficulties due to States' reluctance to provide information about minorities and their situations. Nonetheless, in 1979 he produced an excellent report entitled, 'The Study on the Rights of Persons Belonging to Ethnic, Religious and Linguistic Minorities' containing the most significant definitional attempt so far. It defines minorities as follows (at paragraph 568):

> A group numerically inferior to the rest of the population of a State, in a non-dominant position, whose members being nationals of the State, possess ethnic, religious or linguistic characteristics differing from those of the rest of the population and show, if only implicitly, a sense of solidarity, directed towards preserving their culture, traditions, religion or language.

Capotorti's definition was hailed as "the widest recognition in theory and practice" (Nowak, 1993:487; Thornberry, 1991b:152; Gilbert, 1996:164; Ermacora, 1983:292; Roth, 1992:184). Yet, the definition proposed by Capotorti was not taken seriously by the Commission on Human Rights and the Economic and Social Council.

The definitional issue was the subject of extensive discussions in the 1980s. In particular, at the 30th session in 1981 it was emphasised, as a matter of principle, that the notion of minority should be elaborated in legal terms in order to identify them. However, the Working Group, which was established in pursuance of resolution 5 (xxx) of the Commission on Human Rights, after a lengthy debate decided that it was better to postpone any deliberation until a future session due to the complexities of the issue.[23] In 1983, in an open-ended discussion at its 39th session, the desirability of a definition was stressed again but without any agreement being reached. Later, the Working Group despite the absence of any agreed definition produced a Conference Paper[24] which contained no definition. Nonetheless, it decided to continue its work. But, instead of embarking further upon this contentious issue, the Working Group requested the Sub-Commission to take responsibility for drafting a suitable definition.

By Resolution 1984/62 of 15 March 1984, the Commission on Human Rights asked the Sub-Commission to prepare a draft including a definition. This was a significant development considering its continual opposition to the Sub-Commission's earlier efforts. In 1985, Jules Deschenes, a Special Rapporteur, presented a report containing a definition to the Sub-Commission. The proposed definition was as follows:

> A group of citizens of a State, constituting a numerical minority and in a non-dominant position in that State, endowed with ethnic, religious or linguistic characteristics which differ from those of the majority of the population, having a sense of solidarity with one another, motivated, if only implicitly, by a collective will to survive and whose aim is to achieve equality with the majority in fact and in law.[25]

This is slightly different from the definition provided by Capotorti. Yet in substance, both definitions are similar (Gilbert, 1996:164; Thornberry,[26] 1991b:7). As was expected, it attracted much criticism, especially from State parties. Deschenes' report, together with the report of the ensuing debate, was sent to the Commission on Human Rights for its consideration.[27] Nonetheless, the Commission on Human Rights at its 42nd session in 1986 failed to move forward with Deschenes' definition due to the objections of State representatives.[28] Moreover, the Sub-Commission also agreed to postpone consideration of the question of definition until a later stage.[29]

Against such fierce opposition, the Working Group decided in 1991 not to proceed further with this matter to avoid conflicts between different States' representatives.[30] Members of the Working Group thought it would not be able to finish a draft Declaration on minorities if they tried to find a universally agreed definition before commencing the major task, e.g. a draft on measures for the protection and promotion of minorities' rights (see details Omanga, 1991:34). Disagreements prevailed over the terminology. Some members argued that it should concentrate only on 'national minorities'. Others emphasised that 'suitable adjectives' might prevent any difficulties caused by not having a definition. The Working Group justified its decision as follows:

> Delegates expressed the view that the present declaration did not necessarily have to contain a definition of the term "minority", as such a definition was absent in other human rights instruments. It was pointed out that the draft, by the use of the adjectives national, ethnic, religious, and linguistic in front of the term, already specified what scope it would have and whom it was intended to benefit...It was also stated that the declaration could function perfectly well without precisely defining the term as it was clear from its classical meaning to which groups the term referred in concrete cases.[31]

Responses received by Special Rapporteur Deschenes[32] also demonstrate how deep opposition to any attempt at finalising a definition was. The following is an indication of the position of many contemporary States as reported by Deschenes.

> Widely differing views had been expressed as to the advisability, usefulness and need for a definition of minorities as requested by the Commission. Mr. Khalifa, for instance, had expressed reservations as to the principle itself of a definition and, while agreeing with the rest of the Special Rapporteur's work, had stated that, in his view, it was an 'almost impossible task'. Mr. Mazilu saw no need to have a definition in order to draw up a draft declaration on the rights of persons belonging to national, ethnic, religious and linguistic minorities; and Mr. Yimer, to paraphrase his words, thought that the game was not worth the candle. As to Mr. Joinet, he too had endorsed Mr Yimer's view, after having expressed some doubts, and Mr. Bossuyt had made a statement which in many ways was constructive but had none the less questioned whether it was possible to arrive at a definition. Mr. Bandare did not think it was possible to find a complete definition. Mrs. Gu Yijie, for her part, considered that a definition was unnecessary and Mr Dahak felt it would be preferable not to have one. Mr. Al Khasawneh was sceptical about the possibility of defining the term 'minority'. Mr George took the view that it was an academic exercise and, lastly, Mr Martinez Baez considered that, in law, all definitions were dangerous.[33]

States representatives' argument that adjectives can be used as an alternative to a comprehensive definition and that adjectives themselves are capable of clarifying the scope of the term *minority* is not a convincing one. It can be argued however that adjectives on their own cannot stand for what nouns are meant to be. They can modify and give new meanings to nouns. In this instance it was decided illogically to rely upon few selected adjectives instead of a legally defined noun, 'minority'. However, one cannot rely wholly upon adjectives since "they are meaningless in the absence of the noun". On the other hand, "adjectives themselves are uncertain...to say something is 'green' is not very helpful if one has no idea to what it applies." (Packer, 1993:57). Without having a defined noun in legal terms, how can adjectives convey any ideas in clear terms about the communities or groups who are to benefit from the rights guaranteed by international and human rights laws? Adjectives may only be useful in terms of the protection and promotion of the rights of a particular group if there is a precise definition identifying that group (Gilbert, 1996:169). Reliance irrationally on a selected bunch of adjectives, as Packer correctly argues (1993:57), may even "lead to perverse effect". Indeed for much of the time the Working Group did engage, as mentioned above, in a meaningless debate on whether the term 'national minorities' should replace the traditional terms, 'ethnic', 'religious', and 'linguistic' minorities.

Thus the Declaration on Minorities[34] was produced without a definition after a 13 year tug-of- war between State representatives, and is strong evidence to suggest that States do not want a definition at all.

2.3 *States' Attitudes: "The Game is Not Worth the Candle"*

States tend to regard that any attempt at finding a definition of *minority* as inadvisable believing that such an initiative would create unrealistic aspirations. Some States were of the view that *minorities* could not be defined and attempting to arrive at a definition would prove not only extremely time-consuming but also counter-productive for the advancement of the activities of the Working Group.[35] Other objections are more or less based on the following grounds: a) due to the inherently uncertain and dynamic nature of the concept;[36] it would be difficult to arrive at an acceptable definition,[37] or b) it is "an almost impossible task to find a complete definition";[38] for the simple reason that a minority is not definable;[39] c) there is no point in indulging in a "long debate" on definition as it has been already proved difficult and useless in both the United Nations and the Council of Europe, and such an attempt therefore would be both time-consuming and counter-productive;[40] d) "in law all definitions are dangerous";[41] e) it is not necessary to have a definition of the term minority, because definitions are absent in other human rights instruments;[42] and f) use of the adjectives national, ethnic, religious and linguistic in front of *minorities* is sufficient to identify the persons whom it is intended to benefit.[43] Moreover, some are not sure of the wisdom of having a theoretical discussion arguing that it is enough to have "a working definition in the light of concrete example".[44] These objections are seen by some critics as a strategy, which has continuously been deployed to deny the lawful rights of minorities (Packer, 1993:26). A few States have been in favour of a precise definition. For example, Mexico has emphasised the importance of having a "universally acceptable definition covering the protection of vulnerable groups which made up minorities in a given society".[45] However, they are only a minority.

Most States have generally opposed a definition of the term *minority*. Haiti, representing many doubters' views, asked "what after all is this shifting, imprecise, and vague notion which we term a minority"?[46] The former Yugoslav Republic was rather pessimistic. Its fear was based on the belief that a universally accepted definition of *minority* might give unnecessary "prominence to the classical thesis of minorities versus majorities" (Capotorti report, 1979:7). Subjective elements, in the view of Yugoslavia, should not be emphasised unnecessarily (Capotorti report, 1979:8). According to the delegate of USSR without fulfilling the duties of States towards minorities it was futile to embark upon drafting a definition.[47] In principle, France did not oppose drafting a definition, but it "should apply to *recognised and satisfied* minorities".[48] At the same time France was, and still is not prepared to accept even the existence of *minorities* in France.[49] What is meant by the "recognised and satisfied minorities" was not explained by Mr Spanien, the representative of France. Latin American countries have generally been cautious and negative. In general there has been a marked reluctance to accept that there are communities identified as minorities in their territories.[50] They feared that such attempts would interfere with their domestic affairs. Brazil's representative Mr Albuquerque Mello admitted that it was necessary to define the word 'minorities'. However, he argued that:[51]

> For a minority to exist, a group of people must have been transferred 'enblock' without a chance to express their will freely, to a State with a population most of whom differed from them in race, language or religion. Thus, groups which had been gradually and deliberately formed by immigrants within a country could not be considered minorities, or claim the international protection accorded to minorities. That was why Brazil and other American States, which gave immigrants the same legal status as aliens and the same fundamental rights as

their own nationals, did not recognize the existence of minorities on the American continent.

He pointed out that "mere coexistence of different groups in a country do not make minorities in legal terms".[52] Therefore any attempt at finding a definition of *minority* should be carried out very carefully. Having agreed with Mello, the Chilean representative cautioned that the "concept of minority was difficult to define", and emphasised that his country did not have minorities.[53] In his view, "the formation of minority groups in Latin America would seriously impede the efforts of the States to strengthen their national unity". He also he emphasised that "aliens of European origin living in the Latin American countries should not be encouraged to claim the status of minorities".[54] Venezuela,[55] Ecuador,[56] and Mexico[57] followed a similar approach. Brazil emphasised that the American states did not recognise the existence of minorities on the American continent.[58] India's position was not much different to that of the above Latin American countries. Having experienced bloody ethnic conflicts since partition, India has been very cautious on this delicate issue and has never adopted the extremely negative stance, which has characterised observations made by the Latin American delegations. India has not tried to deny the existence of minorities in its country. In 1950, the Indian representative, Mr Masani supported the Sub-Commission's attempt even though he thought that it was engaged in "abstract matters".[59] India's delegate questioned why the Sub-commission had tried to embark upon such an "unnecessary effort to prepare a comprehensive definition".[60] It was not clear to him why either the Commission on Human Rights or the Economic and Social Council needed a definition.[61] However, with regard to drafting a definition, India's position was that *minority* should be limited only to 'citizens' of the State in which they live,[62] a position which attracted the support of many other State representatives.[63] Having examined the motives behind such a negative campaign against minorities Capotorti (1979:35) explained:

There is a political reason. The fact of granting rights to minorities and thus endowing them with legal status might increase the danger of friction between them and the state, in so far as the minority group, as an entity, would seem to be invested with authority to represent the interests of a particular community vis-à-vis the state representing the interests of the entire population. Moreover, the freedom of each individual member of a minority to choose between voluntary assimilation with the majority and the prevention of his own distinctive characteristics might be disregarded by the organs of the entity formed by the minority group, in its concern to preserve the unity and strength of the group".

As is apparent from the above discussions it seems that some countries even find the term *minority* itself unacceptable. For example, in responding to Capotorti, Romania contended that it was wrong to use the term 'minority' because it was too 'broad and indeterminate', not suitable for differentiating between racial, sexual, religious or national groups (Capotorti report, 1979:8). The term 'ethnic, religious and linguistic minorities' was rejected by the former USSR (Capotorti report, 1979:8; see also article 36 of the USSR Constitution, 1977). The representative of the Philippines remarked that it would use 'national cultural communities' to identify non-dominant groups (Capotorti report, 1979:8). Hungary (Capotorti report, 1979:111), the former Czechoslovakia (Capotorti report, 1979:110), and the former Yugoslavia (Capotorti report, 1979:8) have been prominent amongst States which have opposed the use of 'minority'. The Austrian government's statement summarises the core of these objections:

> With respect to the theoretical question raised, it may be remarked that these problems have been under discussion in the relevant literature ever since scholars started to examine minority problems. They have not so far succeeded in formulating a generally accepted definition of the concept of minority-whether ethnic, religious or linguistic. In view of these unsuccessful efforts, it may be doubted whether a satisfactory solution of this problem is possible.[64]

2.4 *European Response*

Europe has not followed a different approach to that of the United Nations (Capotorti report, 1979:11) or of the Latin American countries. For example, at the Ohrid seminar in 1974, several speakers commented: [65]

a) Diversity of historical, economic and social conditions all over the world was considered a significant problem for the elaboration of a general concept;

b) Its contextual concept and the usage of the term *minority* are varied from one geographical location to another. For example, in Africa tribal populations do not differentiate one tribe from another by the term *minority*. In the Indian sub-continent, different community groups identify themselves according to castes; it is therefore difficult to finalise a universally agreed term;

c) Some countries do not feel comfortable with the term *minority* because it has a negative connotation. Such an opinion was expressed particularly by the former Communist regimes in Eastern Europe; and

d) Even the term 'minority' should be abandoned because it lacks a universal meaning.

The Council of Europe itself, due to objections and the disagreement amongst its members, found that it was extremely difficult to provide any satisfactory definition acceptable to all member States (Capotorti report, 1979:11; see further Gilbert, 1992:81). Is this due, as McGoldrick (1993:157) suggests, to the fact that European initiatives have "concentrated on better ways of protecting minorities, rather than on substantive questions of definition..."? It might be argued that European States have also been concerned with the danger of embarking upon such a bold adventure where the United Nations feared to tread. In the opinion of the observer for Switzerland one reason for the failure to find a definition is due to the fact that each minority had its own specific problems and characteristics.[66] Significantly, the Council of Europe's Framework Convention on the Protection of Minorities, 1994 failed to provide a definition. A feeble reason given by the drafters was that it was impossible to arrive at a definition capable of mustering general support of all the members of the Council of Europe.[67] Within the system of the Council of Europe the question of definition did not initially raise serious questions since the collective rights of minorities were not advocated. On the other hand, the European States have not shown much interest in minorities' rights being internationalised (Rosas, 1993:9). For example, the European Convention on Human Rights and Fundamental Freedom, 1950 guarantees only individual rights although it vaguely refers to 'national minorities'. The rights enshrined in the Convention are identified in individualistic terms.

There have, however, been some developments in recent times. For instance, in May 1990, the European Commission For Democracy Through Law (ECommDL) adopted a proposal including a definition[68] emphasising ethnic, religious or linguistic features. The European Charter for Regional or Minority Languages, 1992[69] of the Council of Europe has also identified certain elements of a minority group (nationals of a State who form a group numerically smaller than the rest of the population) but even these by no means represent a comprehensive definition. Among these, Recommendation 1201, 1993 on an Additional Protocol on the Rights of National Minorities to the European Convention on Human Rights is worthy of mention. The proposed definition is however confined to national minorities. Article 1 provides, "For the purpose of this convention the expression 'national minority' refers to a group of persons in a State who: a) reside on the territory of that State and are citizens thereof; b) maintain long standing, firm and lasting ties with that State; c) display distinctive ethnic, cultural, religious or linguistic characteristics; d) are sufficiently representative, although smaller in number than the rest of the population of that State; e) are motivated by the concern to preserve together that which constitutes their common identity, including their culture, their traditions, their religion and their language".[70] However plausible this attempt might be, member States of the Council of Europe did not take steps to adopt it.

Strong opposition to any attempt at arriving at a definition has been the major stumbling block. For example, at the Fourth follow-up meeting of the CSCE on 24 March -10 July 1992, the French delegation vehemently objected to any definitional attempts. This is not surprising taking into account the continued refusal of France to admit the existence of *minorities* in its territories. At the Plenary Meeting of the Experts on National Minorities at Geneva on 2 July 1992, Hungary declared that "it was superfluous to dwell on the problem of the definition of the term 'national minority' within the CSCE, since even the best definition would be lacking some important elements, which in turn would adversely affect our basic objectives and commitments".[71] Ireland thought such an exercise would be futile.[72] It argued that "it would not be wise to devote too much of our limited time to trying to reach agreement on a single precise definition of national minorities since it is clear already that each participating State, in the light of its own experience, has its own view on what constitutes a national minority".[73] Turkey demanded that any attempt to define a minority should be avoided.[74] The Bulgarian delegation thought that the elaboration of a generally acceptable definition of the term 'minority' was hardly a realistic task and "should not be in the focus of our efforts".[75] However, a few States supported the definitional attempt. The Bulgarian delegation stated as follows:

> It is clear nonetheless, that we have reached a stage when our common desire for specific and viable commitments in this field requires unambiguous and commonly understood terms. In our view the exclusive use of the term 'national minorities' does not meet these requirements. It is not exhaustive and allows for arbitrary interpretations, which leave without protection the rights of persons belonging to objectively existing minorities. We find such a situation difficult to accept, since what is at stake is, after all, the effective protection of human rights.[76]

2.5 *From Racial Minorities to National Minorities?*

There is another dimension to this problem. Contemporary UN and regional human rights documents continually use adjectives such as 'national', 'ethnic', 'religious', and 'linguistic' to differentiate non-dominant groups from the rest of the population of a State and to differentiate them from each other. This trend emanated from the regime of the League of Nations. In the *Greco-Bulgarian Communities* case (1930, PCIJ, Ser. B/17), the Permanent Court of Justice, in compliance with the practice of the League of Nations placed emphasis on racial, religious, linguistic and cultural aspects of minorities. This traditional approach has been followed by the United Nations. The UN General Assembly in its resolution 217 C (III), 1948 recognised 'national minorities' in addition to racial, religious and linguistic minorities.

Up until 1950 the term, 'ethnic minorities' was not prominent in UN documents. Instead, the term 'racial minorities' appeared (Capotorti report, 1979:34). Gradually this approach has changed. The Sub-Commission on Minorities began to employ only ethnic, religious and linguistic minorities thus dropping the terms racial and national minorities in its programmes.[77]

The adjective *racial* preceding *minorities* has gradually lost its significance in the definitional debate due to fierce opposition both from the international community and liberal academics. Banton and Harwood (1975) point out that as a way of categorising people, 'race' is based upon a delusion. It was argued that the frequent misuse of 'race' has acquired unpleasant and distressing connotations. Some even questioned the logic of the retention of the term 'race' to identify a group of peoples because they could not justify it in contemporary vocabulary. Another distinguished scholar, L. C. Dunn (1950: 249-250) argued:

> The word race as generally used has no clear or exact meaning at all, and through frequent misuse has acquired unpleasant and distressing connotations. Many people become confused when the direct question is put to them as it is in some official documents. To what race do you belong? ... The existence of that question is evidence of past misuse.... Owing to its bad connotations and the absence of such an objective list, doubts have been expressed whether there is any valid and useful meaning of the word at all which would justify its retention in our vocabulary.

The connotations associated with 'race' or 'racial groups' have been subjected to criticism in the Sub-Commission. In particular, abuse of this term by the Nazis during the Second World War caused much resentment among international lawyers. The biological and genetic connotations associated with it in the light of Nazi emphasis on the purity of blood and nations raised suspicion among many State representatives. On the other hand, some believed that it was much narrower in meaning than the terms 'ethnic' or 'ethnicity'.

'Race' does envisage and identify a specific category of people different from the other groups in terms of physical or biological characteristics. Therefore 'racial minority' is not included in most contemporary international law documents to identify or differentiate a particular group of peoples (Sigler, 1983:9). One of the main reasons given for this by Capotorti is the "non-scientific basis of racial categorisation and the more inclusive meaning of 'ethnic' as a reference to cultural, historical and biological characteristics, as opposed to 'racial', which refers only to inherited characteristics" (Capotorti report, 1979:34). He states that 'ethnic' can be used as a broad expression to cover racial elements as well. Asbjorn Eide, the Special Rapporteur to the Sub-Commission in his report in 1990 adopting a similar line refused to use the term 'race' to identify a particular group of peoples of a State. His finding was that the word 'race' could not be used to classify human beings because it is negative in character and practically meaningless in modern pluralist polities.[78] He concluded, "Whatever is intended by it in a positive way will probably be covered by the word 'ethnic'. Even though 'race' is still used in some UN documents when they refer to non-discrimination[79] it is not used in the biological sense. Contemporary international law has thus turned to less controversial phrases such as 'ethnic, religious, linguistic and national minorities'.

'Ethnic' is not however without its difficulties. This term is often thought elusive, descriptive, mystical and is frequently romanticised (Wirsing, 1981:5), and can therefore make it difficult to define what is meant by 'ethnic minority' (Nowak, 1993:491). Ethnic is normally used therefore to a category of people or nation possessing some degree of coherence and solidarity, being aware of their common origin and cultural interests. An ethnic group is not therefore a mere aggregate of people or a section of a population, but a self-conscious collection of people united, or closely related by shared experiences (Claydon, 1975:26), and "who feel somehow marginal to the mainstream of society" (Cashmore, 1984). Ethnic groups are also seen as pressure groups fighting for survival in competitive societies (Rosens, 1989; see also Glazer and Moynihan eds. 1975). Cultural and historical aspects of ethnic groups provide some of the leading criteria according to contemporary international documents. It should also be mentioned that the terms 'culture' and 'ethnic' are used interchangeably.

Thus, it is used to refer to a community which has wider characteristics or diversities than its other rivals such as racial, religious or linguistic minorities (see further Jones and Welhengama, 2000).

Ethnic groups, writes Rushashyankiko, are "linked and characterised by certain linguistic, cultural or religious ties".[80] Ermacora (1983:294) noted that "the particularity of an ethnic minority is the so-called 'volkstum' which the minority wants to preserve; it is more than just culture, it is the remembrance of history, of the origin of fathers and forefathers, it is the group consciousness". Subjective and objective criteria, according to this theory, should be preserved. Particular attention is paid to sentimental factors, i.e., the will of the people to unite behind the things which they think most important to differentiate them from other groups.

The majority of UN documents prefer 'ethnic minorities' to 'national minorities'. The former is very often used by North American sociologists and human rights jurists alike instead of the latter. The European tradition seems to be quite different from that of North America. Many European scholars believe that these two terms demonstrate separate stages of the development of 'national minorities'. They argue that ethnic, religious, and linguistic criteria depict different characteristics of 'national minorities'.

However, it should be mentioned that 'national minority' is also an "inherently fluid social phenomenon, i.e. a phenomenon that intrinsically defies precise definition" (Akzin, 1970:259). This continuously causes problems for international lawyers (Gilbert, 1996:169). It has often been said that "it would be difficult or even impossible to set up legal distinctions between national and ethnic groups".[81]

To date there is no commonly accepted definition for the term 'national minority' either (Tabory, 1992:195). There is no unanimous opinion as to how it has originated or developed (Hannum, 1991:1431; Veiter, 1974:274). According to Ramage, it is a product of European academics (Ramaga, 1992:420-421). Hannum (1991:1454) gives the following explanations:

> The concept of 'national minorities' seems to me to be something that only Europeans can explain. It is a concept that is very much founded in the last century of European history, and it does seem to include nations, as you call them, with a certain historical and territorial content. It is not necessarily applicable to all ethnic or cultural or all religious groups.

During the formative years of the UN some European States, notably the USSR, Czechoslovakia, the Ukraine Soviet Republic and their allies attempted to include 'national minorities' in major UN documents. In particular, the representative of the USSR tried to include a special provision on national minorities in the proposed international covenants on human rights. It is worthy of mention that the USSR proposal contained a definition. It described a 'national minority' as "an historically framed community of people characterised by a common language, a common history, a common economic life and a common psychological structure manifesting itself in a common culture".[82] It further argued that the expression 'ethnic, religious or linguistic groups' was narrower in scope than 'national minorities', since a group of persons could be called an 'ethnic, religious or linguistic group' before attaining the status of a national minority.[83] The USSR also suggested that that limiting protection to ethnic or linguistic groups might amount to a denial of protection to national minorities (see details in Ramaga, 1992: 421). Capotorti (1979:35) noted that "the omission of any reference to national minorities, when coupled with the substitution of 'ethnic' for 'racial' minorities implied that the broadest expression was sought and that racial and national minorities would be subsumed within the category of ethnic minorities". There are also other reasons for this approach. Since the Second World-War "nation-States have perceived the idea of protecting 'national minorities' as an affront to their jealously guarded sovereignty" (Ramaga, 1992:421), because many saw them as a strong political entity whose interests conflicted with the socio-legal infra-structure of the State in which they lived. Due to these unfounded reasons and prejudices, 'national minorities' was replaced in the 1950s by 'ethnic minorities', which has since then been very much in prominence in UN documents.

However, this trend seems to be being reversed. Deviating from the long-standing tradition of the UN, the Sub-Commission in particular has been using 'national minorities' along with ethnic, religious and linguistic minorities. Both terms, 'ethnic minority' and 'national minority', are frequently used (Tabory, 1992:196). This may perhaps be due to the influence of European academics and to the practice of European institutions. Recent developments in the field of minority protection in the Council of Europe and the OSCE indicate that European institutions are now employing the term 'national minorities' to cover ethnic, religious and linguistic minorities as well.[84] However, there are still differences of opinion on this. For example, in 1973 the Committee of Government Experts of the CSCE concluded that:

> Whilst article 14 of the European Convention on Human Rights referred to national minorities, article 27 of the Covenant referred to ethnic, religious or linguistic minorities. The first question, therefore, was whether these two terms covered the same thing; some of the experts felt that they did, whilst others did

not. This difficulty of interpretation led the Committee to consider the definition of national minorities, since its terms of reference were concerned with the rights of national minorities.

They continued:

> In most cases a 'national minority' would also constitute an ethnic, linguistic or religious minority. On the other hand, there are clearly certain ethnic, linguistic or religious minorities which do not constitute 'national minorities'... These different factors illustrate further the difficulty of finding any generally accepted definition of the term 'national minority'. For this reason, indeed, the experts found it difficult to provide any satisfactory definition of 'national minorities'.[85]

Again in 1991, the Experts on National Minorities of the CSCE concluded that "not all ethnic, cultural, linguistic or religious differences necessarily lead to the creation of 'national minorities'.[86]

However, it remains a major problem that neither the UN nor regional human rights organisations have so far been able to provide a clear-cut definition of what these adjectives. i.e. 'national', 'ethnic', 'religious' and linguistic' mean, and how they differ from one another. Thus *minorities* have been left to decide themselves. In these circumstances, it is not surprising that minorities are not satisfied with the reasons given for the failure to agree upon a universally recognised term. Their complaint seems to be that if the international community cannot finalise a definition, how can the UN or other international bodies provide protection and guarantee the very existence of minority groups?

Conclusion

It is submitted that the reluctance of the majority of States to reach a conclusive and constructive definition has been a major factor in impeding the development of minorities' rights. It would not be impossible to find a suitable and less controversial definition if the international community genuinely wanted to do so. For the past 50 years or more since the formation of the UN, States have been dragging their feet on this crucial issue. Certainly, the rights of minorities and their affairs now fall within the scope of international concern. To assure them full equality and the opportunity to develop their own cultures States must be able to identify those peoples entitled to claim protection under a system of minority guarantees. As Thornberry (1991a: 7) argues "the failure to formalize a definition to give it legal status by inscription in a text, is a failure of will, born not of a failure to understand the world, but of a refusal to do so".[87]

Special Rapporteur Aide noted: "All efforts to obtain a general definition have so far failed, and it is submitted that they will continue to fail".[88] There is no clear sign yet of substantial results being achieved in the foreseeable future (Wolfrum, 1993:154).

Notes

[1] For example see the delegate of Saudi Arabia's statement, A/C.3/SR. 487, 28 September 1953, para. 8, p. 18. See also A/C.3/49/SR. 6, 31 October 1994, para. 25, p. 6. A similar view was expressed by the Sudanese delegate, see details A/C.3/49/SR.8, 25 October 1994, para. 16, pp. 5-6.

[2] UN Doc. E/CN.4/Sub.2/1993/34, 10 August 1993, *Possible Ways and Means of Facilitating the Peaceful and Constructive Solution of Problems Involving Minorities*, para. 4, p. 3.

[3] *The Oxford English Dictionary,* vol. vi, L-M (1970), 2nd ed, Clarendon Press: Oxford, p. 479.

[4] *The Study of the Rights of Persons Belonging to Ethnic, Religious and Linguistic Minorities*, UN Doc. E/CN.4/Sub.2/384/Rev.1, UN sales no. E. 78, XIV. 1, 1979, (Capotorti report).

[5] UN Sale no. 1950. XIV. 3, *Definition and Classification of Minorities*, p.11.

[6] For example see *Minority Schools in Albania* [1935], Series AB/ 64, *PCIJ*, p 17.

[7] The Commission on Human Rights was mandated by the Economic and Social Council in its resolution 9 (II) of 21, June 1946 to establish a sub-commission to deal with non-discrimination and minorities. See ESCOR (II) Annex 14, 1946, p. 402. When the Sub-Commission on Prevention of Discrimination and Protection of Minorities was established in 1947 it was composed of "twelve persons selected by the Commission in consultation with the Secretary General and subjected to the consent of the government of which the persons are nationals", see ESCOR (IV), Suppl. no. 3, E/259, p. 5. The 'persons' were not expected to be experts on minorities and related issues. They are, however, required to play an independent role detached from the countries in which they are nationals. For useful discussion on this see Salzberg, J. P. (1973), *The United Nations Sub-Commission on Prevention of Discrimination and Protection of Minorities: Functional Analysis of Independent Expert Body Promoting Human Rights*, Michigan: USA, pp. 28-40. See further on this Humphrey, J. P. 'The UN Sub-Commission on Prevention of Discrimination and Protection of Minorities', 62 *AJIL* 1968, pp. 869-888.

[8] See UN Doc. E/CN.4/52, Sec. V, 6 December 1947, pp. 13-14.

[9] *Definition and Classification of Minorities*, as above.

[10] See details in UN Doc. E/CN.4/Sub.2/194, para. 18, p. 8.

[11] UN Docs. E/CN.4/Sub.2/119, para. 32; E/CN.4/Sub.2/140, Annex 1, draft resolution 11 and E/CN.4/Sub.2/149, para. 26.

[12] UN Doc. E/CN.4/641, Annex 1, Res. II.

[13] UN Doc. E/CN.4/Sub.2/194, para. 26, p. 11.

[14] UN Doc. E/CN.4/Sub.2/194, para. 12, p. 6.

[15] See UN Docs. E/CN.4/Sub.2/711, 4 February 1955; E/CN.4/Sub.2/L 83, 1955.

[16] UN Doc. E/CN.4/Sub.2/1985/31, para. 3, p. 3.

[17] *Definition and Classification of Minorities*, as above, para. 48, p. 12.

[18] See A/C.3/SR. 1103, 14 November 1961, para. 8, p. 213.

[19] See for example the statement made by the Secretary General of the Sub-Commission, UN Doc. E/CN.4/ Sub.2/ SR. 66, 17 October 1951, p.10.

[20] *Definition and Classification of Minorities,* as above, para. 48, p 12.

[21] *Ibid.* pr 37.

[22] UN Doc. E/CN.4/Sub.2/286, Resolution 9 (xx), 1967. See further, Centre for Human Rights (1994), *United Nations Action in the Field of Human Rights*, New York and Geneva. See for critical analysis on this, Omanga, B. I. (1991), 'The Draft Declaration of the United Nations on the Rights of Persons Belonging to National, Ethnic, Religious and Linguistic Minorities', 46 *Review* of the International Commission of Jurists, pp. 33-41.

[23] UN Doc. E/CN.4/L 1579, 1981.

[24] UN Doc. E/CN.4/1983/WG. 5.

[25] See UN Doc. E/CN.4/Sub.2/1985/31/ Corr. 1, 14 May 1985, para. 181, p. 30.

[26] Thornberry made the following comments when comparing definitions provided by both Deschenes and Capotorti: "the Deschenes definition differs from Capotorti's in minor respects. One improvement is the replacement of 'numerically inferior to rest of the population of a State' by 'constituting a numerical minority'. This is more than *elegantia juris*; the term 'inferior' is avoided even though in Capotorti it clearly refers to a number and is not a cultural value-judgment. Deschenes prefers 'citizens' to 'nations' (of a State), dispelling potential criticism on the vagueness of the Capotorti term. 'Equality in fact and in law' is explicit in Deschenes, but only implicit in Capotorti. Both formulae perhaps carry an incorrect implication through contrasting 'the rest of the population' (Capotorti) and 'the majority' (Deschenes) with minorities, as if the majority were a monolithic cultural block in opposition to the minority, which is not the case in many States. An earlier refinement of Capotorti proposed by Canada had contrasted 'others of the population' with the minority, which can be reconciled with a general cultural heterogeneity in the State. There is not much to choose between the definitions and the present work adopts Capotorti as the longest establishment of the two. It is doubtful if any international instrument of the future attempting a definition will depart greatly from this line of approach".

[27] UN Doc. E/CN.4/Sub.2/1985/SR. 13- 16.

[28] See UN Docs. E/CN.4/1986/5 and E/CN.4/Sub.2/1985/SR. 13-16.

[29] UN Doc. E/CN.4/1986/43, para. 12.

[30] See UN Doc. E/CN.4/1991/53, pp 3-6.

[31] See the report of the Working Group on the rights of persons belonging to national, religious and linguistic minorities, UN Doc. E /CN.4/1991/53, 1991, 5 March 1991, para. 9, p.3.

[32] See details in UN Docs. E/CN.4/Sub.2/1985/31 para. 181 and E/CN.4/ Sub.2/ 1985/SR.16, 20 August 1985, para. 21, p. 7.

[33] UN Doc. E/CN.4/Sub.2/1985/SR. 16, 20 August 1985, para. 31, p. 7.

[34] The Commission's working group completed a first reading of its draft declaration in 1990 (UN Doc. E/CN.4 /1990/41), and completed work on the second reading of the preamble and the first two articles in 1991, see UN Doc. E/CN.4/1991/53. It was adopted on 21 February 1992. This Declaration was approved by the General Assembly, see GAOR, A/Res/47/135, 18 December 1992; See Thornberry, P. (1993), 'The UN Declaration on the Rights of Persons Belonging to National or Ethnic, Religious and Linguistic Minorities: Background, Analysis and Observations', in Phillips. A. and Rosas, A. eds. *The UN Minority Rights Declaration*, Turku: Abo, pp. 11-72.

[35] UN Doc. E/CN.4/Sub.2/1996/2, 30 November 1995, para. 76, p. 17, report of the Working Group on Minorities on its First Session.

[36] UN Doc. E/CN.4/Sub.2/1996/2, 30 November 1995, para. 87, p. 19.

[37] See the observations made by the delegations of Islamic Republic of Iran and the United States of America, UN Doc. E/CN.4/Sub.2/1996, 30 November 1995, p. 18.

[38] UN Doc. E/CN.4/Sub.2/1985/SR.16, 20 August 1985, para. 20, p. 5. See also Chile's statement A/C.3/SR. 1103, 14 November 1961, para. 20, p. 214.

[39] UN Doc. E/CN.4/Sub.2/1996/2, 30 November 1995, para. 85, p. 19.

[40] See for example the statement of the Chairman-Rapporteur of the Working Group on Minorities, Asbjorn Eide, UN Doc. E/CN.4/Sub.2/1996/2, 30 November 1995, para. 88, p. 19.

[41] Cited by Eide, *ibid.* para. 88, p. 19.

[42] UN Doc. E/CN.4/1991/53, 5 March. 1991, para. 9, p. 3.

[43] *Ibid.* para. 9, p. 3.

[44] See Venezuela's observations, UN Doc. E/CN.4/Sub.2/1996/2,30 November 1995, para. 82, p. 18.

[45] UN Doc. E/CN.4/Sub.2/1996/2, 30 November 1995, paras. 77 and 80, pp.17-18.

[46] See *LNOJ*, vol. 9, 6 June 1928, p. 888.

[47] UN Doc. E/CN.4/Sub.2/SR.66, 17 October 1951, p. 7.

[48] UN Doc. E/CN.4/Sub.2/SR.66, 17 October 1951, p. 8 (emphasis added).

[49] See UN Docs. E/CN.4/1991/53, p.7; E/CN.4/Sub.2/SR 2, 1947, p.20; See also *T.K v France;* communication no. 220/1987, 2 Report of the HRC, 1990, UN Doc. A/45/40, Annex X. A Appendix II, 11 *HRLJ* 1990, p.300; *M.K v France,* communication no. 222/1987 HRC, Annex X.B, Appendix II; *S.G v France,* communication no. 347/1988, UN Doc. A/47/40,1992 Annex X.F; *G.B v France,* communication no. 348/1989, UN Doc. HRC A/47/40, Annex X.G; *Dominique Guesdon v France,* UN Doc. A/45/40, Annex IX. G. France's opposition registered in respect of Article 30 of the UN Convention on the Rights of the Child, UN Doc.

CRC/C/2, 22 August 1991, pp. 10, 16-17. A similar reservation was deposited in respect of Article 27 when it ratified the ICCPARA. Its position was that it has only 'French citizens', see UN Doc. CCPR/C/2 Rev. 2, 12 May 1989, p. 18. See France's report under Article 40 of the ICCPR to the Human Rights Committee, HRC, CCPR/C/22/Add. 2, where it has stated: "Article 2 of the constitution of 4 October 1958 declares that France should be a Republic, indivisible, secular, democratic and social. It shall ensure the equality of all citizens before the law, without distinction of origin, race or religion. It shall respect all beliefs. Since the basic principles of public law prohibit distinctions between citizens on grounds of origin, race or religion. France is a country in which there are no minorities and, as stated in the declaration made by France, Article 27 is not applicable as far as the Republic is concerned". This position was reiterated in 1991 in the Working Group on the Rights of Persons belonging to National or Ethnic, Religious and Linguistic Minorities. See UN Doc. E/CN.4/ 1991/53, para. 30, p. 6. It is worthy mentioning that France and others' denial of the existence of minorities in their territories have been criticised by the Human Rights Committee in its general comments as 'wrongly contended'. See HRC General comments 1994, reprinted in 15 (4-6) *HRLJ* 1994, p. 235.

[50] UN Doc. E/CN.4/1991/53, para. 48, p.10 and 23.

[51] A/C.3/SR. 1103, 14 November 1961, para. 12, pp. 213-214.

[52] A/C.3/SR. 1103, 14 November 1961, para. 11, p. 213.

[53] *Ibid.* para. 20, p. 214. See further A/C.3/SR. 489, 30 September 1953, para. 39, p. 31. ("Chile had no minorities and practised no discrimination").

[54] A/C.3/SR. 1103, 14 November 1961, para. 21, p. 214.

[55] A/C.3/SR. 1103, 14 November 1961, para. 28, p. 214.

[56] "Ecuador could rightly and objectively claim there were no minorities on its territory", see A/C.3/SR. 1103, 14 November 1961, para. 43, p. 215.

[57] A/C.3/SR. 487, 28 September 1953, paras. 28-29, p. 20.

[58] See A/C.3/SR. 1103. 14 November 1961, para. 11, p. 214.

[59] UN Doc. E/CN.4/Sub.2/109, 19 January 1950.

[60] India's position was rather unpredictable. For example, in 1951 the Indian representative with the support of the Ecuadorian and Swedish representatives submitted a draft convention on the prevention of discrimination and the protection of minorities, see UN Doc. E/CN.4/Sub.2/127, 9 August 1951.

[61] *Ibid.*

[62] A/C.3/SR. 1103, 14, November 1961, para. 38, p. 215.

[63] For example see Iraq' statement A/C.3/SR. 1104, 14 November 1961, p. 219.

[64] *Ibid.* para. 33, p. 8.

[65] ST/TAO/HR/49, 1974, prs. 29-36, cited in *Capotorti report* 1979 (as below), para. 50, p. 10 and para. 559, p. 95.

[66] UN Doc. E/CN.4/Sub.2/1996/2, 30 November 1995, para. 84, p. 19.

[67] See details, *Explanatory Memorandum on the Framework Convention for the Protection of National Minorities*, 16 (1-3) *HRLJ* 1995, para. 12, p. 102.

[68] See UN Doc. E/CN.4/Sub.2/1990/ 46, Annex. III, para. 4, p.20, see 1 (6-7) *HRLJ* 1991, pp. 270-273. Article 2 (i) states, "For the purpose of this Convention, the term

'minority' shall mean a group which is smaller in number than the rest of the population of a State, whose members, who are nationals of that State, have ethnical, religious or linguistic features different from those of the rest of the population, and are guided by the will to safeguard their culture, traditions, religion or language; (ii) Any group coming within this definition shall be treated as an ethnic, religious or linguistic minority; (iii) To belong to a national minority shall be a matter of individual choice and no disadvantage may arise from the exercise of such choice.

[69] The full text can be found in 14 (3-4) *HRLJ* 1993, pp. 148 -152.

[70] See 16 (1-3) *HRLJ* 1995, p. 108.

[71] Statement made by Geza Entz, Head of the Hungarian delegation at the opening session of the CSCE Expert Meeting on National Minorities, Geneva, 2 July 1992, details, Eddison, as below, p. 5.

[72] *Ibid.* p. 5.

[73] *Ibid.* p. 5.

[74] The opening statement by Riza Turmen, the Head of Turkish Delegation at the opening session of the CSCE Expert Meeting on National Minorities, Geneva, 2 July 1992. *Ibid.* p. 5.

[75] *Ibid.* p. 5.

[76] *Ibid.* p. 5. The statement of the Delegation of the Republic of Bulgaria at the opening session of the CSCE Expert Meeting on National Minorities, Geneva 2 July 1992.

[77] See UN Docs. E/CN.4/Sub.2/108, 1950; E/CN.4/Sub.2/112, 1950; E/CN.4/Sub.2 /358, 1950; and E/CN.4/Sub.2/L.564, 1972.

[78] UN Doc. E/CN.4/Sub.2/1990/46, para. 14, p. 4.

[79] See for example articles 2 and 26 of the ICCPR 1966; article 2 of the ICESCR 1966; article 14 of the European Convention on Human Rights 1950. See also International Convention on the Elimination of all Forms of Racial Discrimination 1966.

[80] See *Study of the Question of the Prevention and Punishment of the Crime of Genocide*, UN Doc. E/CN.4/Sub.2/416, 1978, pp. 18-20.

[81] UN Doc. E/CN.4/1991/53, 5 March 1991, para. 10, p. 3.

[82] UN Doc. E/CN.4/SR. 369, 1953, para. 16. See further, Thornberry, as below, 1991b, p.160.

[83] UN Doc. E/CN.4/SR.369, 1955, p. 13.

[84] See for example Article 5 (1) of the Framework Convention for the Protection of National Minorities, 16 (1-3) *HRLJ* 1995, pp. 98-101.

[85] The report of the Committee of Experts on Human Rights to the Committee of Ministers, Council of Europe, DH/EXO (73), 47, 9 November 1973, see further Capotorti report, para. 51, p. 11.

[86] See the report of the CSCE Meeting of Experts on National Minorities, 1991, 12 (8-9) *HRLJ* 1991, p. 332.

[87] *Thornberry*, 1991a, as below, p. 7.

[88] UN Doc. E/CN.4/Sub.2/1990/46, para. 31, p.8.

References

Akzin, B. (1970), 'Who is a Jew? : A Hard Case', 5 *ILR*, pp. 259-273.

Alfredsson, G. (1992), *Minority Rights and Democracy*, Discussion Paper, Third Strasbourg Conference on Parliamentary Democracy, Parliamentary Assembly of the Council of Europe.

Alfredsson, G. and Zayas, A. D. (1993), 'Minority Rights: Protection by the United Nations', 14 (1-2) *HRQ*, pp. 1-9.

Andrysek, O. (1989), *Report on the Definition of Minorities*, 8 *SIM Special*, Ultrech: Netherlands Institute of Human Rights, cited in Packer, below.

Bagley, T. H. (1950), *General Principles and Problems in the Institutional Protection of Minorities*, Imprimeries Popularies: Geneva.

Banton, M. and Harwood, H. (1975), *The Race Concept*, David and Charles: Newton and Abbot.

Capotorti, F (1979), *The Study of the Rights of Persons Belonging to Ethnic, Religious and Linguistic Minorities*, UN Doc. E/CN.4/Sub.2/384/Rev. 1.

Cashmore, E. (1984), 'Ethnicity', in *Dictionary of Race and Race Relations*, Routledge and Keegan Poul: London, p. 214.

Claydon, J. (1975), 'The Transnational Protection of Ethnic Minorities: A Tentative Framework for Inquiry', in *CYIL*, pp. 25 - 60.

Dunn, L. C. (1950), 'Race and Biology: The Significance of Racial Differences', in *UNESCO Statement on Race*, UNESCO, pp. 249-250.

Dyke, V. van, (1995), 'The Individual, the State and Ethnic Communities in Political Theory', in W. Kymlicka (ed), *The Rights of Minority Culture*, Oxford UP: Oxford, pp. 31-56.

Eddison, E. (1993), *The Protection of Minorities at the Conference on Security and Co-operation in Europe*, no. 5, Published by the Human Rights Centre of the University of Essex.

Eide, A. (1991), 'Minority Situations: In Search of Peaceful and Constructive Solutions' 66 *Notre Dame LR*, pp. 1311-1355.

Ermacora, F. (1983), 'Protection of Minorities Before the Law', 182 *Recueil Des Cours*, pp. 251-370.

Gilbert, G. (1992), 'The Legal Protection Accorded to Minority Groups in Europe', 23 *NYIL*, pp. 67-104.

Gilbert, G. (1996), 'The Council of Europe and Minority Rights', 18 (1) *HRQ*, pp. 160-189.

Glazer, N. and Moynihan, D. eds. (1975), *Ethnicity: Theory and Experience*, Harvard University Press.

Gurr, T. R. and Scaritt, J. R. (1989), 'Minorities Rights at Risk: A Global Survey', 11 *HRQ*, pp. 375-405.

Hannum, H. (1991), 'Contemporary Developments in the International Protection of the Rights of Minorities', 66 *Notre Dame LR*, pp. 1431-1448.

Humphrey, J. P. (1968), 'The UN Sub-Commission on Prevention of Discrimination and Protection of Minorities', 62 *AJIL*, pp. 869-888.

Jones, R. and Welhengama, G. (2000), *Ethnic Minorities in English Law*, Trentham Books: London.

Lerner, N. (1991), *Group Rights and Discrimination in International Law*, Martinus Nijhoff.

Malinverni, G. (1991), 'The Draft Convention for the Protection of Minorities: The Proposal of the European Commission for Democracy Through Law', 12 (6-7) *HRLJ*, pp. 265-269.

McGoldrick, D. (1993), 'The Development of the Conference on Security and Co-operation in Europe: From Process to Institutions', in B. Jackson, and D. McGoldrick (eds), *Legal Vision of the New Europe: Essays Celebrating the Centenary of the Faculty of Law*, Graham and Trotman: London, pp. 135-182.

Nowak, M. (1993), *UN Convention on Civil and Political Rights: CCPR Commentary*, N. P. Engel, Kehl : Strasbourg.

Omanga, B. I. (1991), 'The Draft Declaration of the United Nations on the Rights of Persons Belonging to National, Ethnic, Religious and Linguistic Minorities', 46 *The Review* of the International Commission of Jurists, pp. 33-41.

Packer, J and Myntti, K. eds. (1993), *The Protection of Ethnic and Linguistic Minorities in Europe, Institute of Human Rights*: Abo-Akademi University: Finland.

Packer, J. (1993), 'On the Definition of Minorities', in Packer, and Myntti, *The Protection of Ethnic and Linguistic Minorities in Europe*, as above, pp. 23-65.

Pejic, J. (1997), 'Minority Rights in International Law', 19 (3) *HRQ*, pp. 665-685.

Ramaga, P. V. (1992), 'The Bases of Minority Identity', 14 (3) *HRQ*, pp. 409-428.

Rodley, N. (1995), 'Conceptual Problems in the Protection of Minorities', 17 (1) *HRQ*, pp. 48-71.

Rosas, A. (1993), 'The Protection of Minorities in Europe: A General Overview', in Packer and Myntti (eds), as above. pp. 9-14.

Rosenne, S. (1993), 'The Protection of Minorities and Human Rights', in Y. Dinstein, and M. Tabory (eds), *The Protection of Minorities and Human Rights*, Kluwer: Dordrecht, p. 515.

Rosens, E. E. (1989), *Creating Ethnicity: The Process of Ethnogenecies*, SAGE: USA.

Roth, S. (1992), 'Towards a Minority Convention: Its Needs and Content', in Dinstein,. and Tabory (eds), as above, pp. 83-117.

Rushashyankiko, N. (1978), *Study of the Question of the Prevention and Punishment of the Crime of Genocide*, UN Doc. E/CN.4/Sub.2/416.

Salzberg, J. P. (1973), *The United Nations Sub-Commission on Prevention of Discrimination and Protection of Minorities: Functional Analysis of an Independent Expert Body Promoting Human Rights*, University Microfilms International, Michigan: USA.

Shaw, M. N. (1991), 'The Definition of Minorities in International Law', 20 (14) *IYHR*, pp. 13-43.

Sigler, J. A. (1983), *Minority Rights: A Comparative Analysis*, Greenwood Press: London.

Sohn, L. B. (1981), 'The Rights of Minorities', in L. Henkin (ed), *The International Bill of Rights, New York*: Colombia UP, pp. 270-289.

Stoel, M. v. d. (1993), *Key-note Address to the Human Dimension Seminar, Case Studies on National Minorities Issues*, Warsaw 24-28 May 1993, reprinted in 1 (1) *CSCE ODHR Bulletin*, p. 22.

Tabory, M. (1992), 'Minority Rights in the CSCE Context', in Dinstein, and Tabory (eds), as above, pp. 187 - 211.

Thornberry, P. (1991a), *Minorities and Human Rights Law*, Minority Rights Group: London.

Thornberry, P. (1991b), *International Law and the Rights of Minorities*, Clarendon Press: Oxford.

Thornberry, P. (1993), 'The UN Declaration on the Rights of Persons Belonging to National or Ethnic, Religious and Linguistic Minorities: Background, Analysis and Observations', in A. Phillips, and A. Rosas (eds), *The UN Minority Rights Declaration*, Turku: Abo, pp. 11-72.

Veiter, T. (1974), 'Commentary on the Concept of National Minorities', 7 *Rev. Des. Droits De. L'Homme*, pp. 273 - 290.

Wirsing, R. C. (1981), 'Dimensions of Minority Protection', in R. C. Wirsing (ed), *Protection of Ethnic Minorities: Comparative Perspectives*, Pergamon Press: New York, pp. 3-17.

Wolfrum, R. (1993), 'The Emergence of New Minorities as a Result of Migration', in C. Brolmann, R. Lefeber, and M. Zieck (eds), *Peoples and Minorities in International Law*, Martinus Nijhoff: Dordrecht/Boston/London, pp. 131-148.

Wright, J. (1996), 'The OSCE and the Protection of Minority Rights', 18 (1) *HRQ*, pp. 190-205.

3 Peoples, All Peoples, Nations and Minorities

Introduction

Even during the early years of the United Nations regime some States declared that the right to self-determination entitled *peoples* and *nations* to constitute independent States and to determine the form of governments they wished to adopt.[1] This right does not, as stated by the UK delegate during the debate on the Recommendation Concerning International Respect for the Self-determination of Peoples, end with the formation of free and independent sovereign States. It is a continuing process.[2]

Interestingly, it was also argued to mean, "the right of *individuals within a nation* to preserve their ethnic, cultural or religious characteristics".[3] It is a right, which can be enjoyed in an independent State.[4] However, there has been confusion not only amongst States but also amongst jurists since the 1950s as to the exact social or political unit to which this right has been attributed. For example some States' understanding was that "every people", whether or not they constituted independent nations, had a right to decide independently by invocation of the right to self-determination what manner of State they wished to have.[5]

Even after the adoption of the UN Charter, the Covenants on human rights, and the various General Assembly resolutions, the opinions of States are not in consensus as to the exact political or social groups which come under the category of *peoples* or *nations*. For example, in the view of both the Czech Republic[6] and the former USSR,[7] the right of self-determination belongs to *nations*. Some identified *Independent peoples,*[8] or *all peoples*[9] as right holders. It was also pointed out that both *all peoples* and *individuals* could enjoy this right.[10] However, most States are in consensus on one important issue, that is, that *minorities* are not intended by *peoples* or *all peoples*.

This apparent confusion was further augmented by new claims by some minority groups who live compactly together in part of the territory of a sovereign State that they are also entitled as separate political or social units to exercise the *peoples' right* to self-determination,[11] and most importantly, if they wish to secede and set up independent States by virtue of this right (see details Brilmayer, 1991:179; see details Alfredsson, 1996:58). Special Rapporteur observed:[12]

> The controversy over the understanding of 'peoples' as beneficiaries of the right to 'self-determination' had, prior to the 1993 Vienna Declaration and Programme of Action, become heightened. It had been further complicated by the increasingly numerous understandings sought to be given to the content of self-determination. Some of the most vehement parties to the present violence in Bosnia and elsewhere seek to justify it by exaggerated and misconceived interpretation of the right to self-determination. Bosnia- Herzegovina was and should still be seen as a sovereign State whose territorial integrity and political unity should be respected; the acts of aggression in encouragement of group claims for self-determination have demonstrated the dangers inherent in vague and elusive interpretations of the right to self-determination.

Most minority groups tend to identify themselves with *peoples, all peoples* or *nations*, the words continually appearing in the UN treaties, covenants, declarations, and resolutions as the repositories of the right to self-determination.

Before embarking upon a discussion on autonomy or of the legitimacy of the right to secession, I will now examine whether *minorities* come under *nations, peoples* or *all people* in the context of the right to self-determination. A brief reference to regional human rights documents will also be made where appropriate.

3.1 *Peoples and Nations' Right to Self-Determination: Who are the Right Holders?*

Robert Lansing's (1921:97) question whether "the bearer of the right of self-determination was to be a race, a territorial area, or a community" is still a valid one given the ambiguous nature, "slogan like quality" and "potentially explosive character" of the right to self-determination.[13] Casses (1995:5), remarks "the concept of self-determination is both radical, progressive, alluring and, at the same time, subversive and threatening".

Since the League of Nations, the most controversial and romanticised terms have been 'peoples' and 'peoples' right to self-determination' (see McGoldrick, 1991:14; Wilson, 1988:55; Crawford, 1979:85; Sinha,

1973:263; Higgins, 1994:111).[14] Although it is repeatedly said that it is *peoples* who can exercise the right to self-determination, it is difficult to find the legitimate standard bearers of the right to self-determination without knowing who these *peoples* are. Sir Ivor Jennings (1956:56) said, "on the surface it seemed reasonable: let the people decide. It is in fact ridiculous because the people cannot decide until somebody decides who are the people". Some States also argued that "the concept of a people or nation was difficult to define".[15] This could, as argued by Cyprus, "present very complex problems".[16] Politically biased various interpretations given to *peoples* do not help either. Often *peoples* and peoples' right to self-determination has been used in a very vague and uncommitted way.[17] In *re: Secession of Quebec* (1998) 2 SCR 217,[18] the Supreme Court of Canada concluded: "International law grants the right to self-determination to 'peoples'. Accordingly, access to the right requires the threshold step of characterizing as a people of the group seeking self-determination. However, as the right to self-determination has developed by virtue of a combination of international agreements and conventions coupled with State practice, with little formal elaboration of the definition of 'peoples', the result has been that precise meaning of the term 'people' remain somewhat uncertain".

Consequently, a wide interpretation of the word *peoples* left enough room for ethno-nationalists to further their cause, i.e., the right to secession. However, as will further be discussed in chapters 9 and 10, it is worth mentioning that there is no strong or reliable evidence to suggest that minorities as *peoples* or *nations* can proclaim independence by virtue of the right to self-determination (see re: *Secession of Quebec*). Although a few States advanced the theory that self-determination should be granted to "all peoples and all national groups"[19] it has never been clear whether it was intended that a section of a population, for example an ethnic or religious group operating as *peoples*, should be granted the right to secede by virtue of the peoples' right to self-determination.

The UN has not spelt out the beneficiary of the right though some earlier UN resolutions identified *inhabitants* in non-self-governing territories and the trust territories. For example, GA Res. 9/1 of February 1946 contained 'political aspirations of peoples' and 'the interests of the inhabitants'. 'Inhabitants' right to self-government' was again emphasised in numerous UN resolutions.[20] The inference can be drawn, as far as the earlier resolutions are concerned that *inhabitants* was intended to mean the whole native population of a territory with foreigners being excluded. This assumption is supported by the UN resolution on Eritrea which specifically mentioned that rights should be "exercised as citizens",[21] by the citizens of the whole territory. It is not surprising that in certain situations, as stated in the *Western Sahara* (Advisory Opinion) case,[22] UN practice has been that a certain segment of a population may not be considered a *people* who can exercise the right to self-determination.[23] The position adopted by the pre-sixties UN resolutions as to the right holders does not demonstrate a great deal of variation. For instance, GA Res. 421 D (V) December 4, 1950; GA Res. 545 (vi) February 5, 1952; GA Res. 637 (viii) December 16, 1952,[24] and GA Res. 1314 (xii) December 12, 1958[25] recognised *peoples* and *nations* as the right holders whilst *all peoples* and *all nations* were identified as the right holders by the proposal on the draft Covenant submitted by the Commission on Human Rights.[26]

In the early 1950s, the phrase, 'the nations and peoples' right to self-determination' appeared in many statements made by various States.[27] Both the West and the Communist countries also followed a similar approach.[28] In subsequent debate on the subject of the right to self-determination this has been used by many States, perhaps without giving any serious consideration to the likelihood of minorities misappropriating the term, in particular by equating *nation* with *minorities* to justify their claims. Generally there is a tendency for *minorities* to desire to be identified with *nations* since this status gives them greater protection and political identity.

It is clearly evident from UN practice that the terms *nations* and *inhabitants* (except indigenous peoples), had gradually disappeared or been intentionally dropped to avoid situations which might otherwise have been misused by ethno-nationalists. The term *nation* was replaced by *States* from the latter part of the 1950s.[29] For example, GA Res. 2181 (xx) December 12, 1966 has dropped 'nation' in preference of 'States' ('friendly relations and co-operation among States'). Gradually, *peoples* or *all peoples'* right to self-determination became the popular catchword in international and human rights documents. The UN Charter (*peoples*), GA. Res. 1514 (XV) December 14, 1960 (*all peoples*), GA. Res. 2160 (XXI) November 30, 1960 (*peoples*), GA. Res. 2625 (XXV) October 24, 1970 (*peoples*), the Helsinki Final Act 1975 (*people* and *all peoples*), article one of both the Covenants on human rights (*all peoples*), and the Arab Charter on Human Rights (*all peoples*).[30] The African Charter on Human and Peoples' Rights, 1981[31] identified *all peoples* and *colonised* or *oppressed peoples* as right holders of the right to self-determination. I submit that the UN's practice strongly indicates that *peoples* or *all peoples* were used to identify a totality of peoples organised as a political unit in a State. Ethnic, national or other minority groups are not intended by *peoples, every people* or *all peoples* as will be shown below. There is no credible evidence to infer from the UN documents that a *minority* is synonymous with *peoples*. *Peoples* are the totality of peoples living in a State.

3.2 *No Ethnic Connotations Were Meant in the Charter by 'Peoples' and 'All Peoples'*

The UN Charter is regarded as "the first authoritative legal document to uphold the principle of self-determination" (Cassese, 1979:137-138 and 165) Article I (2) states:

> To develop friendly relations among *nations* based on respect for the principle of equal rights and self-determination of *peoples,* and to take other appropriate measures to strengthen universal peace (emphasis added).

Article 55 states:

> With a view to the creation of conditions of stability and well-being which are necessary for peaceful and friendly relations among *nations* based on respect for the principle of equal rights and self-determination of *peoples*, the United Nations shall promote... (emphasis added).

Under article 73 of the UN Charter, *peoples* of the Non-Self-Governing Territories and Trust Territories were to achieve the status of self-government or independence as the situation warranted with the close co-operation of the administering powers and to a certain extent with the assistance of the other States.

The discussion on the GA Res. 2625 (xxv) October 24, 1970 (Declaration on Friendly Relations) reveals that some argued (by referring to articles 1 (2), 55 and 73 of the UN Charter) that when reading these articles together, "the principle seemed to mean that substantial groups with a national character desiring to govern themselves and able to do so should be accorded self-government".[32] However, by close examination of how these terms *peoples* and *nations* are used in both articles 1 (2) and 55, only one conclusion can be safely arrived at. That is that two different notions are intended. The wording in the Preamble in the UN Charter also supports this position. For example, in comparing the phrase, "the equal rights of men and women and of nations large and small..." with "We the peoples of the United Nations determined", it is clearly evident that the word *nations* was used for both small and large States. One should not forget the fact that, as has been seen in chapter 1, during World War II and its aftermath, the allied powers had not been enthusiastically engaged in the promotion of the rights of minorities, fearing that such steps would put the territorial integrity and political unity of the nation-State at risk. It was a time during which both small and large States, having fought to protect or restore the sovereignty of their respective countries against the Axis aggressors, were anxious to protect their political unity against both external and internal enemies in the aftermath of war.

It is noteworthy that the Dumbarton Oaks Proposals, which initiated the proceedings for founding the United Nations, continuously emphasised how "to develop friendly relations among nations and to take other appropriate measures to strengthen universal peace".[33] In fact the Dumbarton Oaks documents were silent about the peoples' right to self-determination. The origin of both these articles goes back to the San Francisco Conference, 1945 (officially known as the United Nations Conference on International Organisation).[34] Purposes no. 2 of Chapter One and no. 2 of Chapter Nine - 'Purposes and Relationship' were[35] adopted verbatim in the present articles 1 (2) and 55 of the UN Charter.

The word *peoples* (proposed by the USA and subsequently approved by the USSR, Ukrainian SSR, China, France and the Latin American countries) was preferred to 'High Contracting Parties' (which was proposed by South Africa) in the San Francisco documents. This was because it was principally agreed that the UN Charter must, by its nature, be an agreement between the Governments of the United Nations. Thus, *peoples* was used for the nation-State. The San Francisco debates reveal that the representatives of participant States repeatedly used *peoples* and *nations* interchangeably. However, the preferred word for the nation-State was *nations.* During the debate on the Declaration on Friendly Relations at the 6th Committee of the General Assembly, the representative of the UK referring to *peoples* in the UN Charter said:[36]

> What was meant by people? That was the principal difficulty which the Committee would have to overcome in elaborating the principle of self-determination. In the context of the Charter, *'peoples' meant essentially those who were so organized as to constitute a State in the territory which they occupy.* That was clear from the Preamble, which declared that the Charter had been concluded in the name of the 'peoples' of the United Nations (emphasis added).

Indeed, it has been continually emphasised since the 1950s that *peoples* referred to in the UN Charter (in both articles 1 (2) and 55) were those found in the Trust territories, the Non-Self-Governing Territories, and peoples living in colonies as a whole,[37] or "those living under the authority of other nations".[38] It was correctly pointed out by some States that the authors of the UN Charter had not been thinking of minorities when they included the peoples' right to self-determination in articles 1 (2) and 55.[39] In its context, the word *people,* it was argued by Syria, "clearly meant the multiplicity of human beings constituting a nation, or the aggregate of the various national groups governed by a single authority".[40]

In fact, as Claude (1955:113) correctly points out, the Charter did not focus on minorities or problems associated with them. This was mainly because most leading States representative's attitudes towards minorities were "largely negative in character" (Thornberry, 1989:872; Boven, 1995:470). In fact, one representative was quoted as saying during the San Francisco Conference that "What the world needs now is not protection for minorities, but protection from minorities" (see details Helgesen, 1992:159-186). On the other hand, in both articles 1(2) and 55, these references were made in the context of development of peaceful and friendly relations amongst nations which is central to the Charter and upon which the "peaceful and friendly relations was to be achieved by the UN".[41] *Nations* was used in both articles in the Charter to identify *nation-States* so adhering to the early practice of the League of Nations.[42] The UN Secretariat concluded that, "The word 'nation' is broad enough to include colonies, mandates, protectorates and quasi-States as well as States... and 'nation' is used in the sense of all political entities, States and non-States, whereas 'peoples' refers to groups of human beings who may, or may not, comprise States or nations".[43] It was also argued that these two terms are identical in the context of the right to self-determination.[44]

It was also suggested that peoples' right to self-determination was related to the future of any territory constituting a distinct geographical entity.[45] Juridically, the world was not made up of peoples, argued the US delegate, but rather of political entities called States;[46] therefore it is States which become the ultimate beneficiary of this right. To define these two terms, *peoples* and *nations,* the Commission on Human Rights was required to examine them fully by resolution 586 (xx) at the 889th Plenary Meeting on 29th of July 1955.[47] But there is no evidence that the Commission ever fulfilled this obligation. This has in effect created difficulty and confusion whenever these two terms have appeared in UN treaties or resolutions.

3.3 *'All Peoples' Instead of 'Peoples' and 'Nations' in the Covenants*

In compliance with some early resolutions of the General Assembly, most notably with the GA Res. 545 (VI) of 5 February, 1952, the following term was proposed by the Draft Resolution, E/2256, Annex V, Draft Resolutions A and B (submitted by the Economic and Social Council to the Third Committee) for the proposed human rights conventions:[48]

> Member States should: (1) uphold the principle of self-determination of peoples and nations and respect their independence; and (2) recognise and promote the realization of the right of self-determination of the peoples of Non-Self-Governing and Trust Territories who were under their administration and grant that right on a demand for self-government on the part of those peoples, the popular wish being ascertained in particular through a plebiscite held under the auspices of the United Nations.

The Western powers and their allies on the one hand were not pleased with the phrase 'peoples and nations', believing that the proposed article on the right to self-determination would be applied only to peoples in the Non-Self-Governing Territories, Trust Territories and the peoples living in the colonies. It was in their view, (i discriminatory against the powers which controlled those territories; and (ii initiated by the Socialist countries of Eastern Europe with the tacit approval of the newly independent countries of Asia, Africa and the Middle East to create problems for the West. Presenting an amendment to the Resolutions A and B mentioned above, the UK urged that "every member of the United Nations, in conformity with the Charter, should respect the maintenance of the principle of equal rights and self-determination of peoples everywhere". Paragraph 2 states:

> The State members of the United Nations shall recognize this principle and promote its application in relation to the peoples of all territories and nations under their control; shall do so in a manner appropriate to the particular circumstances of each territory or nation and the interests of the peoples concerned; and shall respect its application in other States. [49]

Having presented an amendment to the draft resolution 'A', E/2256, Annex V, the US delegate proposed that "the States Members of the United Nations shall uphold the principle of self-determination of all peoples and nations".[50] The insistence of other Western powers, i.e., Belgium, the Netherlands, Australia,[51] and France, that the right to self-determination be applied universally won the argument. *All peoples* in all territories, including independent States has finally been adopted instead of *peoples*. The Western powers' amendments received significant help from the Fifteen Power's resolution which called for the "self-determination of all peoples" to be recognised by the United Nations.[52]

On the other hand, some Asian and a few Latin American and Arab countries were concerned about the possible consequence for independent States if the phrase 'all peoples and nations' right to self-determination were to be included in the proposed human rights covenants. Their fear was based on the possibility of a scenario in which *minorities,* sheltering behind the cloak of *all peoples* and *nations* might exploit it to make their own claims to self-determination and independence. Therefore, another resolution was submitted suggesting that 'all peoples and nations right to self-determination' be replaced with 'the rights of peoples to self-determination'.[53] Iraq and Pakistan again presented a similar resolution making amendments to India's resolution by proposing that 'of all peoples right to self-determination' be replaced with that 'of the peoples'.[54] It is worth mentioning that even though in India's amendment, the phrase 'the right of self-determination of all the peoples' was included to recognise the universality of the principle, it had never been intended to infer that minorities as *peoples* or as segments of *all the peoples* had any legitimate claim to self-determination as a political units.[55] Such an admission, as the delegate of India said, "was fraught with dangerous consequences".[56] 'The Twenty Power' regarded in their proposal the right holders of the right to self-determination as 'peoples and nations',[57] yet none of them admitted, implicitly or explicitly that this phrase had any ethnic connotations.

The majority of Western powers and emerging nation-States in Latin America, Eastern Europe, the Middle East and Asia were unanimous in not wanting the phrase 'all peoples or peoples' to be identified with *minorities*. It was also argued that a segment of a population of the State occupying a particular area could not claim to be the *peoples*.[58] The UK delegation was also concerned about the uncertainty surrounding *peoples,* and did not apparently want a minority population of foreign origin or indigenous race, or irredentist factions to be identified as *peoples*. Its delegate further questioned:[59]

> Could any group of people, however small or scattered, regardless of the territory it occupied and of its geopolitical locality, of the political unit to which it belonged and of the interests of other peoples and other States, claim to exercise that right in full? It was obvious that the recognition of such an unbridled right would be a potent cause of friction and would be one of the very first things to

upset friendly relations among nations and to threaten the domestic peace of the States themselves.

Many feared that this right might be misused in the future by minority groups within sovereign States if care was not properly observed.[60] Therefore, it was urged that member States must make sure that there would only be "the smallest number of problems"[61] when the principle of the right to self-determination of all peoples was to be included in the Covenant.

The Netherlands representative expressed his fear that the resolutions A and B to be included in the Covenant might arouse unrealistic expectations amongst certain segments of the population.[62] It was emphasised by Austria that if *peoples* meant ethnic or racial groups, a strict interpretation would imply a fragmentation of existing States. The difficult question of minority groups, as argued by the Austrian delegate, could not be solved by a facile reference to the principle of self-determination.[63] Many States were in consensus that the draft resolutions A and B did not identify minority groups in the context of peoples' right to self-determination.[64]

Finally, the word *peoples* in article 1 of the Covenants was understood to mean "peoples in all countries and territories, whether independent, trust or non-self-governing".[65] The inference is obvious, *minorities* are not meant by *peoples* or *nations*. Virzijl[66] (1968:322) also rejected the argument that nation has anything to do with ethnic group. Special Rapporteur Eide referring to 'nation' explained:[67]

'Nations' will be understood as the aggregate, permanent population of a sovereign State. The nation in Bosnia and Herzegovina consists of Moslems, Serbs, Croats, other minorities, and persons of mixed descent. It is a technical and legal concept, linked to the notion of citizenship in its legal sense. Article 15 of the Universal Declaration of Human Rights, stating that everyone has the right to a nationality, means that everyone has the right to hold the citizenship of a State, which makes her or him a part of the nation. It carries no necessary implication of solidarity among the different groups within society; even when they are antagonistic towards each other they are part of the nation simply by being citizens thereof.

The summary of the Third Committee's report to the General Assembly noted:

Much of the discussion on Article 1 had related to the question of self-determination to the colonial issue, but that was only because the peoples of non-self-governing and Trust Territories had not yet attained independence. The right would be proclaimed in the Covenants as a universal right and for all time. The dangers of including the article had been exaggerated. It was true that the right could be and had been misused, but that did not invalidate it. It was said that the article was not concerned with minorities or the right to secession, and the term 'peoples' and 'nations' were not intended to cover such questions.[68]

3.4 *Peoples in the 'Declaration on Friendly Relations'* (GA Res. 2625 (xxv) 1970)

When the contents of the first paragraph in the Declaration on Friendly Relations[69] were discussed, the phrase 'all peoples to self-determination' was proposed by many Afro-Asian countries with the help of some eastern European States.[70] State representatives' statements during the debate on the Report of the Special Committee on Principles of International Law Concerning Friendly Relations and Co-operation among States (which lead to 2625 GA Resolution) followed the approach taken by their predecessors in earlier UN covenants and resolutions. Some States opposed the formulation of the concept as a right of peoples primarily because of the difficulty of defining the repository of the right.[71]

There appeared to be a consensus that *peoples* or *all peoples* did not have ethnic connotations.[72] Otherwise, as one representative argued, territorial integrity and political independence would be endangered. It is clearly evident from the statements of State delegates that many were afraid of the revival of secessionist movements similar to that of Katanga within the territories of an independent States. As with the arguments raised during the debate on the proposed Covenants on human rights it was pointed out if *peoples* was not properly understood, "there would be some danger that peoples could be misled into attempting to invoke such rights to justify the dislocation of a State within which various ethnic communities had been successfully living together for a long time".[73] Therefore, *peoples* meant 'peoples of a territory as a whole',[74] or those still living under colonial domination. Thornberry correctly argued that the focus of the Declaration on Friendly Relations was on 'whole territories' or 'peoples' rather than 'ethnic groups' (Thornberry, 1989:877).

The approach taken by the above UN documents has been followed by other regional human rights documents, such as the African Charter on Human and Peoples Rights, 1981 (African Charter)[75] and the Helsinki Final Act, 1975. Even though Article 20 of the African Charter used the term *all peoples*[76] and *colonized* and *oppressed peoples*'[77] right to self-determination, as Gittleman says (1982:679), *minorities* are not meant to be synonymous with *all peoples, oppressed* or *colonized peoples* (see also Kiwanuka, 1988:80- 101).

The Helsinki Final Act 1975 excluded national minorities from the principle of self-determination as enshrined in Principle VIII ("By virtue of the principle of equal rights and self-determination of peoples, all peoples always have the right, in full freedom, to determine, when and as they wish, their internal and external political status, without external interference, and to pursue as they wish their political, economic, social and cultural development"). The main emphasis, *inter alia*, was placed on the inviolability of frontiers (principle III) and the territorial integrity of State (principle IV).

Hannum stated (1996:22), "Again, the proper interpretation turns on the definition of 'peoples', and there is no indication that sub-groups were meant to be able to determine their external political status or pursue political and economic development 'as they wish' without any reference to the larger population of the State". Cassese (1995:283) points out that Eastern and Western European States are unanimous on this. The main reason for the omission of minorities from Principle VIII, according to Cassese (1995:283) was to avoid any secessionist movements fighting for the division of the territories of independent States in the European countries (see also Boven, 1995: 471).

In *re Secession of Quebec* (1998) 2 SCR 217 the Supreme Court of Canada came to a conclusion that "people may include only a portion of the population of an existing State". If further said:

> The right to self-determination has developed largely as a human right, and is generally used in documents that simultaneously contain reference to 'nation' and 'state'. The juxtaposition of these terms is indicative that the reference to 'peoples' does not necessarily mean the entirety of a State's population. To restrict the definition of the term to the population of existing States would render the granting of a right to self-determination largely duplicative. Given the parallel emphasis within the majority of the source documents on the need to protect the territorial integrity of existing states, and would frustrate its remedial purpose.

The statement that 'a segment of a population' can be considered 'peoples' is a significant departure from the majority views on the meaning of 'peoples'. It should be mentioned that the above judgment did not refer to any UN documents to prove its conclusion.

The opinions of international jurists reflect the difficulty in finding what 'people' meant in the above mentioned treaties, covenants, declarations etc (Stavenhagen, 1996:1-11). This difficulty arose because there was still no text or guidance provided by UN organs to determine what a *people* meant (Alfredsson, 1996:58-86). As noted by McGoldrick (1991:250) even the Human Rights Committee failed to address this issue despite being well-placed to do so. The opinions of international jurists and UN practice support the conclusion that any ethnic connotations are absent in *people* in the context of the right to self-determination (Higgins, 1963:104: Crawford, 1979:91-93. See for different views, Anaya, 1993:131-164). Special Rapporteur Aureliu Cristescu concluded that 'people' should not be confused with ethnic, religious or linguistic minorities, whose rights are recognized in article 27 of the ICCPR.[78] Eide (1995:353) analysing the conceptual background of the term *people* came to the conclusion that *people* is used to identify "the permanent, resident population of the territory concerned, not the separate ethnic or religious groups, whether dominant or not in the territory. It refers to *demos*, not to *ethnos*". Although it may sound arbitrary and unsatisfactory, during the process of decolonization, the word *people* was consistently understood as the population as a whole.[79] Higgins (1994:124) rightly observed:

> The emphasis in all the relevant instruments, and in the State practices (by which I mean statements, declarations, positions taken) on the importance of territorial integrity, means that 'peoples' is to be understood in the sense of *all* the peoples of a given territory. Of course, all members of distinct minority groups are part of the peoples of the territory. In that sense they too, as individuals, are the holders of the right of self-determination. But minorities *as such* do not have a right of self-determination. That means, in effect, that they have no right to secession, to independence, or to join with comparable groups in other States.

Clearly *minority* and *people* are two different concepts in international law. The full beneficiaries of the right to self-determination are the *people* of a territory.

Most jurists are of the view that article 1 of both the Covenants refers to the whole people of an established State (Simma ed. 1994:2). It implies the universal character of peoples' right to self-determination (Cassese, 1995:62). It cannot therefore have any racial or ethnic character. However, some scholars see a somewhat weak interrelationship between self-determination and minorities in particular in the context of the Declaration on Friendly Relations. (see Rosenstock, 1971:732). In certain situations, some inference can be drawn from paragraph 7 of this Declaration, that is, a minority may be considered 'peoples' and as such they can benefit from the right to self-determination. According to the obligations imposed by this paragraph it is essential that the protection of paragraph 7 be conferred only on States "possessed of a government representing the whole people belonging to the territory without distinction as to race, creed or colour" (Rosenstock, 1971:732). If a segment of a peoples within a territory "are treated in a grossly discriminatory fashion by an unrepresentative government", states Thornberry (1989: 876), then their claim to self-determination "cannot be defeated by arguments about territorial integrity". Examples of such a scenario are that of the Bangladesh insurrection and perhaps the present Kosovo Albanians' struggles for independence. Thus, in both these instances, it can be argued that East Pakistan Bangladeshis and Kosovo Albanians can claim legitimacy by virtue of peoples' right to self-determination. Oppressed groups, in such a case can legitimately operate as *peoples*, but not as *minorities*.

Conclusion

In conclusion, p*eoples* as used in the above discussed UN documents, the African Charter and the Helsinki Final Act should not be confused with ethnic, religious or linguistic minorities. *Minorities* are not intended by *peoples* or *all peoples*. It is the *peoples* of one territorial unit who become the ultimate repository of the right. Indeed, *minorities* are an important unit of *peoples* and in that sense they too are beneficiaries.

Notes

[1] The debate on the Recommendations Concerning International Respect for the Self-determination of Peoples, E/2256, Annex V, A/2165, B/2172, Chapter V, s.1, see A/C.3/SR. 444, 13 November 1952, para. 34, p. 157 (Brazil), and A/C.3/SR. 397, 21 January 1952, para. 5, p. 300 (Syria). See also GA Res. 545 (vi) 5 February 1952 ("Fundamental Human Rights of Peoples and Nations").

[2] E/2256, Annex V, Resolutions A and B, 1952, *ibid*, see A/C.3/SR.456, 26 November 1952, para. 3, p. 229. See also Principle VIII of the Helsinki Final Act 1975.

[3] Emphasis added. A/C.3/SR. 450, 20 November 1952, para. 43, p.199 (Israel).

[4] A/C.3/SR. 447, 18 November 1952, paras. 6, 7 and 8, p. 172 (the Netherlands).

[5] A/C.3/SR.931, 16 November 1966, para. 19, p. 186 (USSR); see also A/C.6/SR.935, 22 November 1966, para. 26, p. 211 (Mongolia).

[6] A/C.3/49/SR. 8, 25 October 1994, para. 4, p. 3.

[7] A/C.3/45/SR 7, 30 October 1990, para. 71, p. 17.

[8] A/C.3/49/SR.8, 25 October 1994, para. 16, p. 5 (The Sudan).

[9] A/C.3/47/SR.9, 27 October 1992, para. 40, p. 10 (Egypt).

[10] A/C.3/47/SR.4, 19 October 1992, para. 25-26, p.7 (Australia).

[11] UN Doc. E/CN.4/Sub.2/1993/34, 10 August 1993, para. 73, p. 16, *Possible Ways and Means of Facilitating the Peaceful and Constructive Solution of Problems Involving Minorities.*

[12] *Ibid.* para. 79, p. 17.

[13] See for example A/C.3/SR. 444, 13 November 1952, para. 29, p. 157 (the UK). See also *Cassese* (1995), as below, p. 23.

[14] There is a widely published literature on the right to self-determination. See Cobban, A. (1945), *National Self-Determination*, Oxford UP: London / New York and Toronto; Umozurike, U. O. (1972), *Self-Determination in International Law*, Archon Books: Hamden, Connecticut; Pomerance, M. (1982), *Self-Determination in Law and Practice: The New Doctrine in the United Nations*, Martinus Nijhoff: The Hague/Boston and Lancaster; Tomuchat, C. ed. (1993), *Modern Law of Self-Determination*, Martinus Nijhoff: Dordrecht/ Boston/ London; Casses, A. (1995), *Self-Determination of Peoples: A Legal Reappraisal*, Cambridge UP: Cambridge; Musgrave, D. (1997), *Self-Determination and National Minorities*, Oxford University Press: Oxford, 1997; *Rigo-Sureda*, A. (1973), *The Evolution of the Right of Self-Determination*, AW Sijthoff: Leiden; Hannum, H. (1990), *Autonomy, Sovereignty, and Self-Determination: The Accommodation of Conflicting Rights*, University of Pennsylvania Press: Philadelphia; Halperin, M. H. and Scheffer, D. J. with Small, P. L. (1992), *Self-Determination in the New World Order*, Carnage Endowment: Washington.

[15] See Belgium delegate's statement, A/C.3/SR. 361, 7 December 1951, para. 10, p. 84. See also Dinstein, Y. (1976), 'Collective Human Rights of Peoples and Minorities', 25 *ICLQ*, p. 104; see also McCorquodale, R. (1992), 'Self-Determination Beyond Colonial Context and its Potential Impact on Africa', 4 *AJCIL*, p. 594.

[16] A/C.3/47/SR.9, 14 October 1992, para. 88, p. 18 (Cyprus).

[17] See for example interpretation offered by Byelorussia, A/C.3/SR.401, 24 January 1952, para. 2, p. 327.

[18] See the full text, http//:www.mbnet.mb.ca~psim.can-law.html.

[19] Statement of Mr. Lannung, the delegate of Denmark, A/C.3/SR. 401, 24 January 1952, para. 21, p. 329.

[20] See GA Res. 185 (S-2), 26 April 1948, Protection of the City of Jerusalem and its Inhabitants: Reference to the Trusteeship Council; GA Res. 387 (v) 17 November 1950, 307th plenary mtg. ('inhabitants of Libya'); GA Res. 390 (v) 14 December 1950 ('inhabitants of Eritrea').

[21] GA Res. 390 (v) 14 December 1950, 325th plenary mtg. para. 6 (c).

[22] Order of 3 January 1975, *ICJ Reports* 1975, 12 at 33.

[23] *Western Sahara (Advisory Opinion),* order of 3 January 1975, *ICJ Reports*, 1975, p. 33.

[24] 'The Rights of Peoples and Nations to Self-Determination'.

[25] 'Recommendation Concerning International Respect for the Right of Peoples and Nations to Self-Determination'.

[26] E/2256, Annex V, Resolutions A and B, para. 91, cited in A/C.3/SR.443, 12 November 1952, para. 6, p. 149.

[27] GAOR, Agenda Item 58, 9th session, 1954, Doc. A/2808 and Corr. 1, Report of the 3rd comt. para. 42, p.11. See A/C.3/L 186 Add 1.This resolution was popularly referred to as the 'Thirteen Power Resolution' which was later instrumental in the formation of article 1 (2) of the International Covenant on Civil and Political Rights 1966. It was presented by the following States: Afghanistan, Burma, Egypt, India, Indonesia, Iran, Iraq, Lebanon, Pakistan, The Philippines, Saudi Arabia, Syria and Yemen.

[28] A/C.3/SR. 360, 5 December 1951, para. 52, p. 81 (Israel); A/C.3/SR.359, 4 December 1951, para.7, p.74 (USSR); Byelorussia, *ibid.* para. 21, p.75; A/C.3/SR.361, para. 10, p. 84 (Belgium); A/C.3/L.29/ Rev.1, para. 3 (US), GAOR, 7th session, Annexes, Agenda Item 30, 1952-53, p. 3.

[29] See also GA Res. A/6799, 26 September 1967, para. 182 ("The Development of Friendly Relations and Co-operation among States").

[30] The Arab Charter on Human and Peoples' Right, 1981, reprinted in 4 (3) *IHRR* 1997, pp. 850-857.

[31] Reprinted in Brownlie, I. (1992), *Basic Documents on Human Rights,* 3rd ed. Clarendon Press: Oxford, pp. 551-558.

[32] GAOR, 21st session, Annexes (xxi) Agenda Item. 87, 1966, Report of the Special Committee, A/6230, para. 478, p. 94.

[33] See Chapter 1, article 1 (2) of the Dumbarton Oaks Proposal 1944, reprinted in the *YBUN,* 1946-1947 Published by the Department of Public Information, UN: New York, 1947, p. 4.

[34] See *United Nations Documents 1941- 1945,* published by the Royal Institute of International Affairs (1946), London/ New York, pp. 145-176.

[35] See, San Francisco Conference document 1945, chapter 1, *Purposes,* nos. 2 and 1 of the Chapter IX, Section A, *Purpose and Relationship.* See YBUN 1946-1947, respectively, p. 14 and p. 16.

[36] A/C.3/SR. 890, 3 December 1965, para. 19, p. 303.

[37] See for example, A/C.3/SR. 366, 12 December 1951, para. 25, p.115 (Liberia). Also see A/C.3/SR. 398, 22 January 1952, paras. 34, 35, 36, 37, pp. 309-310 (Saudi Arabia).

[38] A/C.3/SR. 399, 23 January 1952, para. 2, p.311 (India). Venezuela, Colombia and Belgium had similar views, see Microfilmed minutes of the debates of the First Committee of the First Commission of the San Francisco Conference, 14-15 May and 1 and 11 June 1945, unpublished, Library of the Palais des Nations, Geneva, cited in Cassese (1995), as above, p. 39. See also Thornberry, P. (1989), 'Self-Determination, Minorities and Human Rights: A Review of International Instruments', 38 *ICLQ,* pp. 871-875.

[39] A/C.3/SR. 399, 12 December 1951, para. 29, p.116 (Liberia).

[40] A/C.3/SR. 397, 21 January 1952, para. 5, p.300 (Syria).

[41] See UN Doc. A/6799, 26 September 1967, para. 181. See also GAOR, Agenda Item 90-94, Annexes (xxii), 22nd session, 1967, para. 181, p.30.

[42] During the debate on the naming of the new League of Nations after the first World-War, it was suggested by the British delegate that the difference between 'nations' and 'States' was a very small one. Later, instead of the League of States, the 'League of Nations' was confirmed. See Miller, D. H. (1928), *The Drafting of the Covenant*, vol. 1, G.B. Putnam and Sons: New York and London, p.135, cited in Cassese (1995), above, p.27.

[43] UNCIO Docs. vol. xviii, pp. 657-658, cited in *Thornberry* (1989), p. 871.

[44] A/C.3/SR. 396, 21 January 1952, para. 58, p. 297 (Afghanistan).

[45] A/C.6/SR. 892, 7 December 1965, para. 24, p. 320 (Cyprus).

[46] A/C.6/SR. 893, 8 December 1965, para. 16, p. 329 (the USA).

[47] Report of the Commission on Human Rights, 889th plenary mtg. 29 July 1955, ESCOR, 20 session, supplement no. 1, Res. 586 (xx) p. 12.

[48] E/2256, Annex V, Draft Resolution A and B, GAOR, 7th session, Annexes, Agenda Item 30, 1952- 1953, p. 9. This was criticised by many States. For example, the delegate of Bolivia criticising the Draft Declaration said that it was concerned only with "one aspect of the problem, the peoples of the Non-Self-Governing and Trust Territories, not with the problems of self-determination as a whole". See A/C.3/SR. 459, 29 November 1952, para. 51, p. 255.

[49] Resolution A/C.3/L.299, 25 November 1952. See also GAOR, 7th session, Annexes, Agenda Item 30, 1952-1953, pp. 5-6.

[50] See GAOR, 7th session, Annexes, Agenda Item 30, 1952-1953, p.3 (this amendment was adopted by 33 votes to 6 votes with 11 absentees). See US delegate Mrs Roosvelt's statement, A/C.3/SR.457, 28 November 1952, paras. 32 and 34, p. 240.

[51] A/C.3/SR.458, 28 November 1952, paras. 13, 14 and 15, p.246 ("Universal Application of the Principle of the Right to Self-determination"). See US resolution A/C.3/L.297/Rev.1, 25 November 1952. The US delegate later submitted another amendment to this, see Res. A/C.3/L.294.

[52] The following Latin American countries presented this resolution, A/C.3/L.304, 28 November 1952, (amendment to the Resolution submitted by India, A/C.3/L. 297/Rev. 1): Brazil, Chile, Colombia, Costa Rica, Dominican Republic, Equador, El Salvador, Guatemala, Haiti, Honduras, Mexico, Nicaragua, Panama, Uruguay and Venezuela. See, GAOR, 7th session, Annexes, Agenda Item 30, 1952-1953, p. 6.

[53] This was proposed by Afghanistan, Argentina, Chile, Guatemala, Iraq, Lebanon, Mexico and Pakistan. See A/C.3/L.317, 3 December 1952, GAOR, 7th session, Annexes, Agenda Item 30, 1952-1953, p. 9.

[54] See A/C.3/L309 Rev. 1, December 1952, GAOR, 7th session, Annexes, Agenda Item 30, 1952-1953, p.97.

[55] See India's view in support of its resolution A/C.3/L.297/Rev. 1, A/C.3/SR. 457, 28 November 1952, paras. 51, 52 and 53, p. 241.

[56] *Ibid.* paras. 51, 52 and 53, p.241.

[57] Afghanistan, Bolivia, Burma, Chile, Egypt, Greece, Haiti, India, Indonesia, Iraq, Lebanon, Liberia, Pakistan, the Philippines, Saudi Arabia, Syria, Thailand, Uruguay, Yemen and Yugoslavia, A/C.3/L.427, Add. 1, GAOR, 7th session, Annexes, 1952-1953, Agenda Item 30.

[58] A/C.3/SR. 400, 23 January 1952, para. 23, p.321 (New Zealand).

[59] *Ibid.* para. 26, p.156

[60] A/C.3/SR. 401, 24 January 1952, para. 28, p. 329 (the UK) and A/C.3/SR.358, 30 November 1951, para. 35, p. 70 (Mexico).

[61] A/C.3/SR. 402, 24 January 1952, para. 12, p. 336 (Sweden).

[62] A/C.3/SR.447, 18 November 1952, para. 8, p. 172.

[63] UN Doc. A/2309 and Corr. 1, Report of the Third Committee, para. 40, p. 163, GAOR, 7th session, Annexes, Agenda Item 30, 1952-1953.

[64] See for example A/C.3/SR. 446, 17, November 1952, paras. 16 and 17, p.166 (Belgium).

[65] See UN Doc. E/CN.4/SR.253, p. 4.

[66] Verzijl, J. H. (1968), *International Law in Historical Perspective*, vol. 1, A. W. Sijthoff: Leiden.

[67] UN Doc. E/CN.4/Sub.2/1993/34, 10 August 1993, para. 35, p. 8, *Possible Ways and Means of Facilitating the Peaceful and Constructive Solution of Problems Involving Minorities.*

[68] UN Doc. A/3077, 1955, para. 39.

[69] See Rosenstock, R. (1971), 'The Declaration of Principles of International Law Concerning Friendly Relations', 65 *AJIL*, pp. 713-735.

[70] Algeria, Burma, Cameroon, Dahomey, Ghana, India, Kenya, Lebanon, Madagascar, Nigeria, Syria, the United Arab Republic and Yugoslavia proposed this amendment. See the text, GAOR, 21st session, Annexes (xxi), Doc. A/6230, Report of the Special Committee on Friendly Relations, 1966, Agenda Item. 87, para. 458, p.91, A/AC.125/L. 31 and Add. 1-3. See also, UN Doc. A/6799, 26 September 1967, para. 190.

[71] GAOR, Agenda Item 87, Annexes (xxii) 22nd session, 1967, para. 192, p. 32.

[72] *Ibid.* para. 194, p. 32.

[73] UN Doc. A/6799, 26 September 1967, para. 221.

[74] A/C.3/SR. 938, 23 November 1966, para. 22, p.231 (Cyprus). See also GAOR, 21st session, Annexes (xxi) Agenda Item. 87, 1966, Special Comt Rept. Doc. A/6230. para. 69, p.127.

[75] 21 *ILM* 59 [1982], 27, OAU Doc. CAB/LEG/67/3, Rev. 5, 1981.

[76] Article 20 (I) states: "All peoples shall have the right to existence. They shall have the unquestionable and inalienable right to self-determination. They shall freely determine their political status and shall pursue their economic and social development according to the policy they have freely chosen."

[77] Article 20 (II) states, "Colonial or oppressed peoples shall have the right to free themselves from the bonds of domination by resorting to any means recognized by the international community".
[78] UN Doc. E/CN.4/Sub.2/404/Rev. 1, pr. 279, UN Sales no. E. 80. XIV. 3, 1981, *The Right to Self-Determination, Historical and Current Development on the Basis of United Nations Instrument.*
[79] UN Doc. E/CN.4/Sub.2/1993/34, para. 76, p.17 and para. 82, and p. 18.

References

Alfredsson, G. (1996), 'Different Forms of and Claims to the Right of Self-Determination', in D. Clark, R. Williamson (eds), *Self-Determination: International Perspectives*, Macmillan Press Ltd: London, pp. 58-86.

Anaya, J. (1993), 'A Contemporary Definition of the International Norm of Self-Determination', in 3 (1) *Transnational Law and Contemporary Problems*, pp. 131-164.

Boven, T. van. (1995), 'Human Rights and Rights of Peoples', 6 (3) *EJIL*, pp. 461-476.

Brilmayer, L. (1991), 'Secession and Self-Determination: A Territorial Interpretation', 16 (1) *YJIL*, pp. 177-201.

Cassese, A. (1979), 'Political Self-Determination - Old Concepts and New Developments', in A. Cassese (ed), *UN Law / Fundamental Rights: Two Topics in International Law*, Sijthoff and Noordhoff: Alphen aan den Rijn.

Cassese, A. (1995), *Self-Determination of Peoples: A Legal Appraisal*, Cambridge UP: Cambridge.

Claude, I. L. (1955), *National Minorities: An International Problem*, Harvard UP: Cambridge.

Crawford, J. (1979), *Creation of State in International Law*, Oxford UP: Oxford.

Cristescu, A. (1981), *The Right to Self-Determination: Historial and Current Development on the Basis of United Nations Instruments*, UN Doc. E/CN.4/Sub. 2/404/Rev. 1, UN Sales no. E. 80. XIV. 3, para. 279.

Dinstein, Y. (1976), 'Collective Human Rights of Peoples and Minorities', 25 *ICLQ*, pp. 102-120.

Eide, A. (1995), 'The National Society, Peoples and Ethno-Nations: Semantic Confusions and Legal Consequences', 64 *Nord. J.Int.L*, pp. 353-367.

Gittleman, R. (1982), 'The African Charter on Human and Peoples Rights: A Legal Analysis', 22 (4) *Va.J.I.L*, pp. 666-713.

Hannum, H. (1996), 'Self-Determination in the Post-Colonial Era', in Clark, and Williamson (eds), as above, pp. 12-44.

Helgesen, R. (1992), 'Protecting Minorities in the Conference on Security and Co-operation in Europe (CSCE) Process', in A. Rosas, and J. Helgesen (eds), *The

Strength of Diversity, Human Rights and Pluralist Democracy, Martinus Nijhoff: Dordrecht/Boston/London, pp. 159-186.

Higgins, R. (1963), *The Development of International Law Through the Political Organs of the United Nations*, Oxford UP: London.

Higgins, R. (1994), *Problems and Progress: International Law and How We Use It*, Oxford UP: Oxford.

Jennings, I. (1956), *Approach to Self-Government*, Cambridge UP: Cambridge.

Kiwanuka, R. N. (1988), 'The Meaning of 'People' in the African Charter on Human and Peoples' Rights', 82 *AJIL*, pp. 88- 101.

Lansing, R. (1921), *The Peace Negotiations: A Personal Narrative*, New York and Boston.

McCorquodale, R. (1992), 'Self-Determination Beyond the Colonial Context and its Potential Impact on Africa', 4 *AJCIL*, pp. 592-608.

McGoldrick, D. (1991), *The Human Rights Committee, Its Role in the Development of the International Covenant on Civil and Political Rights*, Clarendon Press: Oxford.

Rosenstock, R. (1971), 'The Declaration of Principles of International Law Concerning Friendly Relations: A Survey', 65 *AJIL*, pp. 713-735.

Simma, B. ed. (1994), *The Charter of the United Nations*, Oxford UP: Oxford.

Sinha, P. (1973), 'Is Self-Determination Passe?', 12 (3) *CJIL*, pp. 260-273.

Stavenhagen, R. (1996), 'Self-Determination: Right or Demon?', in Clark and Williamson (eds), as above, pp. 1-11.

Thornberry, P. (1989), 'Self-Determination, Minorities and Human Rights: A Review of International Instruments', 38 *ICLQ*, pp. 871-875.

Wilson, H. (1988), *International Law and the Use of Force by National Liberation Movements*, Clarendon Press: Oxford.

4 Claims for Autonomy With Shared-Sovereignty

Introduction

Former UN Secretary-General Boutros Ghali, reporting in pursuance of the statement adopted by the Summit Meeting of the Security Council, said that the international community was entering an era compounded by one of the greatest political upheavals which was "marked by uniquely contradictory trends". He focused on the "new assertions of nationalism and sovereignty", and their resultant detrimental effects on the cohesion of the nation-States.[1] Though minority groups' claim for greater political power with shared-sovereignty in the form of autonomy is not a new development, a sudden burst of such claims by 're-energised and contesting ethnic groups' in recent times has surprised many statesmen and jurists alike (Thornberry, 1998:97). "Often ethnic minorities", states Henry J. Steiner (1991:1539-1559), "have understandably viewed those regimes as necessary not simply to assure their cultural survival, but principally to avoid oppression and violence". Such claims are political in nature and more controversial than traditionally understood 'minority rights', some of which, i.e., religious, linguistic and cultural rights, are now enunciated in article 27 of the ICCPR. Nor is such a right enshrined in the UN Declaration on Minorities, 1992, (see generally Thornberry, 1993:11-71) though the Draft UN Declaration on the Rights of Indigenous Peoples [2] (draft Declaration on indigenous peoples), recognises indigenous peoples' right to autonomy.

Given the seriousness and the controversial nature of such claims, a majority of States are opposed to any enlargement of minority rights to accommodate greater autonomy with 'shared-sovereignty', in particular when this has territorial implications. On the other hand, if they cannot resist such claims, as Friedlander (1981:136) states, autonomy has been used by States to frustrate independence movements of ethnic groups or to "offset secessionist pressure". Whilst analysing the conceptual aspects of autonomy, and its interrelationship with federalism and sovereignty this chapter examines its relevance to minorities' claims for greater political power.

4.1 *Autonomy*

Autonomy has been at the experimental stage for centuries. A few States from time to time have used autonomy as a political tool to appease or suppress minorities and their movements with a little success. Autonomy is, however, not a new phenomenon. In fact, as Sohn (1980:181) points out, discussions on autonomy or autonomous regimes had been a popular subject of scholarly debates in the late 19th century and early 20th centuries (see also Thornberry, 1991, in particular chapter 2; Robinson, 1943). International treaties, the League of Nations and the constitutional practice of States have been instrumental in moulding the notion of autonomy as an important element in democratic governance which, as many argued, can be operated in pluralist societies more effectively. Some of these were formulated to accommodate individuals belonging to minority groups and others were created in collective terms taking into consideration ethnic, religious and linguistic characteristics. Extensive power for self-governments as well as for local administrative units was also amongst the earlier autonomous models.

Some elements of cultural autonomy can be seen in pre-UN multilateral or bilateral treaties. For example, the Treaty of Versailles, 1919 (Treaty between Poland and Principal Allied and Associated Powers), the Treaty of Saint-Germain-en-Laye, 1919 (involving Austria), the Treaty of Paris, 1919 (between Principal Powers and Romania), the Treaty of Lausanne, 1924 (between Principal Allied and Associated Powers and Greece), Neuilly-sur-Seine, 1919 (between Bulgaria and Principal Powers) were prominent amongst them.[3] However, Baron Heyking (1928:37) points out that with the exception of political autonomy in respect of the Ruthenes in the region of South Carpathians and religious autonomy for the Saxons and Czechs in Transylvania the minorities treaties do not contain any special mention of autonomy or political powers to minority groups (see also Hannum, 1993:8).

The Mosquito Indian Territory in Nicaragua (under a treaty with the UK, 1860), The Memel Territory under the sovereignty of Lithuania in 1924,[4] the German-Polish Convention relating to Upper Silesia, 1922, the Aaland Islands created in 1921 under the aegis of the League of Nations (agreement between Sweden and Finland),[5] the Eritrean autonomous region within the sovereignty of the Ethiopian Crown in 1952,[6] the Faeroe

Islands,[7] Greenland,[8] the Cook Islands under New Zealand, Kurdistan in Iraq,[9] the Catalan and Basque regions of Spain, and South Tyrol/Alto Adige in Italy are other prominent autonomy models which came into force since the 19th century.

'Autonomy' derives from two Latin terms, '*auto*' (self), and '*nomos*' (law, or rule), (see Lapidoth, 1997:29; Dinstein, 1981:291; Ostwald, 1969; Hannikainen, 1998:79; Eide, 1998:251) and was originally used by sociologists (Heintze, 1998:7; Harhoff, 1986:31). It expresses the idea of one's own right to make rules and regulation over one's own affairs, or according to Jellinek (1960 cited in Lapidoth, above:30), "authority to govern, to administer, and to judge". Autonomy as a legal concept is, however, vague and imprecise (Harhoff, 1986:31) and "inhabits a famous imprecise area of international law and international relations" (Kampelman, 1996:xi). Friedlander (1981:136) even questioned its validity as a legal norm. According to Suksi (1998:xi), autonomy "seems to be very elastic and capable of stretching into a multitude of social and legal relationships." He further argues that autonomy seems to be having "full of loose ends of all kinds". Thornberry (1998:98) states that autonomy is a protean term which is a somewhat flexible notion, "Coming apart at the seams, lacking a definite shape. Shapeless or not, it is, like collective rights in general, a site of polemics in the fields of international law, despite the number and scope of domestic examples". Therefore, argues Thornberry (1998:122), "a preliminary rush to judgement suggest that autonomy is hardly there in the minority rights texts, but close examination discovers strands and whispers of autonomy or something like it". He confesses (at 123, above) his uneasiness about extended meanings in the light of the many adjectives offered to qualify the term. "It could be that the manifold uses of autonomy do not grasp an essence, but express only the fiercest nominalism". He further writes (at 123):

> In the context of minority rights, autonomy appears as hortatory or pragmatic politics, refusing to convert itself into a coherent norm and perhaps dissolving into conceptual sub-constituencies before our eyes. It is too little for indigenous peoples. Suggestions that they should adopt the concept of autonomy as a general focus for their claims do not appeal. Autonomy is seen as a grant, not a right; it is viewed as static, not dynamic.

This conceptual confusion is also highlighted by Hannum and Lillich. They state that "autonomy is not a term of art or a concept which has a generally accepted definition in international law". Quoting John Chipman Gray (1909) they point out (1981:215-254) that it is due to "so much loose writing and nebulous speculation by jurists without properly interpreting the term and its application in modern nation-states" (see also Hannum and Lillich, 1980:215). However they (1980:860) provide the following characteristics of autonomy:

> Autonomy is understood to refer to independence of action on the internal or domestic level, as foreign affairs and defence normally are in the hands of the central or national government, but occasionally power to conclude international agreements concerning cultural or economic matters also may reside with the autonomous entity...autonomy in theory and practice will provide a description and analysis of the degree of independence and control over its own internal affairs that an autonomous entity generally enjoys.

Sohn (1980:190) suggests that the concept of autonomy is in between the concept of a non-self-governing territory and an independent State, that is 'short of independence', enabling the inhabitants of the territory to control its economic, social and cultural affairs. It indicates a certain degree of independence, or as noted by Heintze (1998:7), "a partial independence from the influence of the national or central government", for a group or a delineated region in dealing with defined areas of activities agreed by both the central government and the province (see also Harhoff, 1986:31). It is, according to Harhoff (at 32), "between full-fledged state like sovereignty and full subordination under national authority". However, as Crawford (1979:111-112) correctly points out, autonomous regions or units always exist without being detached from the State of which they remain a constituent part.

It is worth mentioning that autonomy is a political tool often used both by minority groups and States to strengthen their respective claims and power bases. It has, however, been identified in terms of the protection of minority rights which within a democratic environment enables the people of a given territory to participate effectively in cultural, religious, social, and economic life at regional or personal level. In this context, the right to 'independence' is not envisaged[10] although a degree of independence from the central or federal government for a region or particular ethnic group is clearly evident (Hannum and Lillich, 1980:885; Harhoff, 1986). By referring to autonomy Harhoff explains (at 32): "It signifies some level of political, economical or cultural independence vis-à-vis national authorities, based on differences mainly in culture and language, and established with a local institutional structure through legal provisions in the constitution, in national legislation or in particular agreements concluded with the national governments".

Various terms are used in documents dealing with autonomy of which 'self-government' (Lapidoth, 1997:52), or 'self-rule', 'local administration' or 'autonomous administration',[11] 'local government', and 'home rule'[12] are the ones frequently found in international and bilateral treaties and constitutions dealing with minorities and indigenous peoples. Since autonomy has not yet been established as a principle in international law, researchers have to rely on the analysis of jurists and publicists to understand the concept of autonomy and its application to minority groups.

4.2 *Autonomy Means Self-government?*

Autonomy is not a well-defined legal concept in a legal and political sense. According to Harhoff (1986:31), the concept of autonomy is difficult to apply in a legal context. Nonetheless, autonomy means, in the view of Dinstein (1981:291), self-government, which is seen as government by consent of the people of a given territory. Often, the terms 'autonomy' and 'self-government' are identified as synonyms (Hannikainen, 1998: 79). Sohn (1980:180-190), Thornberry (1998:79), and Elazar (1991) also see an analogy between self-government and autonomy. Autonomy, in the view of Heintze (1998:7), in a democracy is part of the self-government which enables the "authority to regulate their own affairs by enacting legal rules". According to Nordquist (1998:59), self-government is embedded in any arrangement of autonomy. Self-rule and self-government are related concepts according to Sohn (1980:180-190). Suksi (1997:104) says autonomy culminates in the achievement of self-government (see further Hannum and Lillich, 1981:249). Often constitutions dealing with autonomous arrangements employ the term 'self-government' to imply autonomy. For example, the Constitution Act of Finland, 1994 (new chapter iv (a), see detail Palmgren, 1997: 86), the Constitution of Spain, 1978 (articles 143 (1) and (2), and the Southern Provinces Regional Self-Government Act 1972 (Sudan) all employ 'self-government'. On the other hand, some international treaties[13] and documents, notably, the Draft UN Declaration on Indigenous Peoples, 1994 uses autonomy and self-government interchangeably.[14] 'Self-government' is what is sought by many minority groups and indigenous peoples to identify greater autonomy in territorial terms. It can be, in their view, used to take control over their own affairs effectively without interference from the centre and to preserve their cultural identity, their customs and traditions, and their institutions in the way they like. For instance, Chief Mercredi, who is the National Chief of the Assembly of the First Nations in Ottawa argued

(1993:163) that what Canadian Indians (notably his tribe, Mohawk) sought was 'self-government' to protect their way of life in a collective sense through their own institutions. He was not asking simply for local government or municipal units with a few decentralized powers. A similar view was expressed by the Aboriginal and Torres Strait Islander Commission to the UN Working Group on Indigenous Population in 1993 ('self-government by indigenous peoples of their own communities or lands'; see detail Thornberry, 1998:119). In *Delgamuukw* v *British Colombia*,[15] Mr Justice Wallace said that a claim of self-government by the Gitksand and Wet'suwet'en tribes was a right to govern the territory themselves in accordance with their laws and customs. Many other tribal groups also prefer 'self-government' to regain control over their affairs.

However, some scholars see a significant difference between self-government and autonomy. Autonomy signifies, according to Crawford (1979: 211-212), a preliminary stage of the development of self-government. Willemsen (cited in Lapidoth, 1997, see chapter 10) argues that if autonomy is a house, then self-government is only one room in it. Malberg (1920:169-170, cited in Lapidoth, 1997:30) refutes the suggestion that these two concepts, autonomy and self-government, have the same meaning. In his view, 'autonomy' as an entity may be considered autonomous only when it has its own non-derivative original powers of legislation, administration and adjudication, whereas self-government is an inferior form of legislative power subordinate to a superior entity which can effectively control it. Lapidoth (1997) also points out that even though there is similarity between autonomy and self-government to a greater extent, differences between these two concepts cannot be overlooked. "The term self-government implies a considerable degree of self-rule, whereas autonomy is a flexible concept, its substance ranging from limited powers to very broad ones. In addition, self-government usually applies to a specific region, whereas autonomy can be personal" (Lapidoth, 1997:53-54). This semantic debate is of little value. All these terms suffice, as pointed out by Alfredsson (1992), as long as the central government agrees to a meaningful shared sovereign power in the form of autonomy.

The forms of self-government vary in different territories, from extensive legislative and executive powers entrenched in a constitution or statute to a limited delegated power exercised by local government (sometimes called 'local autonomy'). The latter is essentially an inferior institution (see Page, 1992:1), which is therefore not generally attractive to minority groups. For example, *'collectivite territoriale'*, a self-governing sub-unit operated in Corsica is perceived by Corsicans to be no more than local government (Suksi, 1997:111). Cultural autonomy for national minorities in Finland, Estonia, Latvia, Lithuania, Croatia, Slovenia, Norway, Finland and Sweden operates at local self-government level (Suksi, 1997:104; see also Bernhardt, 1981:27). For instance, many local authorities in Portugal are not fully autonomous, but they contain elements of autonomy having democratically decentralized administrations.[16] However, they lack any significant political powers. Instead, they may be useful to central government by integrating the whole system of State institutions to reach the local population more effectively. A close political integration between local governments and central government is clearly visible where greater autonomous powers are not conferred upon the region, that is, where no significant diffusion of constitutional power is involved.[17] Often, 'localism' is the criterion taken into consideration when local-self-governments are created irrespective of minority identities. Whilst they are more likely to be vulnerable (Page, 1992:2), local self-governments display some elements of models of autonomy in the sense that they are representative democratic institutions which the local people can participate in.

In Europe the idea of local self-government as an alternative to autonomy is emerging. For example, the European Charter of Local Self-Government, 1985 advocated the idea that local self-government ('elected assemblies with meaningful powers') through local authorities can be used to further the interests of the local population.[18] "Appropriate local or autonomous authorities" was one of the options suggested in the Recommendation 1201/1993 by the Experts of the CSCE on National Minorities.[19] Similarly, the Documents of the Copenhagen Meeting on the Human Dimension of the CSCE, 29 June 1990 suggested that "appropriate local or autonomous administrations" could be used to "create conditions for the promotion of ethnic, cultural, linguistic and religious identity of certain minorities".[20] It was further recognised that such arrangements can be implemented on a territorial basis. Most importantly, the Experts of the CSCE on National Minorities in their recommendation promoted the idea of "local bodies and autonomous administration" in terms of "decentralised or local forms of government".[21]

4.3 *Categories of Autonomous Models*

There are two categories of autonomous models in the scope and application of autonomy, that is personal or cultural autonomy and territorial autonomy. Whilst territorial autonomy applies to a delineated part of a territory irrespective of differences amongst population, cultural or personal autonomy aims at a particular ethnic, religious or linguistic groups irrespective of their place of birth or origin. According to Eide (1998:252), cultural autonomy is different from territorial autonomy in three different ways; a) the management of affairs in cultural nature is allocated to culturally different groups as opposed to a territorially defined group; b) it applies only to cultural aspects; and c) only to those who belong to that cultural group. Commenting on the term 'cultural autonomy', Eide (1998: 252) says that "the phrase cultural autonomy is doubly vague: it carries with it the ambiguity of autonomy and adds to it the elusive term 'culture', so much more difficult to define than territory". Nonetheless, Eide provides the following definition (at 252):

> Provisionally, cultural autonomy will here be understood as the right to self-rule, by a culturally defined group, in regard to matters which affect the maintenance and reproduction of its culture.

Cultural autonomy is a very restricted one which allows minority groups a certain degree of independence to regulate areas such as traditional ways of life, i.e., hunting, fishing and farming, minority symbols, protection of monuments and memorial places, languages, education, religious and marital affairs, birth and death registration, and the like not involving or directly affecting the territory or State's authority. Personal laws, customs and religious practices are the main elements of personal autonomy which, according to Steiner (1991:1542), "can provide an important degree of autonomy and cohesion even for minorities that are territorially dispersed" (see also Lapidoth, 1997:37-40).

Personal autonomy (cultural autonomy) was introduced as a radical theory by Austrian Social Democrat Karl Renner (1918) and Otto Bauer (1907, cited in Eide, 1998:267) at the beginning of the 20th century mainly to protect minority groups in the Austro-Hungarian empire (see also Dinstein, 1981:29; Lapidoth, 1997:33). Renner rejected centralization of power around the State (*atomistische-Zentralistische Schule*) arguing that it would not reflect the proper structure of the society. In his view, the State is a 'federation of nations' (*Nationalitatenbundesstaat*) which is based on a dual principle, territorial and cultural. Cultural groups are free to administer their own cultural matters which the State should not interfere with. He was confident that by granting personal autonomy to minority groups, States could solve so-called minority problems. It was experimented with in Eastern Europe in particular, with a view to promoting minorities' rights after World War I, but without notable success (see Eide, 1998:271-272). Maintenance of educational and charitable, religious and social institutions was the focus of this system. This also promised "to grant adequate facilities to enable nationals whose mother tongue was not the official language to use their own language, orally or in writing, before the courts" (Thornberry, 1991:24; see further Robinson, 1943:91; see also *Minority Schools in Albania*[22]). One of the reasons for such a glaring failure, in addition to States' reluctance to honour such arrangements, was the reluctance of minority groups to accept such limited rights, which in their view, were no more than glorified individual rights derived from western liberal political philosophy. This was vividly explained by the founding father of Israel, David Ben Gurion (1924, cited in Dinstein, 1981:293), when the offer of personal autonomy to the Jews living in Palestine was made. His main argument was that "in the absence of territorial autonomy, personal autonomy is groundless". But personal autonomy might be a practical solution in the promotion and protection of minority rights where ethnic and other sub-groups are interspersed throughout the State, because territorial autonomy involving any form of constitutional diffusion or other ordinary legislation is inconceivable or impractical in such cases (Dinstein, 1981:292). This was also the view expressed by observers during the debate on the Working Group on Minorities. It was emphasized that cultural autonomy could be a valuable regime to accommodate the needs of minorities and ensure the preservation of their characteristics.[23] However, personal autonomy applies only to people "who opt to be members of the group" living in a State irrespective of their place of residence (see Lapidoth, 1997:39).

One of the successful experiments in cultural autonomy under the Ottoman Empire was that of the *Millet* system which, according to Cobban (1969:238), was practised and developed by the Iranian and Arab Empires. *Millets* empowered the non-Islamic religious communities, i.e., Christians, Jewish, Armenian and Roman Catholics to organise and manage their personal life. In fact it enjoyed a 'considerable degree of self-government' in the administrative and judicial fields, in particular control of properties, education, church affairs, marriages, records of birth, death and wills, and civil rights (Cobban, 1969:238; see further Thornberry, 1991:29; Laponce, 1960; Capotorti report, 1979: paragraph 6; Hannum and Lillich, 1980:884; see further on *Millet* system, Karpat, 1973). Even tax imposing powers were granted provided a portion of tax be given to the Sultan. The operation of cultural/personal autonomy should, however, be "within the limits of the law of the State" (Lapidoth, 1997:38). Contemporary personal autonomy models in Estonia (Law on Cultural Autonomy for National

Minorities, October 26, 1993), Latvia (Law on the Free Development of National and Ethnic Groups of Latvia and Their Right to Central Autonomy, March 19, 1991), Russian Federation (Law on National-Cultural Autonomy, June 25, 1996), Croatia (Constitutional Law of Human Rights and Freedoms and the Rights of National and Ethnic Communities or Minorities in the Republic of Croatia, December 4, 1991), Slovenia (Law on Self-Managing Ethnic Communities, October 5, 1994), Belgium linguistic communities, and Sami assemblies in Nordic countries (Norway, Sweden and Finland) provide examples of modern cultural autonomies (see Suksi, 1997:120; Ahren, 1995:461).

Territorial autonomy may be the result of a direct response to the demands of ethnic or other sub-groups of the population of the State (the proposed autonomy for the Kosovo province by the Six-Nations Contact group, 1999, a Constitutional Framework for a Special Autonomy for East Timor, 1999[24] (between the UN and Indonesia before the August referendum in 1999) Southern Sudan autonomy in 1972, autonomous provincial councils for the northern and eastern provinces in Sri Lanka under the 1987 constitutional amendment),[25] or by recognition of geographical or linguistic differences (Australia and India respectively), or due to historical reasons (the Swiss model). Most importantly, it can emerge as a mechanism to prevent ethnic conflicts as in the case of Basques, Catalans in Spain,[26] the Serbs dominated Sprska in Bosnia and Herzegovina, and the proposed autonomous regional government in Northern Ireland by the Good-Friday Agreement, 1999 (see further Harhoff, 1986; Nordquist, 1998). The operation of territorial autonomy may be limited only to a designated province or a region in the State yet it has a direct effect on every individual and group of people living within that territory (Dinstein, 1993:235; 1981:292 and Eide, 1993:90). Thus, individuals belonging to sub-groups will have a greater opportunity within a territorial autonomy to preserve, protect and promote cultural and traditional values of ethnic groups (Hannum, 1990:4) than where personal autonomy is operated (Solozabal, 1996:247). The political power of autonomous units or regions might be greater in a State which contains a homogenous population or where less divisions in terms of ethnicity or similar characteristics are evidenced between population groups, in contrast to the State which is pluralist or divided along the lines of ethnicity. If autonomy is granted due to pressure of ethnic elements, the powers may not be too significant because the State from the very beginning may have come to the negotiating table with a reluctant heart and mind. In brief, the effectiveness of autonomy depends upon the degree of independence possessed by the autonomous region over the affairs of the people in its territory, in particular in the areas of legislation and its implementation. In the end, the determining factor will be the extent to which the parties to the autonomous arrangement are prepared to co-operate with each other and make it work (Steiner, 1991:1542). It is also of importance to note that in order to exercise sovereign power effectively, an autonomous territory also needs a government free from interference from the State (Sohn, 1980:190).

4.4 *Variations of Autonomous Models: "From a Classic Federation to Various Forms of Cultural Home Rule"*

Elazar (1991: introduction) states that there are at least 100 functioning examples of autonomous models ranging from classic federation to various forms of cultural home rule. However, according to Lyck (1995:481) there are 500 autonomous units worldwide. Most of them differ from each other to a varying degree involving a wider range of different arrangements. There is no uniform pattern in autonomous arrangements with respect to the degree of the transfer of power to the region or structure of the autonomous unit. Hannum and Lillich (1981:216) accept that autonomy is necessarily limited though a "wide-ranging transfer of powers" can be seen in some models" (see also Crawford, 1979:211-212). Greenland/Kalaallit Nunaat,[27] the Faeroe Islands[28] and the Aaland Islands provide examples of extensive autonomous power. By a comparison of autonomy of the Aaland Islands with an *Oblast* or *Okruga* in the Republic of Russia, one can immediately observe a significant difference between these two models. The Aaland Islands operate as one territorial unit, and are close to a territorial autonomy, considering its distinctive geographical identity.[29] It possesses substantial legislative, administrative and executive powers though it constitutionally comes under the sovereignty of Finland. An Aalandic member of Finnish Parliament, relying on his own experience with the operative aspects of Aaland autonomy, stated that Aalandic autonomy ever since the 1920s has been developing and growing stronger. Since 1954 it has had its own flag, and separate postage stamps since 1980, since 1993 it owns its own postal administration. Since the 1970s it has become a member of the Nordic Council and has the right of participation in the meeting of Nordic Ministers. It has been granted power to deal with culture, religion, education, and some administrative functions with legislative powers. Most importantly, the Aaland's legislative competence is very extensive (Jansson, 1997:1; Palmgren, 1997:85-97). On the other hand, the competence of the kind of *oblast* or *okruga* model is relatively modest and minimal (Lapidoth, 1997:84-92). They stand at the bottom of the federal structure of the former Soviet Union and the present Russian Federation. They are confined to small local areas and their powers are limited to local, cultural, and administrative matters. Whilst all major nations (*natsiya*) were given either Union Republic or autonomous republic status (which was defined on a territorial basis having at least 80,000 to 100,000 people), less developed small national (*narodnost*) were given either the *oblast* or *okruga* autonomy models.[30] In fact the former were given their own governments with legislature, executive and judiciary. Both *oblast* and *okruga* come under the authority of a union republic. Therefore any acts of these autonomous regions or areas can be amended or repealed by the Union republics. Lapidoth says "that the autonomous areas and the autonomous regions had very limited, purely administrative autonomy- if the expression is at all appropriate".[31]

However, as points out by Palley (1978:13), there are certain characteristics common to any autonomous model. First of all, both the center and the autonomous territorial units exercise divided sovereignty whilst coordinating and complementing each other. The competence of each level of government is identified and often constitutionally defined and guaranteed. However, the center exercises the most important tasks relevant to the whole State while the competence of regional autonomous units is confined to the region. Both parties' aim is to prevent conflicts and disagreements so as to preserve the sovereign integrity of the State while preserving their diversities in dignity and honour. "In such a system", as stated by Palley (1978:13), "units and center are more committed to working together than to disagreeing and fragmenting".

States are, however, more cautious in conferring or maintaining autonomous powers on the province or regionally based sub-groups, as is evident from the Kosovo, Sri Lanka, Kurdistan and East Timor disputes, fearing that new autonomous regions will become a threat to the empowering State. Therefore, States seek to ensure that autonomous regions or provinces operate in compliance with the constitutional or international arrangements (by way of treaties) agreed upon by both parties. This is normally carried out by constitutional or other international arrangements which may provide for the involvement of administrative and executive branches of both the center and the region to remedy any breach of constitutional structure and to make sure that the system operates smoothly. But, some States are opposed to any involvement of international mediation. For instance, before the withdrawal of Serb military forces from the Kosovo province, Serbia's (FRY) opposition to NATO's involvement in the implementation process in the event of any arrangement being made for autonomy for the Kosovo province can be presented as an example.

4.5 *Autonomy with 'Shared' or 'Divided Sovereignty'*

Sovereignty is both a friend and an enemy of autonomy. It is a friend in the sense that autonomy achieves its legal base for its existence from sovereignty. However, sovereignty constrains the functioning power of autonomous region or unit by imposing parameters within which autonomy has to operate. As stated in the *Lighthhouses in Crete* and Samo,[32] *Memel*,[33] even greater autonomy cannot challenge the authority of sovereignty (see also *Lighthouses* case[34]). It is generally assumed that the residual powers inhere in the sovereign State as stated in the *Memel* case (see details in Dinstein, 1981:298-301). "There exists a sovereign above the autonomous authority and that sovereign has the highest authority" (see also Hannikainen, 1998:86). Full sovereignty always rests with an independent State.

Minorities' claims for 'shared' or 'divided' sovereignty within the framework of autonomy are one of the most contentious issues in international law. If we were to accept the theory that sovereignty belongs to the nation-State, and it has therefore nothing to do with minorities or other sub-groups, then minorities' claims for autonomy with shared or divided sovereignty would fail. Recognition of their claims would create problems for nation-States. Any significant changes to the traditional understanding of the concept of sovereignty[35] would significantly weaken the nation-State system.

The view that sovereignty could be restricted, for example by way of constitutional arrangements, is gaining acceptance amongst publicists. Divisibility of sovereignty has been popular since the 18th century. It became clear with the transformation of the USA, Germany and Switzerland from confederal into federal systems that the divisibility of sovereignty between federal governments and the union States was no longer such a contentious issue. Because both federal State and union States are sovereign; both units enjoy sovereignty within their competence. Restrictions can be imposed on sovereignty through internal and external arrangements thus limiting its competence. Oppenheim (see 1992 ed:124 and 249) rightly concluded that sovereignty is divisible, most importantly in federal States. However, he pointed out, "the supreme authority which a State exercises over its territory would seem to suggest that on one and the same territory there could exist only one full sovereign State, and that for there to be two or more full sovereign States on one and the same territory is not possible" (Oppenheim, above:165). The sovereign State is the one which "posses independence all round, and therefore full sovereignty". Union States in federal States are "not-full sovereign States or full subjects of international laws". They, however, possess authority over certain matters "as far as their competence reaches" (Oppenheim, above:245). However, in federations, union States ('non-full sovereign States') could enjoy less sovereign powers.

Contemporary international jurists assert that the divisibility of sovereignty is prominent in pluralist societies. As Lee (1994:52) points out that inward or downward development from State to sub-state entities exists in most States. This clearly contrasts with upward or outward development from States to inter-government organisation exists in Westphalian model nation State system (Lee, 1994:52). Franck (1994:53) also admits that the State is subdividing itself into sub-groups (sub-actors) which can, in his view, be regions or populations. In modern polities, there may be many instances where sovereignty is exercised by more than one organ. Regional governments or union States, in particular in federal structures, exercise powers which legitimately come within their competence. In such cases it is 'divided sovereignty' which is exercised by both the federal State and its member-States as pointed out by Oppenheim (above:564-65 and 571). Does then a degree of autonomy in the form of shared-sovereignty conferred upon a region have any relevance to minority and other sub-groups? Can at least a certain element of sovereignty be exercised by a segment of the population of a State, for instance by minority groups living within a designated region within the State? Lee (1994:52) argues that elements of sovereignty can be passed down to a region and to peoples within it. Sovereignty does have corresponding obligations and commitments to the sub-elements existing within sovereign States. Its obligation to groups (ethnic, indigenous and other weaker groups such as women) is emphasised by many contemporary scholars (Chinkin, 1994:73; Frank, 1994:73; Lee, 1994:52). According to Deng (1994:56), it brings with it serious obligations, most notably commitment to human rights. However, these progressive analyses of sovereignty have met with dissent. For example, Ratner (1994:75) states that such arguments ignore the essential nature of sovereignty. Sovereignty, in his view, is "the entitlement of a state to act as it wishes at the international level - the ability to resist intervention from the international community". Higgins (1994:73) also expressed a similar opinion.

Redistribution of sovereignty is seen by Khan (1994:54) as a reallocation of some functions. It does not, however, in Khan's view, "approach a displacement of the idea of state sovereignty". Fox (1994:57) also argues that the 'reallocation of sovereignty' involving especially human rights strengthens the sovereign State as a political unit. The abiding political ethic within such a system is tolerance. All members of the sub-group or groups living in the autonomous State, it can be argued, possess some elements of sovereign power through their representative governments. In such cases, sovereignty can be seen in autonomous rights or federal rights, because these rights ultimately emanate from sovereignty. Thus, autonomous States created in response to the agitation of sub-groups or minority groups will become 'non-full sovereign States' or regions.

Current understanding of human rights and democratic governance enhances and strengthens the arguments that minorities living in autonomous regions/provinces can exercise shared-sovereignty with the central or federal government. This sharing is aimed at the strengthening and stabilising of nation-States so as to avoid conflicts and anarchy. Thus, minorities as a segment of a people can claim certain rights emanating from sovereignty by adhering to norms recognised by international law. This implies that minorities can enjoy their legitimate rights within autonomy or, short of secession involving a federal solution. It can further be argued that there may be a slim relationship between minority groups and sovereignty (Rosenau, 1995:192). This can be described by examining the concept of 'responsive sovereign State' which requires the fulfilment of States' obligation to its peoples and sub-groups, i.e., minorities. States' responsibilities, in the final analysis, are necessarily associated with human rights (see Deng, 1994).

Rosenau (1995:192) interprets sovereignty pointing out that it "can be treated as a psychological concept and it can be used to explore the behaviour of ethnic groups, nationalism, and peoples' sense of community and territoriality". This is, however, more political than current theories of international law are prepared to uphold. Nevertheless, it should also be noted that sovereignty cannot float in a vacuum, nor is it a non-negotiable institution (Soyinka, 1996). Sovereignty, as admitted by many States in their constitutions, exists among people.[36] Modern States possess sovereignty as trustees rather than owners or simply being rulers. Thus it can be argued that minority groups can claim shared or divided sovereignty through both personal and territorial autonomy within a unitary, confederal or federal structure. Sovereign power or State sovereignty is therefore no longer the unquestionable and noble concept it was. "The time of absolute and exclusive sovereignty, however, has passed; its theory was never matched by reality".[37] It has now come under great pressure and increasingly become controversial (Khan, 1994:54). Sovereignty has also been weakened to a considerable extent by continued attack by the federalists.[38] A prominent member of the World Federal Association suggested that it was time we should "talk about sovereignty of people instead of sovereignty (Hoffmann, 1994:64-65). They contend that union States of a federal structure are entitled to a certain degree of independence as in the case of the USA, Germany, Canada and Switzerland. In fact, union States of federal structure are often described as sovereign States. Some human rights scholars also view the polity "as a matrix of overlapping, interlocking units, powers and relationships" (Elazar, 1991:introduction). Moreover, sovereignty's most important appurtenance – territorial integrity[39] of the State - has become a legitimate target of many minority groups who are fighting for either self-government with greater autonomy or independent statehood. Most notably, many minority groups seem to think that the traditional meaning and understanding of sovereignty is no longer valid in contemporary multiethnic societies (Goldman and Wilson eds., 1984, see in particular chapter 10). Most minority groups refuse to believe in indivisible sovereignty. For example, the leader of the movement of autonomy in the 'Sverdlovsk Ural Republic' in the Ural Mountains, Eduard Ergartovich Rossel stressed that sovereignty was not exclusively the possession of central government. It exists in every component part of the State system (Easter, 1997:631).

However, minority groups, as pointed out by Fowler and Bunck (1995:17), are showing enthusiasm for re-possessing or recreating sovereignty because it is associated with an assortment of privileges and rights. "They are keenly aware of the benefit of entry into the private clubs of sovereign states" (Fowler and Bunck, 1995:17; see also Kingsbury, 1994:4). On the other hand, this shows their inconsistent attitudes towards sovereignty, because whilst attacking sovereignty they themselves try to possess it by achieving statehood. Without sovereignty they know very well that independent States cannot exist, because it is highly unlikely that the international community will ever be prepared to accept non-sovereign entities as members of their exclusive clubs. Anarchic societies are not what the UN and other regional and international bodies like to see.

Sovereignty does have different dimensions when it comes to indigenous peoples. It is said that 'indigenous sovereignty' can take on multiple meanings ranging from 'cultural integrity' to 'internal management' (Corntassel and Primeau, 1995:361). Indigenous groups justify their struggle arguing that it is to win back or restore their 'lost sovereignty' (Williams, 1992). The concept of 'prior sovereignty' or 'original sovereignty' is presented by some indigenous groups as a strategy to achieve greater autonomy in the areas in which they live. Corntassel and Primeau (1995:361) write, "prior sovereignty refers to the argument that antecedent to the invasion of the North American continent by the European powers, Indian communities exercised sovereignty over themselves and that, at least in the initial stages of contact, this sovereignty was formally recognized by the colonial powers via the treaty-making process". Quoting a landmark judgment, *Worcester* v *The State of Georgia,*[40] it was argued by Hutchins, Hilling and Schulze (1995:253-254) that when aborigines (indigenous peoples) did enter into treaties with colonial powers they gave up only 'external sovereignty' while retaining 'internal sovereignty'. A similar opinion was expressed in the majority judgment in *Casimel* v *Insurance Corporation of British Colombia.*[41] Thus sovereignty has now become a part of indigenous peoples' lexicon in an ongoing quest for greater autonomy" (Corntassel and Primeau, 1995:361).

4.6 *Autonomy Within a Federal Structure*

Federalism originates from a Latin word *foedus*, meaning a 'covenant'. Partnership among various elements in a common cause is envisaged (Elazer, 1991:introduction). A federal State is a union of several sovereign States (*Bundesstaaten*) (Oppenheim, above:248-249). Federalism in a very broad sense means the distribution of powers between a federal State and regions or union States (Bernhardt 1981:23), or "two orders of government: the federal government on the one hand, and the provinces on the other" (*re Secession of Quebec* (1998) 2 SCR 217). It is a kind of "combining self-rule with shared rule" (Elazar, 1991:introduction) involving individuals, groups and often geographical variations. When models of autonomy operate in a 'quasi-federal'[42] or 'federal' structure, both federal and union States can make policies common to both units. Thus, they exercise their powers within their competence without encroaching upon each other's and, in such a way as to maintain their respective entities. Elazar (1991:introduction, xv) noted that "basic policies are made and implemented through negotiation in some form so that all can share in the system's decision-making and executive powers".

Federalism is a political concept and it has "a long, rich and diverse history and encompasses a wide variety of political forms" (Forsythe, 1996). It is a mechanism which delegates certain subjects to the central government whilst leaving other subjects to the sub-regions (Opinion no. 1 of the Badinter Committee).[43] In federalism, the emphasis is on non-centralisation of power, constitutional diffusion and sharing of power between various institutions. It, as held in the *Quebec* case (above), "recognizes the diversity of the component parts of confederation or a federation and the autonomy of provincial governments to develop their societies within their respective sphere of jurisdiction". Federal units operate within fixed boundaries thus respecting the territorial integrity and national unity of the State. Special Rapporteur Eide states that federalism might be the result of 'limited unification' of various units which "have joined together but retained a reserved domain within their territorial units".[44] Dinstein (1993:221) argues that federalism does not mean a federation of independent States because there can be only one federal State.

It is worthy of mention that there are different varieties of federal States, from the most restrictive (eg. the former Eritrean model) to the most extensive (eg. the Swiss, German, and US models). In the former category, the central government holds extensive powers, whilst in the latter powers come within the competence of the constituent States of the Federation. However, the common feature of a federal system is the division of legislative powers. Such Union States and federal government derive their powers from the constitution, which acts like an arbitrator or source of power. During the debate on the proposed federal clause to the ICCPR it was argued that, "the central government could not assume responsibilities which were not within its competence without endangering the basic compromise of federation and, ultimately, the federation itself".[45]

The federal State operates with a number of component units (Dinstein, 1993:222; see also Elazar ed. 1991:introduction), (they may be called, cantons, lander or provinces, union States or, as in the case of the USA, 'states'). It is, therefore, in a better position than the unitary State to accommodate ethnic, linguistic and other regional variations, because wide powers to the regions will be attractive to sub-groups (Dinstein, 1993:221). Moreover, federalism favours tolerance, mutual understanding and respect between the various entities which make up the State.[46] When a federation is created taking into account ethnic, religious and linguistic differences, then it reflects the desire of the constituent parties to accommodate self-rule for minority groups in those areas in which they are mainly concentrated.

Federalism as a constitutional strategy has been applied in many parts of the world to accommodate linguistic and ethnic differences. Its application to minority groups is immense. It is widely accepted that federalism could effectively address issues relating to minority groups and promote their rights by granting a certain degree of legislative, judicial and financial autonomy. The Swiss delegate states: "well-organized federalism was a means to ensure the perpetuity of the state as it was the expression of an institutionalised dialogue that required the constant search, in the common interest, for a common denominator between often contradictory interests".[47]

Federalism is not, however, a concept embedded in international law. According to Schreuer (Schreuer, 1993:449), international law "has a tendency to turn a blind eye to federal structures and regard their distribution of functions as internal matter". Most States are of the view that the "distribution of power between the central government and local or regional authorities was merely an internal problem which was of no concern to international law".[48]

It can be argued that reluctance to consider federalism as a vital part of international law might be due to the horizontal nature of international law. A parallel system or asymmetrical federal structure has a tendency to create conflicts between the centre and the federal provinces. In contrast to regional or cantonal governments in a federation, Westphalian model nation-States operate horizontally (Franck, 1994:53). This implies that there cannot be other subgroups operating in asymmetrical or more alarmingly in vertical ways that would challenge the authority of the State. Therefore, they are not welcome by the nation-State system in general.

In contrast to the principle of federalism, autonomy is a relatively new concept. Although autonomy may operate within a federal or confederal structure it is not a branch of federal theory nor are they synonymous (Hannum and Lillich, 1980:858-889). Common aspects can be detected in both systems. They are, as correctly pointed out by Bernhardt (1981:23), "distinct phenomena in modern history with basically different underlying philosophies" with different political background (see also Dinstein, 1993:234).

4.7 *Autonomy is Non-derogable?*

It is said by some jurists that once autonomy is granted it cannot unilaterally be abolished. This theory seems to be based on both constitutional and international law without properly examining the State practice. It is true that many modern autonomous States or regions are created through either constitutional or normal legislative mechanisms. In both these instances there may be some entrenchment in constitutions or legislation making it difficult for either an autonomous region or a central government to make any amendments or to abolish unilaterally without consulting the other party. For example, the Spanish constitution guarantees that the Spanish parliament alone cannot make any changes to it or take steps to abolish the autonomous States unilaterally. There are certain procedures to be followed as stipulated by section 168 of the 1978 constitution. According to Suksi (1997) the self-governments of Portuguese Azores and Medeira also possess such constitutional guarantees. Suksi (1997:110) says that "a certain entrenchment of the principle of autonomy" can be seen in section 288 of the *Constitution of Portugal*. Any changes to the autonomy through legislative means have to be made by mutual consent of both the regions and the centre. Changes can be introduced by the Portuguese Parliament only after consideration of the opinions of the autonomous regions except in a state of siege or emergency as stipulated by section 19 (I) of the *Portuguese constitution* (Suksi, 1997:110). Similarly, any amendments to the existing autonomous regions should be carried out in Italy only with the co-operation of the autonomous regions although autonomy is not entrenched in the Constitution. Amendments to the Aaland autonomy Act must also have the consent of the Legislative Assembly of Aaland. Referring to legal rights created by the *Autonomy Act of Aaland*, 1991, Palmgren (1997:86) states that "the right given to Aaland can never be taken away without the consent of a qualified majority of the Legislative Assembly" although there is no such right entrenched in the constitution or any other statutes. Where autonomous regions are created as a result of international treaty or under the aegis of the UN or other regional bodies it can be argued that the "State would not be entitled unilaterally to revoke or substantially reduce the autonomy", because; a) States are obliged by their international commitment, and b) autonomies created by international organizations or by a treaty are considered important institutions having *sui generis* character (Suksi, 1998:157; see also Hannikainen, 1998:88). Specially, autonomy granted for indigenous peoples, as argued by Harhoff (1986:40), cannot be revoked unilaterally by the State party. He contends (at 40):

> Once a certain level of degree of autonomy has been achieved, it cannot be revoked unilaterally by the metropolitan State. Thus, indigenous autonomy is subject only to improvements according to international law. Consequently, any

partial or total withdrawal of powers transferred to the institutions of an (indigenous) autonomy represents a violation of international law to the extent in which this takes place against the will of the autonomous structure. This implies in turn that the indigenous populations in general are considered entitled as well to invoke such violations at the international level, but it has been debated whether subjects other than States can bring cases before the United Nations... .

The above arguments are also based on the notion that sovereign States have obligations and duties to their constituent parties. States are obliged not to renege on what they promised when they entered into agreements with their constituent parties. Once autonomy arrangements have been introduced by the Constitution or by an ordinary Act of parliament, states Suksi (1997:113-114), "a state is under an obligation not to worsen or abolish them without the consent of the inhabitants concerned. It is a legal protection under international law". For instance, referring to the Faeroe Islands' home rule, some scholars argue that the powers (legislative, executive and judicial) conferred upon the *Landsstyre* (legislative assembly) of the Faeroe Islands by the Danish Parliament cannot be taken back without the consent of the islanders. Yet there is no consensus on this. Suksi (1997:113-114) argues that the Faeroe's autonomy can be reclaimed by the Danish parliament since its powers are a kind of delegation of power.

Although there are constitutional safeguards preventing the State taking unilateral action in amending or abrogating the autonomous arrangement, State practice suggests such constitutional guarantees or international involvement may not restrain States when they are determined to see the end of any autonomous States in their territories. Classic examples of this are the abolition of the autonomous regions of Spain by Franco's military regime in 1939, the destruction of the Eritrean autonomous model by the Ethiopian monarch in 1962, the revocation of the Kosovo autonomous provincial government by the Serbian parliament in 1989-1990, the suspension of the regional government of the North and East provinces of Sri Lanka in 1990, and the abolition of the self-government of Nagorny Karabakh in November 1991 by Azerbaijan. One of the most recent cases is that of the termination of the three-year-old Crimean autonomy by the Ukrainian Parliament on 17 March 1995 (Suksi, 1997:125). International law or UN or other regional practices do not have any viable means for preventing such arbitrary decisions though they can keep immense pressure on the recalcitrant States. It can therefore be argued that autonomy is a permitted right which can be enjoyed only as far as the State is prepared to go along with such arrangements. In practice, the survival of models of autonomy depends upon the goodwill of the empowering State.

Conclusion

Autonomy with shared-sovereignty, from the minorities' perspective, strengthens their position in any regional arrangement within a unitary, federal or confederal structure. For example, the representative of Espacio-Americano called on the Working Group on Minorities to consider autonomy as a means to ensure the effective participation of minorities.[49] Psychologically the term 'autonomous government' may provide much satisfaction and political leverage against the central government. It reflects the desire of different ethnic groups in a State structure to remain separate from others yet in certain areas to work with the majority community on an equal footing.

Notes

[1] *An Agenda For Peace*, UN Doc. A/47/277, para. 11; S/24111, 17 June 1992.

[2] UN Doc. E/CN.4/Sub.2/1994/56, 28 October 1994.

[3] See League of Nations (1927), *Protection of Linguistic, Racial and Religious Minorities by the League of Nations*, cited in *Special Protective Measures of an International Character for Ethnic, Religious or Linguistic Groups*, UN Publication: New York, 1967, part II, p. 47. See further Thornberry, P. (1991), *International Law and the Rights of Minorities*, Clarendon Press: Oxford, pp. 41-42.

[4] Lithuania was given sovereignty over Memel upon the advice of the League of Nations. Great Britain, France, Italy, Japan and Lithuania were the parties to the Treaty which was signed on 8 May 1924. The main aim was to give self-rule to the German speaking people. The Memel Territory did not survive the Second World War. See Lapidoth, R. (1997) *Autonomy, Flexible Solutions to Ethnic Conflicts*, United States Institute of Peace Press: Washington DC, 1997, p.78.

[5] The Aaland Islands were granted autonomy first on 6 May 1921 by *Guarantee Law* by Finland. Later, a resolution adopted at its thirteenth session by the League Council effectively affirming it. See *LNOJ*, Suppl. 5, 1921, p. 24, cited in Hannum, H. (1990), *Autonomy, Sovereignty and Self-Determination*, University of Pennsylvania Press: Philadelphia, p. 371.

[6] The UN has initiated a federal solution to the Eritrean problem by the *Federal Act of 1952* in pursuance of its resolution GA Res. 390 (V) 2 December 1950. On 3 May 1952 the UN Commission in Eritrea presented a draft constitution which was adopted by the Eritrean Assembly on 10 July 1952 with some amendments. On

11 August 1952 the Emperor of Ethiopia ratified it. The Eritrean Constitution came into force on 11 September 1952. See Ghali, B. B. (1996), 'Overview', in *The United Nations and the Independence of Eritrea,* Department of Public Information, UN: New York. See further Meron, T. and Pappas, A. M. (1981), 'The Eritrean Autonomy: A Case Study of a Failure', in Y. Dinstein (eds), *Models of Autonomy,* Transaction Books: New Brunswick and London, p.183.

[7] See *infra* footnote 28.

[8] See *infra* footnotes 12 and 27.

[9] The Kurds in Iraq were granted autonomous status by *The Law of Autonomy in the Region of Kurdistan,* Act no. 33 of 11 March 1974 (as amended in 1983) even though it has never been fully implemented as promised by the Iraqi regime. English text is included in *Settlements of the Kurdish Problem in Iraq,* Ath-thawra Publication: Baghdad, 1974, pp. 185 –198. See generally Kreyenbroek, P. G. and Sperl, S. (1992), *The Kurds: A Contemporary Overview,* Routledge: London and New York, 1992. See further Hannum, H. eds. (1993), *Documents on Autonomy and Minority Rights,* Martinus Nijhoff: Dordrecht, pp. 317-24. Sohn, L. B. (1980), 'The Concept of Autonomy in International Law and the Practice of the United Nations', 15 (2) *ILR,* p.182.

[10] UN Doc. E/CN.4/Sub.2/1990/46, *Possible Ways and Means of Facilitating the Peaceful and Constructive Solution of Problems Involving Minorities,* para. 23, p.6.

[11] See paragraph 35 of the Copenhagen Meeting on the Human Dimension of the Conference on Security and Corporation, 29 June 1990 ("appropriate local or autonomous administrations corresponding to the specific historical and territorial circumstances"), 29 *ILM* 1305 [1990].

[12] Greenland autonomy is mentioned as 'home rule' for Greenlanders, see *Greenland Home Rule Act,* no. 577, 1978. It entered into force on 1 May 1979.

[13] See the Declaration of Principles on Interim Self-Government Arrangements Concerning Gaza and Jericho, 13 September 1993, 32 *ILM* 1525 [1993], pp. 1525-1544.

[14] See article 31 of the Draft UN Declaration on Indigenous Peoples, 1994, which states, "Indigenous peoples, as a specific form of exercising their right to self-determination, have the right to autonomy or self-government in matters relating to their internal and local affairs, including culture, religion, education, information, media, health, housing, employment, social welfare, economic activities, land resource management, environment and entry by non-members, as well as ways and means for financing these autonomous functions".

[15] 104 *DLR* (4th) BCCA (1993) pp. 591-92, cited in Hutchins, P. W. Hilling, C. and Schulze, D. (1995), 'The Aboriginal Right to Self-Government and the Canadian Constitution: The Ghost in the Machine', 29 (2) *UBC Law Review,* pp. 251-302.

[16] Article 6 of the Constitution of Portugal says that the State is a unitary one organised to respect the principle of the autonomy of local authorities. See Suksi, M. (1997), 'The Constitutional Setting of the Aaland Islands Compared', in L. Hannikainen and H. Horn (eds), *Autonomy and Demilitarisation in International*

Law: The Aaland Islands in a Changing Europe, Kluwer Law International: The Hague/London/Boston, see footnote 1, p.120.

[17] It should be noted that diffusion of power is not always done by way of constitution in the creation of autonomous regions. For instance, autonomous status of Greenland and Faeroe Islands was created through ordinary legislations.

[18] Council of Europe (1993), *Conference on the European Charter of Local Self-Government*, Studies and Texts, no. 27, see articles 3. 2 and 4. 8, p. 7.

[19] Reprinted in 16 (1/3) *HRLJ* p. 112.

[20] Principle IV, para. 35. 29 *ILM* 1990, pp. 1305-1321.

[21] 30 *ILM* 1692 [1991], pp. 1692-1702

[22] *PCIJ*, Ser. A/B, No. 64, 1935, pp. 4-36.

[23] UN DOC. E/CN.4/Sub.2/1996/2, 30 November 1995, para. 61, p. 15.

[24] See http://www.un.org/peace/etimor/agreement.

[25] This amendment to the constitution of Sri Lanka is popularly known as the 'Thirteenth Amendment' which came into force on 12 November 1987, see Marasinghe, M. L. (1988), 'Ethnic Politics and Constitutional Reform: The Indo-Sri Lankan Accord', 37 *ICLQ*, pp. 551-583.

[26] See Ben-Ami, S. (1981), 'The Catalan and Basque Movements for Autonomy', in Dinstein, as above, pp. 67-84.

[27] Greenland's autonomy has notably increased since the 1950s and it was conferred an extensive autonomous powers in 1978 by the *Home Rule Act*. See Lyck, L. 'Lessons to be Learnt on Human Rights From the Faeroes Situations Since 1992', 64 (3) *Nord. J.Int.L* 1995, 82, p.482. See also Foighei, I. (1981), 'A Framework for Local Autonomy: The Greenland Case', in Dinstein (ed), as above, pp. 31-52.

[28] The Faeroes Islands achieved self-government status by the *Home Rule Act* of 1948, Danish Law no. 137, 23 March 1948, reprinted in *UNYBHR* 1950, cited in Olafsson, A. (1995), 'Relationship Between Political and Economic Self-Determination: The Faeroes Case', 64 (3) *Nord. J.Int.L*, p. 467.

[29] See sec. 1 and 2, Annex 3, *Act on the Autonomy of Aaland*, 1991, Act no. 1144, 16 August 1991.

[30] Autonomous models experimented with under the former USSR were not only complex but also demonstrates distinctive characteristics. They are different from other autonomous models in many ways. There were Union Republics (SSR), autonomous republics (ASSR), then autonomous regions (*oblast*), and autonomous areas (*okruga*). These arrangements were structured within a federal structure. See Lapidoth, R. (1997), *Autonomy: Flexible Solutions to Ethnic Conflicts*, United States Institute of Peace Press: Washington DC, p.85.

[31] *Ibid.* p. 89.

[32] *PCIJ* Ser. A/B, No. 7, 1934.

[33] *Memel* case, *PCIJ* Ser. A/B, No. 49, 1932.

[34] *PCIJ*, Ser. A/B, no. 62, 1934.

[35] From a theoretical point of view, the classical understanding of the concept of sovereignty is that of 'omnipotence'. According to Bodin (1530-1596), the pioneer

of the classical doctrine of sovereignty, the person who exercises sovereign power can exercise absolute power and introduce law at whim and pleasure at any time regulating the behaviour of citizens. See Bodin, J. (1577), *De La Republique,* cited in Jennings, R. Y. and Watts, A. eds. (1992), *Oppenheim's International Law, PEACE* vol. I, 9th ed, Longmans: Essex, para. 36, p. 124. Hobbes, T. (1928 ed.) *Leviathan,* EP Dutton and Co: London and Toronto. Bodins's theory was further expanded by Hobbes (*Leviathan,* 1651) arguing that sovereignty was above religious laws during the 17th century and later by Calhoun in *A Disquisition on Government,* 1851 (cited in Oppenheim, *ibid.* p. 124). Sovereignty was necessary, suggested Hobbes, to avoid conflicts and could be used as a weapon to maintain law and order against horrible calamities created by 'masterless men', Hobbs, *ibid.* p. 95. In their view, sovereignty could not be restricted and it is indivisible. Even Rousseau (*Le Contrat Social,* 1762) advocated and defended the indivisibility of sovereignty, *ibid.* p. 124.

[36] See *The Constitution of Sri Lanka,* Arts. 3 and 4. Article 3 states: "In the Republic of Sri Lanka sovereignty is in the People and is inalienable. Sovereignty includes the powers of government, fundamental rights and the franchise".

[37] *An Agenda For Peace,* as above, para. 17, p.959.

[38] During the 18th century federalists defending the American revolution justified a certain degree of independence for union States within a federation. Alexander Hamilton, James Madison, and John Jay were prominent federalists who presented the theory of concurrent sovereignty of the federal State and its member States. *See Oppenheim's, International Law,* vol. 1, as above, para. 69, p.118.

[39] 'Territory' is the most important part of the sovereign State. According to Oppenheim, territory is "totally independent of the racial characteristics of the inhabitants of the State. The territory is the public property of the State, and not of a nation in the sense of a race". Lauterpacht, H. ed. (1962), *Oppenheim's International Law, A Treatise, PEACE, vol. 1,* Longman: Essex, para. 169, p. 408. He further said, "the importance of State territory lies in the fact that it is the space within which the State exercises its supreme authority". *Ibid.* para. 172, see also para. 173-175, pp. 415-419.

[40] 31 US 350, 6 Pet 515 [1832]

[41] 106, *DLR* (4th) 720 (BCCA) (1993), p.728.

[42] The current Spanish constitution is designed within a quasi-federal structure according to Solozabal. See Solozabal, J. J. (1996), 'Spain: A Federation in the Making', in J. J. Hesse, and. V. Write (eds), *Federalizinf Europe?* Oxford UP: Oxford, pp. 325-360.

[43] 31 (6) *ILM* 1494 [1992], p. 1495.

[44] UN Doc. E/CN.4/Sub.2/1993/34, 10 August 1993, *Possible Ways and Means of Facilitating the Peaceful and Constructive Solution of Problems Involving Minorities,* para. 255, p. 55.

[45] See A/C.3/SR. 292, 26 October 1950, para. 17, p. 134.

[46] UN Doc.E/CN.4/Sub.2/1996/2, 30 November 1995, para.51, p.13 (Switzerland).

[47] *Ibid.* para. 51, p. 13 (Switzerland).

[48] For example see A/C.3/SR.293, 26 October 1950, para. 2, p.141 (Poland) and A/C.3/SR.292, 26 October 1950, paras. 78-79, p. 139 (Cuba).
[49] UN Doc. E/CN.4/Sub.2/1996/2, 30 November 1995, para. 52, p. 13.

References

Ahren, I. (1995), 'Small Nations of the North in Constitutional and International Law', 64 (3) *Nord. J.Int.L*, pp. 457-463.

Alfredsson, G. (1992), *Discussion Paper on Minority Rights and Democracy*, Third Strasbourg Conference on Parliamentary Democracy, Published by Parliamentary Assembly of the Council of Europe: Strasbourg.

Bauer, O. (1907), *Die Nationalitatenfrage und die Sozialdemokratie* (The Nationalities Question and the Social Democracy), cited in Eide, below, 1998.

Bernhardt, R. (1981), 'Federalism and Autonomy', in Y. Dinstein (ed), *Models of Autonomy*, Transaction Books: New Brunswick and London, pp. 23-30.

Capotorti, F. (1979), *Study of the Rights of Persons Belonging to Ethnic, Religious and Linguistic Minorities*, UN Doc. E/CN.4/Sub.2/384, UN Sales no. E. 78. XIV. 1, 1979.

Chief Mercredi, O. (1993), 'First Nations and Self-Determination', in K. E. Mahoney and P. Mahoney (eds), *Human Rights in the Twenty-First Century: A Global Challenge*, Martinus Nijhoff: Dordrecht/Boston/London, pp. 161- 166.

Chinkin, C. (1994), Commentary on 'The End of Sovereignty?' *ASIL Proceedings* (6-9 April), p. 73.

Cobban, A. (1969), *The Nation State and National Self-Determination*, T.Y. Crowell : New York.

Corntassel, J. J. and Primeau, T. H. (1995), 'Indigenous Sovereignty and International Law: Revised Strategies for Pursuing Self-Determination', 17 (2) *HRQ*, pp. 343-365.

Crawford, J (1979), *The Creation of States in International Law*, Clarendon Press: Oxford.

Deng, F. (1994), Commentary on 'Multiple Tiers of Sovereignty', *ASIL Proceedings* (6-9 April), p. 56.

Dinstein, Y. (1981), 'Autonomy', in Dinstein (ed), *Models of Autonomy*, as above, pp. 291-303.

Dinstein, Y. (1993), 'The Degree of Self-Rule of Minorities in Unitary and Federal States', in C. Brolmann, R. Lefeber, and M. Zieck (eds), *Peoples and Minorities in International Law*, Martinus Nijhoff: Dordrecht/Boston/London, pp. 221-235.

Easter, G. M. (1997), 'Redefining Centre- Regional Relations in the Russian Federation: Sverdlovsk Oblast', 49 (4) *Europe-Asia Studies,* pp. 617-635.

Eide, A. (1993), 'Approaches to Minority Protection', in A. Phillips, and A. Rosas (eds), *The Minority Rights Declaration*, Tuku/Abo/London, pp. 81- 93.

Eide, A. (1998), 'Cultural Autonomy: Concept, Content, History and Role in the World Order', in M. Suksi (ed), *Autonomy: Applications and Implications*, Kluwer Law International: The Hague/London/Boston, pp. 251-272.

Elazar, D. J. ed. (1991), *Federal Systems of the World: A Handbook of Federal, Confederal and Autonomy Arrangements*, Longman: London.

Forsythe, M. (1996), 'The Political Theory of Federalism: The Relevance of Classical Approaches', in J. J. Hesse and V. Writes (eds), *Federalizing Europe?* Oxford UP: Oxford, pp. 353-386.

Fowler, M. R. and Bunck, J. M. (1995), *Law, Power and Sovereign State: The Evolution and Application of the Concept of Sovereignty*, The Pennsylvania State University Press: Pennsylvania.

Fox, G. H. (1994), Commentary on 'Multiple Tiers of Sovereignty', *ASIL Proceedings* (6-9 April), p. 57.

Franck, T. M. (1994), Commentary on 'Multiple Tiers of Sovereignty: The Future of International Governance', *ASIL Proceedings* (6-9 April), p. 53.

Friedlander, R. A. (1981), 'Autonomy and the Thirteen Colonies: Was the American Revolution Really Necessary?', in Dinstein (ed), as above, pp. 135-148.

Goldman, R B. and Wilson, A. J. eds. (1984), *From Independence to Statehood: Managing Ethnic Conflict in Five African and Asian States*, Frances Printer: London.

Gray, J. C. (1909), *The Nature and Sources of the Law*, cited in Hannum, H. and Lillich, R. B. (1981), 'The Concept of Autonomy in International Law', in Dinstein (ed), as above, pp. 215-254.

Gurion, D. B. (1924), 'National Autonomy and Neighbouring Relations', 9 (no. 172) *Kuntress,* pp. 36-38, cited in Dinstein (ed), as above.

Hannikainen, L. and Horn, H. eds. (1997), *Autonomy and Demilitarisation in International Law: The Aaland Islands in a Changing Europe*, Kluwer Law International: The Hague/London/Boston.

Hannikainen, K. (1998), 'Self-Determination and Autonomy in International Law', in Suksi (ed), as above, pp. 79-95.

Hannum, H. (1990), *Autonomy, Sovereignty, and Self-Determination: The Accommodation of Conflicting Rights*, University of Pennsylvania Press: Philadelphia.

Hannum, H. (1993), 'Rethinking of Self-Determination', 34 *Va JIL*, pp. 1- 69.

Hannum, H. and Lillich, R. B. (1980), 'The Concept of Autonomy in International Law', 74 *AJIL*, pp. 858-889.

Hannum, H. and Lillich, R B. (1981), 'The Concept of Autonomy in International Law', in Dinstein (ed), as above, pp. 215-254.

Harhoff, F. (1986), 'Institutions of Autonomy', 55 *Nord. Jint.L*, pp. 31-40.

Heintze, Hans-Joachim, (1998), 'On the Legal Understanding of Autonomy', in Suksi (ed), *Autonomy: Applications and Implications*, as above, pp. 7-32.

Heyking, B. (1928), 'The International Protection of Minorities: The Achilles' Heel of the League of Nations', 13 *Problems of Peace and War*, pp. 31- 51.

Higgins, R. (1994), Commentary on 'End of Sovereignty', *ASIL Proceedings* (6-9 April) p. 73.

Hoffmann, W. (1994), Commentary on 'Multiple Tiers of Sovereignty: The Future of International Governance', *ASIL Proceedings* (6-9 April), pp. 64-65.

Hutchins, P. W. Hilling, C. and Schulze, D. (1995), 'The Aboriginal Right to Self-Government and the Canadian Constitution: The Ghost in the Machine', 29 (2) *UBC Law Review*, pp. 251-302.

Jansson, G. (1997), 'Introduction', in Hannikainen and Horn (eds), as above, pp. 1-7.

Jellinek, G. (1960), 3rd ed. *Allgemeine Staatslehre*, Hermann Gentner Verlag: Bad Homburg, cited in Lapidoth (1997), as above.

Jennings, R. Y. and Watts, A. eds. (1992), *Oppenheim's International Law*, vol. 1, *PEACE*, 9th ed. Longmans: Essex.

Kampelman, Max. M. 'Forward', in Lapidoth, as below, pp. IX- XII.

Karpat, K. (1973), *An Inquiry into Social Foundations of Nationalism in the Ottoman State: From Social Estates to Classes, From Millet to Nations*, Princeton University: New Haven

Khan, P. W. (1994), Commentary on 'Multiple Tiers of Sovereignty', *ASIL Proceedings* (6-9 April), p. 57.

Kingsbury, B. (1994), 'Whose International Law: Sovereignty and Non-State Groups', *ASIL Proceedings* (6-9 April), p. 4.

Lapidoth, R. (1997), *Autonomy: Flexible Solutions to Ethnic Conflicts*, United States Institute of Peace Press: Washington DC.

Laponce, J. A. (1960), *The Protection of Minorities*, University of California Press: Berkeley and Los Angeles.

Lauterpacht, H. ed. (1962), *Oppenheim's International Law, A Treatise*, vol. 1, PEACE, Longman: Essex.

Lee, R. S. (1994), Commentary on 'Multiple Tiers of Sovereignty: The Future of International Governance', *ASIL Proceedings* (6-9 April), p. 52.

Lyck, L. (1995), 'Lessons to be Learned on Autonomy and on Human Rights From the Faeroes Situation Since 1992', 64 (3) *Nord. J.Int.L*, pp. 481-487.

Malberg, R. C. de. (1920), *Contribution a la Theorie generale de l'Etat Specialement d'apres les donnees fournies par le Droit Constitutionnel Francais*, vol. 1, Sirey : Paris, cited in Lapidoth (1997) as above.

Marasinghe, M. L. (1988), 'Ethnic Politics and Constitutional Reform: The Indo-Sri Lankan Accord', 37 *ICLQ*, pp. 551-583.

Nordquist, Kjell-Ake, (1998), 'Autonomy as a Conflict-Solving Mechanism: An Overview', in Suksi (ed), as above, pp. 59-74.

Olafsson, A. (1995), 'Relationship Between Political and Economic Self-Determination: The Faeroes Case', 64 (3) *Nord.J.Int.L*, pp. 465-480.

Ostwald, M. (1969), *Nomos and the Beginning of Athenian Democracy*, Oxford University Press: London.

Page, E. C. (1992), *Localism and Centralism in Europe: The Political and Legal Bases of Local Self-Government*, Oxford UP: Oxford.

Palley, C. (1978), *Constitutional Law and Minorities*, Report no. 36, Minority Rights Group: London.

Palmgren, S. (1997), 'The Autonomy of the Aaland Islands in the Constitutional Law of Finland', in Hannikainen, and Horn (eds), as above, pp. 85- 97.

Ratner, S. (1994), Commentary on 'End of Sovereignty', *ASIL Proceedings* (6-9 April), p. 75.

Renner, K. (1918), *Das Selbstbestimmungsrecht der Nationen in besonderer Anwendung auf Osterreich*, Leipzig and Vienna: Franz Deuticke, cited in Lapidoth, above, 1997.

Robinson, R. (1943), *Were the Minorities Treaties a Failure*? Institute of Jewish Affairs: New York.

Rosenau, J. N. (1995), 'Sovereignty in a Turbulent World', in G. M. Lyons and M. Mustanduno (eds), *Beyond Westphalia? State Sovereignty and International Intervention*, The John Hopkins University Press: Baltimore and London, pp. 191-227.

Schreuer, C. (1993), 'The Waning of the Sovereign State: Towards a New Paradigm for International Law? ', 4 (4) *EJIL*, pp. 447-471.

Sohn, L. B. (1980), 'The Concept of Autonomy in International Law and the Practice of the United Nations', 15 (2) *ILR*, pp. 180-190.

Solozabal, J. J. (1996), 'Spain: A Federation in the Making', in Hesse and Wrights (eds), as above, pp. 240-265.

Soyinka, W. (1996), *The Open Sore of a Continent*, Oxford UP: Oxford.

Steiner, H. J (1991), 'Ideals and Counter-Ideals in the Struggle Over Autonomy Regimes for Minorities', 66 *Notre Dame LR*, pp. 1539-1559.

Suksi, M. (1997), 'The Constitutional Setting of the Aaland Islands Compared', in Hannikainen, and Horn (eds), as above, pp. 99-129.

Suksi, M. (1998), 'On the Entrenchment of Autonomy', in Suksi (ed), as above, pp. 151-168.

Thornberry, P. (1991), *International Law and the Rights of Minorities*, Clarendon Press: Oxford.

Thornberry, P. (1993), 'The Declaration on the Rights of Persons Belonging to National or Ethnic, Religious and Linguistic Minorities: Background, Analysis and Observations', in Phillips and Rosas (eds), *The UN Minority Rights Declaration*, as above, pp. 11-71.

Thornberry, P. (1998), 'Images of Autonomy and Individual and Collective Rights in International Instruments on the Rights of Minorities', in Suksi (ed), as above, pp. 97-121.

Williams, S. A. (1992*), International Legal Effects of Secession by Quebec*, Centre for Public Law and Policy: New York/Ontario, cited in Fowler and Bunck (1995), as above.

5   Claims For Autonomy Through the Right to Self-determination?

Introduction

Opposition to autonomous rights for minorities is well-documented. Blociszewski argued in 1922 (in Revue des Sciences Politique, cited in Heyking, 1928:44):

> We must prevent the minority from transforming itself into a privileged caste and taking definite form as a foreign group instead of becoming fused in the society in which it lives. If we carry the *exaggerated conception of the autonomy of minorities* to the last extreme, these minorities will become disruptive elements in the State and a source of national disorganisation (emphasis added).

However, minority rights campaigners argue not only that *minorities* are entitled to autonomy with shared sovereignty but also that this right attains its legitimacy through the right to self-determination, thus giving the impression that autonomy is a settled principle of international law. It is obvious that "autonomy captures the sense and meaning of the concept of self-determination,"[1] but what is less clear is whether autonomy is an established component of the right to self-determination. Opinion is divided on this issue amongst scholars. The validity of such claims and whether there is any evidence in international law to suggest that autonomy is a recognised right are examined in this chapter by referring to the opinions of jurists and UN and other international documents.

5.1 *Autonomy as a Part of Self-determination?*

The goal of self-determination is no longer regarded as being confined to the now almost defunct decolonisation process. Having played its historic role in assisting in particular in the course of third world liberation struggles against imperialism and colonialism (Tomuschat, 1993:1), it is continuing to evolve in the post-colonial world in forms which are essentially human rights. Emphasis is placed on democratic governance, thereby promoting such values as participatory rights and the right of peoples to elect a government at periodically held genuine elections. For example *the kinds of rights* enshrined in article 21 (3) of the UDHR and article 25 of the ICCPR is gaining prominence. The latter states: "Every citizen shall have the right and the opportunity, without any of the distinctions mentioned in Article 2 and without unreasonable restrictions:

> a) to take part in the conduct of public affairs, directly or through freely chosen representatives;
> b) to vote and to be elected at genuine periodic elections which shall be by universal and equal suffrage and shall be held by secret ballot, guaranteeing the free expression of the will of the electors;
> c) to have access, on general terms of equality, to public service in his country".

This was further affirmed in principle VIII of the Helsinki Final Act of 1975 which says: "By virtue of the Principle of equal rights and self-determination of peoples, all peoples always have the right, in full freedom, to determine, when and as they wish, their internal and external political status, without external interference, and to pursue as they wish their political, economic, social and cultural development". This also ensures in particular the rights of peoples within independent States to enjoy rights without internal interference. Paragraph 35 of the Document of the Copenhagen Meeting of the Conference on the Human Dimension of the (CSCE), 1990 says:

> The participating States will respect the right of persons belonging to national minorities to effective participation in public affairs, including participation in the affairs relating to the protection and promotion of the identity of such minorities. The participating States note the efforts undertaken to protect and create conditions for the promotion of the ethnic, cultural, linguistic and religious identity of certain national minorities by establishing, as one of the possible means to achieve these aims, appropriate local or autonomous administrations corresponding to the specific historical and territorial circumstances of such minorities and in accordance with the policies of the state concerned." (See on this, Buergenthal, 1990:217-246).

The democratisation of States' structures is considered paramount in any system of participatory democratic governance. Respect for pluralism, diversity, multiculturalism and "the right of popular participation in the government of the State as an entity"[2] are emerging as new values in this developing process. Internal aspects of self-determination form the centre around which these new norms are beginning to take shape (Franck, 1992:54). Not only does democratic governance legitimise the existence of independent States and their institutions it also ensures that the rights guaranteed under international and human rights law are properly observed without distinctions as to race, ethnicity, religion or linguistic bias. States are, argues Tomuschat (1993:9), "no more sacrosanct". The determining factor in this new environment is democratic governance which provides an environment in which individuals as well as groups of peoples can determine their political, economic and social activities (Franck, 1992:47). This newly emerging role assigned to self-determination is becoming the most important aspect of the right to self-determination, that is internal self-determination. Even though there is little consensus as to the exact context of this new principle it flows from the writing of scholars and even more so from comments of the UN Human Rights Committee (Sanders, 1993:80). Internal self-determination, according to Irene-Daes, the Chairperson-Rapporteur of the Working Group of Indigenous Populations (WGIP), empowers "a people to choose its political allegiance, to influence the political order in which it lives, and to preserve its cultural, ethnic, historical or territorial identity".[3]

At the other end of the spectrum, autonomy is increasingly gaining international recognition as an important component of internal self-determination. It is gradually evolving as a dynamic force in internal political structures, shedding its old image by which it was largely associated with local matters. It is apparent that some States are ready to experiment with autonomous models as a response to ethnic conflicts and the political demands of minorities whilst at the same time trying to preserve the *status quo* by whatever means possible. For this, States have to adapt their centralised political power bases to more federal or decentralised systems acceptable both to the centre and to regional sub-groups. Autonomy, in this context, has been used by some States as a vital part of the democratisation of contemporary multi-ethnic societies. However, there are some obstacles to be overcome. On the one hand, States, albeit reluctantly, seem to be ready to exploit the benefits of autonomy to strengthen the social and political order. On the other hand, States are afraid of using autonomous models to address domestic problems, because, as will be shown in chapter 7, such experiments will in the view of most States ultimately result in their dismemberment. Moreover, as Sanders (1993:72) rightly points out the sovereign State system is still operating as an obstacle to the further development of autonomous experiments in terms of international law. Any proposed experiment for power sharing with sub-groups is met with vehement opposition since such steps necessarily limit the sovereignty of States.

Uncertainties and difficulties are further increased when regionally based minority groups respond to any grant of autonomy by asserting that their demands cannot be meaningfully met by a limited devolution of political power alone. Autonomy unlike self-determination is not enthusiastically embraced by minority groups due to its lack of appeal and romanticism. Humphrey (1984:193) wrote, "that every peoples should freely determine its own political status and freely pursue its economic, social and cultural development has long been one of which poets have sung and for which patriots have been ready to lay down their lives". But how many will be ready to become martyrs for the cause of autonomy as stated by Thornberry elsewhere? These trends are continually hampering any further development of autonomy as a valid and practical cure for the contemporary ills of ethnic conflicts in contemporary multiethnic polities. The problem with autonomy is, as has been seen earlier, its lack of appeal to minority groups. Robert A. Friedlander (1981:136) writes, "In almost every instance, grants of autonomy were reluctantly given and ungratefully received". This inevitably creates uncertainties, mistrust, and a hostile environment for both proponents and opponents alike. Thus, squeezed between States and regionally based minority groups the progress of autonomy is constantly hindered in most States.

In fact, autonomy is one of the models through which the rights emanating from internal self-determination can be meaningfully exercised. Thus, it can be argued that these two concepts, autonomy and internal self-determination, are increasingly being seen as two sides of the same coin. Moreover, the development of the concept of self-determination in the post-colonial era can be further developed to accommodate minorities' demands for participation in the political and economic process or to find solutions for ethnic conflicts. Thus, the continuing evolution of the development of the most progressive concept in international law in the post-world-war era, that is internal self-determination, may depend on the extent to which new ideas and concepts such as autonomy can be absorbed by it.

The terms 'autonomy' and 'self-determination' are, however, different concepts (Sohn, 1981:5; Harhoff, 1986:32). The former empowers only the right to self-government whilst the latter empowers peoples within a given State to determine without external interference the form of State or political system they would like to have (Hannikainen, 1998:79).

Whilst the whole population of a given territory is the beneficiary of the right to self-determination, autonomous models are often designed to appease a segment of the population in a designated region or regions of the State on historical, political, cultural or economic grounds. Autonomy thus has the capacity to protect and promote minority rights, because it allows the people inhabiting the autonomous region/s to deal with matters of direct concern to them whilst leaving more important matters such as foreign policy, security, immigration etc. to the competence of States. For this reason, it attracts the attention of international law and is increasingly being considered as a valid option within international law (Suksi, 1998:150- 171).

There are other significant differences between autonomy and self-determination. Whilst the right to independence and full sovereignty are fundamental to the right to self-determination, only partial independence in terms of self-government or self-rule is implied by autonomy (Harhoff, 1986:31-33). Although it can be argued that shared-sovereignty is involved in any autonomous arrangements, full sovereignty is excluded by such models. This does not mean that autonomy is entirely different from self-determination since autonomy possesses some basic characteristics of internal self-determination. As admitted by Harhoff (1986), there is an apparent link between autonomy and self-determination (see also Heintze, 1998:9). Both systems emphasise democratic governance. Most importantly, peoples' right to participation in the political process through fair and genuine periodic elections,[4] and the right to engage in economic and social activities are some of the values highlighted by them. However, autonomy gains its strength by relying on the right to self-determination. In fact, autonomy is one of the most important ingredients embedded in the right to self-determination within liberal democracies.

It is widely held view that "international conventions or other UN documents do not provide for any general right of autonomy to regions or regional minorities" (Hannikainen, 1998:84). Suksi (1997:102) argues that there is a slim chance of autonomy being transformed into "some kind of half-way house short of secession". Although international law does not create any direct right to autonomy, states Suksi, national arrangements leading to the creation of autonomous areas may signify a certain recognition of the right to self-determination. Such arrangements whether created by constitutional or ordinary legislation, may sometimes be protected by the principle of self-determination (Suksi, 1997:113).

Some encouraging developments are now taking place. Autonomy is interpreted by some political scientists and philosophers in terms of 'consociational democracy', a theory, which is considered a further development of internal self-determination. It is a system which is operated within a democratic environment and supports "pluralism in togetherness whereby different groups could maintain and develop their own identity and characteristics"[5] (see also Raikka, 1998; Williams, 1995; Kymlicka, 1995 (a) and 1995 (b); Rickard, 1994). States are supposed to take appropriate measures to ensure that minorities will have an opportunity for the actual enjoyment of human rights and fundamental freedoms within democratic political frameworks. For example, Principle VII of the Helsinki Final Act of 1975 states, "The participating States on whose territory national minority exist will respect the right of persons belonging to such minorities to equality before the law, will afford them the full opportunity for the actual enjoyment of human rights and fundamental freedoms and will, in this manner, protect their legitimate interests in this sphere".[6]

Lijphart (1995:275-287), a political scientist, and one of the main theoretical analysts of consociational democracy, has identified autonomy as one of the crucial elements in 'consociational democracy', not least because it creates opportunities by promoting minorities' interests. It represents, according to Lijphart, a significant stage of the development of the right to self-determination. It is inherently a power-sharing democracy utilising democratic means to maintain a balance of power amongst competing sub-groups. This may involve a 'grand coalition method' based on executive power-sharing and a certain degree of self-determination for each group whether they live together or separately (Eide, 1993:89). Consociational democracy, in Lijphart's view, also provides an opportunity for ethnic groups (identified as segments of sub-groups) to administer their cultural matters better than in any other system. In other words, autonomy in a consociational democracy is synonymous with 'territorial federalism' (Lijphart, 1995). In particular, Eide (1993:89) noted that consociational democracy can be used as an alternative to a majoritarian type of democracy and "it is more suitable for good government in plural societies divided by ethnic, linguistic, religious or cultural differences, where the groups are clearly identifiable".

According to Cassese (1995:332), autonomy can be used as a "possible form of realizing internal self-determination" for a segment of a population (see also Rosas, 1993:225-252). Others see a more important role for autonomy in addressing the issues relating to minorities. Autonomy in the narrower sense, argues Bernhardt (1981:26), "has to do with the protection and self-determination of minorities", a notion which has been angrily rejected by many States, as will be shown in chapter seven. Both minorities and indigenous groups, in the view of Hannum (1996:473-474), can exercise a "meaningful internal self-determination" through autonomy, which allows them to control their own affairs in a way they like, yet is not inconsistent with the ultimate sovereignty.

Claims for autonomy by minority groups are seen by Kimminich (1993:100) as claims for limited self-determination. Autonomy through self-determination, in his view, is a *modus operandi* which can be used in pluralist societies to accommodate the legitimate rights of minority groups within a federal structure. Kimminich (1993:92) points out that where the State violates the fundamental human rights of minority groups, then they can invoke the right to self-determination in order to bring about constitutional changes aimed at achieving minority protection through autonomy or a suitable federal structure. If they cannot achieve justice from the recalcitrant State, then, argues Kimminich, oppressed minority groups could secede by invoking the right to self-determination. Brownlie (1992) is also of the view that autonomy is one of the models inherent in the right to self-determination to which minorities are entitled whatever the traditional meaning of autonomy and the doctrine of the right to self-determination might be. Brownlie (1992:48) argues that "the exercise of self-determination involves a wide range of political choices, including independent statehood, federal union, and various forms of autonomy or associated statehood".

Special Rapporteur Eide is more cautious although he sees some interrelationship between autonomy and minorities. Eide points out that some form of territorial sub-divisions may be applied within a sovereign State allowing sub-groups to enjoy greater political powers.[7] He concludes:

What is less clear is whether groups have a right to some local self-government, or autonomy within the state, on the basis of the right to self-determination...some form of territorial sub-division may in some cases be a practical way to ensure the existence and identity of an ethnic group, provided it is given a democratic, not ethnocratic content. Whether there exists a general right is much more doubtful.[8]

Hannum (1996:453) argues that autonomy is "one step above minority rights, one step below full self-determination". Special Rapporteur Eide also came to a similar conclusion. In his view, autonomy is "the highest or maximum aspiration" or the "highest possible level of rights" which minority groups can enjoy in domestic law whilst remaining within the State.[9] Thus, minorities are put in an advantageous position given that they may enjoy a right to autonomy in addition to minorities' rights. However, autonomy is not a specific right assigned to minorities alone since sometimes regional differences are also instrumental in the introduction of autonomous models.

5.2   *The Right to Autonomy Under International Law: "Artificial Concept of Dubious Legal Consequence"?*

The concept of autonomy, according to Sohn (1980:180) and Sanders (1986:17), is present both in constitutional and international law. However, some scholars are not so convinced. In the view of Suksi (1998:152), autonomy "obviously exists" at constitutional level although it can be used as an option in terms of internal right to self-determination. Simply because international law recognises certain collective rights, argues Suksi, it does not automatically follow that there exists the right to autonomy under it. Suksi (1998:152) emphasises:

> There is undoubtedly no right to autonomy at the level of general international law. Autonomy is thus not a specific human right, formulated as such. However, various documents and instruments at the level of international law indicate the possibility of autonomy arrangements, a possibility which may even be viewed as expressing a mode of internal sovereignty.

Friedlander (1981:137) writes:

> Those who seek to obtain a juridical definition of autonomy from international law (treaties and books) will quest in vain. Although self-determination has been elevated by many to the status of an international human 'right', or at the very least a normative principle, autonomy has been often neglected and on occasion totally disregarded by legal scholars and commentators. Viewed from the perspective of international law, autonomy is therefore an artificial concept of dubious legal consequence. Admittedly, it is still invoked by politicians, historians, and political analysts, though its twentieth-century historical role has only been that of a political instrumentality.

Even though decentralisation of power and autonomy at regional level have increasingly become popular in the 1990s, and are being used in national and international affairs in particular as a solution to ethnic conflicts (Heintze, 1998:10; Hannikainen, 1998:86), autonomy does not have a strong basis in international law. Internal domestic arrangements such as autonomies fall within the sphere of constitutional law, which are normally beyond the control of general international law although they can influence States' behaviour in domestic matters. "As long as a state has not assumed any specific obligation to consent to autonomous arrangements, it is up to that state whether to provide autonomy or not" (Hannikainen, 1998:87). However, when such arrangements are implemented, the benefits emanating from such autonomies, argues Suksi (1998:164), "can be understood to be protected under principle of self-determination".

Special Rapporteur Eide, clarifying UN practice and the position of international law, voiced his doubts about the claim that there already existed a general right of autonomy in international law.[10] However, he admits the possibility that autonomy could evolve as a general right through instruments relating to minority rights or the rights of the UN Declaration on Minorities or a future Universal Declaration on the Rights of Indigenous Peoples.[11] Nonetheless, the Special Rapporteur does not deny the importance of territorial arrangements in suitable cases provided such sub-divisions occur without harming existing boundaries.[12] Wherever possible, States should find suitable arrangements to facilitate the accommodation of different ethnic or linguistic groups.[13]

It is submitted that autonomy has to overcome many barriers before it can be considered a part of international law. However, the reluctance to introduce any substantial law in terms of international law guaranteeing autonomy as a legal right to minorities, except indigenous peoples, is evident. A case in point is the UN Declaration on Minorities, 1992. The strongest inference that can be drawn from the Declaration is article 2 (3) which refers to the participatory rights of minorities. It states:

> Persons belonging to minorities have the right to participate effectively in decisions on the national and, where appropriate, regional level concerning the minority to which they belong or the regions in which they live, in a manner not incompatible with national legislation.

The participatory right advocated by this article does not amount to the right to autonomy. Moreover, it is based on an individual right. Any persons belonging to a minority have the right to take part in the decision making process at either national or regional level if they wish to do so. Tomuschat states (1993:15):

> A literal reading of Article 2, paragraph 3 would seem to indicate no more than that members of minority groups must have a right to participate in decision-making processes affecting their destiny within the framework of the general institutions of the State concerned, but that, on the other hand, no requirement to establish specific institutions for them is postulated.

Although article 4 (2) appears to be making recommendations favourable to autonomy, it can be argued that it relates to no more than personal or cultural autonomy:

> States shall take measures to create favourable conditions to enable persons belonging to minorities to express their characteristics and to develop their culture, language, religion, traditions and customs, except where specific practices are in violation of national law and contrary to international standards.

The right to territorial autonomy is not entrenched in either of these articles. Both articles, however, encourage diversity and pluralism within a structure of democratic governance or consociational democracy. Thornberry (1993: 42-43) states: "There is no specific right to autonomy in the Declaration, but 'effective' participation through local and national organizations may necessitate the creation of autonomies to achieve the Declaration's standard".

5.3 *Indigenous Peoples' Right to Autonomy: "We are not Looking to Dismember Your States and You Know It"*

Both minorities and indigenous peoples possess some common characteristics. Both are vulnerable, have been in constant struggle to preserve and protect their identity, traditions and customs, and above all their way of life. Both groups are non-dominant in the modern nation-State structure and therefore are often subject to exploitation and discrimination (Thornberry, 1995:64). Nonetheless, as Shaw (1997:269) rightly points out, indigenous peoples are "different conceptually and practically from those of ...conventional minorities." Also, indigenous rights are different from other rights as stated by Chief Justice Lamer, in *R v Van der Peet* (1996) 2 SCR 507 (Canada), because such rights could be exercised only by indigenous peoples. Moreover, indigenous rights are collective rights as opposed to individual rights or minority rights (Kyle, 1997:299).

Indigenous peoples have been transformed in the 1990s from defenceless, scattered tribal groups to a formidable force with considerable bargaining power (Kingsbury, 1998:414; Anaya, 1996). Now most indigenous peoples are well organized and have been fighting for greater regional autonomy, sometimes even resorting to violence as in the case of the Mohawk Indians at Oka,[14] and Mayas in Guatemala (the Unidad Revolucionaria Nacional Guatemaltec). However, indigenous peoples generally prefer to have a power-sharing structure with greater autonomy within existing territorial boundaries. Indigenous or aboriginal rights have become legitimate concerns on the international human rights agenda (Sanders, 1993:55; Yukich, 1996:251) emerging as new norms in international law (Torres, 1991; Barsh, 1986:369-385). Their demands have attracted a wider and sympathetic audience in recent decades (Lapidoth, 1997:17). This has been mainly due to increased efforts by indigenous peoples since the 1970s to win back their 'lost rights' (Reisman, 1995:350), and in particular, to claim the lands which have been taken away from them. These claims have been found to be reasonable and justifiable by many UN and other international organizations. For instance, it was admitted by Special Rapporteur Martinez Cobo that "indigenous peoples have a natural and inalienable right to keep the territories they possess and claim the lands which have been taken from them."[15] Most States in which indigenous peoples live have been exploring the possibilities of advancing indigenous rights through both the international and domestic arenas (Barsh, 1986:369). For instance, the *Indigenous Peoples Rights Act* of 1997 enacted by the Philippines is considered a significant step in the recognition of indigenous peoples' right to self-government. Other States adopting similar measures have been the USA (Indian Self-determination and Educational Assistance Act, 1975; whilst in addition at least 280 indigenous reservations have been established), Canada (the creation of autonomous regions such as Nunuvut in North East Canada; and introduction of section 35 to the Canadian Constitution Act in 1982 by recognising existing aboriginal and treaty rights of the aboriginal peoples of Canada), Australia, New Zealand (the establishment of Waitangi Tribunal in 1975 and Maori Trust Boards), the Nordic States (the establishment of Saami Parliaments, see details in Kingsbury, 1998:439). In particular, the international institutions have taken many positive standard-setting measures to advance the claims of indigenous peoples. Amongst them the most important step was taken by the ILO

Convention, no. 107 of 1957 and 169 of 1989. The main step taken in this direction was the establishment of the Working Group on Indigenous Populations (WGIP) in 1982 to review "the evolution of standards concerning the rights of indigenous populations" taking into account both the similarities and differences in the situations and aspirations of indigenous populations throughout the world.[16]

Indigenous peoples' claim to manage their own affairs, as Kingsbury (1998:436-437) correctly points out, is not dependent on one single factor or concept alone (see further Yukich, 1996:235). The source of their rights goes back to the "pre-colonial legal order" (Sanders, 1993:72). Justification of their claims in particular to self-government and other rights such as territorial rights has often been based on an amalgamation of various factors. These includes indigenous rights/law (see the following cases *Sparrow*; *Van der Peet*; *Gladstone*; *Guerin*; Calder),[17] treaty law (*Guerin* case),[18] environmental law (*Dagi*: *Yosofa Alomang*; *Tom Beanal*),[19] diplomatic protection (*Cayuga* case),[20] common law concepts such as the doctrine of fiduciary duty (Guerin; Cherokee Nation and Mabo, no. 2),[21] estoppel, abuse of rights and natural justice, (principle of equality, fair dealing and justice).[22] In addition, indigenous peoples have been relying on article 27 of the ICCPR (see the following cases of HRC, *Lubicon Lake Band*; *Sandra Lovelace*; *Ominayak*; *Kitok*),[23] self-determination, and general human rights (*Unocal* case).[24]

The right to govern their traditional homelands and territories according to their own way of life has often been based on the right to self-determination as will be discussed further below. However, it should be emphasised that indigenous peoples are not obsessed with legal terminologies. Nor are they worried about whether they are covered by 'peoples' as understood in international law and human rights conventions and treaties. Most indigenous groups identify themselves as such (by self-identification) regardless of legal ramifications (see *RL et al* v *Canada*).[25] In fact, some prominent indigenous groups have opposed any attempt at finding a definition for 'indigenous' arguing that in their struggles against colonisers such endeavours were irrelevant (see Kingsbury, 1998:442-446; Barsh, 1986:374-375).[26]

Their main concerns, *inter alia*, are to reclaim the sovereignty of their traditional territories (see *Lubicon Lake Band* case), to protect and preserve natural resources and environment (see *Sparrow* case), and to preserve their indigenous laws/customs and cultures (see *Unocal* case and *Dagi* case). As Special Rapporteur Martinus Cobo observes, the indigenous peoples are "determined to preserve, develop and transmit to future generations their ancestral territories, and their ethnic identity, as the basis of their continued existence as peoples, in accordance with their own cultural patterns, social institutions and legal systems".[27] The final communiqué adopted by the Preparatory Meeting of Indigenous Peoples in 1987 stated what they have been fighting for:

> Indigenous nations and peoples are entitled to the permanent control and enjoyment of their aboriginal ancestral-historical territories. This includes air space, surface and subsurface rights, inland and coastal waters, sea, ice, renewable and non-renewable resources, and the economies based on those resources.[28]

The backbone of their argument is that they are the inheritors or inhabitants of those States. Therefore they do not want to see a fragmentation of their countries. For example, in 1985 Samis in Norway, Finland, Sweden and indigenous peoples in the Aaland Islands, the Faeroe islands, and Greenland convened a Convention to discuss the possibility of setting up a *Samiid Aednan* to fight for their rights. In their final communiqué they emphasised that they would not seek an independent and sovereign nation-State breaking away from the existing States because the areas in disputes were their inherited lands. It is worth mentioning that they expressed their desire to have citizenship in the countries in which they live. Similar attitudes were demonstrated by the MISURASTA, an organisation of the Miskito, Sumo and Rama nations in the Atlantic coastal area of Nicaragua in April 1987. Having agreed with a provision in the Treaty of Peace they declared that they would exercise their inherent right within existing boundaries of Nicaragua (Hannum, 1990: 211- 212).

The above position is more or less true in the case of aborigines in Australia, Maoris in New Zealand, Amerindians in America, Samis and other Indian tribes/ nations in the Nordic countries and Veddhas in Sri Lanka. Traditional land disputes and the exploitation of natural resources are some of the most important issues arising between States and these indigenous peoples. For example, the Veddahs in Sri Lanka, the oldest community in the island, instead of turning to violence sought legal remedies in the Badulla District Court in 1988 by way of a possesory action to recover their ancestral forest-lands when the Mahaweli Authority started to divert the River Mahaweli for hydro-agricultural developments via their traditional hunting lands. Thisahamy, the leader of the tribe, tried to secure their traditional lands and forests from the outsiders. No territorial rearrangement was sought in this case. They sought the right to self-determination over their traditional lands without interference from the Mahaweli Authority and the outside settlers. Generally, land is the *raison d'etre* of indigenous peoples' culture (Barsh, 1996: 801).

Their uncompromising stance on these issues was evident in their statement to the WGIP that States should recognize "the special relationship of indigenous peoples to their land... land rights and natural resources should not be taken away from them... Discovery, conquest, and unilateral legislation are no legitimate bases for States to claim or retain the territories or natural resources of indigenous peoples. In no circumstances should indigenous peoples or groups be subjected to adverse discrimination with respect to their rights or claims to land, property or natural resources".[29] Similarly, Bohlin (1995:495), a member of the Natural Union of the Swedish Saami Peoples stated:

> It is our inalienable right to preserve and develop our economic activities and our communities in keeping with our own common conditions, and together we wish to preserve our lands, natural assets and national heritage for future generations.

Many indigenous peoples stress that arrangements in the form of autonomy are an expression of and realisation of self-determination (Bohlin, 1995: 495-499). They do not generally attempt to rely on modern theories of international law to justify their claim to self-determination which, in their views, flows from traditional indigenous rights (Sanders, 1993:75). It is in a wider sense, self-government beyond self-regulation of a community of people through their own institutions in order to regulate their own conduct toward each other, and to have control over the natural resources, environment, traditional way of life (hunting, fishing, and the like). They strongly believe that as inheritors "they have the inherent right to self-determination" in the territories which they occupy or to lands which they claim.[30] For example a tribunal set up in 1993 by indigenous activists at Hawaii in *Ka Ho'oklokolonui Maoli* upheld that indigenous peoples have the inherent right to sovereignty and self-government which can be realized through self-determination (Hutchins, Hilling and Schulze, 1995:280; see further Alfredsson, 1993:41-54; Daes, 1993:1-11; Torres, 1991:127-175). It is said by Michael Dodson, the Commissioner for the Aboriginal and Toress Strait Islanders' Social Justice Commission, "self-determination is the river in which all other rights swim" (see Scott, 1996:814: see also Langton, 1988:88). This position has continually been maintained by most indigenous groups. Arrangements in the form of autonomy in respect of indigenous peoples are often considered in terms of internal self-determination. Apart from a few indigenous groups such as the Nagas in India,[31] the Cree Indians in Quebec, Mohawak Indians at Oka, the Mayas in Guatemala, the right to secession is not generally advocated by these arguments.[32] As pointed out by Thornberry (1998:121), "most indigenous peoples are uninterested in secession" and many groups want to reconstruct the State infra-structure without dismembering it (see also Kingsbury, 1998:437: Alfredsson, 1998:131; Venne, 1996:292), This process has been described by some as "belated State-building" which allows indigenous peoples as equal partners to take part in democratic governance (Daes, 1996:53-54). This constitutional reconstruction is the most vital part of self-determination because it ends the marginalisation of indigenous peoples from the main-stream political structure. It, above all creates an environment which empowers them to negotiate freely their political, economic and social structures within new State infra-structure (Daes, 1996:53).

Emphasis on self-determination is being used as a bargaining tool and many indigenous peoples are prepared to fight for realistic rights such as lands and resources (Alfredsson, 1998:131). It is worthy of mention that indigenous peoples are under no illusion that strict adherence to the meaning of self-determination provides them with an opportunity to secede from the States in which they live (see Langton, 1988:84). It was said by the National Coalition of Aboriginal Organizations (Australia):[33]

> We define our rights in terms of self-determination. We are not looking to dismember your states and you know it. But we do insist on the right to control our territories, our resources, the organisation of our societies, our own decision making institutions, and the maintenance of our own cultures and ways of life.

Sharon H. Venne, a member of the Blood Tribe within the Treaty Seven territory, vehemently denied the allegation that indigenous groups are trying to secede using self-determination as a pretext from the States in which they live. In referring to a Canadian Government statement Venne said (1996:292):

> Dismemberment of the State has never been the stated goal of any indigenous group living within the territory known as Canada. The Government of Canada is more concerned with continuing their control of our political, economic, social and cultural rights.

In fact, the demands submitted jointly by indigenous peoples to the WGIP were from the beginning based on autonomy and self-government. Their main statement was that, "all indigenous nations and peoples have the right to self-determination, by virtue of which they have the right to whatever degree of autonomy or self-government they choose".[34] A representative of the Aboriginal and Torres Strait Islander Commission to the UN Working Group on Indigenous Populations (WGIP) stated in 1993:

> Self-determination is an aspirational concept which embraces a widening spectrum of political possibilities, from self-management by indigenous peoples of their own affairs to self-government by indigenous peoples of their own communities or lands... recognition of self-determination does not provide a mandate for secessionist separatism... rather, self-determination represents the conceptual basis for the progressive empowerment of indigenous peoples (cited in Thornberry, 1998:119).

Coulter (1995:131), a member of the Citizen Band Potawatomi Tribe and Executive Director of the Indian Law Resource Centre clarifying the general opinion of the indigenous peoples stated:

> Practically no indigenous representatives have spoken of a right to secede from an existing country... It is clear that indigenous leaders mean self-determination to include freedom from political and economic domination by others; self-governments and the management of all their affairs; the right to have their own governments and laws free from external control; free and agreed-upon political and legal relationship with the government of the country and other governments, and the right to control their own economic developments.

A similar view was adopted by the International Organization of Indigenous Resource Development in June 1992.[35]

5.4 Maximum Right: "Only Self-Government Through Internal Self-determination"?

The theory that indigenous peoples do not have a legal right to autonomy according to the "current status of international law",[36] is gradually losing ground. As argued by Kingsbury (1998:439) the application and understanding of self-determination is constantly evolving in response to the demands of indigenous peoples. There has been significant progress made in this particular area since 1989. With a view to enhancing the life of indigenous peoples the ILO Convention no. 169 (1989) on Indigenous and Tribal Peoples[37] took a much more progressive and liberal approach than had previous been adopted (Gayim, 1994:38; Anaya, 1996:47-54). Above all it recognised the need for protection of social, cultural, religious and spiritual values and practice of indigenous peoples (see article 5). Article 7 states:

> The peoples concerned shall have the right to decide their own priorities for the process of development as it affects their lives, beliefs, institutions and spiritual well-being and the lands they occupy or otherwise use, and to exercise control, to the extent possible, over their own economic, social and cultural development. In addition, they shall participate in the formulation, implementation and evaluation of plans and programmes for national and international development which may affect them directly.

Emphasis is on the participatory rights of indigenous peoples should they wish to exercise them. Most scholars commenting on this article admit that it is the most important provision in the Convention (Yukich, 1996:253; Alfredsson, 1998:127). Although the validity and justification of indigenous claims to self-government was apparently recognised by this Convention, it explicitly failed to refer to them in terms of autonomy or the right to self-determination. In fact, article 1.3 of the Convention states that the use of the term 'peoples' "shall not be construed as having any implications as regards the rights which may attach to the term under international law". This was reiterated in the Provisional Record issued by the Committee.[38] However, Alfredsson (1998:128-130) argues that all the characteristics of autonomies are visible throughout the provisions of the Convention no. 169 of 1989. The ratifying States are under an obligation to recognise the indigenous institutions and "or to allow their creation so that these institutions can carry out the assigned self-governing and participatory functions in a democratic and representative manner" (Alfredsson, 1998 :128). Article 13 states:

> In applying the provisions of this Part of the Convention governments shall respect the special importance for the cultures and spiritual values of the peoples concerned of their relationship with the lands or territories, or both as applicable, which they occupy or otherwise use, and in particular the collective aspects of this relationship.

Indigenous peoples' right to autonomy through the right to self-determination was recognised by the UN Experts in 1991 when they concluded, "the Meeting of Experts shares the view that indigenous peoples constitute distinct peoples and societies with the right to self-determination, including the rights of autonomy, self-government, and self-identification".[39] They concluded that autonomy and self-determination are prerequisites for achieving equality, human dignity, freedom from discrimination and the full enjoyment of all human rights. However it is the Draft UN Declaration on the Rights of Indigenous Peoples, 1994 which has made a significant progress (Yukich, 1996:255; Gayim, 1995:12-45; Anaya, 1996:53) by recognising the right to autonomy in terms of the right to internal self-determination.[40] The rights enshrined in the Draft UN Declaration as a whole are seen by indigenous representatives to the WGIP as comprehensive and a manifestation of the legitimate aspirations of indigenous peoples.[41]   Collective rights contained in the Draft UN Declaration, in the view of Chairperson-Rapporteur of the WGIP, exhibit the characteristics of internal self-determination[42] (see further Brolmann and Zieck, 1995:103-104).

However, in 1991 there were some significant attempts to limit the application of the right of self-determination. It was proposed:

> Indigenous peoples have the right to self-determination, in accordance with international law. By virtue of this right, they freely determine their relationship *with the States in which they live*, in a spirit of co-existence with other citizens, and freely pursue their economic, social and cultural and spiritual development in conditions of freedom and dignity.[43] (emphasis added).

Thus, indigenous peoples were expected to achieve their goals and aspirations whilst respecting the boundaries of the States in which they live. Later, in 1992, this was further amended to:

> Indigenous peoples have the right of self-determination, in accordance with international law by virtue of which they freely determine their political status and institutions and freely pursue their economic, social and cultural development. An integral part of this is *the right to autonomy and self-government*.[44] (emphasis added).

Article 3 of the Draft UN Declaration, as it stands now, recognises the most important right, i.e. the right to self-determination of indigenous peoples:

> Indigenous peoples have the right to self-determination. By virtue of that right they freely determine their political status and freely pursue their economic, social and cultural development.

The right entrenched in this article is unqualified. This is more extensive than what the earlier version of the original Drafts UN Declaration proposed. Internal aspects of self-determination, in particular autonomy, are further clarified in article 31, which is connected with article 3:

> Indigenous peoples, as a specific form of exercising their right to self-determination, have the right to autonomy or self-government in matters relating to their internal and local affairs, including culture, religion, education, information, media, health, housing, employment, social welfare, economic activities, land and resource management, environment and entry by non-members, as well as ways and means for financing these autonomous functions.

The specific rights which indigenous peoples can exercise are further identified in article 26:

> Indigenous peoples have the right to own, develop, control and use the lands and territories, including the total environment of the lands, air, waters, coastal seas, sea-ice, flora and fauna and other resources which they have traditionally owned or otherwise occupied or used. This includes the right to the full recognition of their laws, traditions and customs, land-tenure systems and institutions for the development and management of resources, and the right to effective measures by States to prevent any interference with, alienation or encroachment upon these rights.

It is apparent that the right to self-determination can be achieved by way of autonomy as provided in the Draft UN Declaration. Is then autonomy the maximum which is guaranteed by the Draft UN Declaration?

Article 3 is the most controversial and politically sensitive one in the Draft UN Declaration. Most scholars are of the view that article 3 refers only to internal self-determination whilst emphasising that indigenous peoples cannot as of right achieve independence by virtue of the right to self-determination (see Eide, 1995:365; Brolmann and Zieck, 1995; Gayim, 1995; Sanders, 1993; Alfredsson, 1998:135). Eide (1995:365) states that, "in relation to indigenous peoples, however, the right to 'self-determination' is normally not understood as a right to an independent State, but rather to some limited form of autonomy on ethnic grounds". He further points out (at 365), that "the term 'right to self-determination' (Article 3) when read in conjunction with draft Article 4,[45] apparently also intends to provide for a right to autonomy short of independence". He concludes (at 366) that "the right to self-determination of indigenous peoples must therefore be understood to mean some form of autonomy".

Thus, the thrust of this article appears to promote a right to autonomy and self-government (see also Tomuschat, 1993:13).

To dispel any misgivings and misunderstanding, the Working Groups' Chairperson and Rapporteur Erica-Irene A. Daes was compelled to issue a separate Explanatory Report clarifying the extent of article 3 rights in the Declaration.[46] She states that the rights mentioned in article 3 are essentially limited, and that indigenous peoples must operate within the nation-State system, unless the system is "so exclusive and non-democratic that it no longer can be said to represent the whole of the population". She, however, recognises the possibility of a restructuring of power-sharing arrangements between States and indigenous communities through constitutional reforms. She emphasised that article 3 recognised only internal self-determination, by virtue of which indigenous peoples could choose the political order in which they live, and to preserve their cultural, ethnic, historical or territorial identity.[47] She stressed, "I believe that the right of self-determination would ordinarily be interpreted as the right of these peoples to negotiate freely their political status and representation in the State in which they live"[48] (see also Daes, 1996:47- 54). It was further emphasised that:

> The principle of self-determination as discussed within the Working Group and as reflected in the draft declaration was used in its internal character, that is short of any implications which might encourage the formation of independent States.[49]

Only the nature and degree of autonomy can be negotiated with the State concerned by the indigenous peoples "in good faith, on sharing power within the existing State, and to the extent possible, to exercise their right to self-determination by this means".[50]

Some attempts have also been made elsewhere, that is, at the Vienna World Conference on Human Rights, 1993, to stress that indigenous peoples cannot exercise the right to self-determination as 'peoples'. The Vienna Declaration carefully and shrewdly selected the word 'people', i.e., in the singular form to preclude claims by indigenous communities (Eide, 1995: 365).

Thus, the common consensus seems to be that however progressive and far reaching the rights enshrined in the Draft UN Declaration may be, they should not be interpreted as anything other than a right within the context of participatory democracy or consociational democracy (Brolmann and Zieck, 1995:108). It is argued that the right to autonomy is the maximum that the indigenous peoples can consider if they decide to do so, as provided by article 4, by staying in the State in which they live (see in particular articles 31, 32 and 33). However, the controversy surrounding the exact extent and meaning of self-determination does not simply disappear (Alfredsson, 1998:133). By reading articles 3 and 31 together, it can be argued that indigenous peoples are entitled to both aspects of self-determination, that is internal self-determination (by way of autonomy), and the right to external self-determination (the right to establish their own States). Most indigenous peoples and organisations have continually been maintaining that the entire Draft UN Declaration is based on the right to self-determination, that is both internal and external[51] (see Alfredsson, 1998:130).

The autonomy rights contained in this Declaration are more expansive than mere cultural autonomy and are certainly more specific than the ILO Convention mentioned above (Alfredsson, 1998:128). Hutchins *et al* (1995: 279) argue by referring to ILO Convention no. 169 (1989) and the Draft UN Declaration that these international documents "recognised the right of aboriginal peoples to self-government not as a new right but as an inherent right that always existed". Thus, it has clearly been evident for some time now that "practice and meaning of self-determination are evolving in response to the claims and circumstances of indigenous peoples" (Kingsbury, 1998:439).

Articles 4, 19, 21, 23, 25, 27, 30, 32 and 33 deal with traditions and customs, indigenous legal systems, indigenous political and economic institutions, the right to keep lands, territories, waters, coastal seas, and 'other resources' which have traditionally been owned and occupied by indigenous peoples. These rights constitute, according to article 42, "minimum standards for the survival, dignity and well-being of the indigenous peoples". In contrast to article 27 of the ICCPR which offers only limited rights for individuals belonging to minority groups, or the UN Declaration on Minorities, 1992 (articles 2 (3) and 4 (2)) the above articles represent a higher standard of minority rights and signal a move away from traditional international law.

5.5 *Human Rights Committee and the Claim of the Right to Self-determination by Indigenous Peoples: "Article 1 (ICCPR) Is Our Goal, Our Vision"*

Some indigenous peoples, notably, north American Indian tribes contested before the Human Rights Committee (HRC) that their right to self-determination has been violated by the State in which they live and have sought remedies under the first Optional Protocol to the ICCPR.[52] Article 1 states:

> A state Party to the Covenant that becomes a party to the present Protocol recognizes the competence of the Committee to receive and consider communications from individuals subject to its jurisdiction who claim to be victims of a violation by that State Party of any of the rights set forth in the Covenant. No communications shall be received by the Committee if it concerns a State Party to the Covenant which is not a party to the present Protocol.

Article 2 provides:

> Subject to the provisions of Article 1, individuals who claim that any of their rights enumerated in the Covenant have been violated and who have exhausted all available domestic remedies may submit a written communication to the Committee for consideration.

The HRC concluded in all the cases mentioned below that an individual could not claim to be the victim of a violation of the right to self-determination enshrined in article 1 of the Covenant. [53]

5.5.1 *AD, The Grand Captain of Mikmaq Tribal Society v Canada*[54]

Jigap'ten of Santeoi Mawa'iomi, Grand Captain of the Mikmaq Tribal Society submitting a communication dated 30 September 1980 on behalf of the Mikmaq peoples, alleged that the Government of Canada had denied and continued to deny to the people of the Mikmaq Tribal Society the right of self-determination in violation of article 1 of the ICCPR. His main objective was to get the traditional Government of the Mikmaq Tribal Society recognised as such and the Mikmaq nation recognised as a State. He stressed that the Grand Council, which consisted of the Grand Captain, the Assistant Grand Chief, and the Grand Chief, constituted the traditional Government of the Mikmaq Tribal Society. He also vehemently denied any suggestion that the territory which his tribe occupied known as 'Mikmaq Nationimouw' was ceded or surrendered to Great Britain or subsequently to Canada. Questioning the validity of the State party's contention that self-determination is only a collective right, he maintained that it could be enjoyed both by peoples and individuals. In the event of the HRC deciding not to adjudicate on his communication on the grounds that it was beyond its competence, the Grand Captain asked the HRC to refer the issue to the Economic and Social Council with a recommendation that an advisory opinion be sought from the ICJ.

In a further submission to the HRC dated 29 December 1980 the Grand Captain reaffirmed that the Communication was concerned essentially with the violation of article 1 of the ICCPR. The author stressed, "Article 1 is our goal, our vision...." He claimed that his tribe could determine its political future independently of Canada by virtue of this article. He did not want his Communication to be considered under other provision of the ICCPR, and especially not under article 27.

Responding to the claims of the author, the Government of Canada argued that the Grand Captain's claim should be declared inadmissible on the grounds that article 1 of the ICCPR could not affect the territorial integrity of a State nor the principles asserted in the Colonial Declaration (GA Res. 1514 (xv) December 14, 1960) and the Declaration on Friendly Relations (GA Res. 2625 (xxv) October 24, 1970). It was also argued that the remedy sought by the Grand Captain was beyond the competence of the HRC. The State party further submitted that Grand Captain could not claim that his own rights had been violated, because, according to article 1 of the ICCPR, the right of self-determination was a collective right and nothing to do with indigenous or minority groups. It was also pointed out that Grand Captain lacked *locus standi* because he was not duly authorised under the relevant provisions of the Optional Protocol to act on behalf of the Mikmaq peoples.

By upholding the objections raised by the State party the HRC came to the conclusion that since Grand Captain had not proved that he was authorized to act as a representative on behalf of the Mikmaq tribal society, he could not maintain his Communication under the Optional Protocol.

5.5.2 *Bernard Ominayak, Chief of the Lubicon Lake Band v Canada*[55]

Bernard Ominayak is the Chief and the representative of the Lubicon Lake Band in the province of Alberta in Canada. The Band is a self-identified and relatively autonomous group, which has been living in this particular territory of 10,000 square kilometers located in northern Alberta.

By a communication dated 14 February 1984 Canada was accused by Ominayak of violating the Band's right to determine freely its political status and to pursue its economic, social and cultural development as guaranteed by article 1 (1) of the ICCPR. It was further alleged that by the destruction of the environment and the undermining of the Band's economic base and by the expropriation of its territory for the benefit of private corporate interests (e.g. leases for oil and gas exploration), the Band had been deprived of its means of subsistence and of the enjoyment of the right of self-determination guaranteed in the above article. It was further alleged that the undertaking of energy exploration in the Band's territory without consulting the Band constituted a violation of article 1 paragraph 2 of the ICCPR.[56] In refuting the validity of these allegations, the Canadian Government stressed that the Lubicon Lake Band did not constitute a people within the meaning of article 1 of the ICCPR, and therefore the Band was not entitled to assert under Optional Protocol the right to self-determination. In considering the structure of the ICCPR and taking it as a whole, the State party argued that, self-determination was a collective right available only to 'peoples'. It was further argued that since indigenous groups are not entitled to be regarded as a 'people' they could not claim any right of self-determination.

In response to the HRC, the author (complainant) by a further submission dated 12 June 1982 apparently tried to change the main premise of his previous Communication by maintaining that he was not seeking "a territorial decision". It seems that the HRC did not want to examine whether the Lubicon Lake Band was entitled to the right to self-determination, and most importantly to the right to external self-determination. Instead, relying on procedural grounds, the HRC held (see paragraph 13.3) that as an individual the author Ominayak could not claim under the Optional Protocol to be a victim of a violation of the right of self-determination enshrined in article 1 of the Covenant, because it deals with rights conferred upon 'peoples' as such. The HRC held:

> While all peoples have the right of self-determination and the right freely to determine their political status, pursue their economic, social and cultural development and dispose of their natural wealth and resources, as stipulated in Article 1 of the Covenant, the question whether the Lubicon Lake Band constitutes a 'people' is not an issue for the Committee to address under the Optional Protocol to the Covenant. The Optional Protocol provides a procedure under which individuals can claim that their individual rights have been violated. Those rights are set out in part III of the Covenant, Article 6 to 27, inclusive. There is, however, no objection to a group of individuals, who claim

to be similarly affected, collectively to submit a communication about alleged breaches of their rights (paragraph 32.1).

5.5.3 *Ivan Kitok v Sweden*[57]

By a communication dated 2 December 1985 and subsequent submissions dated 5 and 12 November 1986, Ivon Kitok, a Saami in Sweden alleged that he became a victim of violation by the Government of Sweden under articles 1 and 27[58] the ICCPR. His position was that Saami peoples have the right to self-determination under article 1, paragraph 1 of the ICCPR. He contended that the old Lapp villages must be looked upon as small realms, not States, with a right to neutrality in war. This was the Swedish position during the reign of Gustavus Vasa and is well expressed in royal letters issued in 1526, 1543 and 1551(see paragraph, 5.2).

Responding to Kitok's allegation the State party argued that the Communication could not be maintained because the Saami could not constitute a 'people' within the meaning of article 1 of the ICCPR. Therefore, it was argued, that article 1 was not applicable to the case at issue and it should therefore be declared inadmissible under article 3[59] of the first Optional Protocol to the ICCPR. In agreeing with the objections raised by the State party the HRC held:

> With regard to the State party's submission that the communication should be declared inadmissible as incompatible with Article 3 of the Optional Protocol or as manifestly ill-founded, the Committee observed that the *author, as an individual, could not claim to be the victim of a violation of the right of self-determination enshrined in Article 3 of the Covenant.* Whereas the Optional Protocol provides a recourse procedure for individuals claiming that their rights have been violated, Article 1 of the Covenant deals with rights conferred upon peoples, as such. (pr. 6.3) (emphasis added).

It is worth mentioning that in the above cases the HRC did not reject the claim of indigenous peoples that they are entitled to exercise the right to self-determination. It seems that the HRC tried to avoid politically sensitive issues such as whether indigenous or minority groups have the right to external self-determination.

Conclusion

Autonomy in the form of internal self-determination is still evolving, and there are signs that it might in future be developed into a principle of international law within the context of the principle of self-determination thereby enhancing its internal aspects. International law does not prohibit arrangements designed to provide mechanisms involving regional autonomy for any ethnic or indigenous groups, who, in turn, are expected to exercise these rights in compliance with the laws of the empowering State. The establishment of adequate autonomous measures is in the hands of the nation-States. But it is not a legal right that can be exercised as of right in international law. It is a half-way house between claims and rights. However, a claim is the first step towards acquiring legal rights.

Notes

[1] Nicaragua's statement cited in Barsh, R. L, (1996), 'Indigenous Peoples and the Commission on Human Rights: A Case of the Immovable Object and the Irresistible Force', 18 (4) *HRQ*, pp. 782- 820 at 797.

[2] UN Doc. E/CN.4/Sub.2/1992/37, para. 165, p. 33.

[3] UN Doc. E/CN.4/Sub.2/1993/26/Add. 1, para. 9.

[4] See for example GA Res. 45/150, 18 December 1990 ("Enhancing the Effectiveness of the Principle of Periodic and Genuine Elections"). See also Article 21 (3) of the UDHR which states, "The will of the people shall be the basis of the authority of government; this will shall be expressed in periodic and genuine elections which shall be by universal and equal suffrage and shall be held by secret vote or by equivalent free voting procedures".

[5] UN Doc. E/CN.4/Sub.2/1996/2, 30 November 1995, para. 38, p.10.

[6] 1975, 14 *ILM* 1292, [1975], p.1295.

[7] UN Doc. E/CN.4/Sub.2/1993/34, 10 August 1993, *Possible Ways and Means of Facilitating the Peaceful and Constructive Solution of Problems Involving Minorities*, p. 6.

[8] *Ibid.* para. 88, p. 19.

[9] UN Doc. E/CN.4/Sub.2/1990/46, *Possible Ways and Means of Facilitating the Peaceful and Constructive Solution of Problems Involving Minorities*, para.23, p.6.

[10] *Possible Ways and Means*, above, 1993, para. 88, p. 19.

[11] *Ibid.* para. 88, p. 19.

[12] *Ibid.* para. 124 (a), p. 27.

[13] *Ibid.* paras. 124, 126, 140-145 and 247.

[14] They resorted to armed struggle over ancestral lands in the 1980s. See the report submitted by Canada under Article 40 of the ICCPR, Official Report of the Human

Rights Committee, 1990/91, CCPR/10, CCPR/C/51/Add.1 and CCPR/C/64/Add. 1, paras. 16-17, p. 9.
[15] See for example Jose R. Martinez Cobo's report, UN Doc. E/CN.4/Sub.2/1983/ 21, Add. 8, para. 513.
[16] See Commission on Human Rights Res. 1982/19, 10 March 1982 and ECOSOC Res. 1982/34, 7 May 1982.
[17] It was alleged in the *Sparrow* case that the net length restriction imposed by the Federal Government was contrary to the indigenous laws and customs. This case is considered a 'milestone' in the fishing rights of indigenous peoples. See *R* v *Sparrow* (1990) I SCR 1075, no. 1598 (Canada). Hunting and fishing have been a critical component of indigenous life, see Kyle, R. (1997), 'Aboriginal Fishing Rights: The Supreme Court of Canada in the Post-Sparrow Era', 31 (2) *UBC Law Review*, p. 293. See also *R* v *Van der Peet* (1996) 2 SCR 507; *R* v *Gladstone* (1996) 2 SCR 723; *Guerin* v *The Queen* (1984) 2 SCR 335; *Calder* v *British Colombia* (AG) (1973) 34 DLR (3rd) 145 SCC.
[18] See *Guerin* v *The Queen* (1984) 2 SCR 335 (Canada).
[19] See *Dagi* v *BHP* (No. 2) 1997, IVR 428 (Australia); see also *Dagi* v *BHP* (No. 10) 1995, VIC LEXIS 1182 (Australia). It was alleged that the Australian mining company BHP caused enormous damages to the OK Tedi and Maun Rivers and to the local indigenous peoples in Papua New Guinea. See details in Kingsbury, (1998: 436), as below. See also *Yosofa Alomang* v *Freeport-McMoran* (1996) US Dist. LEXIS 15, 908, 17 October 1996; *Tom Beanal* v *Freeport -McMoran* (1997) WL 178, 10 April 1997. In this latter case the McMoran mining and metal milling company was prosecuted for causing damage to the environment in West Irian.
[20] *Cayuga Indians (Gr Brit)* v *US* 6 RIAA 173, 1926. The British Government brought this action on behalf of Cayuga Indians in Canada alleging that the State of New York had failed to honour the agreement entered into between the Indian Band and the New York state. The Cayugans were awarded $100,000. See details in Reisman (1995: 351) as below. It should be mentioned that the court did not recognise the Cayuga tribe as a legal unit in international law. See Anaya (1996: 23) as below.
[21] A fiduciary duty arises where a person or representative "undertakes or agrees to act for, or on behalf of, or in the interests of another person in the exercise of a power or discretion which will affect the interests of that other in a legal or practical sense", see *Hospital Products Ltd* v *US Surgical Corporation* (1984) 156 CLR 41, pp.96-97, the judgment of Mason J. Both in the USA and Canada it is now accepted that the Crown can owe a fiduciary duty to indigenous peoples, see *R* v *Guerin* (1985) mentioned above and *Cherokee Nation* and *Mabo* (no.2) (1992) 175 CLR 1. In *Mabo* (no. 2) Brennan J with an agreement of Mason J and McHugh J pronounced at p. 60: "If native title were surrendered to the Crown in expectation of a grant of tenure to the indigenous title holders, there may be a fiduciary duty on the Crown to exercise its discretionary power to grant a tenure in land so as to satisfy the expectation." See further *Wik Peoples* v *State of Queensland* (1996) 141

ALR 129. See Buti, T. (1998), 'Removal of Indigenous Children From their Families: The Litigation Path', 27 *Western Australian Law Review*, pp. 203-226.

[22] See *Guerin* v *The Queen* (1984) 13 DLR (4th) 321, Dickson CJ's finding. It was held in this case that the Canadian government's conduct in dealing with indigenous peoples should maintain a "high standard of honourable dealing". It was further held that "the way in which a legislative object is to be attained must uphold the honour of the Crown and must be in keeping with the unique contemporary relationship, grounded in history and policy, between the Crown and Canada's aboriginal peoples", *ibid*. p. 1110.

[23] *Lubicon Lake Band* v *Canada*, Communication no. 167/1984; *Sandra Lovelace* v *Canada*, Communication no. 24/1977; *Mikmaq Tribal Society* v *Canada*, Communication no. 78/1980, declared inadmissible on 29 July 1984; *Kitok* v *Sweden*, Communication no. 197/1985, views adopted on 27 July 1988; see also *Kasivarsi Reindeer Herders' Cooperative* v *Ministry of Trade and Industry*, sup. Admin. Ct. Fin. 15 May 1996; *Kayano and Kaizawa* v *Government of Japan*, Hanrei Jiho, no. 1598, 1997, Sapporo Dist. Ct. 27 March 1997 (discussed the application of ILO Convention, no. 169). See further details in Kingsbury (1998: 437-438, below).

[24] *National Coalition of Union of Burma* v *Unocal*, 176 FRD 329, CD Cal. In this case Unocal oil company was prosecuted on the grounds that the company's exploration activities resulted in a relocation and dispersal of a large number of indigenous peoples, some of whom were used by the company as forced labourers. See also In *Re Public Service Employee Relations Act* (1987) I SCR 313. Dickson J held at 348 in this case that, under international law of human rights "the nations of the world have undertaken to adhere to the standards and principles necessary for ensuring freedom, dignity and social justice for their citizens".

[25] *RL et al* v *Canada*, Communication no. 358/1989, views adopted by the Human Rights Committee on 5 November 1991.

[26] See also UN Doc. E/CN.4/Sub.2/1993/29, paras. 39-75. See further UN Doc. E/CN.4/Sub.2/ 1997/14, Report of the Working Group on Indigenous Population. Referring to definitional issue, Brownlie states that there are no specific rules or principles as to the exact meaning of 'indigenous' in customary or general international law (Brownlie, 1992: 61, below). There are various terms which appear to identify indigenous peoples at present. Of these, natives, aboriginal and indigenous are popular. It should be mentioned that any lack of progress in finalising a definition is due to the reluctance of States to define the term 'indigenous' due to their unfounded fear that any such attempt would undermine the security and stability of nation-State system. The ILO and the UN have both tried to find a definition although neither has been successful. The UN Special Rapportuer Jose Martinus Cobo provides the following definition: "Indigenous communities, peoples and nations are those which, having a historical continuity with pre-invasion and pre-colonial societies that developed on their territories, consider themselves distinct from other sectors of the societies now prevailing in those territories, or parts of them. They form at present non-dominant sectors of

society and are determined to preserve, develop and transmit to future generations their ancestral territories, and their ethnic identity, as the basis of their continued existence as peoples, in accordance with their own cultural patterns, social institutions and legal systems". ILO Convention 169 (1989) provides the following definition in Article 1 (1): "The Convention applies to, a) tribal peoples in independent countries whose social, cultural and economic conditions distinguish them from other sections of the national community, and whose status is regulated wholly or partially by their own customs or traditions or by special laws or regulations; b) peoples in independent countries who are regarded as indigenous on account of their descent from the populations which inhabited the country, or a geographical region to which the country belongs, at the time of the conquest or colonisation or the establishment of present state boundaries and who, irrespective of their legal status, retain some or all of their own social, economic, cultural and political institutions". It should be mentioned that Article 1 (3) of the above Convention emphasises that the use of the term 'peoples' in the Convention shall not be construed as having any implications as regards the rights which may attach to the term under international law. The Draft UN Declaration on Indigenous Peoples made no attempt to define 'indigenous'. Instead, Chairperson, Mrs Erica-Irene Daes stressed that the Draft Declaration should be applicable to the category of indigenous peoples defined by UN Special Rapporteur Cobo. See UN Doc. E/CN.4 /Sub.2/AC.4/ 1992/3 Add. 1, p.21. See further Brownlie, I. (1992), *Treaties and Indigenous Peoples*, Clarendon Press: Oxford, chapter 3, 'Indigenous Peoples: A Relevant Concept'? pp. 55-75.

[27] UN Doc. E/CN.4/Sub.2/1986/7/Add. 4, paras. 378- 80.

[28] UN Doc. E/CN.4/Sub.2/1987/22, Annex V, para. 4.

[29] UN Doc. E/CN.4/Sub.2/AC. 4/1984/WP. 1.

[30] The statement of the Miskito, Sumo, and Rama nations in the Atlantic Coastal area of Nicaragua (MISURASATA). See Hannum (1990: 257-262) as below.

[31] Naga separatists argued that their case was different and distinct from most indigenous peoples who were willing to accept greater autonomy within existing nation-State structures. They insisted that as an indigenous people under force occupation they were entitled to establish an independent State. See the statement made by Naga Peoples' Movement for Human Rights to the UN Working Group on Indigenous Population, July 1993, para. 2, cited in Thornberry (1995: 83), as below. See also Upadhyaya, A. S. (1996), 'Quest For Self-Determination in the Indian Sub-Continent: The Recent Phase', in D. Clark and R. Williamson (eds), *Self-Determination: International Perspectives*, Mcmillan Press Ltd: London, pp. 159-161.

[32] See the submission made by the Gitkson and Wet'suwet'en tribe in *Delgamuukw v British Colombia* 104 *DLR* (4th) BCCA (1993), pp. 591-592. See also UN Doc. E/CN.4/Sub.2/1994/30, paras. 37-39.

[33] The statement made during the 75th session of the International Labour Conference, June 13, 1988, cited in Anaya (1996:64) as below.

[34] UN Doc. E/CN.4/Sub.2/AC.4/1984/WP.1.

[35] See UN Doc. E/CN.4/Sub.2/AC.4/1992/3/Add. 1, p. 5.

[36] See the Report of the Inter-American Commission on Human Rights on the Situation of Human Rights of a Segment of the Nicaraguan Population of Miskito Origin, OAS Doc. OAE/Ser.L/V II, 61, 1984 cited in Hannum, (1990:79-221), as below. A similar view was expressed by the Sami Rights Committee on the Legal Situation of the Sami Population (appointed by Norway).

[37] 28 *ILM* 1382 [1989], pp. 1384-1392.

[38] International Labour Conference, Provisional Record 25, 76th session, 1989, para. 31, p.25.

[39] Report of the Meeting of Experts on Indigenous autonomy and self-government. See Stamatopoulou, E. (1994), 'Indigenous Peoples and the United Nations: Human Rights as a Developing Dynamic', 16 (1) *HRQ*, p. 79.

[40] See Articles 2, 21, 31, 32 and 33 of the Draft UN Declaration on Indigenous Peoples 1994. See also Zieck. Y. A. (1995), 'Some Remarks on the Draft Declaration on the Rights of Indigenous Peoples', 8 *LJIL*, pp. 103-113.

[41] UN Doc. E/CN.4/Sub.2/1994/30, para. 133.

[42] UN Doc. E/CN.4/Sub.2/1994, para. 19, Explanatory Report of Erica-Irene Daes, Chairperson-Rapporteur of the WGIP.

[43] See UN Doc. E/CN.4/Sub.2/1991/40, Rev.1, p. 30, 3 October 1991. Report of the 9th session of the UN Working Group on Indigenous Populations.

[44] See UN Doc. E/CN.4/Sub.2/1992/33, Annex II.

[45] Article 4 of the Draft UN Declaration states: "Indigenous peoples have the right to maintain and strengthen their distinct political, economic, social and cultural characteristics, as well as their legal systems, while retaining their rights to participate fully, if they choose, in the political, economic, social and cultural life of the State".

[46] See the explanatory note by the Rapporteur of the Working Group on Indigenous Peoples, UN Doc. E/CN.4/Sub.2/1993/26/Add. 1

[47] *Ibid.* para. 19.

[48] *Ibid.*

[49] UN Doc. E/CN.4/Sub.2/1992/33, Annex II.

[50] See the explanatory note by the Rapporteur of the Working Group on Indigenous Peoples, UN Doc. E/CN.4/Sub.2/1993/26/Add. 1, paras. 19, 21 and 23.

[51] See UN Doc. E/CN.4/ Sub.2/1994/30, para. 39.

[52] The first Optional Protocol came into force on 23 March 1976. See details McGoldrick, D. (1991), *Human Rights Committee, Its Role in the Development of the International Covenant on Civil and Political Rights*, Clarendon Press: Oxford.

[53] Article 1 (1) states: "All peoples have the right of self-determination. By virtue of that right they freely determine their political status and freely pursue their economic, social and cultural development".

[54] Communication no. 78/1980, declared inadmissible, 29 July 1984 at the 22nd session of the HRC.

[55] Communication no. 167/1984, views adopted on 26 March 1990 at the thirty-eight session.

[56] Article 1 (2) states: "All peoples may, for their own ends, freely dispose of their natural wealth and resources without prejudice to any obligations arising out of international economic co-operation, based upon the principle of mutual benefit, and international law. In no case may a people be deprived of its own means of subsistence".

[57] Communication no. 197/1985, views adopted on 27 July 1988 at the thirty-third session of the HRC.

[58] Article 27 of the ICCPR provides: "In those States in which ethnic, religious or linguistic minorities exist, persons belonging to such minorities shall not be denied the right, in community with the other members of their group, to enjoy their own cultures, to profess and practice their own religion, or to use their own language".

[59] Article 3 of the Optional Protocol to the ICCPR states: "The Committee shall consider inadmissible any communication under the present Protocol which is anonymous, or which it considers to be an abuse of the right of submission of such communications or to be incompatible with the provisions of the Covenant".

References

Alfredsson, G. (1993), 'The Right of Self-determination and Indigenous People', in C. Tomuschat (ed), *Modern Law of Self-Determination*, Martinus Nijhoff: Dordrecht/ Boston and London, pp. 41-54.

Alfredsson, G. (1998), 'Indigenous Peoples and Autonomy', in M. Susksi (ed), *Autonomy: Applications and Implications*, Kluwer Law International: The Hague/London/Boston, pp. 125-136.

Anayay, J. S. (1996), *Indigenous Peoples in International Law*, Oxford UP: New York.

Barsh, R. L. (1986), 'Indigenous Peoples: An Emerging Object of International Law', 80 *AJIL,* pp. 369-385.

Barsh, R. L. (1996), 'Indigenous Peoples and the UN Commission on Human Rights: A Case of the Immovable Object and the Irresistible Force', 18 (4) *HRQ,* pp. 782- 820.

Bernhardt, H. (1981), 'Federalism and Autonomy', in Y. Dinstein (ed), *Models of Autonomy*, Transaction Books: New Brunswick and London, pp. 23-30.

Bohlin, J. (1995), 'Human Rights and Access to Natural Resources', 64 (3) *Nord. J. Int.L,* pp. 495- 499.

Brolmann, C. M. and Zieck, Y. A. (1995), 'Some Remarks on the Draft Declaration on the Rights of Indigenous Peoples', 8 (1) *LJIL,* pp. 103- 113.

Brownlie, I. (1988), 'The Rights of Peoples in Modern International Law', in J. Crawford (ed), *The Rights of People*, Clarendon Press: Oxford, pp. 1-16.

Brownlie, I. (1992), *Treaties and Indigenous Peoples*, Clarendon Press: Oxford.

Buergenthal, T. (1990), 'The Copenhagen CSCE Meeting: A New Public Order for Europe', 11 *HRLJ,* pp. 217-246.

Cassese, A. (1995), *Self-Determination of Peoples: A Legal Reappraisal*, Cambridge UP: Cambridge.

Coulter, R. T. (1995), 'The Draft UN Declaration on the Rights of Indigenous Peoples: What is It ? What does it Mean ?", 13 *NQHR*, pp. 123- 138.

Daes, Erica-Irene, A. (1993), 'Some Considerations on the Right of Indigenous Peoples to Self-Determination', 3 *Transnational Law and Contemporary Problems*, pp. 1- 11.

Daes, Erica-Irene, A. (1996), 'The Rights of Indigenous Peoples to Self-Determination in the Contemporary International Law', in D. Clark and R. Williamson (eds), *Self-Determination: International Perspectives*, Macmillan Press Ltd: London, pp. 47- 54.

Eide, A. (1993), 'Approaches to Minority Protection', in A Phillips and A. Rosas (eds), *The UN Minority Rights Declaration*, Abo Academic Institute for Human Rights and Minority Rights Group International: Turku/Abo/London, pp. 81 -93.

Eide, A. (1995), 'The National Society, Peoples and Ethno-Nations: Semantic Confusions and Legal Consequences', 64 (3) *Nord J.Int.L*, pp. 353- 367.

Franck, T. M. (1992), 'The Emerging Right to Democratic Governance', 86 *AJIL*, pp. 46 -91.

Franck, T. M. (1994), 'Commentary on 'Multiple Tiers of Sovereignty: The Future of International Governance', *ASIL Proceedings* (April 6-9), pp. 54-55 and 61 -62.

Friedlander, R. A. (1981), 'Autonomy and the Thirteen Colonies: Was the American Revolution Really Necessary?, in Y. Dinstein (ed), *Models of Autonomy*, Transaction Books: New Brunswick, USA and London, pp. 135 -148.

Gayim, E. (1994), *The UN Declaration on Indigenous Peoples: Assessment of the Draft Prepared by the Working Group on Indigenous Populations*, University of Lapland: Rovaniemi.

Gayim, E. (1995), 'The Draft Declaration on Indigenous Peoples: With Focus on the Rights to Self-Determination and Law', in E. Gayim and K. Myntti (eds), *Indigenous and Tribal Peoples' Rights - 1993 and After*, Northern Institute for Environment and Minority Law: Rovaniemi, pp. 12 -45.

Hannikainen, L. (1998), 'Self-Determination and Autonomy in International Law', in Suksi (ed), as above, pp. 79- 95.

Hannum, H. (1990), *Autonomy, Sovereignty and Self-Determination: The Accommodation of Conflicting Rights*, University of Pennsylvania Press: Philadelphia.

Hannum, H. (1996 ed.), *Autonomy, Sovereignty and Self-Determination: The Accommodation of Conflicting Rights*, University of Pennsylvania Press: Philadelphia.

Harhoff, F. (1986), 'Institution of Autonomy', 55 *Nord. J.Int.L*, pp. 31- 40.

Heintz, H. J. (1998), 'On the Legal Understanding of Autonomy', in Suksi (ed), as above, pp. 7 -32.

Heyking, B. (1928), 'The International Protection of Minorities: The Achilles' Heel of the League of Nations', 13 *Problems of Peace and War*, pp. 31- 51.

Humphrey, J. P. (1984), 'Political and Related Rights', in T. Meron (ed), *Human Rights in International Law, Legal and Policy Issues*, vol. 1, Clarendon Press: Oxford, pp. 171- 203.

Hutchins, P. W. Hilling, C. and Schulze, D. (1995), 'The Aboriginal Right to Self-government and the Canadian Constitution: The Ghost in the Machine', 29 (2) *UBC Law Review*, pp. 251 -302.

Kimminich, O. (1993), 'A Federal Right of Self-Determination', in Tomuschat (ed), as above, pp. 83- 100.

Kingsbury, B. (1998), 'Indigenous Peoples in International Law: Constructivist Approach to the Asian Controversy', 92 (3) *AJIL*, pp. 414- 457.

Kyle, R. (1997), 'Aboriginal Fishing Rights: The Supreme Court of Canada in the Post-Sparrow Era', 31 (2) *UBC Law Review*, pp. 293- 316.

Kymlicka, W. (1995a), *The Rights of Minority Culture*, Oxford UP: Oxford.

Kymlicka, W. (1995b), *Multicultural Citizenship*, Clarendon Press: Oxford.

Langton, M. (1988), 'The United Nations and Indigenous Minorities: A Report on the United Nations Working Group on Indigenous Populations', in B. Hocking (ed), *International Law and Aborignial Human Rights*, The Law Book Company Ltd: North Ryde, NSW, pp. 83- 92.

Lapidoth, R. (1997), *Autonomy: Flexible Solutions to Ethnic Conflicts*, United States Institute of Peace Press: Washington, DC.

Lerner, N. (1993), 'The 1992 UN Declaration on Minorities', 23 *IYHR*, pp. 111- 128.

Lijphart, A. (1995), 'Self-Determination Versus Pre-Determination of Ethnic Minorities in Power-Sharing Systems', in W. Kymlicka (ed), *Multicultural Citizenship*, Clarendon Press: Oxford, pp. 275 - 287.

Murswiek, D. (1993), 'The Issue of a Right of Secession: Reconsidered', in Tomuschat ed. above, pp. 21- 39.

Raikka, J. (1998), 'On the Ethics of Minority Protection', in Suksi (ed), as above, pp. 33- 42.

Reismen, W. M. (1995), 'Protecting Indigenous Rights in International Adjudication', 89 (2) *AJIL*, pp. 350- 362.

Rickard, M. (1994), 'Liberalism, Multiculturalism, and Minority Protection', 20 *Social Theory and Practice*, pp. 143- 170.

Rosas, A. (1993), 'Internal Self-Determination', in Tomuschat (ed), as above. pp. 225 -252.

Sanders, D. (1986), 'Is Autonomy a Principle of International Law', 55 *Nord. J. Int.L,* pp. 17- 21.

Sanders, D. (1993), 'Self-Determination and Indigenous Peoples', in Tomuschat (ed), as above, pp. 55- 81.

Scott, C. (1996), 'Indigenous Self-Determination and Decolonisation of the International Imagination: A Plea', 8 *HRQ*, pp. 814- 820.

Shaw, M. (1997), 'Commentary on Anaya, J. S. (1996), Indigenous Peoples in International Law', 63 *BYIL*, pp. 269- 270.

Sohn, L. B. (1980), 'The Concept of Autonomy in International Law and the Practice of the United Nations', 15 (2) *ILR*, pp. 180- 190.

Sohn, L. B. (1981), 'Models of Autonomy Within the United Nations Framework', in Y. Dinstein (ed), *Models of Autonomy*, Transaction Books: New Brunswick/London, pp. 5- 22.

Suksi, M. (1997), 'The Constitutional Setting of the Aaland Islands Compared', in H. Hannikainen and F. Horn (eds), *Autonomy and Dimilitarisation in International Law: The Aaland Islands in a Changing World*, Kluwer Law International: The Hague/London/Boston, pp. 99- 129.

Suksi, M. (1998), 'On the Entrenchment of Autonomy', in Suksi (ed), as above, pp. 150- 171.

Thornberry, P. (1989), 'Self-Determination, Minorities and Human Rights: A Review of International Instruments', 38 *ICLQ*, pp. 867- 889.

Thornberry, P. (1993), 'The UN Declaration on the Rights of Persons Belonging to National or Ethnic, Religious and Linguistic Minorities: Background, Analysis and Observations', in A. Phillips and A. Rosas (eds), *The UN Minority Rights Declaration*, Abo-Academic University Institute for Human Rights and Minority Rights Group International, Turku/London, pp. 11- 72.

Thornberry, P. (1995), 'On Some Implications of the UN Draft Declaration on Minorities for Indigenous Peoples', in Gayim and Myntti (eds), as above. pp. 46- 64.

Thornberry, P. (1998), 'Images of Autonomy and Individual and Collective Rights in International Instruments on the Rights of Minorities', in Suksi (ed), as above, pp. 97-121.

Tomuschat, C. (1993), 'Self-Determination in a Post-Colonial World', in Tomuschat (ed), as above, pp. 1- 20.

Torress, R. (1991), 'The Rights of Indigenous Populations: The Emerging International Norm', 16 *Yale J Int'l L*, pp. 127 -175.

Venne, S. H. (1996), 'Self-Determination Issues in Canada: A First Person's Overview', in Clark and Williamson (eds), *Self-Determination: International Perspectives*, as above, pp. 291- 301.

Williams, M. (1995), 'Justice Towards Groups: Political Not Juridical', 23 *Political Theory*, pp. 67- 91.

Yukich, K. C. (1996), 'Aboriginal Rights in the Constitution and International Law', 30 (2) *UBC Law Review*, pp. 235- 278.

6 Models of Autonomy and Movements for Autonomy

Introduction

The purpose of this chapter is to analyse the main characteristics of selected models of autonomy whilst examining the current trends within movements fighting for autonomy and their impact on modern nation-States. How and why sub-groups in multiethnic polities agitate for greater autonomy with shared sovereign power is further examined.

Do minority groups genuinely want power-sharing schemes based on autonomous structures located within the boundaries of nation-States? Or are there other ambitions behind their claims? Do they seek to use autonomy as a stepping stone to independent statehood? These are questions to which a definite general answer cannot be found given the complexities of these issues. Some ethnic groups genuinely want power sharing arrangements so as to realize their rights. Other groups may not.

Claims for regional autonomy with extensive political powers raise a new dimension to minority rights. Ethnic groups perceive autonomous regimes to be necessary, "not simply to assure their ulterior survival, but principally to avoid oppression and violence" (Steiner, 1991:1540; see further Kymlicka, 1995:7; Hannum, 1989:3-4). Another author remarked that "autonomy is for the minority like water for a fish".[1] Ethnically defined and segregated autonomous enclaves will not only re-kindle ethnic consciousness but may also function as ethnic fortresses which demarcate boundaries between 'them' and 'others'. Ethnic and cultural peculiarities are expected to be strengthened, and protected from dilution. Ethnically pure enclaves having autonomous regimes purport to be fortresses which provide protection against other ethnic groups, and in particular against the State in which they are located.

Globalization of State institutions, in the view of many ethnic groups, stands in the way, constraining and hindering any development of ethnic traditions, cultures and other salient ethnic institutions. Although small ethnic groups existed in primitive and non-industrialized societies

159

segregated or completely isolated from the outside world, modern globalized societies do not create an environment in which ethnic groups can survive without being 'polluted' by others. Faced with the threat of assimilation or in some rare cases fusion, most ethnic groups now appear to be struggling to protect their ethnic inheritance based on mythologies and collective achievements. The perceived wisdom amongst most ethnic groups is that, if they fail to take preventive measures, they will be subsumed by dominant groups. Recent violent clashes between different tribes in Indonesia demonstrate that members of a tribe are prepared to go to any length to erect ethnic fortresses to protect themselves against those who are perceived as enemy groups. The creation of enclaves which offer ethnic groups a kind of safe havens requires a political power base or a certain degree of independence from the central authorities. The determining factor in such a context is whether a group or a region has the necessary political power, that is, executive, legislative and judicial powers. These areas function as geographical barriers against encroachment by outsiders.

The survival of ethnically pure groups in modern polities is not easily achieved. The perceived fear of being swamped by other groups always pushes ethnic groups into taking protective measures and in extreme case leads to violence. Faced with such uncertain and precarious circumstances, most ethnic groups consider that group protection is necessary for their survival against other competing groups. The tools required are not only the traditional community networks but also a strong political power base which can be used to ensure survival against any threat by outside ethnic groups. If a minority is numerically weak and non-dominant in a State, then a certain degree of political power, that is, partial independence from the State, may be viewed as a desirable option, at least in the short term. This is now increasingly being identified as autonomy and is becoming popular amongst ethnic groups and minority right campaigners.

From the minorities' perspective, without having greater political power in terms of territorial autonomy, they are effectively being deprived of their legitimate rights to determine the political, economic and cultural way of living they would like. Henry J. Steiner (1991:1546) notes the thrust of that argument appears to be that "only an autonomy regime could give the minority and its members the kind of fair or equitable political participation". On the other hand, modern nation-States are continually struggling to cope with the renewed claims for ethnically defined autonomous regions. The "incremental effect such claims will have upon the international legal order" is immense and unpredictable (Hannum and Lillich, 1981:858).

As recent history witnessed, claims for autonomy by minority groups may result in the emergence of 'ethnic provinces' as rival power bases undermining the authority of the nation-States. A case in point was the Kosovar Albanian 'shadow-State'. Mr. Ibrahim Rugova, the leader of the Democratic League of Kosovo (DLK) had been able to create a virtual parallel ethnic Albanian 'shadow State' in the province of Kosovo during the period between 1991-1999 by building various institutions in direct challenge to Serbia's claim to Kosovo. Rugova was elected President of the self-declared Republic of Kosovo in 1992 and in 1998. The Kosovars' intention is to achieve an 'intermediate sovereignty' is as a basis for further development towards independence.[2] Similar developments are taking place in the Northern and Eastern provinces of Sri Lanka and in the Kwazulu kingdom in South Africa.

6.1 *Autonomy as a Strategy: "First Equality, Then to Priority and in Extreme Cases to Exclusivity"?*

The campaigns of minority groups for greater territorial autonomy in contemporary polities seem to be politically divisive, and detrimental to national unity. Some of these claims seem to be eccentric and militant. Claims often start from "equality, then proceed to priority and in extreme cases to exclusivity" (Horowitz, 1985:197). Such claims are often based on a right to a particular geographical area alleged to be defined or inherited by natural boundaries associated with a particular ethnic or racial group. Initially, they appear to be politically neutral, innocent, harmless and reasonable, but their consequences can be very deep and destructive in actual political terms (Horowitz, 1985:196).

There is a certain methodology in this mayhem. Claims for regional autonomy with greater political power often begin in small clusters of disgruntled individuals, extend to a mass circle of organized groups and then develop into clandestine militant political movements. This often gives rise to violence and long-drawn-out wars. This is particularly true of the LTTE (see Gunasekara, 1996), the Chittagongs in the Chittagong Hill Tracks in Bangladesh, and the KLA in Kosovo (Phillips, 1996:821-832; see also Bugaijski, 1995). The most horrendous contemporary example has been that of the Serbs' abortive attempt to carve a pure-Serb autonomous State out of Bosnia and Herzegovina and Croatia. The International

Criminal Tribunal for the Former Yugoslavia in its findings described the strategy adopted by the Serbs as follows:

> In April 1991 several communities joined a Serbian association of municipalities. These structures were formed in areas predominantly inhabited by Bosnian Serbs, generally by vote of the predominantly Bosnian Serb Local Assemblies. At first, this association was a form of economic and cultural coorperation without administrative power. However, separate police forces and separate Assemblies rapidly developed. In September 1991, it was announced that several Serb Autonomous Regions in Bosnia Herzegovina had been proclaimed, including Krajina, Romanjija and Stara Herzegovina, with the aim of separating from the Republican government agencies in Sarajevo and creating a Greater Serbia".[3] ...Crisis Staff were formed in the Serb Autonomous Regions to assume government functions and carry out general municipal management.[4]

A similar strategy has been applied by the Kosovo Liberation Army in its campaign for independence (see *infra* chapter 11 for further details). As these cases suggest, a claim for autonomy by an ethnic group in a State often results in conflict with the interests of other nationals and undermines the stability of the nation-State (Mullerson, 1994:85).

Generally, before embarking on violent clandestine struggles, minorities claiming autonomy focus initially on issues of morality and justice. Equality and non-discrimination are the main theme of the initial stage of campaigns for autonomy. Often affirmative action and positive discrimination are advocated to correct injustices and prejudices. These claims are in fact being presented as demands which the liberal democracies advocate (Steiner, 1991:1543). A departure from the existing constitutional structures is often urged in favour of a territorial re-arrangement in order to realize the minority rights in the areas of natural resources, value systems, cultures, religions and linguistic matters (Soynika, 1996; Hannum, 1990: 457-458). These may involve proportional representation in executive, legislative and the judiciary. Coalition governments in which a certain number of ethnic minority ministers are elected, and the power of veto for ethnic politicians whenever their rights are threatened are also some of the initial demands of most ethnic minority groups in their quest for independence. Belgium, Lebanon and Cyprus are examples of this. At the second stage, campaigns for autonomy may involve demands for political control over territories inhabited by minority groups. Territorial re-arrangements are promoted to achieve a certain degree of political independence. Unlike the former category of demands, claims for territorial re-arrangements in terms of ethnic or linguistic differences often result in conflicts between ethnic groups and dominant majority groups. Against this background, autonomous arrangements are welcome because they allow ethnic political leaders to wield power in the name of their groups. Moreover, they guarantee their group will not be swamped or assimilated by the dominant culture. Without political power it is difficult to protect and promote ethnic minority cultures and their community structures. Normally political power in autonomous regimes comes at the least with a police force dominated by ethnic groups thereby bringing a sense of security. Judicial powers provide a safe environment by protecting and strengthening personal laws, customs and particular ethnic value systems. One such example is the legal entitlement of the Tamils in the Jaffna province to practise 'Thesavalamai law' in respect of property and land disputes. This prevents any possible encroachment by other ethnic groups on the Tamils' homeland areas. Executive powers can take effective political measures through a network of administrative institutions and power structures. Therefore, both territorial and personal autonomy operate in autonomous regions through greater political power.

A recent example was that of hastily arranged informal local opposition groups in the former USSR. They "began to present demands for the official recognition of their languages, the teaching of their national culture and history, the protection of their environment, and the self-determination of the economy" (Kux, 1996:328). Another example is the claim of the Hungarians in the Republic of Slovakia for linguistic and cultural rights, that is, the right to teach in the Hungarian language, the right to use it for road signs, the demand for the State's assistance for cultural projects etc. As the Slovak government began to implement most of these demands, a new set of demands for greater autonomy for the southern region, known as 'the Komarno Proposal', was presented by the Hungarian national group in 1994 by using a secret map to justify their claims. Refusing to yield to these demands, the Slovaks branded them as a first step to secession (Bakker, 1998:28-29). As these cases demonstrate, claimants take extreme care to present their demands in the guise of a power-sharing mechanism with the majority population on an equal footing for the benefit of all. Expected changes are claimed within existing territorial boundaries. For example, the Albanians living in Tetvo and surrounding villages (a relatively small area in Western Macedonia) are demanding constitutional changes that will "give them more autonomy", stressing that constitutional re-arrangement with greater autonomy will "boost educational and job opportunities".[5] The Silesian movement for autonomy in Upper Silesia in Poland led by Rudolf Kolodziejczk wants to "concentrate everything except the police, the army, the courts and foreign policy" in the 'historical region of Upper Silesia'. The Silesian campaign for autonomy is slowly taking off the ground attracting many supporters in recent times. In the autumn 1997 election, demands for autonomy were backed by more than 100,000 people, 8% of the total population in the region. Its leaders were reported to have sought 'advice' from the Catalan and Basque separatist leaders. More disturbingly, Rudolf Kolodziejczk is alleged to have recently discussed autonomous strategy with the leader of the 'Republica of Padania', Mr. Umerto Bossi.[6] Sometimes, a change from a federal structure to a 'confederation' or at least to a loose union of States akin to the EU[7] is advocated. For instance, before the secession from the former Socialist Federative Republic of Yugoslavia (SFRY), Croatian and Slovenian politicians with the approval of Macedonia and Bosnia-Herzegovina in 1990 demanded that constitutional changes be made to create a union of States akin to a confederation in which different autonomous regions could exercise sovereignty.[8] The Sudan Peoples' Liberation Movement (SPLM) informed the Khartoum administration in November 1997 that "South Sudan should have a choice of becoming an independent state or remaining part of a united Sudan on the basis of a confederation of north and south Sudan under a central authority. It should be a secular state."[9] Similar claims have been made by the self-proclaimed 'Trans-Dniester Moldavian Republic' (a small area between the Dniester river and the Ukraine) in Moldova -"for the creation of a federation with their own constitution, army, currency and foreign policy" (see Jungwiert and Nowicki, 1994:390). Some Afrikaaner groups are also demanding that they should be allowed to establish an 'Afrikaaner People's State (*valkstaat*) "within the borders of South Africa" (Dugard, 1997:87). The Inkatha Freedom Party in South Africa, representing the Zulu people, has made known its claims for a provincial State with greater autonomy within a federal structure of the South African Republic (Dugard, 1997:87). Russian nationals in Narva and Sillamae (predominantly Russian towns) in Estonia have recently voted overwhelmingly in favour of autonomy in response to Estonia's discriminatory citizenship legislation against non-Estonians. The Russian Christian Union has been threatening that it would prefer separatism to integration with Estonia.[10] These claims are rapidly arousing international concern.

6.2 *Reasons Behind the Emergence of Movements for Autonomy*

Claims for greater autonomy may occur, *inter alia,* when a minority group feels that it has been subjected to discrimination at the hands of the State in which it lives or if it feels that it is better off having greater political power to control its own 'affairs' without interference from outsiders. Various other reasons are also advanced to justify these claims. A reason for the Sileseans' demand for autonomy, according to its proponents, is the rejection of their Silesian ethnic identity by the Polish political leaders. It is reported that the Polish Appeal Court has rejected the proposition that there is a separate Silesean ethnic community in Upper Silesia. The Silesians also believe that they have been the "butt of industrial exploitation and discrimination" ever since the region was absorbed by Poland due to its "Polonisation Policy".[11] Movements arising in such circumstances cannot easily be suppressed or ignored as was the case of South Tyrol in Italy and the violent political campaign of the separatist Sikhs in Punjab. For example, the Sikhs have been fighting for decades for greater autonomy for Punjab. Shiromani Akali Dal, the main political stream of the Sikh nationalism, in its Anandpur Sahib Resolution, 1973, declared its determination to achieve union State status for Punjab within a federation in which all States are equally represented at the centre" (Hannum, 1993:310-313). Paragraph 1 (b) says, "In this new Punjab, and other states the central intervention should be restricted to Defence, Foreign affairs, Post and Telegraphs, Currency and Railways. The rest of the departments should be under the direct control of Punjab". Akalis' main demands were centered around bread and butter issues such as control over river water, control of the capital city (Punjab), and agricultural subsidies (Kohli, 1997:335-338). This would be federal in the real sense although gradually that demand turned out to be for a separate 'Khalistan' due to mishandling by the Indian government of the Punjab issue (Morris-Jones, 1993:171; see also Singh, 1995:493; Nayer, 1989). The majority of Sikhs are of the view that they have been deprived of their political, economic and cultural rights due to the centralizing tendencies unleashed by the post-Nehruvian leadership (Brass, 1990 cited in Singh, 1995) and particularly by Indira's uncompromisingly tough regime (Kohli, 1997:335- 338).

Crimean Tartars in the Crimean Peninsula in Ukraine (see generally Mullerson, 1994:chapter 2), the Albanians in Macedonia,[12] Nepali speaking Gurkhas of West Bengal, Kachins, Chins, Shans, Mons in Myanmar (formally the Republic of Burma), the Muslims in Eastern province of Sri Lanka are some other known candidates for regional autonomy. The leader of the Tamils of Indian descent[13] in the hill country in Sri Lanka, Saumya Moorthy Thondaman, a parliamentarian, trade union leader and a cabinet minister during 1979-1999, had been for a considerable time campaigning for a regional assembly for 'hill country Tamils of Indian origin'. He openly said that he and his party were opposed to the break up of Sri Lanka. But his close association with the leader of the LTTE undermines his credibility. Bretons and Basques in France are also claiming regional autonomy within a federal structure (Claydon, 1975:28). The Basques[14] and Catalans fought the 'parasitic and moribund' Spanish regime until they secured extensive autonomous powers,[15] *estado autonomico* or *estado de las autonomias territoriale*,[16] respectively for the Basque country and Catalonia. Even during the 19th century, the Spanish authorities had employed various strategies to destroy the Catalan identity, mercantile law, legal system, and the use of the Catalan language. During the military regime of General Franco, the oppression of Catalans was intensified. Yet autonomy movements for Catalans could not be stopped (see Cobban, 1969:251). Their demand for regional autonomy was achieved in 1932, and later in 1978 the present autonomy status was granted. The Faeroe nationalist movements campaigned for centuries until they secured 'home rule', less than full independence, by the *Home Rule Act* of 1948.[17] The Kurds' struggle goes back centuries, yet there is no clear sign of political settlement or abeyance of their military campaign. The Jura movement campaigned for nearly 160 years until it succeeded in securing a separate Jura canton in 1979 within a federal structure of Switzerland.[18] The Marshall Islands composed of 34 atolls gained autonomous status in 1980 from the USA.[19] South Tyrol (Alto Adige) achieved regional autonomy "partly by terrorism and partly through willingness by the Italian government" (Palley, 1978:14; see further Alcock, 1970).[20] These cases strengthen the argument that when the bandwagon of autonomy movements begins to roll it cannot easily be stopped or suppressed either by democratic or military means. As Cobban correctly points out, ordinary rights containing village assemblies, local councils or limited cultural autonomy are not enough to appease such movements.

There are various other factors which contribute to the multiplication of claims for autonomy. States' failure to understand the aspirations of sub-groups, neglect of ethnic, religious and cultural differences, the organized politics of nationalism, undue dominance of majority over minorities and unequal distribution of national income are some of the main factors which exacerbate this process (Steiner, 1991:1541). There are many contemporary examples. Sudan's unequal and discriminatory treatment and alleged exploitation of natural resources such as oil and water in Southern Sudan is alleged to have led to the escalation of a claim for regional autonomy for Southern Sudan.[21] In justification of the struggles for autonomy, the Andalusians and the Galicians have alleged that their regions had been exploited by the Spanish imperialists for centuries as if they were 'African colonies' (Ben-Ami, 1981:80). The Punjabi Sikhs' struggle for autonomy is based, amongst other things, on the Indian Central government's alleged exploitation of the natural resources of Punjab. A similar allegation was leveled against Pakistan by its erstwhile wing, East Pakistan, before the latter successfully achieved separation from the former. This allegation was found to be proved by the investigation conducted by the International Commission of Jurists.[22] The Ogoni peoples living in the oil-rich Ogoniland of the Republic of Nigeria also make similar allegations against the republic of Nigeria.[23] The Movement for the Survival of the Ogoni people (MSOP) and its Campaign for Democracy's allegations are based on, *inter alia*, the exploitation of petroleum and gas by the Nigerian Government in Ogoniland with the complicity of the multinational petroleum companies (see generally Soyinka, 1996). It is reported that in 1994 alone $30 billion worth of oil was extracted from Ogoniland (see Skogly, 1997:49). Before the overthrow of the former President Mobutu's regime, Kasai and Shaba, southern provinces of Zaire, renewed their claims for autonomy against the Republic of Zaire alleging that the government had been exploiting its natural resources- copper and cobalt.[24]

6.3 *Self-government through Autonomy Depends on the Good Will of the Empowering State?*

Independent statehood via autonomy is not the only way by which minorities can achieve their aspirations (Rosenau, 1995:202). Various other political arrangements and policies which recognize and accommodate minorities' concerns and legitimate interests may serve the same purpose. However, greater autonomy, from minorities' perspective, provides an opportunity for minority groups to establish their own way of administration, political system and to enjoy a certain degree of independence within the modern nation-State system (Rosenau, 1995:202; see further Chandrahasan, 1993: 129-145). The transfer or delegation or decentralization of power from the center to the province at regional level offers an opportunity to a particular segment of a population or a region to participate in decision-making and implementation more effectively than a centralised system.

The granting of autonomy is also used by States as a means of hanging on to the *status quo* by preventing a discontented segment of their population from leaving them for good. The former USSR under Mikhail Gorbachev and the Russian Federation under Boris Yeltsin provide examples. When the signs of disintegration of the former USSR appeared, Gorbachev tried to keep regional provinces in a loose union promising them unprecedented autonomous powers. This strategy went wrong heralding the collapse of the Soviet Empire. Kux noted that the centrifugal force of ethnicity had played a pivotal role in destruction of the former USSR (Kux, 1996:325-358). Under the 'Lebed-Maskhadow' peace plan of 1996, Chechnya was cajoled into accepting greater autonomous status within a federal structure of the Russian Federation initially for five years; at the same time Chechnya and the Russian Federation committed themselves to reaching an agreement by 31 December 2001, *inter alia*, respecting the right of self-determination of Chechen ethnic groups and establishing "programs for the restoration of the socio-economic structure of the Chechen Republic".[25] Before launching a military attack in the summer of 1995, similar tactics were used by Croat politicians to keep minority Serbs living in Krajina within the Croatian Republic. Autonomous status for the Krajina province within the Croatian republic was offered in the Constitutional Act on *Human Rights and Freedoms of National and Ethnic Communities or Minorities in the Republic of Croatia*[26] because the Croatian army felt that it would not be able to defeat the local Serb separatists militarily. The Aceh region in Indonesia has been offered greater autonomy on a matter of local government and allocation of economic resources by the new Indonesian regime headed by President Abdurrahman Wahid in November 1999 to prevent the Aceh region breaking away from Indonesia (Sunday Business, 14 November 1999). The offer for greater autonomy in the form of union status within a federal structure for the north-east Tamils by the Sri Lankan government has also been branded by the LTTE as a 'political conspiracy'[27] to defeat the Tamil minority groups' claim for a separate State. Models of autonomy have so far successfully been used by Spain in the 1978 constitution principally to keep the Basques and Catalans within a 'half-way-federal' Spain (Solozabal, 1996:240) which according to some scholars is "probably one of the most successful innovations in recent times" (Eide, 1993:90-91; Hannum ed. 1993:144-145; Elazar, 1991: introduction).

Autonomous bodies can play a significant role in shaping and restructuring internal political and administrative mechanisms. However, autonomous regions in some federal States may be allowed to deal only with such limited areas as cultural and linguistic matters as in the case of linguistic communities in Belgium,[28] and also some present local arrangements implemented in Nordic countries in respect of indigenous peoples. In a few cases, autonomous regions are allowed to enjoy greater control over legislative, executive, political, administrative matters, social services, health and environmental matters, regional taxation, transport and education systems, local government etc (Hannum and Lillich, 1980:887). For example, Greenland was granted extensive powers by the *Greenland Home Rule Act*, 1978. It has power to levy taxes, enact rent legislation, deal with housing subsidies and housing administration, environment and protection, to maintain religious institutions, fishing, hunting, agriculture, reindeer-breeding, preservation of wild life, country planning, trade and monopolies legislation, social questions, labour market conditions.[29] The Faeroe Islands are another successful autonomous model enjoying great autonomous power. They have been granted powers over 'special Faeroes matters' in which the Faeroes Islands' Legislative Assembly have legislative, executive and administrative authority to deal with vast areas such as taxation including import duties, income tax through municipalities, power to introduce rules and regulations in respect of education, social and health affairs, matters relating to trade and land including hydroelectric production, control over living marine resources and sub-soil resources. It can determine the form of the national flag as well as taking decisions on matters relating to passports. Olafssson observes that the main characteristics are those of political and economic self-determination (Olafsson, 1995:467). The cantonal governments in Switzerland have since 1874 been very successful in the operation of power sharing at Cantonal level which has been structured by virtue of law and customs more in terms of linguistic differences than other characteristics of minority groups.[30] Hong Kong also seems to be enjoying greater legislative, executive and administrative powers seemingly without much interference from the mainland China. Its autonomy is guaranteed by the Joint Declaration of the Government of the United Kingdom of Great Britain and Northern Ireland and the Government of the Peoples' Republic of China.[31] The regional governments in Germany,[32] the provincial governments in Australia and the Republic of India[33] can also be seen as examples of regional governments that have been allowed to exercise greater political, legislative and economic power. They cannot theoretically speaking be identified as models of autonomy though their regions or provincial governments exercise greater autonomous power within a federal structure.

The authority and competence of the autonomous regions depend very much on the mutual understanding and constitutional arrangements between the center and the region. Yet the degree of autonomy concerning sensitive areas such as security and the economic and political sphere, apart from religious and cultural areas, often proves to be contentious. Most models of autonomy are not given authority to deal with monetary policy, issues of currency and coinage, international relations, national defence, customs, immigration policy, airports and other national ports, protection of national and external borders and frontiers.[34] Modern nation-States are particularly concerned about "matters of foreign affairs or defence" which should, in the view of many, be dealt with only by the central government.[35] In rare cases, autonomous regions are granted authority to deal with the international community in limited areas specifically identified by both the central government and the autonomous regions, i.e., in the areas of cultural and economic cooperation (Lapidoth, 1997:32-35). For instance, each Emirate in the UAE is allowed to keep membership in the OPEC. However, Emirates do not have competence to enter into international treaties as separate States (Hannum and Lillich, 1980:252). The Basque country[36] has been given power to control major ports which has became a controversial issue amongst Spaniards. Quebec in Canada,[37] the Flemish and Walloons in Belgium[38] are other examples of autonomous models which have been granted limited power to deal with the international community in cultural affairs.[39] The Archipelago of Azores and Medira are empowered by article 229 (1) (t) of the Constitution to engage in co-operation with other foreign regional entities and to strengthen their interrelationship with them in conformity with the foreign policy (Suksi, 1997:120). Article 28 of The Charter for the Kingdom of the Netherlands 1954[40] allows its autonomous regions, the Netherlands Antilles, to have international relations in limited areas. The new federal autonomous entities created by the General Agreement for Peace in Bosnia and Herzegovina in its constitution are allowed "to establish special parallel relationship with neighbouring states consist with the sovereignty and territorial integrity of Bosnia and Herzegovina".[41] It is worth mentioning that each of the eighteen 'semi-autonomous' regions in the Russian Federation was granted "the right to independently participate in foreign relations and foreign economic affairs, to govern itself based on its own constitution and to choose its own anthem, flag and state symbol" by President Boris Yeltsin in March 1992[42] by the Treaty of Federation and it was further elaborated in the 1993 Constitution of the Russian Federation.

Conclusion

The speed and the progress made by many movements for autonomy seems to have lost momentum as nation-States have demonstrated firmness in resisting them. Yet when a campaign for autonomy emerges with its cultural, religious, linguistic and ethnic baggage it is not easy to confine it within fixed boundaries, however much the international community may want to do so. Some movements may in the course of their struggles disappear after failing to achieve their objectives and to win strong international support. Others may achieve autonomy with self-rule and may be satisfied.

The form and nature of autonomous models depends on the circumstances in which they emerge. When they occur in a relatively homogeneous environment and without great acrimony, autonomous models will have a chance of success. However, when autonomous models are created in situations similar to that of Eritrea and Kosovo there is every possibility that they will eventually fail either moving towards secession or by collapsing completely.

Notes

[1] Tabajdi. C. (undated) *Current Questions of International Minority Protection at the End of 1994* cited in Thornberry, P. (1989), 'Images of Autonomy and Individual and Collective Rights in International Instruments on the Rights of Minorities', in M. Suksi (ed), *Autonomy, Applications and Implications*, Kluwer Law International: The Hague/London/Boston, p. 97.

[2] See Http://www.int-crisisgroup.org/projects/balkans/reports/kos09. Robinson, A. 'Kosovo Violence Starts Alarm Bells Ringing', *The Financial Times*, 4 March 1998, See also Dinmore, G. 'Ethnic Albanians Bury Massacre Victims', *Financial Times*, 4 March 1998.

[3] *Prosecutor* v *Dusko Tadic* a/k/a "Dule", case no. IT-94-I-T, 7 May 1997, 4 *IHRR* 1997, p. 667.

[4] *Ibid.* p. 668.

[5] Hope, K. 'The Albanian Minority: Barometer of Ethnic Tension', *Financial Times*, 15 November 1996.

[6] Anonymous author, 'Poland: Not So Pure', *The Economist*, 29 November- 5 December 1997, p. 52. The Upper Silesian issue goes back to the 1930s when Silesean nationalism was not so developed in the province. See Cobban, A. (1969), *The Nation State and National Self-Determination*, TY Crowell: New York, p. 256.

[7] It is now admitted that 'elements of federalism' can be discerned in the powers of organs of the EU. See Jennings, R. Y. and Watts, A. eds. (1992), *Oppenheim's International Law, Peace*, Vol. 1, 9th ed Longman: Essex, p. 249. Laws, regulations and directives issued by the EU are binding over both States and citizens living in the member States. It is apparent that the European Union (formerly EEC) is transforming itself from a confederated State (Staatenbund) to a loose federation (Bundesstaat). It, however, still contains some elements of confederated system too, the characteristics of which was described by Oppenheim as follows: "Confederated States (Staatenbund) are a number of full sovereign States linked together for the maintenance of their external and internal independence by a treaty into a union with organs of its own, which are vested with a certain power over the member States, but not over the citizens of these States. Such a union of confederated States is no more itself a State than a real union is; it is merely an International Confederation of States, a society of an international character, since the member Sates remain full sovereign States and separate international persons", *ibid.* para. 74, pp. 246-247.

[8] Croatia, Slovenia and Bosnia-Herzegovina were federal Republics within the former Yugoslav Federation, having a greater autonomous power than 'socialist autonomous regions' such as Kosovo and Vojvodina. Lyttle, P. F. (1995), 'Electoral Transitions in Yugoslavia', in Y. Shain and J. J. Linz (eds), *Between States*, Cambridge UP: Cambridge, p. 253. See further Varady, T. (1997), 'Minorities, Majorities, Law and Ethnicity: Reflections of the Yugoslav Case', 19 *HRQ*, p. 49.

[9] Wrong, M. 'Sudan's Rebels Demand Plebiscite', *Financial Times*, 6 November 1997.

[10] Anonymous author, 'Them and Us', *The Economist*, 17 August 1996, p. 68. See also Visek, R. C. (1997), 'Creating the Ethnic Electorate Through Legal Restorationism: Citizenship Rights in Estonia', 38 *HRLJ*, p. 371.

[11] Anonymous Author, 'Poland : Not So Pure', *The Economist*, 29 November- 5 December 1997, p. 52.

[12] Albanians living in Macedonia and Kosovo are separated only by mountains. Often they operate as one unit or have close cooperation with each other in their struggle for independence. See Pettifer, J., 'Encircling Wolves Awaits Their Chance', *The Times*, 9 March 1998.

[13] The Indian Tamils should not be identified with indigenous Tamils living in Northern and Eastern parts of Sri Lanka. British planters brought them to Ceylon during the 19th and early 20th centuries as indentured labourers.

[14] See Ben-Ami, S. (1981), 'The Catalan and Basque Movements for Autonomy', in Y. Dinstein (ed), *Models of Autonomy*, Transaction Books: New Brunswick and

London, pp. 67-84. See also Schreuer, C. (1981), 'Autonomy in South Tyrol', in Dinstein (ed), *ibid.* p. 54.

[15] The most recent amendments to these two autonomous regions were established by the Autonomy Statutes for the Basque Region and Catalonia by Royal Decree-Law, on 13 and 14 September 1979. See Sohn, L. B. (1980), 'The Concept of Autonomy in International Law and the Practice of the United Nations', 15 *ILR*, footnote 11, p. 182. The Basques, Catalans, Galicians and Andalusians have been recognized by the 1978 Spanish constitution as 'historical communities', see UN Doc. E/CN.4/Sub.2/1993/34, *Possible Ways and Means of Facilitating the Peaceful Solution of Problems Solving Minorities*, para. 268, p. 58 (*Possible Ways and Means*, 1993).

[16] The Spanish Constitution 1978, which provides for autonomous regions for some ethnic groups, does not use the term 'estado autonomico', which is said to be popularized by politicians. 'Autonomous communities' is the chosen term in the Constitution. See details Solozabal, J. J. (1996), 'Spain: A Federation in the Making', in J. J. Hesse, and V. Wright (eds), *Federalizing Europe? The Costs, Benefits and Preconditions of Federal Political System*, Oxford UP: Oxford. See for example Articles 137 and 143 of the Constitution and Article 1 of the Statute of Autonomy of the Basque Country, Organic Law 3/1979 of 18 December 1979, for details see Hannum, H. ed. (1993), *Documents on Autonomy and Minority Rights*, Martinus Nijhoff: Dordrecht/Boston/London, p. 156. The Spanish constitution has introduced 17 autonomous self-governing communities. Among them are Catalonia, Galicia, the Basque country, the Valencian community and the Balearic Islands. Article 2 promulgates: 'The constitution is based on the indissoluble unity of the Spanish nation, the common and indivisible country of all Spaniards; it recognizes and guarantees the right to autonomy by the nationalities and regions of which it is composed and solidarity among them all", *Possible Ways and Means, 1993*, as above, paras. 256-267, p.58.

[17] The Faeroe Islands have since 1852 had limited self-government with which the islanders were not satisfied. The Home Rule Act 1948 introduced home rule for Faeroe islanders in recognition of their claims.

[18] The Jura Canton became the 23rd member of the Swiss Federation, see Elazar, D. J. ed. (1991), *Federal Systems of the World: A Handbook of Federal, Confederal and Autonomy Arrangements*, Longman Group: Essex, p. 256. See also Thurer, D. (1996), 'Switzerland: The Model in Need of Adaptation'? in Hesse, and Wright (eds), as above, pp. 219-239.

[19] *N.Y. Times*, 15 January 1980, cited in Hannum, H. and Lillich, R. (1981), 'The Concept of Autonomy in International Law', 74 *AJIL*, p. 858.

[20] The Paris Agreement of 5 September 1946 between Austria and Italy introduced limited authority to South Tyrol/Alto Adige. Article 2 states, "The populations of the above- mentioned zones will be granted the exercise of autonomous legislative and executive regional power." This is implemented by the first Autonomy Statute of 1948, the text of which is printed in the Constitutional Statute of 26 February 1948, Official Gazette, 13 March 1948. A comprehensive autonomous 'package' was not agreed until 1972. The new Autonomy Statute came into force in 1972 by

the Decree of the President of the Republic on 31 August 1972. This is published in the Official Gazette, Raccolta Ufficiale delle Leggi, 3136, 20 November 1972, no. 301, p. 57. Italy has now 20 autonomous territorial units in its territory. For further details, Hannum, H. (1990), *Autonomy, Sovereignty, and Self-Determination: The Accommodation of Conflicting Rights*, University of Pennsylvania: Philadelphia, pp. 432-440. See further Lapidoth, R (1997), *Autonomy: Flexible Solutions to Ethnic Conflicts*, United States of Peace Press: Washington, DC, pp. 100-112.

[21] The Sudanese government refutes these allegations. For details see A/C.3/50/SR.8/30 October 1995, para. 14, p. 5.

[22] See The Secretariat of the International Commission of Jurists (1972), *The Events in East Pakistan*, H. Studer: Geneva.

[23] There are, according to some independent reports, about half a million Ogoni people in Ogoniland which is located in River State in the Niger Delta covering 400 square miles. Due to civil unrest and oppression by the Nigerian government, many intellectuals such as lawyers, doctors, teachers, and many other professionals have already left the Ogoni region. *The Times*, 30 March 1996. See further Skogly, S. I. (1997), 'Complexities in Human Rights Protection: Actors and Rights Involved in the Ogoni Conflict in Nigeria', 15 *NQHR*, p. 48. See also Birnbaum, M. (1995), *Nigeria: Fundamental Rights Denied, Report of the Trial of Ken Saro-Wiwa and Others*, published by Article 19 in association with the Law Society of England and Wales, cited in Skogly, *ibid.* p. 48.

[24] *The Economist*, 23 November 1996.

[25] See *Lebed-Maskhadow Joint Declaration and Principles for Mutual Relations* 17 *HRLJ* 1995 pp. 240-241. This document is very vague and does not guarantee independent statehood for Chechnya by the year 2001. This position has now dramatically changed due to a resumption of war between Chechnya and Russian Federation in October 1999. The Russian Federation insisted that any solution to the current conflicts could be found only after receiving a guarantee from Chechnya that it would remain as a province within the Russian Federation.

[26] Published in Narodne Novine, 34/1992, for details see Varady, T. (1997), 'Minorities, Majorities, Law and Ethnicity: Reflections of the Yugoslav Case', 19 (1) *HRQ*, p. 36.

[27] BBC2, 15 November 1997. See also *Sri Lankan Monitor*, No. 118, November 1997, p.1.

[28] In Belgium, the regionalist autonomous movement was launched first by the Dutch speaking Protestant Flemish movement. At the beginning their demands were centered on 'linguistic equality' and then on 'cultural autonomy'. Later their demands spread to wider areas as well. Now Belgium is divided into three linguistic communities, and four regions. See respectively Cobban, A. (1969), *The Nation State and National Self-Determination*, TY Crowell: New York, pp. 253-254; Hannum, H. ed. (1993) *Documents on Autonomy and Minority Rights*, Martinus Nijhoff: Dordrecht/Boston/London, p. 180.

[29] Greenland Home Rule Act, Act no. 577 of 29 November 1978. It operates within a unitary State. See Article 1 of the Danish constitution. See the full text in Hannum (ed), *Documents on Autonomy,* as above, pp. 213-18. However, Greenland Home Rule does not confer 'unlimited power' to Greenland. Denmark keeps autonomous powers of Greenland under its supervision. It is only a qualified one. For example, defence, treaty-making powers and foreign relations are excluded from the Greenlandic authorities. See Lyck, L. (1995), 'Lessons to be Learned on Autonomy and on Human Rights From the Faeroes Situation Since 1992', *Nord. J.Int.L,* p. 482. See further Foighel, I. (1981), 'A Framework for Local Autonomy: The Greenland Case', in Y. Dinstein (ed), *Models of Autonomy,* Transaction Books: New Brunswick/ London, pp. 36-37.

[30] It should be noted that Switzerland is in-between confederation and federation rather than a union of autonomous regions. See Sigler, J. A. (1983), *Minority Rights: A Comparative Analysis,* Greenwood Press: Westport/Connecticut/ London, p.181.

[31] On the Question of Hong Kong signed on 19 December 1984 and the Basic Law of the Hong Kong Special Administrative Region of the Peoples' Republic of China, Decree no. 26 adopted on 4 April 1990. See the full text in Hannum (ed), *Documents on Autonomy* (1993: 220-272), as above.

[32] Regional governments (Lander) have greater access to EU institutions. The German constitution does not identify Lander, the regional governments, as autonomous units. See Schreuer, C. (1993), 'The Waning of the Sovereign State: Towards a New Paradigm for International Law?", 4 *EJIL,* p. 462. It is also worthy of note that Germany, Australia and the USA do not mention their federal regions as autonomous regions. However, some cultural and religious differences to a greater extent are instrumental in the German model. See further *Possible Ways and Means, 1993,* as above, para. 255, p. 5.

[33] As stated by Atul Kohli, the Republic of India also experimented autonomous models in creating provincial governments using linguistic differences particularly since 1956. See Kohli, A. (1997), 'Can Democracies Accommodate Ethnic Nationalism? Rise and Decline of Self-Determination Movement in India', 56 *JAS,* pp. 334-35. India, has however, neglected ethnic demand to a greater extent structuring their provincial governments alone the line of linguistic differences. The exception also can be seen. Autonomous status for the Punjab province has been based most importantly on Sikh ethnic identity. Some of the Republics in India are not satisfied with the existing political arrangements, most notably, Tamil politicians in the Tamil Nadu province. The leader of the Dravida Munnetra Kalazagham complained that "in Tamil Nadu we had no industry at all and all the powers were concentrated in the north. Even if we wanted to cut the grass in front of the governor's house, we had to seek permission from the federal government". See Goldenberg, S. *The Guardian,* 17 April 1996. Kohli referring to Tamil Nadu states that after achieving regional autonomy at union state level within the Indian Federation, Tamil nationalism lost its steam and settled down to 'realpolitik'. Kohli, *ibid.* pp. 334-35.

[34] See Annex to the New Autonomy Statute 1972 (South Tyrol); Article 149 of the Constitution of Spain 1978 (Basque country); Ninth Schedule, List I to the Constitution of Sri Lanka 1978 (as amended by 1987). See further Hannum, H. and Lillich, R. (1981), 'The Concept of Autonomy in International Law', in Dinstein (ed.), *Models of Autonomy*, as above, footnote. 8, p. 216

[35] See His Serene Highness Prince Hans-Adam II of Liechtenstein's statement to the UN General Assembly, A/48/PV. 36, 11 November 1993, pp. 1-5.

[36] See Official Records of the Human Rights Committee, 1990/91, CCPR/10, CCPR/C/51/ Add. 1 and CCPR/C/64/Add. 1, para. 120, p. 80.

[37] See for example Agreement on Acid Precipitation Between Quebec and the State of New York, 26 July 1982, cited in Schreuer, C. (1993), 'The Waning of the Sovereign State: Towards a New Paradigm for International Law', 4 (4) *EJIL*, p. 450.

[38] The Constitutional amendments of 1998 empowered the regions to enter into international agreements with foreign States in limited areas such as cultural exchanges without prior agreement of the central government, see Hannum, *Autonomy and Sovereignty* (1990: 411), as above.

[39] It should however be noted that the power of sub-state entities in respect of foreign relations is limited to matters assigned to them and is subject to strict federal control. See Schreuer (1993: 450) as above.

[40] Full text in Hannum (ed), *Documents on Autonomy,* pp. 353-369, as above.

[41] Article 2 of the Constitution of Bosnia and Herzegovina, reprinted in 35 *ILM* 118 [1996], p.120. See the full text of the Constitution, pp.118-125. This constitution and other related documents and Annexes are popularly known as 'Dayton Agreement', which was signed on 14 December 1995 at Paris.

[42] Washington Post, 1 April 1992, cited in Moynihan, D. P. (1994), *Pandaemonium: Ethnicity in International Politics*, Oxford UP: Oxford, p. 71.

References

Alcock, A. E. (1970), *The History of the South Tyrol Question*, Joseph: London.

Bakker, E. (1998), 'Growing Isolation: Political and Ethnic Tensions in the Slovak Republic', 9 *Helsinki Monitor*, pp. 28- 29.

Ben-Ami, S. (1981), 'The Catalan and Basque Movements for Autonomy', in Y. Dinstein (ed), *Models of Autonomy*, Transaction Books: New Brunswick and London, pp. 67-84.

Brass, P. (1990), *The Politics of India Since Independence*, Cambridge University Press: Cambridge.

Bugaijski, J. (1995), *Nations in Turmoil: Conflict and Coorperation in Eastern Europe*, 2nd ed. Westview Press: Boulder/Colo.

Chandrahasan, N. (1993), 'Minorities, Autonomy, and the Intervention of Third States: A droit de Regard', 23 *IYHR*, pp. 129- 145.

Claydon, J. (1975), 'The Transnational Protection of Ethnic Minorities: A Tentative Framework for Inquiry', 13 *CYIL*, pp. 25-60.

Cobban, A. (1969), *The Nation State and National Self-Determination*, TY Crowell: New York.

Dugard, J. (1997), 'International Law and the South African Constitution', 8 (1) *EJIL*, pp. 77-92.

Eide, A. (1993), 'Approaches to Minority Protection', in A. Phillips and A. Rosas (eds), *The UN Minority Rights Declaration*, Turku/Abo: London, pp. 81- 93.

Elazar, D. J. ed. (1991), *Federal Systems of the World: A Handbook of Federal, Confederal and Autonomy Arrangements*, Longman Group: Essex.

Gunasekara, S. L. (1996), *Tigers, Moderates and Pandora's Package*, Multi Packs (Ceylon) Ltd: Colombo.

Hannum, H. and Lillich, R. B. (1980), 'The Concept of Autonomy in International Law', 74 *AJIL*, pp. 858-889.

Hannum, H. (1989), 'The Limits of Sovereignty and Minority Rights: Minorities, Indigenous Peoples and the Right to Autonomy', in E. L. Lutz, H. Hannum, and K. J. Burkes (eds), *New Directions in Human Rights*, University of Pennsylvania Press: Philadelphia, pp. 3- 24.

Hannum, H. (1990), *Autonomy, Sovereignty, and Self-Determination: The Accommodation of Conflicting Rights*, University of Pennsylvania Press: Philadelphia.

Hannum, H. (1993), *Documents on Autonomy and Minority Rights*, Martinus Nijhoff: Dordrecht/Boston/London.

Horowitz, D. L. (1985), *Ethnic Groups in Conflict*, University of California Press: Berkeley.

Jungwiert, K. and Nowicki, M. A. (1994), 'Report on the Legislation of the Republic of Moldava', 5 *HRLJ*, pp. 383-394.

Kohli, A. (1997), 'Can Democracies Accommodate Ethnic Nationalism? Rise and Declines of Self-Determination Movements in India', 56 (2) *JAS*, pp. 325- 344.

Kux, S. (1996), 'From the USSR to the Commonwealth of Independent States: Confederation or Civilized Divorce?', in J. J. Hesse, and V. Wright (eds), *Federalizing Europe* ?, Oxford UP: Oxford, pp. 325-358.

Kymlicka, W. (1995), *Multicultural Citizenship: A Liberal Theory of Minority Rights*, Clarendon Press: Oxford.

Lapidoth, R. (1997), *Autonomy, Flexible Solutions to Ethnic Conflicts*, United States of Peace Press: Washington, DC.

Morris-Jones, W. H. (1993), 'South Asia', in R. H. Jackson and A. James (eds), *States in a Changing World*, Clarendon Press Oxford, pp. 157- 176.

Mullerson, R. (1994), *International Law, Rights and Policies: Developments in Eastern Europe and the CIS*, Routledge: London/New York.

Nayer, B. R. (1989), *Minority Politics in Punjab*, Princeton University Press: Princeton, NJ.

Olafsson, A. (1995), 'Relationship Between Political and Economic Self-Determination: The Faeroes Case', 64 (3) *Nord. J.Intl. L*, pp. 465-480.

Palley, C. (1978), *Constitutional Law and Minorities*, Report no. 36, Minority Rights Group London.

Phillips, D. L. (1996), 'Comprehensive Peace in the Balkans: The Kosovo Question', 18 *HRQ*, pp. 821-832.

Rosenau, J. N. (1995), 'Sovereignty in a Turbulent World', in G. M. Lyons and M. Mastanduno (eds), *Beyond Westphalia? State Sovereignty and International Law*, The John Hopkins UP: Baltimore and London, pp. 191- 227.

Schreuer, C. (1981), 'Autonomy in South Tyrol', in Dinstein (ed), as above, pp. 53-65.

Singh, G. (1995), 'The Punjab Crisis Since 1984: A Reassessment', 18 *Ethnic and Racial Studies*, pp. 466-493.

Skogly, S. I. (1997), 'Complexities in Human Rights Protection: Actors and Rights Involved in the Ogoni Conflict in Nigeria', 15 *NQHR*, pp. 47-60.

Solozabal, J. J. (1996), 'Spain: A Federation in the Making?', in J. J. Hesse and V. Wright (eds), *Federailizing Europe? The Costs, Benefits and Preconditions of Federal Political System*, Oxford UP: Oxford, pp. 240- 265.

Soyinka, W. (1996), *The Open Sore of a Continent*, Oxford University Press: Oxford.

Steiner, H. J. (1991), 'Ideals and Counter Ideals in the Struggle Over Autonomy Regimes For Minorities', 66 *Notre Dame LR*, pp. 1539-1559.

Suksi, M. (1997), 'The Constitutional Setting of the Aaland Islands Compared', in L. Hannikainen and F. Horn (eds), *Autonomy and Demilitarisation in International Law: The Aaland Islands in a Changing Europe*, Kluwer Law International: The Hague/London/Boston, pp. 99- 129.

Thornberry, P. (1989), 'Images of Autonomy and Individual and Collective Rights in International Instruments on the Rights of Minorities', in M. Suksi (ed), *Autonomy, Applications and Implications*, Kluwer Law International: The Hague/London/Boston, pp. 97-123.

Visek, R. V. (1997), 'Creating the Ethnic Electorate Through Legal Restorationism: Citizenship Rights in Estonia', 38 (2) *HRLJ*, pp. 315-373.

7 Claims for Autonomy:
The Concerns of States

Introduction

"The international community is composed primarily of States. Any changes in the composition of the international community are of immediate concern to existing States." (Oppenheim, 9th ed. 128). States' practice in respect of any structural changes to States will have a greater impact on other international corporate bodies such as the UN, EU, OAU, OAS, and the like. The decisions taken or opinions expressed by the delegates of States at national and international level shape the norms of international relations. Thus State practice may gradually emerge as coherent principles which may in the end get recognition as norms of international law. Therefore, it is appropriate to examine what State practice is in respect of claims for autonomy by minority groups and to examine whether there is a possibility that autonomy may get recognised as a principle of international law.

Generally, States mistrust minorities. In particular, loyalty has been the focus of criticism by many. There has been, however, a positive development in minority rights in recent times. Some States appear to be prepared to take positive measures to address the concerns of minority groups, in particular on issues relating to language, culture, and religion. Yet, they are, it seems, reluctant to grant political power to minority groups by allowing them to control the regions in which they live. Such initiatives are considered as the creation of rival power bases. The common position seemed to be, "if you give them an inch (or centimeter), they will want a yard (or meter)" (Thornberry, 1997:326). The right to autonomy is therefore considered as something having the potential to destroy territorial integrity and the sovereignty of nation-States. These concerns of the nation-State are examined in this chapter by analysing State practice (selected samples) in the international arena.

7.1 *Autonomy for Minorities: "An Entrance on a Dangerous Path Leading Towards Secession"?*

Claims for autonomy by minority groups raise strong objections from many quarters. There are many reasons for States to be worried about such claims. The consequences of claims for autonomy associated with ethnicity are unpredictable. Greater autonomy for regions in terms of ethnic identity is therefore not universally welcome. Referring to the liberal campaign for regional autonomy for the Yanomami Reserve in Brazil, another prominent politician in Brazil, the Governor of the province, tried to justify such historical fears suggesting that:

> There are ideological problems. There is nothing to stop those who today defend the preservation of Indians like creatures in a Zoo from one day trying to declare an independent Yanomami State in this land of great mineral riches. As Brazilians, we cannot accept this calmly.[1]

Senegal also has a similar opinion about claims of its minority groups for autonomy in Casamance, which the Senegal government identifies as a "secession that must be stopped".[2] The Macedonians are furious about the Albanian minorities' claims for greater autonomy in the Western part of Macedonia. The Macedonian Albanians' struggle for autonomy has not been confined only to political campaigns. Violent clashes between the Macedonian majority community, the Slavs, and the Albanian minority group have already occurred several times. The Western part of Macedonia has already become Macedonia's barometer of inter-ethnic tension. Albanians are threatening that unless their demands for greater autonomy are met to their satisfaction they will "follow the example of Albanians in Kosovo and opt out of Macedonian society altogether".[3]

Moreover, campaigns for autonomy may often lead to violence, destruction, loss of human lives and public property (Mullerson, 1994:60). It is not therefore surprising that autonomy is considered one of the most "dreaded expressions".[4] For example, prior to the creation of Eritrean autonomy province by the Federal Act, 1952, some Ethiopians expressed their anger alleging that it might harm the sovereignty of Ethiopia,[5] and they saw campaigners for autonomy as 'traitors'. Others see 'ethnic autonomy' as a tragedy which could only contribute to the disintegration of the sovereignty of nation-States and the escalation of violence, or - as an Unofficial Commission appointed to inquire into the grievances of the Sinhalese in Sri Lanka found in its interim report - "impractical internal agreement" which would in turn result in the conflict scenario engulfing everyone.[6] Many Italian speaking people who became a minority in the South Tyrol autonomous region feel the same. They are so frustrated that many are now supporting *Movimento Sociale Italiano* (MSI), an Italian Fascist party, and some are leaving the province for good (Lapidoth, 1997:111). Most States are of the view that autonomy might be a first step towards secession (Mullerson, 1994:59), or "an entrance on a dangerous path leading towards the State's dismemberment through external self-determination" (see Steiner, 1991:1558). The political wing of the ETA, Herris Batasuna emphatically demonstrated this, when it decided to accept autonomy for the Basque country in 1979. Issuing a statement to its supporters, *Harris Batasuna* assured them, "autonomy should be embraced and shrewdly used as a first step towards full self-determination and eventual secession from Spain" (Ben-Ami, 1981:83). A similar strategy has being considered by the moderate separatist Kosovar leaders who sought to negotiate autonomy with the Serbs and the Six Nations Contact Group at Rambouillet in 1999. They appeared to be willing to accept autonomy initially for three years, then wanted a referendum to consult the Albanian Kosovars about the status of future Kosovo.[7] Such ambitions would undermine the sovereignty of the State, the scenario that most States want to avoid (see McGoldrick, 1991:257). Apparently influenced by these experiences Kenya argued that the purpose of claims for autonomy by minority groups is to "take control of natural resources for the exclusive use of their community to the detriment of others".[8] The claims for regional autonomy made by separatist groups are seen therefore as a danger to the existence of the nation-State (see Claydon, 1975:39; Symonides, 1991:110). Numerous examples abound. When Southern Sudan was granted regional autonomy in 1972 by the *Southern Provinces Regional Self-Government Act, 1972,*[9] it was alleged that new autonomous status had been used by the Southern Sudanese separatists as a pretext for accelerating their guerrilla activities against the central government - thus putting the whole idea of regional autonomy in jeopardy. In the Kosovo dispute, it was alleged by the Serbian authorities that the autonomous status of Kosovo had been used by Kosovar Albanians "to cleanse the region of non-Albanians. This was to be their first step towards secession" (see Paunovic, 1993). The Serbian President Slobodan Milosevic continually maintains this position alleging that the main aim of Kosovar Albanians "is the disintegration of Serbia and merging that part of the country with Albania" (Phillips, 1996:825). It is also said that the behaviour of the Albanian ethnic group since the 1980s has contributed to a deterioration of the relationship between the Serbs and the Albanians. 'Kosovo is for Albanians', and 'Kosovo - Republika' have been some of the popular slogans used during this period by the Kosovar Albanians. Non-Albanians were alleged to have been intimidated, terrorized and subjected to systematic pressure for decades, which subsequently resulted in the decrease of non-Albanians in 1945 from 30% to 10% in 1990s. This situation, as Paunovic described, created a State within a State, or the possibility of having two Albanian States in Europe, which from the standpoint of non-Albanians, was indeed a dangerous scenario (Paunovic, 1993:145-165; see further Irwin, 1984:72-105). The Serbian authorities are adamant. "If we loose Kosovo, we'll lose Serbia, the Federal Republic of Yugoslavia and our freedom, which should be sacred to us".[10]

States are aware of many other instances where greater autonomous regions in the form of union States or republics in federal structures have been used by minority groups to set the scene for the next stage, independence. It is evident that Croatia and Slovenia[11] succeeded in becoming independent States because their republic status with greater autonomous power helped them in strengthening their power bases against the Serb dominated Yugoslavian military regime, JNA (Lyttle, 1995:253).[12] Yet, the model of Eritrean autonomy provided the more convincing example. Prior to their experience in autonomy, it was said that many Eritreans were not even organized as a strong ethno-political group. As Erlich put it "an Eritrean nationalist movement was non-existent" (Erlich, 1981:173). Nonetheless, since the failure of autonomy in Eritrea, the Eritreans have not only organized as a distinct nation, but they have also been able to establish an independent State.

Mullerson's analysis of the break-up of the former Soviet Union also supports such a fear. Referring to the autonomous provinces of the former Soviet Union, he argues that the break-up of the Soviet Empire accelerated because some autonomous Republics which enjoyed union/ republic status (SSR) were able to secede easily due to their extensive autonomous political power helping them build up a strong power base. When it was apparent that the Soviet Union was on the verge of disintegration, it was not difficult for the provincial union republics to declare independence without facing any significant military action from the Kremlin. For example, Ukraine, Georgia and Byelorussia did not encounter any significant objection from the Kremlin power base. Yet Karelia and Abkhazia[13] did not achieve independence because they had not previously enjoyed greater political power through autonomy unlike Ukraine or Georgia. From 1940 to 1956 Karelia was a constituent autonomous republic of the former Soviet Union. It enjoyed the status of 'Union Republic', but later, in 1956, its political power was reduced by demoting to an autonomous republic with less political power. Abkhazia suffered a similar fate. This has weakened their position in the course of time (see Tskhovrebov, 1995:513). Therefore, both Karelia and Abkhazia did not have an opportunity to strengthen their political and military power bases.

Similarly, when the Republic of Sri Lanka established the Northern Eastern Provincial Assembly with unprecedented powers of autonomy including executive and legislative powers in pursuance of the *Indo-Sri Lanka Accord*, July 29, 1987 the Eelam Peoples' Revolutionary Liberation Front (EPRLF), the elected Tamil militant political party of the Northern and Eastern provinces declared an independent Tamil Eelam in 1990, a few months after its election victory, confirming many doubters' view that minorities are dangerous and may, sometimes, not be trustworthy. This may have a morsel of truth given the destructive tendencies of militant minority groups against States and public property.[14] LTTE's bombing of the Central Bank of Sri Lanka, major oil refineries in Colombo, the World Trade Center in Colombo respectively in 1995, 1996 and 1997, the IRA's bombing of Canary Wharf main buildings in 1996, the Serb minority military junta's virulent and destructive campaign against Muslims in Bosnia-Herzegovina in 1993-95 are telling examples.

7.2 *Claims for Autonomy: Endless Process?*

Moreover, claims for autonomy may be an endless process. Autonomy movements, both democratic and militant, in Assam (in the northeastern part of India/ *Bharat*[15]) provide a classic case in point. First it was granted the status of 'union state' in recognition of its distinct geographical, historical and demographic identity. Assam is an ethnic mosaic containing a myriad of ethnic and tribal groups, each with its own distinct identity going back centuries. In the 1960s, Nagas, Mizories and many other ethnic groups intensified their campaigns, initially for greater autonomy within the State of Assam. Later, however, these demands developed into a separate 'union state-status' within the federation of the Republic of India. The Nagas gained the status of 'union state' status for 'Nagaland', carved out of Assam in 1963. Meghalaya was granted autonomous region status (sub-state) within Assam, and later in 1971 it graduated to the status of union state. The new Meghalaya was also carved out of Assam.

The process does not stop here. Candidates for greater autonomy have mushroomed. Assamese-speaking people living in the Brahmaputra valley also began to campaign for greater autonomous power, in particular, in economic matters. Outsiders, in particular the Bengali Hindus and Muslim migrants became a target as they were seen to obstruct the development of the native Assamese. These political demands terrified the indigenous tribal group, Bodo/ Bodo Kochari, who began to worry about these new developments, particularly about the possibility of their being marginalised due to the increased political and economic power of the Assamese (see Dasgupta, 1997:345-370).[16] The Bodos then began their campaign for *Udayachat* (Bodoland) with greater autonomy, ironically this time with the tacit encouragement of the federal government in New Delhi. Both the political and military campaigns for *Udayachat* increased. Their struggle was met with brutality at the hand of the authorities in Assam, the Assamese speaking Hindus who were, however, unable to suppress Bodo nationalism or their campaign for greater autonomy over their traditional lands and natural resources. Later, the parties came to a compromise. In 1993, the Bodos were given a 'Bodoland Autonomous Council', this time within the State of Assam. The Assamese government's reluctance to implement this new model of autonomy has given rise to a violent campaign with the emergence of Bodoland Liberation Tigers, a separatist movement composed of radical and militant young Bodos. The struggle has been going on ever since (Dasgupta, 1997; see further Prasad, 1994; Pakem, 1993; Chatterjee, 1993). This tendency is very much alive in Sri Lanka. Initially in the 1950s it was the Tamil politicians who demanded greater autonomy for the Northern and Eastern provinces in the island. Later, in the 1990s Muslim minority groups also began to present their claims for autonomy. Now, a leader of one of the factions Mr. Ashrop, who is also a Cabinet Minister in the present Peoples' Alliance (PA), demands that any constitutional amendment should provide for an autonomous region for the Muslims living in the Eastern part of the island. Not surprisingly, the Indian Tamils have also presented their claims for a Tamil Autonomous region in the hill country in which they are principally concentrated. These are only a few examples. A more or less similar process is developing in many parts of the world.

7.3 *Attitudes of the States: "Technically Difficult or Politically Sensitive or Both"*

A system of power-sharing within an existing State structure on a basis of race, ethnicity, religious or cultural differences is not a right guaranteed by general international law. However, it is worthy of note that international law is not generally concerned with the domestic constitutional arrangements which involve decentralization of power from the center to the periphery, perhaps involving minority groups (Hutchins, Hilling and Schulze, 1995:267). The uncertainty of international law on the principle of autonomy is quite well known even though now it has been suggested that autonomy may be used "only in exceptional cases" by way of federal arrangements involving devolution or decentralization of power.[17]

There is now increasing evidence to suggest that autonomous arrangements or federal solutions are encouraged in the form of decentralization of power to regions as a solution to ethnic conflicts as in the case of Bosnia and Herzegovina, Sri Lanka, and Kosovo. Bosnia and Herzegovina was restructured along the lines of ethnicity and religious affiliation by the Dayton Peace Accord.[18] An enormous amount of pressure, the stick and carrot strategy had been applied on the Muslims, Croats and Serbs to accept autonomy as a solution to their problems within a federal structure. Eritrean autonomy within Ethiopia in 1952, the Memel Territory under the sovereignty of Lithuania in 1924, the Aaland Islands in 1921 are other famous examples of federal solutions to ethnic problems which the UN and its predecessors, the League of Nations, experimented with. The Paris Aid Group, the EU, the Nordic countries and the UN have also been applying pressure on the Republic of Sri Lanka to find a solution to Tamils' demands within a federation according them greater autonomy. Current pressure on both Kosovar Albanians and the Serbs in Kosovo by the UN to come to an agreement on autonomous rule for Kosovo is a telling indication that the international community is gradually coming to terms with minorities' claims for autonomy.

Minorities' claims to personal or cultural autonomy do not attract many objections from the nation-States, in contrast to claims for territorial autonomy. Personal autonomy of minority groups, for example, the right to establish schools, practise their religion and cultures, and to exercise limited economic rights are not generally disputed by nation-States.

However, the reaction to greater political power in terms of territorial autonomy is quite different. The response of the international community was exhibited at the debate on the proposal on autonomy put forward by Liechtenstein[19] in the UN General Assembly. It proposed that *communities having a distinctive social and territorial identity* should be able to enjoy autonomy to realize the right of self-determination over their affairs. It is their inherent and inalienable right, it argued further, to decide their political system in the way they like. The proposal went further, suggesting that in suitable cases those communities "having distinctive social and territorial identity" should be allowed to evolve as independent States.[20] Liechtenstein argued:[21]

> The concept of self-determination, namely, the attainment of independence by peoples under colonial domination, has virtually been completed. Since then, the concept of self-determination has evolved, with minorities seeking greater autonomy within the nation State in which they resided. Many conflicts occurred because there were no channels in the parent State through which minorities could assert their distinctive identities. Often, they saw secession as the only solution, even though the parent State was likely to resist the option - by force of arms, if necessary... the realization by minorities of some degree of self-determination was crucial to the maintenance of international peace and security.

This proposal attracted much criticism. Most States furiously opposed it. Some were confused about the scope of the proposal and its implications for the nation-State system. Others were opposed to any kind of proposal, which would promote greater autonomy for a section of the population merely on the grounds of ethnicity or racial differences. It was emphasized that such unwelcome initiatives would have the far-reaching consequences for the nation-State system.

Reactions however were mixed. It is interesting to note that some States admitted reluctantly the wisdom of accommodating some form of limited autonomy for minorities, as circumstances required. Hungary's delegate stated that in his country "minorities were legally autonomous and appropriate measures, including financial provision were taken to protect their identity".[22] However, whilst it is true that the Hungarian State has introduced legislation to grant 'self-government' status for minority groups within its territory (Varady, 1997:36), it does not believe that autonomy will develop into a universal right due to differences of opinions of States.[23] Nepal was certain that "at international level" this principle "remained vague".[24] The delegate for Estonia, agreeing with the above critics, stated that the notion of autonomy was lacking clarity.[25]

Malta's position was that autonomy should be operated within the structure of existing nation-States without harming their territorial integrity and sovereignty. In its view, autonomy is "technically difficult or politically sensitive, or both" due to the "complex nature of the issues" and an "immediate solution" could not therefore be found. However, it admitted that autonomy has in many instances, "provided a practical device for resolving complex situations which would otherwise have denigrated into conflict" and the "fragmentation of States".[26] Slovakia's position was also a positive one.[27]

The delegate for Slovenia pointed out that autonomy could be used to prevent the "escalation of tensions into open conflicts".[28] He claimed that Slovenia has taken some legislative initiatives to grant self-government status to Italian and Hungarian minority groups living in its territory "to carry out certain tasks of state authority" by the Act on Self-Governing National Entities (which was enacted by the Slovenian Parliament on 5 October 1994).[29] It is worthy of note that Slovenia was concerned about the activities of "political elites and clans" in clandestine movements which are ready "to seize and maintain power"[30] in the guise of minorities' rights. The Constitutional Act of Human Rights and Freedoms of National and Ethnic Communities or Minorities in the Republic of Croatia, 1992, provided for cultural autonomy by introducing autonomous regions with special self-governing status in the areas of Glina and Knin, where minorities represent more than 50% of the local population according to the 1991 census (Varady, 1997:36).

The Russian delegate did neither support nor oppose the proposal on autonomy at the General Assembly debate. Nonetheless, he expressed his country's willingness to introduce "constitutional changes" to guarantee equality and non-discrimination for "all the country's inhabitants".[31] The constitution of the Russian Federation (adopted on 12 December 1993) has introduced 21 republics, 6 territories (*kari*), 49 regions (*oblast*), and 2 federal cities, 1 autonomous region and 10 autonomous areas (Gazzini, 1996:93). However, it is not clear as to whether it is ready to grant minority communities autonomous status amounting to internal self-government. In practice, new autonomous regions are discouraged. When Sverdlovsk, an *oblast*, in the Ural Mountains attempted to gain autonomy for the region and sought promotion to the status of Republic within the Russian Federation, the Moscow politicians with the full backing of President Yeltsin were alleged to have taken every step to crush the movement for autonomy. The leader of the regionalist movement, Mr. Eduard Ergartovich Rossel assured the political authorities in Moscow that their campaign was not seeking a dismemberment of the Russian Federation. Their aim was no more than achieving autonomous power within a federal status (Easter, 1997:631; Gazzini, 1996:93). Above all, he was against any campaign for greater political power based on ethnicity, which he genuinely believed should not be allowed to happen. He stressed that the "basis of the federation should be territorial, not ethnic" (cited in Easter:1997:631). Ruslan Avshev, President of Ingushetia, and Tartastan's President, Mintimer Shaimier leveled a similar criticism against the Moscow authorities. Even the Treaty on Social Accord of April 1994 implicitly admitted the fact that the federation has not actually encouraged the policy of decentralization of power in order not to allow local autonomy to flourish (Resler, 1997:96).

In the view of Pakistan, autonomy can be used to overcome political and economic disparities in multiracial and multiethnic societies such as Western Europe, but not in newly independent countries in Asia and Africa.[32] Uruguay's position was that autonomy was a useful device to assure certain political, cultural, ethnic and religious rights. Its representative, supporting the 'noble attempt' of Liechtenstein, tried to allay the fear of African and Asian States by assuring them that the application of autonomy would not "open up a Pandora's box". He explained that he:[33]

> could not understand why some countries had serious reservations about supporting the Liechtenstein's draft proposal. It only allows minorities to negotiate degrees of autonomy allowing them to reaffirm certain political, cultural, ethnic and religious rights, which could not be ignored or denied without triggering armed conflict and violence.

Following a similar line, Armenia argued that autonomy was a "highly useful concept" which can be used to "prevent ethnic conflicts".[34]

Confusion increased further when some States tried to interpret autonomy in terms of the right to self-determination. For example, the delegate for Liechtenstein tried to convince others that autonomy could be used as an "optional mechanism for self-determination"[35] in the realization of human rights. Austria's position was also similar. It pointed out that autonomy could be used as one aspect of self-determination.[36] Hungary agreed.[37] According to the delegate of Ukraine, autonomy implies a decentralization of power, which ensures the "realization of self-determination through a more flexible and gradual process".[38] The delegate of Ukraine informed the Assembly members that his country had already taken some constitutional measures to establish autonomous regions by the *Ukrainian Act on National Minorities* living in the region of Beregovo District of Sub-Carpathia.[39] However, its position remains ambiguous. It has argued that ethnicity could be a divisive factor in the process of nation building - therefore Ukraine was not prepared to consent to more than cultural autonomy. The concept, according to Resler (1997:98), is no more than recognition of individual rights without discrimination as to race and ethnicity. By the *Act on Unrestricted Development and Right to Cultural Autonomy of Latvia's Nationalities and Ethnic Groups,* 1991, the Republic of Latvia recognized the cultural autonomy and self-administration of all nationalities and ethnic groups.[40] The Estonian delegate agreed with Ukraine, Liechtenstein and Austria, although his support was qualified. He further clarified that autonomy implied "cultural-self governments" on a non-territorial basis, which are "equal to local governments".[41] Nonetheless, in his view, autonomy could be used as a flexible model to defuse tensions and to grant rights to those dispersed communities, such as the Romany and Jewish peoples.[42] Estonia has granted cultural autonomy to the Germans, Russians, Swedish and Jewish minorities within its territory by the 1993 *Estonian Act on Cultural Autonomy for National Minorities,* provided that each group consists of at least 3,000 individuals.[43] Uruguay, Hungary, Armenia and Nigeria also entertained similar opinions.

However, some States have serious doubts about the wisdom of interpreting the concept of autonomy in terms of the right to self-determination. Many Asian States in the Indian sub-continent and the African States have vehemently rejected such a proposition. For example, both India and Pakistan were opposed to any attempt to introduce autonomy in the guise of self-determination. Autonomy, in the view of India, should not be identified within the scope of "principle of right to self-determination".[44] They are two different principles applied in different circumstances. The Indian representative further argued that "autonomy related to constitutional theory and the domestic structure of sovereign States" whilst the right to self-determination is a theory developed by the UN concerning the situation of non-independent territories. He warned that any "attempt to blur, if not eliminate, the distinction between domestic law and constitutional law" would not be tolerated. The Indian representative observed that Liechtenstein's proposal "clearly exceeded the scope of the Charter" by failing to distinguish between two different concepts, self-determination and autonomy.[45] Such an endeavour was fraught with danger and would be viewed by many as flagrant interference in the internal affairs of States".[46] Granting autonomy to a particular region is, in the view of the Indian delegate, purely within the powers of respective States. The United Nations in the face of States' opposition cannot take such a crucial decision. Pakistan's position was also based on similar grounds. Its representative further stated that even though self-determination could be applied by European States granting greater autonomous powers in their respective territories, countries that had achieved independence from colonial empires were not obliged to apply such a potentially "destructive policy".[47] Similarly, Nepal was in principle opposed to the application of autonomy in "established political entities" in the guise of the doctrine of self-determination. Its delegate categorically stated that such an interpretation or an application of autonomy "could only encourage the fragmentation" of States,[48] because it could be used to justify the interference by clandestine separatist movements in the internal affairs of States. Possibly he had Indian involvement in his country's affairs in mind when he opposed the proposal, because India's interest in the domestic affairs of Nepal has given rise to misunderstanding between these two nations on many occasions. Nepal contains a sizeable section of citizens of Indian descent in its territory.

Malaysia was opposed to autonomy as a solution to ethnic conflicts in independent States because the concept and scope of the autonomy proposed by Liechtenstein would be "expanded beyond acceptable limits".[49] Malaysia was ready to accept the qualified version of internal self-determination, but it should not be more than certain limited rights, "freedom of choice in free and just national elections".[50] If States were compelled to implement models of autonomy guaranteeing extensive territorial powers in the context of self-determination to satisfy certain ethnic groups within nation-States, such steps would "dangerously undermine the concept of nation-States on which the current international order was founded".[51] The Malaysian delegate warned the international community of the possibility of political unrest arising out of such territorial re-arrangements. In his view such steps would encourage minority communities to "demand rights that were inherently incompatible with national unity".[52] The Indonesian delegate was also not convinced about the practicability of the proposal because it was in conflict with the territorial integrity of States and might hinder the process of nation-building. Indonesia has reason to worry about the consequences of such territorial arrangements since it has 300 different ethnic communities. Should these ethnic groups be allowed autonomous regions with greater political power in recognition of every ethnic and tribal group's distinctive identity this would create, argued the Indonesian delegate, "serious and far-reaching political and legal implications and potential for abuse" of the concept of autonomy.[53] Its objections to Liechtenstein's proposal were threefold, i) it was contrary to territorial integrity, ii) it was against national unity, and iii) it was detrimental to the sovereignty of States.[54] He was in no doubt that autonomy could lead to the fragmentation of newly independent countries[55] and "could pose a serious threat to national efforts to promote unity through diversity".[56] Indonesia as a democratic State, in the view of the Indonesian delegate, was ready to promote freedom of expression or democracy but saw no logic in applying a principle that would create 300 ethnically based mini-States. The Indonesian delegate therefore suggested that instead of encouraging ethnic communities to go their separate ways they should be integrated into the framework of a democratic society. No doubt he was influenced by the Timorese scenario, which has long created problems for Indonesia on the international plane.[57] Slovakia's position was similar in some respects to that of India's stance on this. Autonomy is, according to the Slovakian delegate, clearly a constitutional concept, which has nothing to do with internal self-determination.[58]

Iraq's position was more straight-forward. Iraq's delegate warned that he would oppose any "erroneous attempts to reinterpret the principle of the right to self-determination", that gave wider meaning to autonomy because such attempts would "contravene the spirit of the United Nations Charter".[59] However, it admitted the possibility of the realization of the right to self-determination involving the granting of political and cultural rights to minorities within the existing boundaries "through open dialogue". Iraq's delegate explained his country's experiment with "the autonomy region of Iraq Kurdistan, where legislation and executive power was vested in elected members of the Kurdish community under a pioneering law".[60] Mr. Castro, the delegate of the Philippines, having admitted the applicability of the principle in internal government activities, argued that autonomy should be applied by the nation-States, "within the framework of their national constitution and fundamental laws through democratic and political means",[61] thus indicating the constitutional nature of the notion of autonomy.

African nation-States are, with a notable exception, Nigeria, worried about the possible consequences of the application of autonomy in their countries. For instance, the Ghanaian delegate opposed Liechtenstein's proposal because, i) it would encourage "multiple political loyalty", ii) it would be "destructive to the health of States", and iii) such initiatives "would roll back the progress made toward nations out of diverse communities". It was further pointed out, should autonomy be applied to the African continent there would be "endless balkanization".[62] The

Kenyan representative expressed a similar opinion. He was sceptical about the effective realization of the right to self-determination envisaged through autonomous regions within independent States.[63] Kenya was concerned about the possibility of endless new States on the African continent should autonomy be acceded. It was also not sure whether autonomy would guarantee the "absence of conflicts".[64] The Nigerian delegate remarked that, "realization of the right to self-determination through autonomy was a concept familiar to the experience of his own country."[65] Nigeria, though its practice is dubious, was uncompromisingly in favour of the proposal:

> His delegation believed that *self-determination through autonomy* was a credible alternative to the current tendency towards the fragmentation of States, and could be used constructively to encourage the internal and non-violent resolution of conflicts by reforming government structures with the emphasis on achieving greater responsiveness through decentralization.[66] (emphasis added).

7.4 Developments in Europe: "Like Throwing a Bone to the Yapping Dogs"?

Politicians in Europe are very cautious about the wisdom of the transfer or devolution of power to appease minorities' claims for greater autonomy. For example, making a statement on the proposed devolution to Scotland, Lord Tebbit, the former Cabinet minister and the Chairman of the Conservative Party, stated that devolution to Scotland would cause resentment in England and it would be followed by independence.[67] Referring to claims for regional assemblies to Wales and Scotland, former Prime Minister John Major alleged that the Welsh and Scottish assemblies proposed by the Labour leader Tony Blair "would destroy 1,000 year of British history". He further alleged that "Labour would throw a bone to the yapping dogs in Welsh and Scottish separatism".[68]

Neither the ECHR nor the Framework Convention for the Protection of National Minorities[69] states anything special about the rights of autonomy for minorities. The closest reference to minorities' participatory rights in cultural, social, economic life and public affairs or in the matters affecting them comes in article 15. But on close examination, it does not unambiguously guarantee such a right.[70] A significant change of attitudes towards minorities' claims for autonomy was recognized in July 1991 at a seminar organized by the CSCE (now OSCE) Meeting of Experts on

National Minorities. It recommended in its Report (part iv)[71] that to improve the situation of minorities, "where democratic institutions are being consolidated and national minorities issues are of special concerns," the following measures could be helpful:

> a) local bodies and autonomous administration, as well as autonomy on a territorial basis, including the existence of consultative, legislative and executive bodies should be chosen through free and periodic elections; and
> b) an establishment of self-administration by a national minority in situations where autonomy on a territorial basis does not apply; and
> c) the introduction of decentralized or local forms of government.

The experts advocated decentralization of power at regional level. The report of the CSCE Council from the CSCE Seminar of Experts on Democratic Institutions suggested that in the context of constitutional reform, vertical decentralization and the division of the functions of government on a federal, regional and local basis to accommodate "historical, regional or ethnic distinctions" be adopted.[72] Recommendation 1201 (1993) on an Additional Protocol on the Rights of National Minorities to the European Convention on Human Rights recognized by its article 11:

> In the regions where they are in a majority the persons belonging to a national minority shall have the right to have at their disposal appropriate local or *autonomous authorities* or to have a special status, matching the specific historical and territorial situation and in accordance with the domestic legislation of the State (emphasis added).

One commentator remarked that this recommendation "goes much further than any other political or legal document" concerning minority rights in Europe (see Alexanderson, 1997:55). Nonetheless, neither of these recommendations has been adopted by the OSCE. The Document of the Copenhagen Meeting of the Conference on the Human Dimension of the CSCE (June 29, 1990) contained the following proposal in Principle iv, paragraph 35:

> The participating States will respect the right of persons belonging to national minorities to effective participation in public affairs, including participation in the affairs relating to the protection and promotion of the identity of such minorities.

> The participating States note the efforts undertaken to protect and create conditions for the promotion of the ethnic, cultural, linguistic and religious identity of certain national minorities by establishing, as one of the possible means to achieve these aims, *appropriate local or autonomous administrations* corresponding to the specific historical and territorial circumstances of such minorities and in accordance with the policies of the State concerned (emphasis added; see further Helgesen, 1992:178-179).

The Copenhagen document advocates only a local democracy, which guarantees participation of national minorities in the area of policy making. Autonomy has, however, not been recognized in terms of territorial rearrangements taking into account minorities' or other sub-groups' concerns. However, this undoubtedly demonstrates the willingness on the part of the OSCE to facilitate the aspiration of minorities for autonomous rights, albeit that no action has so far been taken on this. An earlier initiative, the European Charter of Local Self-Government, had promoted the idea of autonomy in the form of enhanced power for local authorities provinces or regions where minorities were concentrated.[73] Article 3 (1) of the Charter states:

> Local self-government denotes the right and the ability of local authorities, within the limits of the law, to regulate and manage a substantial share of public affairs under their own responsibility and in the interests of the local population.

This was further elaborated by article 3 (2), which enshrined the notion of elected local assemblies. Article 4 (8) and 5 respectively provide for meaningful powers for local government at territorial level. At the Barcelona summit in 1992, some delegates, notably the Catalan and Basques delegates, explaining their experiences in their respective autonomous regions further advocated autonomy through decentralization for local areas where minority groups live. Many other members of the Council of Europe also agreed. Describing the position of the Council of Europe in his opening statement, D. Thomas M. Buchsbaum stated:

> The experience of several European countries shows that the problems of minorities can be solved through *greater autonomy at local or regional level.* Of course, this kind of solution is only suited to situations in which communities live as a compact group in a particular area (region, province etc.) of a country. Nevertheless, the other situations (scattered minority or community of travelers) may also benefit from the development of local

democracy and the search for solutions at the level closest to the communities in question.

He further stated:

In Resolution 232 (1992) on autonomy, minorities, nationalism and European Union, the CLRAE recommends the launching of a powerful political and cultural education campaign to increase public awareness, possibly under the title, 'living together in the new multicultural Europe.

Neither OSCE documents nor politicians generally, as Hannikainen argued, favour political autonomy for national minorities (Hannikainen, 1996:13). European States have a reputation for their vacillation in their stance on autonomy. Yet, when non-Western European countries are involved in ethnic conflicts, Western European States preach the virtues of autonomous arrangements to ease tensions and to accommodate minorities' concerns as has been seen in the Kosovo ethnic conflict. A statement by the Chairman-in-Office of the OSCE reflects this policy. He declared on behalf of the OSCE that Nagorny Karabakh should be granted the "highest degree of self-rule"[74] within Azerbaijan to solve ethnic violence.

7.5 *Indigenous Peoples and Autonomy: "They are Assumed to Remain Within Existing Sovereign States"?*

Most States, which contain indigenous peoples, are prepared to accommodate only cultural autonomy and, in a few cases, limited territorial realignments. Referring to indigenous peoples' claims to self-determination, the Australian representative emphasized that in any autonomous arrangements indigenous peoples have to operate within existing boundaries of States. He said, "to suggest that indigenous self-determination was a threat to the territorial integrity of States was to ignore the fact that most indigenous people did not desire independence" (Barsh, 1996:798).

There are some indications in recent years that indigenous groups in many parts of the world are gradually winning their arguments, to a certain extent, for autonomous status for their traditional lands. It is still too early to make any conclusion about the specific nature of such right to autonomy. Some Latin American countries seem to be responding positively to the claims of indigenous peoples. Responding to the Human

Rights Committee, Colombia admitted the legitimate claims of indigenous groups "to own their territory in which to settle, their right to adopt their own organizational structures and elect their own authorities, and the right to study their own living conditions and decide on their development models". Also, it guaranteed their "right to use of renewable natural resources in their territories".[75] However, Colombia does not refer to these territories as 'autonomous regions' or territories. Chile, Bolivia, Mexico, Peru, Venezuela have also taken similar steps to that of Colombia. It is worthy of note that, in particular Chile expressed its concerns about the possible threat to a State's territorial integrity by the claims of an indigenous group (Barsh, 1996:797). Nicaragua was ready to introduce autonomous regions within its borders. It claimed that it has already set up a reserve for indigenous communities on the Atlantic coast with "far reaching status of autonomy".[76] Guatemala was prepared to experiment with a limited cultural autonomy, particularly by way of decentralization of the education of Mayan people, allowing them to pursue their culture and to provide an opportunity for development.[77] Here, 'decentralization' is not intended as territorial autonomy. Indeed, the Guatemalan representative emphasized that his country was hoping to exercise sovereignty without any possible dispute over its whole territory. The recent agreement between Guatemala and the *Unidad Revelucinario Nacional Guatemalteca* promised to confer limited powers on indigenous groups in the form of personal autonomy. Part V (a) in the agreement stipulates that the government "undertake to promote a reform of the constitution". Part V (b) says: "Recognizing the role of the communities, within the framework of municipal autonomy, in exercising the right of indigenous peoples to determine their own development priorities, particularly in the field of education, health, culture and the infrastructure." Part V (c) states: "Taking account of the advisability of having a regional administration based on far-reaching decentralization and deconcentration...the Government undertakes to recognize the administration of the educational, health and cultural services of the indigenous peoples on the base of linguistic criteria."[78] The Mexican constitution includes some provision for (in recognition of the existence of) indigenous rights, and the government has taken some steps to set up reserves (which are not autonomous). It is however not ready to yield to claims of territorial autonomy by indigenous groups.[79] According to Brazil, "the focus on land was inappropriate for an instrument dealing with human rights".[80]

Nordic countries have been following different policies on autonomy. Denmark has granted autonomy status by way of introducing self-government for the Faeroe Islands and Greenland. Denmark has recognized that these autonomous territories could secede and achieve independence if that was what they wanted by exercising their right to self-determination (Hannikainen, 1996:1-71). Similarly the Aaland Islands was given home rule status by Finland. The Samis in Norway have been able to get a separate Sami '*Semetinget*' (parliament) with elected representatives (see details Ahren, 1995:457-463). Eide says that the nature of its authority "is more personal than territorial, but both elements exist".[81] In addition, six municipalities in Northern Norway were formed into administrative areas with extensive power allowing Samis to deal with language and cultural matters. However, continued denial of ownership of traditional territories by the Norwegian government raises some concerns for indigenous peoples in Norway. The representative of Norway at the debate on indigenous rights insisted that his government would support indigenous groups to achieve their "aspirations for greater control over their own destiny" provided that they enjoyed these rights within existing boundaries (Barsh, 1996:799). Finland established a parliament for Samis in 1973.[82] Nonetheless, it has been granted only limited power. According to Hannum (1990:255-256), it is no more than an advisory body. Sweden also followed a similar path establishing a parliament in 1993. Yet the government is alleged to have continually refused to accommodate "real power and force" for indigenous peoples (Hannikainen, 1996:34). It is said that even special hunting and fishing rights for Samis were removed by the very Act which established the Sami parliament. Some elected members are however optimistic. A member of this body, Mr. Ahren, wrote that parliament is a "milestone to the Sami endeavour to achieve self-determination" (Ahren, 1995:460). Norway and Finland are prepared to experiment with personal autonomy to a limited extent, but "maintained that the modalities should be determined jointly by indigenous peoples and the State" (Barsh, 1996:800). However, these more restrictive types of autonomous units are generally empowered to deal only with cultural, traditional, economic, linguistic matters, and the like. In practice, Brazil, Japan, and the USA,[83] have not demonstrated their willingness to share power with indigenous peoples on a collective basis. Canada's position was that the "Federal government remained firmly committed to bringing about aboriginal self-government...within the existing constitutional framework in order to realize their aspiration for more autonomy and control over matters affecting their lives"[84] at communal level. It has, nevertheless conferred self-government on various tribes. Amongst these, the autonomous region of Nunavut in northeast Canada is worthy of mention. But progress on autonomy, from the perspective of tribal groups, is unsatisfactory (Lapidoth, 1997:18-19).

7.6 *Future Directions?*

The traditional position on autonomy, in the light of current developments, is gradually and slowly changing. A few States now seem to be prepared to accept as inevitable that autonomy might in the near future be recognized as a principle of international law. For example, in the view of Austria, autonomy is now an "important concept".[85] Ukraine recognises autonomy as a principle in international law.[86]

   Responding to the criticism, and continuing its campaign for autonomy through self-determination, Liechtenstein has argued that the principle was fully in compliance with well-established principles such as territorial integrity and non-interference in the domestic affairs of States.[87] During the debate on the right to self-determination at the forty-ninth session of the UN General Assembly, Liechtenstein further tried to justify its proposal by emphasizing that "the proposed initiative was designed to offer ways and means for the reasonable expressions of plausible aspiration of that nature through free options ranging from *limited and basic self-administration to virtual internal self-government*".[88] Mrs. Fritsche, its representative, speaking on Agenda item 109, 'Rights of Peoples to Self-determination'[89] stressed that autonomy through self-determination is one of the best channels through which minorities can assert their distinctive identities and, therefore, it is in compliance with existing principles of international law. Such measures, in her view, would help maintain peace and security in multi-ethnic societies.[90] Ecuador's position was cautious, but constructive. Its delegate said:[91]

> The principle of self-determination could not run counter to the equally inalienable principle of respect for the territorial integrity of States. Violation of that principle would threaten further the already fragile international peace... .
> Initiative could be used to improve and implement the concept of governance; it could help to develop methods that would assist member States in their efforts to bring about the full advancement of the various components of their societies...*legitimate aspiration of different communities can be achieved through increasing decision making powers to local authorities* (emphasis added).

He further said that his country has already been following a system involving a distribution of power to the local populations, and emphasized that elements of decentralization of power are involved in this principle. The Estonian delegate welcoming the proposal on autonomy stated that the doctrine of self-determination should take further progressive steps beyond the colonial context and should be allowed to develop in the form of autonomy. He admitted that autonomy is now developing in the context of the right to self-determination.[92] In his opinion such progressive steps would "concomitantly prevent conflicts". Uruguay,[93] Hungary[94] and Armenia[95] did not hesitate to admit the validity of the principle. The latter was of the opinion that, with a view to realizing the right to self-determination, States should elaborate different ways and means, in particular through autonomy. Such a constructive approach argued Armenia, would "help to reconcile the right to self-determination with the principle of territorial integrity".[96] Slovenia remarked that the principle of self-determination should be interpreted by "encompassing new situations".[97] The OSCE in 1996 admitted that the "highest degree of self-rule" could be implemented by means of self-determination. This is no doubt a significant development in European thinking, which has the potential for speeding up the further development of the right to self-determination through autonomy.[98] Some States are not so convinced. Slovakia pointed out that the right of self-determination could be applied in a changing geopolitical world through autonomy, though it is still a constitutional concept, and certainly not a rule of international law.[99] Kenya was not so sure that even in the future autonomy would become a fully-fledged principle of international law.[100] Nepal's position was not so different to that of Kenya.[101]

It is submitted that autonomy with shared sovereignty is not a right recognized by many States in terms of international law. Even though some States and international organisations are prepared to experiment with it. However, it is not possible to say how long it will take for States to recognise autonomy as a valid principle in both domestic and international arenas.

Notes

[1] Cruz, G. 'Brazil's Miners: Military Eye Amazon Tribal Lands', *Washington Post*, 17 April 1987, cited in Hannum, H. ed. (1933), *Documents on Autonomy and Minority Rights*, Martinus Nijhoff: Dordrecht, p.182.

[2] HRC Report, SR 722, cited in McGoldrick, D (1991). *The Human Rights Committee, Its Role in the Development of the International Covenant on Civil and Political Rights*, Clarendon Press: Oxford, footnote. 115, p.265.

[3] Hope, K. 'The Albanian Minority: Barometer of Ethnic Tension', *Financial Times*, 15 November 1996.

[4] Tabajdi, C., (undated) Current Questions of International Minority Protection at the End of 1994, cited in Thornberry, P. (1998), 'Images of Autonomy and Individual and Collective Rights in International Instruments of the Rights of Minorities', in Suksi, M. ed. *Autonomy, Applications and Implications*, Kluwer Law International: The Hague, p.97.

[5] See Erlich, H. (1981), 'The Eritrean Autonomy 1952-1962: Its Failure and Its Contribution to Further Escalation', in Dinstein, Y. ed. *Models of Autonomy*, Transaction Books: New Brunswick USA/ London, pp. 183-212.

[6] *Sri Lankan Monitor*, 1 September 1997, p.2.

[7] Http://www. my.netscape.com/news/TopStories, 22 Feb. 1999.

[8] A/C.3/48/SR.22, 30 November 1993, para. 38, p.9 (Kenya).

[9] The Khartoum government also contributed to the failure of the autonomy experiment. Southern Sudan was granted autonomous status by the 'Southern Provinces Regional Self-Government Act 1972. This is reprinted in *Das Selbstbestimmungsrecht der Volker*, Koln-Wien: Bohlau, 1973, pp. 678-84, cited in Sohn, L. B. (1980), 'The Concept of Autonomy in International Law and the Practice of the United Nations', 15 (2) *ILR*, p.182, footnote 9. See also Hannum, H, (1990), *Autonomy, Sovereignty and Self-Determination: The Accommodation of Conflicting Rights*, University of Pennsylvania Press: Philadelphia, pp. 308-327.

[10] Http://my.netscape.com/news/TopStories, 2 February 1999.

[11] It should be mentioned that they were not identified as autonomous regions although these two republics enjoyed greater autonomous power within a federal structure. See Hannum, H. (1993), *Documents on Autonomy and Minority Rights*, Martinus Nijhoff: Dordrecht, pp. 762-763.

[12] In fact by Basic Principle 1 of the Constitution of former Yugoslavia 1974 (as amended in 1987) recognized the right of every nation to self-determination including the right to secession. But there was not any credible implementation procedure to facilitate any demand for secession. See Mullerson, R. (1994), *International Law, Rights and Politics: Developments in Eastern Europe and the CIS*, Routledge and LSE: London/New York.

[13] See Tskhovrebov, Z. (1995), 'An Unfolding Case of a Genocide: Chechnya, World Order and the Right to Be Left Alone', 64 (3) *NJIL*, p. 513. See further Mullerson (1994:79, above).

[14] See The Center for Human Rights (1994), *United Nations Actions in the Field of Human Rights*, UN Publications: New York and Geneva, para. 1629.

[15] India is also known as *Bharat* in the Indian Constitution 1950. According to article 1 India is a 'Union of States'. See Hannum, ed. *Documents on Autonomy*, above, p. 276.

[16] The Bodo Kochari is a collection of sub-tribes. It is estimated that they account for 4.5 million of the population in Assam. See Dasgupta, J. (1997), 'Community,

Authenticity, and Autonomy: Insurgence and International Development in India's Northeast', 56 (2) *JAS*, pp. 345-370.

[17] Commission of Human Rights, 42nd session, Agenda Item 18, UN Doc. E/CN.4/sub.2/1990/46, 20 July 1990, *Possible Ways and Means of Facilitating the Peaceful and Constructive Solution of Problems Involving Minorities*, para. 23, p.6.

[18] The General Framework Agreement for Peace in Bosnia and Herzegovina signed on 14 December 1995. Signatories to the agreement are the Republic of Bosnia and Herzegovina, the Republic of Croatia, and the Federal Republic of Yugoslavia for itself and on behalf of the Republic of Srpska (the region controlled by the Bosnian Serbs). See *Yearbook*, published by the UN and the International Criminal Tribunal for the former Yugoslavia, 1996, p. 321. Annex 4 to the Constitution of Bosnia and Herzegovina in its article 2 states that Bosnia and Herzegovina shall consists of two 'entities', the Federation of Bosnia and Herzegovina and the Republic of Srpska, see p.118. See the full text in 35 *ILM* 75 [1996], pp. 118-125.

[19] See Liechtenstein's proposal, UN Doc. A/Res/48/147 and Add. 1 1991.

[20] See details A/C.3/48/SR.22, 30 November 1993, para. 5, p.3.

[21] A/C.3/51/SR.27, 13 August 1997, para. 5, pp. 2-3.

[22] *Ibid.* para. 54, p.12.

[23] A/C.2/48/SR.22, 30 November 1993, para. 37, p.9.

[24] *Ibid.* para. 4, p.2.

[25] *Ibid.* para. 11, p.4.

[26] *Ibid.* para. 1, p.2.

[27] A/C.3/48/SR.21, 30 November 1993, para. 45, p.10.

[28] A/C.3/48/SR.21, 26 November 1993, para. 23, p.6.

[29] This was published in Uradni List, Slovenian Official Gazette 65/1994, see Varady, T. (1997), 'Minorities, Majorities, Law and Ethnicity: Reflections of the Yugoslav Case', 19 (1) *HRQ*, p.36.

[30] A/C.3/49/SR.8, 25 October 1994, para. 9, p.4.

[31] A/C.3/49/SR.6, 31 October 1994, para. 54, p.10.

[32] A/C.3/48/SR.22, 30 November 1993, para. 40, p.9.

[33] *Ibid.* para. 47, p.11.

[34] A/C.3/48/SR.21, 26 Nov 1993, para. 12, p.4.

[35] A/C.3/48/SR.22, 30 November 1993, para. 48, p.12.

[36] *Ibid.* para. 51, p.12.

[37] *Ibid.* para. 53, p.12.

[38] *Ibid.* para. 30, p.8.

[39] This Act was enacted on 25 June 1992. See *Ukrainian Official Gazette*, 36/1992. See details Varady, above, p. 30.

[40] This is enacted on 19 March 1991, printed in Latvian Official Gazette, *Augustas Padomes Un Valdibas Zinotajs*, 21/1991, amendments printed in the New Latvian Official Gazette 25/1994. See Resler, T. M. (1997), 'Dilemmas of Democratization: Safeguarding Minorities in Russia, Ukraine and Lithuania', 49 *Europe-Asia Studies*, p. 96. See further Lapidoth, R. (1997), *Autonomy: Flexible*

Solution to Ethnic Conflict, United States Institute of Peace Press: Washington DC, pp. 95-96.

[41] A/C.3/48/SR.22, 3 November 1993, para. 9, and p. 3, para. 11, p.4.

[42] *Ibid.* paras. 12-13, p.4.

[43] This new Act was published in the Estonian Official Gazette, *Riigi Teataja*, 71/1993, which came into effect by Presidential Decree on 11 November 1993, see Articles, 2 (1). For details Varady, above, p. 37.

[44] A/C.3/48/SR.22, 30 November 1993, para. 29, p.7.

[45] *Ibid.* para. 28, p.7.

[46] *Ibid.* para. 29, p.7.

[47] *Ibid.* para. 40, p.9.

[48] *Ibid.* para. 3, p.2.

[49] A/C.3/48/SR.22, 30 November 1993, para. 15, p.4.

[50] *Ibid.* para. 16, pp. 4-5.

[51] *Ibid.* para. 16, pp. 4-5.

[52] *Ibid.* para. 16-17, p.5.

[53] *Ibid.* para. 24, p.6.

[54] *Ibid.* para. 23, p.6.

[55] *Ibid.* para. 25, p.7.

[56] *Ibid.* para. 25, p.7.

[57] The Indonesian Legislative Assembly approved Independence for East Timor on 19 October 1999. See *Financial Times*, 20 October 1999. The final batch of Indonesian soldiers left East Timor on 30 October 1999.

[58] A/C.3/48/SR.22, 30 November 1993, para. 45, p.10.

[59] A/C.3/48/SR.21, 26 November 1993, para. 25, p.7.

[60] *Ibid.* para. 26, p.7. Autonomy for the Kurds was recognized by the Constitution of Iraq, 1970, by its article 8 (c). By Act no. 33 of 11 March 1974 (as amended by 1983) Iraq provided for a Kurdish autonomous region. Article 262 provides: "The region of Kurdistan shall enjoy autonomy and shall be regarded as a separa.te administrative unit endowed with distinct personality within the framework of the legal, political and economic unity of the Republic of Iraq." See Hannum, ed. *Documents on Autonomy, above,* pp. 317-324).

[61] A/C.3/48/SR.21, 26 November 1993, para. 14, p.5.

[62] A/C.3/48/SR. 22, 30 November 1993, para. 7. p. 3.

[63] *Ibid.* paras. 36-38, pp. 8-9.

[64] *Ibid.* para. 38, p.9.

[65] *Ibid.* para. 20, p. 6. Special Rapporteur, Eide was also supportive of Nigeria's decentralization process as a solution to ethnic conflicts, see *Possible Ways and Means, 1993.* UN Doc. E/CN.4/Sub.2/1993/34, para. 256, p.55.

[66] A/C.3/48/SR.21, 26 November 1993, para. 21, p.6.

[67] *BBC News Bulletin*, 16 February 1997. See also Tebbit, N., 'My Challenge to Major: Let the Scots Decide', *The Sunday Telegraph*, 16 February 1997.

[68] See 'Major Derides Labour Devolution Package', *The Times*, 14 February 1997.

[69] See Klebes, H. (1995), 'The Council of Europe's Framework Convention for the Protection of National Minorities', 16 *HRLJ*, pp. 92-115; see also Gilbert, G. (1996), 'The Council of Europe and Minority Rights', 18 (1) *HRQ*, pp. 161-189.

[70] Article 15 states that "the parties shall create the condition necessary for the effective participation of persons belonging to national minorities in cultural, social and economic life and in public affairs, in particular those affecting them". See the full text in 34 *ILM* 351 [1995], p.356. Gilbert, above. pp. 161-89.

[71] Report of the CSCE Meeting of Experts on National Minorities, 30 *ILM* 1692 [1991], pp. 1692-1702.

[72] See 31 *ILM* 374 [1992], p.380.

[73] Council of Europe (1993), *Conference on the European Charter of Local Self-Government, Studies and Texts*, no. 27, p.7. This was reaffirmed in the Final Declaration of the Conference on the European Charter on Local Self-Government at Barcelona on 23-35 of January 1992.

[74] See the statement of the Chairman-in-Office, in *OSCE Decisions, 1996, Lisbon Document*, Annex I, 1996, p.23.

[75] CCPR/C/64/Add. 3, paras. 213, 215, 217, cited in *Possible Ways and Means, 1993*, above, para. 238, p.50.

[76] *Possible Ways and Means, 1993*, above, para. 270, p.58.

[77] A/C.3/49/SR. 32, 5 January 1995, para. 22, p.6.

[78] *Ibid.* para. 23, p.6, see details 36 *ILM*, 258 [1997], p.289.

[79] A/C.3/49/SR.31, 28 December 1994, para. 10, p.3.

[80] Barsh, R. L. (1996), 'Indigenous Peoples and the UN Commission on Human Rights: A Case of the Immovable Object and the Irresistible Force', 18 (4) *HRQ*, p.801.

[81] *Possible Ways and Means, 1993*, above, para. 243, p.52.

[82] CCPR/C/58/Add. 5, paras. 135-142.

[83] The USA set up at least 280 different 'reservations' for indigenous communities. See Lapidoth, above, p.18.

[84] See Canada's statement to the HRC, in HRC, Official Records of the Human Rights Committee, Vol. 1, 1990/1991, CCPR/10, CCPR/C/51/Add.1, and CCPR/C/64/Add. 1, para. 32, p. 11.

[85] A/C.3/48/SR.22, 30 November 1993, para. 52, p.12.

[86] *Ibid.* para. 31, p.8.

[87] *Ibid.* para. 48, p.11.

[88] Emphasis added. See A/C.3/ 49/SR., 25 October 1994, para. 12-13, p.5.

[89] UN Doc. A/51/392, 414 and A/51/532-S/1996/864.

[90] A/C.3/51/SR 27, 13 August 1997, para. 5, pp. 2-3.

[91] A/C.3/48/SR.21, 26 November 26 1993. para. 16, p.5.

[92] *Ibid.* para. 21, p. 6.

[93] *Ibid*, para. 46, pp.10-11.

[94] *Ibid.* para. 55, pp.12-3.

[95] A/C.3/48/SR.21, 26 November 1993, paras. 11-12, pp. 3-4.

[96] *Ibid.* para. 12, p. 4.

[97] *Ibid.* para. 23, p. 6.

[98] See The statement of the OSCE Chairman-in -Office *in OSCE Decisions 1996, Lisbon Document*, Annex I, 1996, p. 23.
[99] A/C.3/48/SR.21, 26 November 1993, para. 45 p. 10.
[100] A/C.3/48/SR.22, 30 November 1993, para.7, p. 3.
[101] A/C3/48/SR.22, 30 November 1993, para. 37, p. 9.

References

Ahren, I. (1995), 'Small Nations of the North in Constitutional and International Law', *Nord. J.Int.L*, pp. 457-463.

Alexanderson, M. (1997), 'The Need for a Generalized Application of Minorities Regime in Europe', 8 (4) *Helsinki Monitor*, p. 55.

Barsh, R. L. (1996), 'Indigenous Peoples and the UN Commission on Human Rights: A Case of the Immovable Object and the Irresistible Force', 18 (4) *HRQ*, pp. 782-820.

Ben-Ami, S. (1981), 'The Catalan and Basque Movements for Autonomy', in Y. Dinstein (ed), *Models of Autonomy*, Transaction Books: New Brunswick USA/London, pp. 67-84.

Chatterjee, P. (1993), *The Nation and its Fragments*, Princeton University Press: Princeton.

Claydon, J. (1975), 'The Transnational Protection of Ethnic Minorities: A Tentative Framework for Inquiry', 13 *CYIL*, pp. 25-60.

Dasgupta, J. (1997), 'Community, Authencity, and Autonomy: Insurgence and International Development in India's Northeast', 56 (2) *JSA*, pp. 345-370.

Easter, G. M. (1997), 'Redefining Center-Regional Relations in the Russian Federations: Sverdlovsk Oblast', 49 (4) *Europe-Asia Studies*, p. 631.

Erlich, H. (1983), 'The Eritrean Autonomy 1952-1962: Its Failure and Its Contribution to Further Escalation', in Dinstein (ed), *Models of Autonomy,* as above, pp. 171-182.

Gazzini, T. (1996), 'Considerations on the Conflict in Chechnya', 17 (3/6) *HRLJ* pp. 93-105.

Goodrich, L. M. (1960), *The United Nations*, Stevens and Sons Ltd: London.

Hannikainen, L. (1996), 'The Status of Minorities, Indigenous Peoples and Immigrant and Refugee Groups in Four Nordic States', 65 (1) *Nord.Jint.L* 1996, pp.1-71.

Hannum, H. (1990), *Autonomy, Sovereignty and Self-Determination*, University of Pennsylvania Press: Philadelphia.

Helgesen, J. (1992), 'Protecting Minorities in the Conference on Security and Co-operation in Europe (CSCE) Process: in A. Rosas and J. Helgesen (eds), *The Strength of Diversity: Human Rights and Plural Democracy*, Martinus Nijhoff: Dordrecht/Boston and London, pp. 159- 186.

Heyking, B. (1928), 'The International Protection of Minorities: The Achilles' Heel of the League of Nations', 13 *Problems of Peace and War*, pp. 31-51.

Hutchins, P. W. Hillings, C. and Schulze, D. (1995), 'The Aboriginal Right to Self-Government and the Canadian Constitution: The Ghost in the Machine', 29 (2) *UBC Law Review*, pp. 251-302.

Irwin, Z. T. (1984), 'Yugoslavia and Ethnonationalists', in F. L. Shiels (ed), *Ethnic Separa.tism and World Politics*, University Press of America: Lanham/London, pp. 72-105.

Jennings, R. Y. and Watts, A eds. (1992). *Oppenheim's International Law*, vol. 1, *PEACE*, 9th ed. Longman: Essex.

Lapidoth, R. (1997), *Autonomy: Flexible Solutiosn to Ethnic Conflict*, United States Institute of Peace Press: Washington DC.

Lyttle, P. F. (1995), 'Electoral Transition in Yugoslavia', in Y. Shain and J. J. Linz.(eds), *Between States*, Cambridge University Press: Cambridge, pp. 237-252.

McGoldrick, D. (1991), *The Human Rights Committee, Its Role in the Development of the International Covenant on Civil and Political Rights*, Clarendon Press: Oxford.

Mullerson, R. (1994), *International Law, Rights and Politics: Developments in Eastern Europe and the CIS*, Routledge and LSE: London/New York.

Pakem, B. ed. (1993), *Regionalism in India*, Har-Anand: New Delhi.

Paunovic, M. (1993), 'Nationalities and Minorities in the Yugoslav Federation and in Serbia', in J. Packer and K. Myntti (eds), *The Protection of Ethnic and Linguistic Minorities in Europe*, Institute for Human Rights: Abo-Akedemi University Press: Turku/Abo, pp. 145-165.

Phillips, D. L. (1996), 'Comprehensive Peace in the Balkans: The Kosovo Question', 18 (4) *HRQ*, pp. 821-832.

Prasad, R. N. ed. (1994), *Autonomy Movements in Mizoram*, Vicas: New Delhi.

Resler, T. M. (1997), 'Dilemmas of Democratization: Safeguarding Minorities in Russia, Ukraine and Lithuania', 49 *Europe-Asia Studies* 1997, p. 96.

Steiner, J. (1991), 'Ideals and Counter-Ideals in the Struggle Over Autonomy Regimes for Minorities', 66 *Notre Dame LR*, pp. 1539-1559.

Symonides, J. (1991), 'Collective Rights of Minorities in Europe', in R. Lefeber, M. Fitzmourice and E. Vierdag (eds), *The Changing Political Structure of Europe*, Nijhoff: Dordrecht, pp. 107-125.

Thornberry, P. (1997), 'Minority Rights', in *Academi of European Law* edited by Collective Course of the Academi of European Law, vol. VI, pp. 307-390.

Tskhovrebov, Z. (1995), 'An Unfolding Case of a Genocide: Chechnya, World Order and the Right to Be Left Alone', 64 (3) *Nord. J.Int.L*, pp. 501-555.

Varady, T. (1997), 'Minorities, Majorities, Law and Ethnicity: Reflections of the Yugoslav Case', 19 *HRQ*, pp. 9-54.

8 Secessionist Movements

Introduction

Claims by minority groups for secession have often resulted in virulent clashes between minority groups on the one hand and the State (which is normally controlled by the majority community) on the other creating a threat to the stability of modern pluralist societies and to international peace. This chapter examines the background of secessionist movements in contemporary multiethnic polities to lay a foundation for an analysis of the legitimacy of secessionist claims in chapters 9 to 10, and a critical examination of the attitudes of the international community to such claims (see chapter 12).

8.1 *Ethnic Revivalism as a Prelude to Secession*

Ethnic revivalism is seen by some as a form of struggle to establish ethnically defined new post-modern-tribal-states.[1] From the perspective of minorities, the decolonisation of Asia, Latin America, Africa and elsewhere let them down. It was often peoples belonging to majority communities who were able to succeed their former colonial masters. Many minority groups feel that not only in newly created States, but also in long established Westphalian model nation-States, they have been discriminated against and unjustifiably excluded from the power structure. So, struggles for new nation-States are being enthusiastically taken up in many parts of the world (Mullerson, 1993:799; Moynihan, 1994 ed.).

    A negative international environment and the failure of the UN, some argue, have to a certain extent been instrumental in awakening ethnic consciousness. Ahmed (1995:6) argues that small ethnic groups have lost their faith in the UN and begun to organise themselves in a search for security and protection through new nation-States. Most prominent examples are the Sikhs in Punjab, and the Kurds in Iraq, Turkey and Iran. They have selected the gun-barrel strategy to achieve their goal of new tribal-States.

Some are critical of such movements. Horowitz (1985:preface) points out that post-modern ethnic revivalism has become a cancer in peoples' lives. Whilst few States have been able to avoid some measure of secessionist conflict, it is equally true that such conflicts have literally engulfed many post-war States in Latin America, Asia, Africa and Europe (Franck, 1996:359-383; see also Stavenhagen, 1996).

A move towards secession may be triggered when a significant proportion of a population begins to question the legitimacy of the existing boundaries of a State (Leff, 1999:206), and a State tries to keep discontented minority groups within its territory without their consent (Soyinka, 1996) or subjects them to extreme forms of discrimination. In the latter situation, a respect for diversity in such States is alarmingly missing. Power is often concentrated in the hands of small cliques of elites whilst in most cases excluding minorities. Despotic leaders exercise power in the name of the interests of the people without relying on the consensus of their citizens (Schreuer, 1993:448). Many post-colonial African and Asian States provide examples. The late Sani Abacha of Nigeria, the former President Mobutu Sese Seko in Zaire, the former self-styled Emperor Jean-Bedel Bokasa in Central Africa, Idi Amin in Uganda,[2] the late Presidents, J. R. Jayawardane and R. Premadasa in Sri Lanka, the former Presidents General Zia, Ayub Khan, and Yahya Khan in Pakistan, the Polpot regime in Kampuchea, the former President Suharto in Indonesia and the present military regime in Myanmar are classic cases in point. Such an environment creates breeding grounds for the claims of minorities for post-modern tribal-states.

8.2 *The Post-modern Tribal-state Scenario*

There is a certain pattern in minorities' claims for greater political power. These claims usually start with autonomy, then may proceed to separatism, whilst a final step would be secession, the post-modern tribal-state or irredentism. These three steps may operate vertically as well as horizontally as the graph below illustrates. When a compromise can be achieved through mutual understanding between a minority group (or groups) and the State concerned, autonomy may develop (as is illustrated in the graph vertically) within unitary, a federal or confederal structure consisting of Union-States. When claims for autonomy fail the resentments of minority groups may develop first into separatism, then into rebellion against the State, which if successful might result in a post-modern tribal-state. On the other hand, autonomy might increase minorities' ambitions to achieve post-modern tribal-States by operating first vertically, then moving horizontally. Even assuming that a minority group achieved autonomy with shared sovereignty within a federation, tendencies towards for a post-modern tribal-State might still operate. Indeed, autonomous power may help a minority group to strengthen its power base. Here, the development is from the federation to a post-modern tribal-State.

Chart- A Hypothetical Pattern of the Movements from Autonomy to Secession

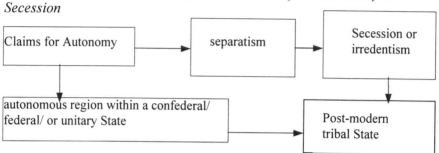

In 1944 Cobban noted that nationalism had passed from the era of State building to State breaking. He observed how 'dormant nationalities' were coming to the surface and had become a threat to the nation-State structure (Cobban, 1944: preface). His prophetic statement anticipated the upheavals of contemporary polities engulfed by secessionist violence. Nationalism has gone through many stages, from nationalism to ethno-nationalism, and then to post-modern tribalism involving "the break-up or serious weakening of states" (Bremmer and Bailes, 1998:131). In many parts of the world secessionist struggles are increasingly becoming the order of the day.

Some research reveals that there are active movements fighting either for secession or greater autonomy in more than sixty nation-States, almost one third of the international community (Halprin, Scheffer, and Small, 1992; see also Stavenhagen, 1996; see generally Buchheit, 1978). This phenomenon has reached a point at which even the smallest minority groups armed with the so-called secessionist right to self-determination are fighting for new nation-States. Buchheit refers to an instance where twenty-nine individuals living in the province of the Hutt River in Western Australia served a declaration of secession on the Australian government. The politics of secessionist struggles have become attractive to a wide range of people- young, old, intellectuals etc. Honour and pride mixed with aggression and militancy play a significant role in the psychology of such movements. No single factor can be attributed to the secessionists' motives. The behaviour of human beings is indeed very complex and is usually beyond our comprehension. Human beings do not normally regulate their behavioural patterns in a rational way nor do they behave in a civilised way. The behaviour of human beings is unpredictable. As Arthur Koestler argues, when human beings lose self-control the inevitable result is over-excitement and a tendency to assert themselves to the detriment of others (Koestler, 1967:117). Reason and wisdom are overcome by fear, uncertainty, insecurity, loneliness, prejudice etc. Human beings naturally tend to group together precisely for these reasons. When this happens, group processes create divisions amongst different groups which cannot easily be erased. This is particularly true of ethnic groups. Ronen (1974) argues very convincingly that ethnic groups (encompassing religious and linguistic groups) often try to rally around their specific groups to avoid the dominance of other groups. Here, the foundation of such groups is based on "a sense of collective destiny on the basis of a collective past and common biological descent" (Lawson, 1996:156). This is seen as a constant struggle, the purpose of which is to control their own lives by themselves without the interference of 'outsiders'. Ethnic identity thus gradually becomes "a rallying point for confrontations" with other similar groups (Ronen, 1974: 42-43). Stephanie Lawson (1996:156) rightly argues that "the single-minded assertion of ethnic differences can overwhelm all other aspects of identity, resulting in the total domination of social and cultural life". This may, as argued by Ronen, (1974:preface), gradually increase pressure towards secession, and the establishment of their own community or, as bluntly pointed out by Franck (1993:21), constitute new "uninational and unicultural- that is, post-modern tribal-states". Existing State structures are perceived as insufficient to cater for ethnic demands or seen as an obstacle to development as a separate nation. Such an environment puts pressure on both minorities and States, and in extreme cases escalates into secessionist violence (Ronen, 1974:49). This has become a concern for more than a third of nation-States at present because secessionist movements do not hesitate to challenge the legitimacy of the present structure of multiethnic polities (Shiels, 1984:1). It is said that nation-States are now being continually hounded by ethnonationalists (Shiels, 1984:1).

Secessionist movements have achieved significant momentum, especially, since the end of Cold War and the collapse of the former USSR and its satellite Socialist States in Eastern Europe (Triesman, 1997: 212-249; Shehadi, 1993:6; see further Mihas, 1997:175-181 and Leff,

1999:205-235). Since 1990 twenty-nine new nation-States have emerged and subsequently been granted membership of the UN. The former Soviet Union was dissolved unexpectedly, and 15 new nation-States emerged. Eastern Europe has followed the same path and some minority groups have been successful in achieving new nation-States (Blum, 1992:830-833). For example, on the 22th of May 1992, the United Nations General Assembly admitted three new members - Slovenia, Bosnia and Herzegovina, and Croatia. On 17 September 1991 constituent parts of the former USSR, Estonia, Latvia and Lithuania were admitted to the UN as new members. Azerbaijan, Armenia, Kazakhstan, Kyrgystan, Moldova, Tajikistan, Turkistan, and Uzbekistan were admitted by the UN on 2 March 1992. Georgia was admitted on 31 July 1992. Belarus (earlier, Byelorussia) and Ukraine were original UN members and therefore no issues arose as to their membership being recognised by the UN. Elsewhere, notably Eritrea broke-away from Ethiopia with the connivance of the international community in 1993 to the delight and satisfaction of minority communities in other parts of the world. Some other secessionist struggles also succeeded. For example, ethnic Slovaks in the former Czechoslovakia were successful in achieving their Slovak nation-State without embarking upon a war against the Czechs. Croatia had achieved its independence by seceding, in the context of a dissolution, from the former Yugoslav Republic after a long-drawn-out-war which claimed the lives of many thousands of men and women. Chechnya has been virtually operating as an independent State already, although legally it is still a component part of the Russian Federation. East Timor's independence was virtually guaranteed with the involvement of the UN and the approval of results of the referendum by the Legislative Assembly of Indonesia on 19 October 1999. Encouraged by East Timor's victory, another tiny part of Indonesia, the Aceh region of the northern tip of Sumatra has stepped up their campaign for independence. It was reported that campaigners for independence held a mass demonstration with at least half a million Acehnes before the mosque in the capital of Aceh, Banda Aceh on 8th of November 1999. The Foreign Minister Dr Alwi Shihab, expressing his fear of disintegration of Indonesia, was reported as saying that the majority of Achenes did not want to secede from Indonesia.[3] Greater autonomy for the province has already been rejected by rebels. The Secessionist forces were adamant that they would explore every avenue in their struggle for independence including "diplomacy, politics and law: (*Financial Times*, November 10, 1999). Indonesians are worried that after East Timor independence flood-gates would open and Aceh would be the first through.

Secessionist movements in other provinces in Indonesia such as Irian Jaya and Ambon have been increasing their independence campaign, apparently encouraged by East Timor's successful independence campaign (*Financial Times*, November 10, 1999). In Europe, another contender for independent statehood Montenegro is threatening to hold a referendum to become an independent sovereign State. Foreign Minister Branko Perovic by giving an interview to the Vienna newspaper *Die Presse* stressed that the Montenegrins wanted to become a nation-State breaking its constitutional ties with the Belgrade regime. "Our demands for democracy", argued Branko Perovic, "and decentralisation are just not compatible with the Milosovic dictatorship" (*Sunday Business*, October 17, 1999). New secessionist movements are emerging day by day in areas such as the Caucasus, and even in the US. Making the 'Asheville Declaration' on 8th of August 1999 it was stated by a group of descendants of the Anglo-Saxons living in the area of Dixie that they wanted to secede from the US. They argued that "the last best hope for constitutional liberty lies with the people of the South, predominantly Celtic and British in culture, true to their Christian faith, inspired by memories and sacrifices of their colonial and confederate forefathers, and jealous of their ancient liberties" (*The Times*, August 9, 1999).

This is now becoming the new paradigm in the international order. Dagestan, Nakhichevan, Nagorny-Karabakh, Tartastan, Chechnya, Kosovo, Jaffna, the Spice Islands and, Bougainville,[4] previously largely unheard names in international politics, have emerged out of obscurity as new candidates for post-modern tribal-States. As Mullerson (1994:19) writes, secessionist movements believe "this is the correct moment to achieve their goals. Now or never". For many minority groups, "separatism seemed the only vehicle for self-expression" (Sigler, 1983:189). But, secessionists have to face new challenges. For example, when minority groups achieve independence through secession, as Stavenhagen (1996:8) correctly points out, "another minority may arise in its bosom, like so many Matrioska dolls". This new danger, as noted by the former UN Secretary-General Boutros Ghali, creates more unstable and fragmented micro-States. He cautioned, "rather than 100 or 200 countries, you may have at the end of the century 400 countries, and we will not be able to achieve any kind of economic development, not to mention more disputes on boundaries" (*The Times*, September 21, 1992, cited in Shehadi, 1983:8). According to the former US Secretary of State Warren Christopher, if we fail to respond quickly, "we'll have 5,000 countries rather than the hundred plus we now have" (Shehadi, 1983:3). Though this may not happen in the near future, secessionist violence has shattered the conventional belief that the UN system would eventually be able to bring peace in the post-war era by respecting and guaranteeing individual's rights on a universal basis.

No doubt, these events encourage minority groups to believe that they are politically as well as legally entitled to secede from existing States by invoking the doctrine of the right to self-determination. Yet the difficulties which they have to overcome are enormous, both on legal and moral grounds.

8.3 *Separatism, Irredentism and Secession*

Separatist, separatism and secessionists all have negative connotations. It is said that it was the former President of France, General de Gaulle, who popularised these terms during the Algerian war (see Tubiana, 1983:23). Various definitions are provided by political and social scientists to identify the phenomenon of *secession*, and to analyse how secession is different from kindred concepts such as *separatism* and *irredentism*. It is common to see these terms used interchangeably. 'Separatism', whilst inherently embedded in ethnic claims for minority rights,[5] nevertheless indicates two different options (Irwin, 1984:105). One is that of the demands of an ethnic group for a new nation-State. Secessionist Tamil guerrillas in Sri Lanka, and Basques ETA in Spain fall into this category. The second option allows separatists to pursue their claims for a lesser alternative, that is for autonomous status for whatever region the minorities make their claims. Kurdish separatists in Iraq and the Catalans in Spain and the moderate Sikh nationalist movements in Punjab come into the second category. When the second option is followed, separatism does not necessarily lead to the establishment of a new nation-State (Horowitz, 1985:231). However, the nature of the claims made is dependent on the level of mutual understanding between the separatists and the State concerned.

8.3.1 *Irredentism*

There is a significant difference between *irredentism* and *secession*. Irredentism presents a different scenario to that of secession. The term *irredentism* is said to have originated from an Italian word, *irredenta*, meaning 'redemption' of the territory conquered by a foreign country (Mayall, 1990). But in modern political jargon it stands for territorial claims by a State to a part of the territory of another State. This may also involve alliances of ethnic groups across the borders (involving kindred ethnic groups in two or more States) whose principal aim is to merge with another State. This is usually on historical or ethnic grounds or both (Mayall, 1990:272). Chechen Muslim rebels' claims for Dagestan, Somalia's claims to the Ogden region in Ethiopia and the Djibouti region in the Northeast province of Kenya, Morocco's claims to Western Sahara, Mauritania's claim to Western Sahara, Argentina's claims to the Malvinas (Falklands), Spanish claims to Gibraltar, the Irish Republic's former claim to Northern Ireland are cases in point. Irredentist movements wish to see a merger of part of a territory to which they claim with another State in which other members of their group live. In the 1950s and 1960s some Tamil separatist movements had advocated the merger of the Dravidian nations across the Palk Strait uniting South Indian Tamils, Malaysian Tamils and Ceylon Tamils in the north-eastern province of Sri Lanka to create a *Dravidastan/ Dravidam*. Similar movements are evident in other contemporary multiethnic polities (Horowitz, 1985:281). It is asserted that the Albanians living in Macedonia and the province of Kosovo have ulterior motives behind their campaigns for greater political power, that is, they hoped to join the Albanian State to create a 'Greater Albania' (Irwin, 1984). Similar attempts have recently been made by the Serbs in Macedonia and Bosnia and Herzegovina to create a 'Greater Serbia' with a view to providing a common home for Serb nationalities in central and Eastern Europe. The attendant consequence of the building of greater Serbia was demonstrated in his interview by Vladimir Srebovic of the Serbia Democratic Party as follows: "The plan was for a division of Bosnia into two spheres of influence, leading to a Greater Serbia and a Greater Croatia. The Muslims were to be subjected to a final solution - more than half were to be killed, a smaller segment converted to Orthodoxy. while a smaller segment still, those with riches, could buy their lives and leave. The goal was to cleanse Bosnia-Herzegovina completely of the Muslim people" (see details Vulliamy, 1998:77). Transylvanians' desire for a merger with Hungary by breaking away from Romania, the Azerbaijanis in Georgia with Azerbaijan are well-known other irredentist cases. The Muslim fundamentalist Wahhabis in both Chechnya and Dagestan have launched the latest irredentist campaign in the Caucasus to create an Islamic Republic by merging Chechnya and Degestan (see *The Times*, September 9, 1999). Due to its international dimension, irredentism thus presents more problems than secession. However, irredentist movements are not in abundance in comparison with secessionist movements at present.

8.3.2 *Secession*

The Supreme Court of Canada in *re Secession of Quebec* (1998) 2 SCR 217 interpreted secession:

> Secession is the effect of a group or section of a State to withdraw itself from the political and constitutional authority of that State, with a view to achieving statehood for a new territorial unit on the international plane. In a federal State, secession typically takes the form of a territorial unit seeking to withdraw from the federation.

Most importantly, secession is a unilateral action of a section of the population for a specific part of the territory. Their Lordships in the above case held, "Rather, what is claimed by a right to secede 'unilaterally' is the right to effectuate secession without prior negotiations with the other provinces and the federal government". Thus, secession is a movement which campaigns for independence for a region of an existing State, and which, if successful, results in the redrawing of the boundaries of the State (see Buchanan, 1991:11; Heraclides 1991:1). For these reasons secession is identified with terrorism. The International Law Commission provides that the following acts constitute terrorism:

> i) Any act causing death or grievous bodily harm or loss of liberty to a Head of State, persons exercising the prerogatives of the Head of State, their hereditary or designated successors, the spouse of such persons, or persons charged with public functions or holding public positions when the act is directed against them in their public capacity;
> ii) Acts calculated to destroy or damage public property or property devoted to a public purpose;
> iii) Any act likely to imperil human lives through the creation of a public danger, in particular the seizure of aircraft, the taking of hostage and any form of violence directed against persons who enjoy international protection or diplomatic immunity;
> iv) The manufacture, obtaining, possession or supplying of arms, ammunition, explosives or harmful substances with a view to the commission of a terrorist act (see Elagab, 1995 at iv).

Secessionists, however, do not see their actions as terrorism. Generally, secessionists neither claim the whole territory of the State nor do they want to change the political or constitutional structure of the State at issue (Buchanan, 1991:11). Most importantly, as Buchanan correctly points out (at 10), the State's authority to govern a province or a region, which is predominantly inhabited by the group represented by secessionists, is severely challenged. The State at issue is identified and described as an occupying force in a given territory. Secession based on territorial claims presents more complexities and difficulties than any other form of domestic unrest. Although they often call themselves liberation armies, secessionist groups are different from national liberation movements. In the latter case the sole purpose is to capture the whole territory by changing the State structure by violent and undemocratic means.

Secession may occur within a province or provinces in the State itself. Demands can be based on a group or regional basis. This is normally associated with minority groups - therefore secession is considered by some as "a special species of ethnic conflicts" (Horowitz, 1985:231). The movement operates at a regional basis and may consist of many ethnic and religious groups, e.g. the Eritrean secessionist movement (Arab Beja, Arab Afar, Black African and Christians), Biafran secession (Ibo,[6] Ibibio, Efik, Ijaw and many other small tribes) and present secessionists in southern Sudan (mainly Christian religious groups with the assistance of other ethnic and tribal groups).[7] However, the most important element of a secessionist claim is, as pointed out by Brilmayer (1991:187-188), the continued claim to a particular piece of land, which would be used, if the secession succeeded, for the future State.

Secessionists advocate the dismemberment of a State, and "intend to abandon their current State, and in so doing, to take with them the land on which they live" (Brilmayer, 1991:187). Secession often emerges and is organised from below (Horowitz, 1985:273) unlike a *coup d'etat* with which the politicians and the officials at higher echelons are often associated (Horowitz, 1985:273). A classic example is that of the LTTE in Sri Lanka. Its leadership comes from the lower castes of the Tamils in the regions of the north and east of the island. Sometimes, elite members of secessionist groups provide leadership, in particular, on the ideological front with international campaigns to win friends, sympathisers and activists. If the struggle succeeds, the region at issue may achieve independent Statehood, which is normally by a unilateral declaration on the part of the secessionists. Sometimes this may happen with the tacit agreement of the international community. Bangladesh is the most quoted example. It may also happen with or without the consent of the majority community or the State at issue. Slovakia seceded with the consent of the Czechs.

8.4 *Secession: "Pregnant With Such Unutterable Calamities"?*

Secession is often seen as the most dangerous phenomenon in the era of post-modern tribalism. There is one significant aspect to this phenomenon-it is, as pointed out by Albert Taylor Bledsoe one and a half centuries ago, "pregnant with such unutterable calamities" (Bledsoe, 1866 cited in Buchanan, 1991:preface). Cobban (1944:75) described secession as "generally a work of destruction and breaking down of established connexions".

Secession can result in civil unrest and chaos. "It can shatter old alliances, stimulate the forging of new ones, tip the balance of power, create refugee populations, and disrupt international communities" (details Buchanan, 1991:2). As Thornberry (1993:104) points out, at worst, secessionist movements may lead to 'genocidal policies of so-called ethnic cleansing'. Eide (1993:140 and 144) views secession as "one of the most serious contemporary threats both to a peaceful evolution of the international order and to the advancement of human rights". Therefore, he suggested that secessionist movements based on 'ethno-nationalism' should be constrained and counteracted. Presenting a very forceful argument, Mullerson (1994:71) emphasised that endless tribalization may increase if secessionism is recognised or encouraged. He also points out that the potential threat of secessionism to international society is too much to warrant any acceptance in international law or political science. Emergence of a multiplicity of small States based on ethno-nationalist ideology may not help the international order. He also sees secessionist leaders as selfish and power crazy, ready to exploit any opportunity to satisfy their ambitions at the expense of non-combatant peace loving civilians (Mullerson, 1994). Above all, secession undermines, as pointed out by Cassese (1995:339), the State structure.

Secession is conspicuous for its unpredictability both in its movements and its impact on the State. Ethnically based secessionism results in deep divisions and tensions amongst different ethnic groups leaving deep scars. Such an environment generates mistrust, fear and insecurity which are neither ideal ground for the development of liberal democracies nor do they help human rights to flourish. Accompanying elements are aggressiveness, hatred, and intolerance towards other ethnic groups. Consequently, other smaller ethnic groups are prompted either to find protection from the largest ethnic group in the polity or to seek separate ethnic enclaves by having their own tribal States (Mullerson, 1994:84-85). For example, the Muslims living in the Northeast provinces of Sri Lanka had never sought ethnically based separate territories before the commencement of the secessionist struggle of the Tamil Eelamists. But now not only do they seek protection against Tamil secessionist groups such as the LTTE but also demand a separate province of their own in the eastern part of the island. Similarly, tribal Indian groups living in the province of Quebec demanded that in the event of a secession by the Quebecois from the Federation of Canada they should be allowed to break-away and set up their own tribal-States where they form a majority.

As such, secession is a variable phenomenon associated with extremism. Secessionist movements operate in both forward and reverse directions. They "slide back and forth between autonomy and independence" (Treisman, 1997:224; see further Kohli, 1997:326). The case in point is the secessionist movement that prevailed in the province of Madras before it was elevated to the status of Union-State. The secessionist Dravidian movements in Tamil Nadu reversed their secessionist strategy preferring greater political power within a federal structure. A similar route was taken by the Northern Nigerian secessionists, mostly Hausa-Fulani people. They abandoned their secessionist goal in 1966, despite many prominent leaders feeling that secession was the only way which guaranteed 'honour and dignity' (Horowitz, 1985:241 and 243). But such constitutional arrangements are still seen by secessionist forces in term of separatism. Some secessionists may move away from autonomy to secession as in the case of Mizo secessionists (Mizo National Front in Mizoram in Northeast India) and the Moro National Liberation Front in the Philippines (Horowitz, 1985:230). Southern Sudan secessionists have changed their positions from autonomy to secession and *vice versa* many times. Each and every secessionist movement does not end in the achievement of independence. The abortive Biafran secessionist struggle is one such case. There is no rule that prevents secessionists from coming to a compromise solution well short of independence. Autonomous status in terms of territory might be such a compromise, as happened in Tamil Nadu, the Basque country and Catalonia.

The paradoxical nature of this phenomenon is such that, sometimes, secessionist tendencies in suppressed groups may never develop into a secession. The Lozi homeland in Zambia is one of the examples provided by Horowitz. Even though the powers of their monarch were limited and many other legislative measures were taken to curtail administrative powers within the region, the Lozis preferred to stay with unitary Zambia (Horowitz, 1985:241-243). Secession is rarely mentioned even when matters deteriorate. Another notable example is the Catalans. Both the Basques and the Catalans had been equally subjected to oppression for many decades, yet the Catalans' secessionist tendencies are insignificant by comparison with the Basques. The latter is described as the most violent, intransigent, always assertive and, above all, "the most difficult to reconcile" (see respectively Horowitz, 1985:231 and 252; Clark, 1984:71).

The target population in a secessionist campaign is of course different. Firstly, the secessionists have to keep the group or the region intact and their ardent supporters together. If that cannot be achieved, then at least the passive support of the target group is expected. Most importantly, the assistance of the international community is needed. Both these objectives may be targeted simultaneously. However, it is only the most advanced secessionist groups such as the PKK (the Kurdish Workers Party, see McDowall, 1992:20), the LTTE, the ETA, and the like which find little difficulty in reaching the international organisations through which the justification of their respectively secessionist and irredentist claims can be effectively defended.

As Heraclides notes (1991:42-43), secessionists use propaganda as a strong weapon to gain legitimacy for their movements. Misrepresentation and distortion of facts and figures are effective tools in their armoury. Beatings as well as pleadings are used to maintain group control and to achieve group loyalty as in the case of the Tamil Tigers in Sri Lanka, the ETA in Spain, the KLA in Kosovo and the IRA movement in Northern Ireland. An alleged exploitation of the community or the region concerned, and the neglect of the group or the region are attributed to the State and to the dominant groups in the State concerned. Propaganda is not so difficult at the initial stage of the conflict due to difficulties of getting accurate information. It may be due to the reluctance of both States and secessionist groups to allow the international media access to the theatres of conflicts.

Moreover, secessionists employ various strategies to justify and strengthen their case. From persuasion by peaceful means to coercion and violence, the latter being a kind of 'propaganda by deed' (Buchheit, 1978: 19). Human sufferings and the sacrifice of a perceived 'enemy group' are seen as justified in the struggle for a worthy cause. The blowing up of buildings, especially those belonging to the State, the theft of property, the random killings of members of the enemy group, kidnapping and inflicting fear and uncertainty are some prominent tactics used by secessionists with a view to bringing their 'just cause' to the attention of the international community and domestic politicians. If the State at issue is not prepared to give up a part of its territory in recognition of a secessionist claim, violence is the ultimate choice adopted by many contemporary secessionist groups in the belief that ultimately the State will be forced to accept secession. For example, the ETA in Basque country in Spain has, from 1968 to 1998, alleged to have killed 768 individuals.[8] Violence in the name of group interests is justified on the assumption that a people has the right to choose its own cause, particularly its political destiny (Gilbert, 1994: chapter 6). Fighting, in the views of secessionists, is not only 'intrinsically important', but also instrumentally valuable' for protection against the enemy group or State and for the survival of the group (Margalit and Raz, 1995:89), and in pursuit of their life as a free people (Ronen, 1974:47).

It is argued that as a separate nation or a region, secession can be justified on moral grounds. The philosophy behind this argument is that individuals or groups have the inherent right to decide whether to stay with the existing polity or leave it and set up their own States. Arguments based on morality are based on liberal principles. Secessionists believe that the right to secession flows from natural rights, which guarantee an inherent right to self-government. They often refer to the American Declaration of Independence and the French Declaration of the Rights of Man and of the Citizen to claim a stake in the moral high ground (Brilmayer, 1991:179). The right to determine their own political system is presented as a strong reason. If the secession does not harm the other communities or groups or individuals then States have a moral obligation not to obstruct it. According to liberal political philosophy, secessionists should be allowed to achieve their aspirations to the maximum without interference by States, because both groups and individuals have an inherent right to decide or select the kind of society, community or the State in which they would like to live. The right to participate in the political process is one of the most essential rights to which any individual is entitled. The State simply cannot violate these basic rights - it is morally bound to safeguard rights within a liberal environment, which is conducive to the enhancement of individual rights. Individuals acquire rights not as citizens of the State, but as human beings. Therefore, an individual's decision alone matters in determining whether he or she should join a society or a polity or break-away at any time he or she chooses to do so. On these grounds, it is argued that secession is a morally justifiable right, which cannot be suppressed by any one (Buchanan, 1991, chapter 2; Dyke, 1955:44-45; Murswieck, 1993:21-40).

The problem with such a liberal attitude is that it creates chaos and anarchy. Do we want to go back to the nomadic era and see the end of the world as it stands today?

8.5 *The Ubiquitous Nature of Secessionist Movements: "Locked in a Life-or-Death Struggle"?*

Most secessionist movements enter "the path of the gun" and are eventually "locked in a life-or-death struggle"[9] against States to achieve their ultimate paradise, the new nation-States. Some of these secessionist movements, as stated by the Armenian delegate, "have escalated into long-standing conflicts or civil wars".[10] Military action of secessionist Serbs to create the Republika Srpska[11] in the Republic of Bosnia-Herzegovina resulted in the most bloody war, the "first general war since 1945" (Denitch, 1994: further see Moynihan, 1994 ed), we have witnessed in recent history (Denitch, 1994; see further Moynihan, 1994:72). Ethnic Albanians living in the Kosovo region have been fighting the Serbian forces for independence "to preserve their language, educational system, traditional culture",[12] or perhaps to join the Albanian Republic.[13] The justification claimed for these struggles is the building of nation-States along the lines of ethnic, religious, linguistic and cultural boundaries. We have not yet seen the end of Yugoslavian ethnic wars. "The only question remaining is how many nations or nearly nations will emerge from the carcass" (Jackson and James, 1993:100; see also Akhavan, 1996:227-248). These dangerous tendencies are gradually spreading over the boundaries of many contemporary nation-States as will be shown below.

On the African continent secessionist movements are active as never before. "From Angola to Somalia, from Burundi to Rwanda to Liberia" conflicts are widespread.[14] Due to these conflicts, in the words of Namibia's Foreign Minister, "Africa is bleeding...the African people are burning in misery and mayhem".[15] Human tragedy and mass killings of innocent people "have gone beyond the bounds of reason".[16] It is common knowledge that in the Democratic Republic of Congo, Uganda, Burundi, Algeria, Ethiopia, Somalia, and Sudan many thousands of non-combatant civilians suffer as a result of violence launched by secessionists. The international community has also witnessed with horror how 'freelance gunmen' operating on a tribal basis launched a suicidal war against each other bringing Somalia into total anarchy.[17] The sole purpose appears to be to carve Somalia into several micro-States (tribal-States) purely and simply on the basis of tribal and clan allegiances. Secessionists in the northern part of Somalia have already set up an independent 'Somaliland' which appears to be gaining international approval indirectly (see *The Economist*, August, 1999). Secessionist wars in Sudan's southern and eastern regions have entered into a new era under the umbrella organisation of 'the National Democratic Alliance' - which consists mainly of non-Muslim groups in the southern[18] and eastern parts of the country. Even the neighbouring countries, Ethiopia, Eritrea and Uganda are alleged to have been involved in assisting the rebels against Sudan (*Financial Times*, February 9, 1997). New claimants are emerging year after year. Amongst these the South African White settler communities, Afrikaners, have already declared their determination to fight for a 'white homeland' (*Valkstaat*), breaking away from the Republic of South Africa. Support for a *Valkstaat*, which is led by the 'Freedom Front', has been gaining ground according to recent reports. Professor Hendrik Robbertz, the Chairman of the *Valkstaat* Council, was reported as saying, "self-determination for Afrikaners will determine whether South Africa will survive as a stable community of secure peoples". He further said, "we don't accept the idea of a pot where you throw in everything and then you have a new nation".[19]

In Europe secessionist movements are on the increase, in particular in Eastern and Central Europe. New nation-States emerging out of the former USSR are grappling with this problem, and there seems to be no end of secessionist claims by new minority groups. The Chechen separatist armed struggle against Russia is a classic case in point. When Boris Yeltsin offered the separatists greater autonomous status including the right to have powers to establish relations with the international community and other economic and cultural organisations, to govern according to their constitutional structure, the right to determine their flag and national anthem, Chechen and Tartastan ethnonationalist politicians rejected his offer because they were not satisfied with anything short of Statehood.[20] The Ossetians and the Abkhazians, who represent respectively 3 per cent and 1.9 per cent of the population of the Republic of Georgia, have declared respectively Ossetia and Abkhazia as independent States. The Abkhazians have attempted several times to break-away from Georgia. In 1990, the Abkhaz Supreme Soviet declared Abkhazia a sovereign Republic.[21] In the hope that the Abkhzians would remain in the Georgian Republic, they were offered "disproportionate representation" by the Georgian government in the legislative council of Abkhzia. This constitutional arrangement has been neglected by the Abkhazian separatist politicians making it clear that it does not match their separatist ambition. Separatist Crimean Tartars in the Crimean peninsula of Ukraine are not satisfied with administrative and territorial autonomy for Crimea.[22] The Armenian minorities' campaign for secession in the Nagorny Karabakh[23] region in Azerbaijan resulted in a large-scale ethnic war between Azerbaijan and Armenia. The Turkish Cypriot separatists are, at present, not even satisfied with the "bicommunal and bi-zonal federation" proposed by the Greek Cypriot President Mr.Glafcos Clerides based on the principle that the future political structure of Cyprus should be composed of two politically equal communities.[24]

Similarly, despite having an autonomous province, ETA secessionists in the Basque country have continually been fighting for a separate State even though they have expressed their willingness to enter into a democratic path. The Guardian columnist Tunku Vardarajan writes that the ETA wants nothing short of total sovereignty. Its members posed the question, "how can we accept political consensus within the Spanish State if we do not accept that State in the first place"?[25] The liberal political analyst may find it hard to grasp why ETA fighters do not want to accept one of the most advanced self-governments in Europe. Perhaps, it is not so surprising - their motto is, *Euzkadi ta a skatassuna'* - land and freedom.

Separatist tendencies are prevalent even in the most advanced democratic systems such as the UK, USA, and Canada. In Great Britain although the Scots have not yet resorted to violence, 52 per cent of 18-23 year olds are in favour of an independent Scotland according to an opinion poll conducted in December 1996 by *Scotland on Sunday*.[26] Secessionist movements are active in Wales in the guise of 'Welsh language groups' although they have not yet resorted to serious violence.

In Canada, Francophile Quebecois have been claiming the right to secede for a long time even though Quebec is enjoying greater autonomous power within a federal structure considered by many liberal constitutionalists to be "one of the most decentralized in the world" (Buchanan, 1991:128). Yet, the majority of Quebecois are in favour of secession and further constitutional arrangements may not suffice to quell secessionists' desires for an independent Quebec. "We want a country, we will wait a bit, but not for long", said Jacques Parizau, a separatist leader.[27] In the USA, Puerto Rican and Alaskan secessionist movements are also campaigning for independent statehood. The latter is alleged to have connections with international terrorist organisations (Moynihan, 1994:76).

Asia is beset by a great number of separatist movements. Given the diverse nature of the various ethnic and tribal populations, especially in northern and eastern parts of the continent, it is not surprising that these demographic diversities should make the region unstable and politically volatile. Secessionist armed struggles by ethnic and tribal groups in Sri Lanka, India, Bangladesh, Pakistan and Myanmar (previously known as Burma) have a long history - and there seems to be no end to such conflicts. Most tribal and ethnic groups in the region are of the view that they have been deprived of their nation-States, first by the British Raj, and then by the newly created States. These resentments have resulted in widespread violence between ethnic or tribal groups and States. Not surprisingly, secessionist armed struggles have resulted in border clashes between States causing the deterioration of inter-States relations. For example, India has had many clashes with Pakistan since it became a new nation-State. India has supported separatist movements in Pakistan and Pakistan has supported secessionist movements operating in India, each merely to hurt or take revenge on its enemy.[28] It is widely reported that many separatist movements in the northern and eastern regions of India have been supported financially, ideologically and militarily by the Republic of China and Pakistan. India's clandestine assistance, both politically and militarily, for the Sri Lankan Tamil secessionist groups has resulted in the deterioration of diplomatic relations between India and Sri Lanka, in particular during 1986-1993. The invasion of Sri Lankan air-space by the Indian Air Force on the instruction of the former Indian Premier, Indira Gandhi, damaged the relationship between these two countries creating an atmosphere of war on the island. When, in pursuance of the Indo-Lanka Peace Accord, 1987,[29] the Sri Lankan government made an offer of autonomous powers to the merged northern-eastern provinces of the island, the hard-core Tamil secessionist group, the LTTE, rejected it outright making it clear that such a move would not fulfil the aspiration of the Tamil nation for a separate Tamil Eelam. The Chittagongs in the Chittagong Hill Tracks were at first prepared to accept greater autonomous status within Bangladesh, yet due to the "spiral of government repression and armed resistance" Chittagong secessionist groups are now fighting for an independent Chittagong and they are gaining ground, in particular since 1975. Separatists in Kashmir and Jammu,[30] the Nagas and the Mizos in the Republic of India are also fighting for respectively, Nagaland and Mizoram. The Nagas commenced their separatist struggle even before India attained independence. This was given impetus by the declaration of independence by Naga national leaders on the eve of the declaration of independence for India by the British Raj. Both British and later post-independent Nehruvian governments refused to grant independent status to

Nagaland. A short-lived independent sovereign 'Federal Government of Nagaland' has never been militarily or politically able to sustain its proclaimed statehood. Nonetheless, with the encouragement of Pakistan and sometimes with the military assistance of the Chinese Republic, the Nagas' secessionist movement, currently the Nationalist Socialist Council of Nagaland, with the secret alliance of Manipur's United National Liberation Front and Poresh Baruash's United Liberation Front of Assam, are continuing their struggle to create a Christian Socialist State in greater Nagaland. Analysing this unusually protracted military struggle, Mahmud Ali writes (1993:37): "Nagas have fought Indian forces for more than three decades and, despite immense odds, continue to do so". The Manipur secessionist struggle launched by the Meitei tribal group is another example of the determined and uncompromising nature of modern secessionist movements. Recognising the legitimacy of some of the claims made by the Meitei secessionist movement the Indian government established the Manipur Hill Council granting greater autonomous powers within the Indian federal structure. Yet, both the Peoples Liberation Army (PLA) and Peoples Revolutionary Government of KunglaPak (PREPAK), the main separatist groups of Meitei, are not satisfied with a limited autonomous status. The secessionists' argument is that, "we are beasts of burden under Mayang colonial rule; let us throw out Mayang rule and build a new society. We want independence, we want liberalism".[31] Extremely concerned with the Marxist-Leninist leaning of both factions, the PLA and PREPAK, the Indian government does not seem to want to come to a compromise with them. The Meiteis' aim is not only to establish a socialist State but also to revolutionise the existing socio-demographic structure in order to remove migrant communities and Indian influence.

In Darjeeling in West Bengal the Gurkhas's struggle for an independent Gurkhaland commenced as far back as 1907. They first tried peacefully to secure a separate constituency to voice their grievances in the national assembly. Later, the campaign turned to the liberation of Gurkhaland, a struggle launched both politically and militarily. The militant groups' struggle has "transformed Darjeeling from a peaceful tourist haven into a potential tinder-box".[32] Pranta Prashad and the Gurkha National Liberation Front (GNLF) were prominent amongst secessionist groups in the 1980s. Even though the central government of India was able to persuade some moderate leaders of the GNLF to accept autonomous status for 600,000 Gurkhas by establishing the 'Darjeeling Gurkha Hill Council' in 1988, the military wing of the GNLF and other small secessionist groups are not satisfied with such a constitutional

arrangement. So the hit-and-run guerrilla campaign against the State authorities and their administration has continued though success seems unlikely, at least in the near future.[33] Baluchis and Pathans in Pakistan have also been unsuccessfully fighting for their own nation-States. Myanmar, Thailand, Indonesia and the Philippines have also experienced similar violent secessionist movements by minority groups. Myanmar's unitary structure has been threatened mainly by Karens since Myanmar gained independence from the British Empire in 1948.[34] Separatist ethnic groups increased their activities against Myanmar after the military coup in 1962. Constitutional changes also triggered the secessionists' struggles since Myanmar was declared a unitary State by the 1974 constitution (Milne, 1993:183).

In conclusion, although only a few secessionist groups have been successful in achieving post-modern-tribal-states there is no sign of a decrease in secessionist struggles. Whilst some have lost momentum others are increasingly active. Ultimately success or failure depends on the extent to which these groups are prepared to carry on their struggles and on the determination of States to resist them.

Notes

[1] The concept of 'post-modern tribal-state' is popularised by Thomas M. Franck and supported by many, including Higgins and Cassese. See Franck, T.M. (1993), 'Postmodern Tribalism and the Right to Secession', in C. Brolmann et al (eds), *Peoples and Minorities in International Law*, Martinus Nijhoff: Dordrecht/Boston/ London, pp. 3-28. See also Higgins, R. (1993), 'Postmodern Tribalism and the Right to Secession, Comments', in Brolmann, *ibid.* pp. 29-36. Cassese, A. (1995), *Self-Determination of Peoples*, Cambridge University Press: Cambridge, p. 338. However, some scholars question the suitability of such a term, notably Patrick Thornberry and the Special Rapporteur, Asbjorn Eide. Thornberry noted that when *tribal* in the descriptive sense is used it might carry some negative connotation. His preferred term is *ethnic fundamentalism*, see Thornberry, P. (1993), 'The Democratic or Internal Aspect of Self-Determination with Some Remarks on Federalism', in C. Tomuschat (ed), *Modern Law of Self-Determination*, Martinus Nijhoff, Dordrecht/ Boston/London, p. 105. Special Rapporteur Asbjorn Eide also uses *ethnic fundamentalism* to identify this new ethnic revivalism and the resulting trend towards secession, see *Possible Ways and Means of Facilitating the Peaceful and Constructive Solution of Problems Involving Minorities, 2nd Progress Report*, UN Doc. E/CN.4/Sub.2/ 1992/37, paras. 16-22. See further Eide, A. (1993), 'In Search of Constructive Alternatives to Secession', in Tomuschat ed. *ibid.* pp. 139-

176. It can be argued that 'ethnic fundamentalism' also implies negative connotations since 'fundamentalism' suggests fringe group extremism in some societies. However this author sees no reason why 'post-modern tribal-states' should not be used. Many of those ethnic militant groups campaigning for secession base their ideologies on tribalism as is evident from most secessionist violence.

[2] Both Bokassa and Idi Amin were alleged to have eaten their political enemies for lunch. See Sympson, J. "Was Cannibal Bokasa's Story All Cooked Up", *The Sunday Telegraph*, 10 November 1996.

[3] Watts, D. 'Half a Million Gather to Defy Jakarta's Rule', *The Times*, 9 November 1999.

[4] See on Bougainville, Lawson, S. (1993), 'Ethno-Nationalist Dimensions of Internal Conflict: The Case of Bougainville Secessionism', in K. P. Clements (ed), *Peace and Security in the Asia-Pacific Region: Post-Cold War Problems and Prospects*, United Nations University Press and Dummove Press: Tokyo, pp. 58-77.

[5] Sigler argues that minority rights, 'for the sake of clarity and logic,' should not be identified with 'separatism'. See Sigler, J. A. (1983), *Minority Rights: A Comparative Analysis*, Greenwood Press: Westport, Conn and London, p. 191.

[6] During the Biafran war (and still), the Biafran secession was identified as ethnic secession launched by the Ibos. See Phillips, C. S. (1984), 'Nigeria and Biafra', in Shiels (ed), as below, pp. 176-177. However, Col. Ojuku who led the separatist campaign rejecting such assertions emphasised that the Biafra struggle was between the 'North and South' and between 'Nigeria and the former eastern region'. *ibid.* p. 178.

[7] They are mainly Negroid. Most tribal groups remain pagan. Southerners are divided into three main linguistic groups, i.e. Nilotis, Nilo-Hamitis, and the Sudanic. Each linguistic group is composed of various sub-tribal groups. For example, the Sudanic includes the Azande, Kreish, Bongo, Moru and Madi tribes. See Whitaker, B. (1972), 'The Southern Sudan and Eritrea', in B. Whitaker (ed), *The Fourth World: Victims of Group Oppression*, Sidgwick and Jackson: London, pp. 77-79.

[8] See details, White, D. 'Basque Politicians Under the Gun', *The Financial Times*, 27 January 1998.

[9] A/C.3/49/SR.8/, 25 October 1992, para. 12, p.5.

[10] A/C.3/48/SR. 21, 26 November 1993, para. 11, p. 4.

[11] See *infra* chapter 11. 11. 5.

[12] A/C.3/47/SR.8, 19 October 1992, para. 48, p. 13 (Albania).

[13] See *infra* chapter 11. 4.

[14] A/51/PV.20, 3 October 1996, p. 9 (Senegal).

[15] A/51/PV. 14, 30 September 1996, p. 6.

[16] Mr. Al-Eryany, the Yemen Deputy Prime Minister's address to the UN, UN Department of Humanitarian Affairs (1994, January-February), *DHA News, Special Edition*, p. 12.

¹⁷ UN Department of Public Information (1995), *The United Nations and the Situation in Somalia*, New York, DPI/1321/Rev. 4, p. 1.
¹⁸ On the historical background to the conflict between the South and North in the Sudan, see Whitaker, ed., above, pp. 80-94.
¹⁹ Kiley, S. 'Afrikaaners Win Backing for Separate Homeland', *The Times*, 7 August 1998.
²⁰ *Washington Post*, 1 April 1992, cited in Moynihan, R. (1994), *Pandaemonium: Ethnicity in International Politics*, Oxford UP: Oxford, p.71.
²¹ See UN Department of Information (1995), *The United Nations and the Situations on Georgia*, New York, DPI/1693, p. 1. See details, *infra* chapter 11.11.7.
²² A/C.3/51/SR.28, 19, September 1997, para.14, p.5 (the Ukraine). See details Packer, J. (1998), 'Autonomy Within the OSCE: The Case of Crimea', in M. Suksi (eds), *Autonomy: Applications and Implications*, Kluwer Law International: The Hague/ London /Boston, pp. 312-314.
²³ See *infra* chapter 11.
²⁴ A/51/PV. 10, 26 September 1996, p. 3. See further A/C.3/47/SR.9, 27 October 1992, para. 89, p. 19. See *infra* chapter 11.
²⁵ *The Guardian*, 23 July 1996.
²⁶ *The Times*, 30 December 1996.
²⁷ Http://www.usatoday.com/news/index/inque 005 htm, 16 March 1999.
²⁸ A/C.3/50/SR.50, 12 January 1996, para. 43, p.8 (India's' allegation against Pakistan).
²⁹ See the full text of the Accord, 26 *ILM* 1175 [1987], pp.1175-1183.
³⁰ A/C.3/47/SR.9, 27 October 1992, para.52, p. 12 (Pakistan).
³¹ For details see Ali, S. M. (1993), *The Federal State: Power, People and Internal Wars in South Asia*, Zed Books: London and New Jersey, p. 47.
³² *Ibid.* pp. 53-54.
³³ *Ibid.* pp. 53-56.
³⁴ Myanmar's Foreign Affairs Minister Mr. Ohn Gyaw stated that there were 16 secessionist groups in his country fighting for independent States. See A/50/PV, 13, 27 September 1996, p. 16.

References

Ahmed, A. S. (1995), 'Ethnic Cleansing: A Metaphor for Our Time', 18 (1) *Ethnic and Racial Studies*, pp. 1-25.
Akhavan, P. (1996), 'Self-Determination and the Disintegration of Yugoslavia: What Lessons for the International Community?' in D. Clark and R. Williamson, (eds), *Self-Determination: International Perspectives*, Macmillan Press: London, pp. 227- 248.
Ali, S. M. (1993), *The Fearful States: People and International Wars in South Asia,* Xed Books: London and New Jersey.

Blum, Y. Z. (1992), 'UN, Membership of the New Yugoslavia: Continuity or Break?', 86 (4) *AJIL*, pp. 830-833.

Bremmer, I. and Bailes, A. (1998), 'Sub-Regionalism in the Newly Independent States', 74 (1) *International Affairs*, pp. 131-147.

Brilmayer, L. (1991), 'Secession and Self-Determination: A Territorial Interpretation', 16 (1) *Yale.J.Int.l.L*, pp. 177-201.

Buchanan, A. (1991), *Secession: The Morality of Political Divorce, From Fort Sumter to Lithuania and Quebec*, Westview Press: Boulder/Sanfrancisco/Oxford.

Buchheit, L. C. (1978), *Secession: The Legitimacy of Self-Determination*, Yale University Press: New Haven and London.

Clark, R. P. (1984), 'Spain and the Basques', in Shiels (ed), as below, pp. 71-104.

Cobban, A. (1944), *National Self-Determination*, Oxford UP: London/New York and Toronto.

Denitch, B. (1994), *Ethnic Nationalism: The Tragic Death of Yugoslavia*, University of Minnesota Press: Minneapolis/London.

Dyke, V. V. (1995), 'The Individual, The State, and Ethnic Communities in Political Theory', in W. Kymlicka (ed), Multicultural Citizenship, Clarendon Press: Oxford, pp. 32-56.

Eide, A. (1993), 'In Search of Constructive Alternatives to Secession', in Tomuschat (ed), as below, pp. 139-176.

Elagab, O. Y. (1995), *International Law Documents Relating to Terrorism*, Cavendish Publishing Ltd: London.

Franck, T. M. (1993), 'Postmodern Tribalism and the Right to Secession', in C. Brolmann, R. Lefeber and M. Zieck (eds), *Peoples and Minorities in International Law*, Martinus Nijhoff / Dordrecht/Boston/London, pp. 3- 27.

Franck, T. M. (1996), 'Clan and Super Clan: Loyalty, Identity and Community in Law and Practice', 90 *AJIL*, pp. 359-383.

Gilbert, P. (1994), *Terrorism, Security and Nationality: An Introductory Study in Applied Political Philosophy*, Routledge: London and New York.

Halprin, M. H. and Scheffer, D. and Small, P. L. (1992), *Self-Determination in the New World Order*, Carnegie Endowment for International Peace: Washington DC.

Heraclides, A. (1991), *The Self-Determination of Minorities in International Politics*, Franck Cass: London.

Horowitz, D. L. (1985), *Ethnic Groups in Conflict*, University of California Press: Berkerly.

Irwin, Z. T. (1984), 'Yugoslavia and Ethnonatinalists', in Shiels (ed), as below, pp. 72- 105.

Jackson, R. A. and James, A. eds. (1993), *States in a Changing World: A Contemporary Analysis*, Clarendon Press: Oxford.

Koestler, A. (1967), *The Ghost in the Machine*, Pan Books Ltd: London.

Kohli, A. (1997), 'Can Democracies Accommodate Ethnic Nationalism? Rise and Decline of Self-Determination Movements in India', 56 (2) *JAS*, pp. 359- 380.

Lawson, S. (1996), 'Self-Determination as Ethnocracy: Perspectives from the South Pacific', in M. Sellers (ed), *The New World Order, Sovereignty, Human*

Rights and the Self-Determination of Peoples, BERG: Oxford/Washington DC, 153-175.

Leff, C. S. (1999), 'Democratization and Disintegration in Multinational States: The Breakup of the Communist Federations', 51 (2) *World Politics*, pp. 205- 235.

Margalit, A and Raz, J. (1995), 'National Self-Determination', in W. Kymlicka. (ed), *The Rights of Minority Cultures*, Oxford UP: Oxford, pp. 79-92.

Mayall, J. (1990), *Nationalism and International Society*, Cambridge UP: Cambridge.

McDowall (1992), 'The Kurdish Question: A Historical Review', in P. G. Kreyenbroek and S. Sperl (eds), *The Kurds: A Contemporary Overview*, Routledge: London and New York.

Mihas, D. E. (1997), 'Romania Between Balkan Nationalism and Democratic Transition', 17 (3) *World Politics*, pp. 175-181.

Milne, R. (1993), 'South East Asia', in Jackson and James (eds), as above, pp. 177-196.

Moynihan, D. P. (1994), *Pandaemonium: Ethnicity in International Politics*, Oxford UP: Oxford.

Mullerson, R. (1993), 'Minorities in Eastern Europe and the Former USSR: Problems, Tendencies and Protection', 56 *MLR*, pp. 793- 811.

Mullerson, R. (1994), *International Law, Rights and Politics: Developments in Eastern Europe and the CIS*, LSE and Routledge: London.

Murswiek, D. (1993), 'The Issues of a Right of a Secession: Reconsidered', in Tomuschat ed., below, pp. 21-40.

Ronen, D. (1974), *The Quest for Self-Determination*, Yale University Press: New Haven and London.

Schiels, F. L. ed. (1984), *Ethnic Separatism and World Politics*, University Press of America: Lanham/New York and London.

Schreuer, C. (1993), 'The Waning of the Sovereign State: Towards a New Paradigm for International Law', 4 (4) *EJIL*, pp. 444-471.

Shehadi, K. S. (1993), *Ethnic Self-Determination and the Break-up of States*, Adelphi Papers 283, Brassey's (UK): London.

Sigler, J. A. (1983), *Minority Rights: A Comparative Analysis*, Clarendon Press: Westport, Conn and London.

Soyinka, W. (1996), *The Open Sore of a Continent*, Oxford UP: Oxford.

Suksi, M. ed. (1998), *Autonomy, Applications and Implications*, Kluwer Law International: The Hague/London/Boston.

Stavenhagen, R. (1996), 'Self-Determination: Right or Demon?', in D. Clark and R. Williamson (eds), *Self-Determination: In International Perspectives*, Macmillan Press Ltd: London.

Thornberry, P. (1993), 'The Democratic or Internal Aspects of Self-Determination with some Remarks on Federalism', in Tomuschat (ed), as below, pp. 101-138.

Tomuchat, C. ed. (1993), *Modern Law of Self-Determination*, Martinus Nijhoff: Dordrecht/Boston/London.

Treisman, D. S. (1997), 'Russia's Ethnic Revival: The Separatist Activism of Regional Leaders in a Post Communist Order', 49 (2) *World Politics*, pp. 212- 249.

Tubiana, J. (1983), 'The Linguistic Approach to Self-Determination', in I. M. Lewis (ed), *Nationalism and Self-Determination in the Horn of Africa*, Ithaca Press: London, p. 23.

Vulliamy, E. (1998), 'Bosnia: The Crimes of Appeasement', 74 (1) *International Affairs,* pp. 73- 91.

Williamson, R. eds. (1996), *Self-Determination: International Perspectives*, Macmillan Press: London, pp. 1-11.

9 The Right to Secession: The Views of Jurists

Introduction

The claim that minorities are entitled to secede from the States they inhabit by virtue of the right to self-determination has become a source of inspiration for many minority groups in contemporary polities. By exercising the right to self-determination, peoples living under colonial or alien domination are entitled to break away from their colonial masters and to establish the form of the State they wish to have. Secessionist rights campaigners argue that a section of a people living in an independent State by reason of ethnic, religious or linguistic origins is also entitled to proclaim independence for a region and secede from that State. Minority groups in contemporary polities, it is argued, are trapped in arbitrarily created territories against their will. Their only way to self-expression lies on the road to secession. This is seen as the emancipation of 'trapped minorities' from the Westphalian model nation-State system. The argument goes on that "only by an act of secession can a trapped minority exercise the right of self-determination" (for details see White, 1981:161). This is clearly an attempt to interpret self-determination in terms of ethnicity by challenging the legitimacy of the State-oriented approach.

The whole territory, in this decolonisation process, becomes a new State. The people of the territory as one unit take part in this process. Peoples who live in a territory under colonial rule do not leave it. This must not be understood as a right to secession as will be shown below.

Secession denotes a different scenario as has been seen earlier. It advocates a break-up of the country. Ethnic differences become demarcating factors in place of territorial boundaries. Secessionists appear as 'peoples' thus placing themselves within 'the boundaries of self-determination'. They are, it is said, as peoples entitled to determine whether to stay within the existing State or opt out of it altogether.

Politicisation of the doctrine of self-determination by 'many European leaders' (Higgins, 1994:121-124 and 128) has given rise to false hopes amongst minorities. It is often said that the right to secession is in accordance with the right to self-determination, and liberal democracy. Such views find favour amongst most ethnic groups. Secessionists often use only 'favourable aspects' of the right to self-determination to justify their struggles for independence "while disregarding the accompanying caveats that the principle does not supersede a state's territorial integrity" (see Brilmayer, 1991:183). Thus, secession is seen as a radical alternative to State-centred international law. The idea of the supremacy of the territory in opposition to the popular sovereignty is seen as the continuation of feudalism and monarchism. It is necessary, from secessionists' perspectives, to identify the moral superiority of self-determination over other concerns such as the sanctity of territorial boundaries. Dissatisfied groups and individuals, it is said, should not be chained to abstract concepts in violation of fundamental human rights. "The idea that government must stem from the consent of the governed seems to allow a disaffected group the right to opt out of an existing state. If consent is the keystone of legitimacy, then a non-consenting individual must be allowed to leave. In this way, principles of democratic government translate into a right of secession" (see Brilmayer, 1991:184). So, minorities "appropriate the vocabulary of self-determination whether governments or scholars approve or not" (Thornberry, 1989:868). For them "secession is really a political process which, in the final analysis, can be realised notwithstanding the absence of legality" (Shehadi, 1993:3).

This is in many respects similar to the situation prevalent in post-World War I Europe and elsewhere. Encouraged by the manifesto of the Bolshevik revolutionaries in the USSR which declared that nations have the right to decide their own destinies, and later by Wilson's advocacy of national self-determination through democratic governance as the expression of the people, small nations "began a wild rush" for independent Statehood "which was to sweep onward until the end of the war and beyond" eventually becoming an "uncontrollable torrent" (Cobban, 1944:12). Reminiscent of these events, the right to self-determination is now increasingly used as a means to their ends by militant minority groups in all corners of the world (Stavenhagen, 1996; Cassese, 1995:5; Alfredsson, 1996:58; see generally Buchheit, 1978:214). This is variously referred to as 'ethnic self-determination', (Shehadi, 1993) 'secessionist self-determination' (Cassese, 1995:339-343), or 'ethnic separatism' (Shiels, 1984).

Before examining claims that the right to secession is an inherent part of the right to self-determination I will first analyse the scope of self-determination and its application in modern international law.

9.1 *Self-determination?: "For Which Poets Have Sung and Patriots Have Laid Down Their Lives"*

Like most norms of international law, the notion of the right to self-determination has evolved over centuries. Various kinds of individuals and peoples took part in this process. Travellers, poets, patriots, soldiers, politicians, liberal philosophers and the like have contributed to the birth and the development of the idea of self-determination. This has resulted in the crumbling of many empires and given rise to the birth of many new nation-States. The enlightenment and the romanticisation of nationalism during the French Revolution of 1789 and subsequent nation-building movements, notably in Italy and Germany, saw the principle of self-determination as a natural human right opposed to autocratic and feudal empires (Ronen, 1974:14). Democratic governance based on the will of the people has been the core element of this principle from its inception.

Self-determination has already passed through two stages, from national self-determination to the right to self-determination. As has been seen in chapter 5, it is still developing, particularly its internal dimension, its most important aspect as far as democratic governance and the human rights of minority groups are concerned. National self-determination originated and was nurtured by Western civilisation. The popular assumption is that the origin of the doctrine can be traced back to the French and American revolutions, but its seeds had existed even before these historical events took place (Kohn, 1958:526-528). Since the French revolution, writes Dov Ronen (1974), the ideal of self-determination has spread throughout the world affecting the whole inter-State relations and the nation-State system. National self-determination has justified its existence by giving birth to many States in Latin America, Europe, and the Mediterranean. England, France, Italy, Germany, and Spain became strong nation-States in Europe whilst the USA emerged as a union of peoples emphasising the importance of the peoples' will as opposed to autocratic regimes. In the early 20th century, a cluster of new nation-States replaced those empires in Europe such as the Ottoman, German and Austro-Hungarian empires (Shehadi, 1993:14-15).

The idea of national self-determination continued to flourish during the first World War and its aftermath. The belief that each nation has an inherent right to constitute an independent State and to determine its own destiny spread like wild-fire amongst ethnic groups (Cobban, 1944). Self-determination as a principle in international relations was popularised by 'strange bedfellows', J. Stalin, V. I. Lenin and the former US President Woodrow Wilson (Cassese, 1995).[1]

Both Lenin and Stalin preached the theory, as will be shown below, that by virtue of self-determination, nationalities and ethnic groups could exercise the right to secession (see Cassese, 1995:20-23). However, some critics doubt the sincerity of the statements made by Lenin and Stalin. Kohn (1958:528) points out that the principle of self-determination was used by both as a political tool against the West. "To communism", argues Hans Kohn (at 528), "persons and nationalities alike were not ends in themselves but instruments to be used in various and opportunist ways".

Wilson's contribution to the development of the right to self-determination was enormous by virtue of his equation of democratic governance with self-determination (see Pomerance, 1982; Cassese, 1995:19-23; Cobban, 1944; Hannum, 1993:7-8). Democratically elected government by popular will (popular sovereignty) without interference was the main plank of Wilson's theory. Self-determination meant, in his view, self-government (see Cassese, 1995:19). For him it was a democratic principle to be achieved by non-violent and orderly means. He presented his idea in the now famous speeches of 8 January 1918 on 'Fourteen Points' and of 11 February 1918 on 'Four Principles' (Cassese, 1995:20; see further Cobban, 1944:13-14 and 19-22; Kohn, 1958). Advocating further his principle at Montana on 11 September 1919, he emphasised that "that the countries of the world belong to the people who live in them, and that they have a right to determine their own destiny and their own form of government and their own policy... ." (Padover ed. 1942:109, cited in Cassese, 1995:20).

It is worthy of mention that Wilson later regretted his unguarded description of some aspects of the principle of self-determination, notably the unit which benefits from it. In a testimony to the Committee of Foreign Relations on 19 August 1919, Wilson apologised for creating false hope amongst various nationalities around the globe (see details in Temperley, 1969, cited in Cassese, 1995:22). His close associate Robert Lansing also severely criticised Wilson's theory of self-determination. He wrote (1921:97-98): "The phrase is simply loaded with dynamite. It will raise hopes, which can never be realised. It will, I fear, cost thousands of lives. In the end it is bound to be discredited, to be called the dream of an idealist who failed to realize the danger until too late to check those who attempt to put the principle in force. What a calamity that the phrase was ever uttered! What misery it will cause!"

However, the application of the principle was limited to a few States in Central and Eastern Europe. This subsequently gave rise to anger and frustration amongst many oppressed minority groups world-wide. The right holders of the principle of self-determination were also not clearly identified and the principle itself was too confused and vague. It was applied very selectively excluding many national groups. In fact, the principle of self-determination was applied on a territorial basis thereby refusing to give any legitimacy to ethnic claims.

9.2 *Emergence From a Principle to a Legal Right "With all its Contradictory, Subversive and Threatening Nature"*

With the adoption of the ICCPR and ICESCR,[2] the principle of self-determination was transformed from a political principle to a legal right, that is the right to self-determination. In its early years, the UN General Assembly in its resolution 421 D (V) December 4, 1950 recognized the 'self-determination of peoples and nations' as a 'fundamental human right'.[3] Although some States are still apprehensive of the doctrine due to its 'contradictory, subversive and threatening nature' (Cassese, 1995), the right to self-determination has gradually emerged as "the foundation of international order".[4] The attitudes of the international community to it have become fairly favourable, so that the principle of self-determination is no longer considered as a mere moral or political postulate. It is, as stated by Judge Weeramantry in his dissenting opinion in the *Case Concerning East Timor (Portugal v Australia)*[5] rather a fundamental norm of contemporary international law. Some early judgments of the ICJ, notably the *Namibia*,[6] and *Western Sahara*[7] cases also came to similar conclusions. It is an unquestionable and inalienable right which "all civilized nations should accept and respect",[8] because "self-determination is a fundamental condition for the effective guarantee and observance of human rights and for the preservation and promotion of such rights".[9]

The right to self-determination is now recognised by many States as "a prerequisite to the full enjoyment of all fundamental human rights",[10] "the corner-stone of the whole edifice of human rights",[11] and is "the very essence of peaceful co-existence" in international relations.[12] As the Algerian delegate to the UN Mr Sharaui stated, the right to self-determination is "a fundamental principle of international relations and a peremptory rule of international law", a violation of which constitute a crime.[13] The German representative Mr. Graf zu Rantzau agreed with the theory that a violation of the right constitutes a violation of human rights.[14] Another State representative argued that a violation of the right amounts not only to an 'offence' but also to 'an international crime'.[15]

As early as 1951, some States stressed that the right to self-determination stood above all other rights". In fact, some States were over-optimistic even during the embryonic stage of the United Nations. Indonesia, for example, said:

> That right was, indeed, basic: nations which, like Indonesia, had just freed themselves from colonialism knew what blood had been shed and what wars had been caused as a result of attacks on that right. His delegation was convinced that by guaranteeing the right of peoples to self-determination, the United Nations could not but help to avert a new world war, or at least to prevent disputes between nations.[16]

Self-determination does not necessarily mean independence. As described by principle VI of the GA Res. 1541 it entitles the population of the territory concerned to take the following options: a) emergence as an independent sovereign State, b) free association with an independent State, and c) integration with another State. However self-determination has to be exercised without harming another equally important principle in the UN Charter, the territorial integrity of the State. The second and third option should be exercised by democratic means and be a result of the free and voluntary choice of the peoples of the territory concerned (see further Sinha, 1973: 269-270).

Our investigation focuses here on whether minorities appearing as a 'people' can exercise the right to secession by virtue of the right to self-determination.

9.3 *The Right to Secession: "An Ultimate Remedy for Trapped Minorities"?*

Lenin, Stalin and other post-Bolshevik revolutionaries, as Anthonio Cassese (1995) points out, advocated that self-determination could be exercised by ethnic and national groups. For instance, in 1917 in transmitting the Soviet Union's peace proposal to other States, Lenin and Stalin repeated among other things that the right to secession could be exercised by nationalities, including ethnic groups (see Simma ed., 1994:58). Stalin wrote (1913:20):

> The right to self-determination means that a nation can arrange its life in accordance to its own will. It has the right to arrange its life on the basis of autonomy. It has the right to complete secession. Nations are sovereign and all nations are equal.

Stalin further pointed out (1913:159) that "the self-determination of nations living in sovereign States was to be primarily realized through secession" and argued for "complete freedom to agitate for secession and for a referendum on secession by the seceding nations".

Secession is attracting more attention than any other issue in contemporary polities. Even though its disastrous legal and political implications for human society are clearly evident, it continues to be advocated by secessionist rights campaigners. Debate on the issue has created deep divisions even amongst jurists. Alexis Heraclides writes in 1992 (at 403):

> Until recently, secessionist nationalism was erroneously treated as passé: an oddity fit for the museum of historical movements. Such claims can no longer be made: Secession has taken centre stage in domestic and international politics... In the wake of the astounding events of the past three years, one can detect a weakening in the existing taboo against secession, indeed the signs of an emerging paradigm shift whereby secession will no longer be treated as unthinkable by the international system.

Nonetheless, it is not easy for theorists of secession to find a sound legal foundation for its legitimacy, because secession itself stands against the most revered principles of contemporary international law, territorial integrity and the sovereignty of States. The theory that peoples have to exercise the right to self-determination without violation of the principle of territorial integrity causes problems for jurists who advocate secession.

Attempts to limit the application of self-determination only to the colonial situation provoke advocates of secession (see details Klabbers and Lefeber, 1993:41). These are seen by them as hypocrisy on the part of the nation-State system which, they allege, stands only for the welfare of the majority population of the State (see also Heraclides, 1992:407). The majority of contemporary polities are seen as artificial monsters created by former colonial Empires. Within these arbitrary boundaries, argues Buchheit (1978:17), minority groups are hapless victims, "pursuant to a paragraph in some medieval territorial settlement or through a fiat of cartographers, annexed to an independent State". If a part of a population is deprived of fundamental human rights and is subjected to persistent oppression on ethnic, racial, religious or linguistic grounds, then, it is argued, why cannot oppressed group secede by resorting to external self-determination? These arguments thus appear to mean that secession can be converted to a part of external self-determination in certain situations.

As a segment of the population of the State, should a minority stay where it is by respecting the territorial integrity of the State? Or, if it decides otherwise, can it opt out of the system altogether by forming its own State?

Lea Brilmayer (1991:179 and 183), who tried to provide a theoretical base for secessionist rights, emphasises that minorities may have a legitimate claim for a secession if they can prove that they:

a) occupy a distinct geographical unit of the part of a State of which they form part;
b) have strong historical ties with the disputed territory; and
c) are 'a true nation' different from the dominant group in the existing State in terms of racial, ethnic, religious and linguistic characteristics; (see also for similar views, McCorquodale, 1992:595; See Buchanan, 1991).

In addition, if they can also prove that they have been subjected to a sustained campaign of discrimination and oppression, and they have been denied the internal right to self-determination then they have a better chance of winning their argument (see White, 1981:161; Buchheit: 1978:220-223; Buchanan, 1991). Brilmayer is of the view that the current interpretation of self-determination distorts the separatist question by giving undue prominence to territorial integrity. *Peoples*, *State* and the *territory* are all embedded in self-determination. Neglect of the relationship between a segment of a population and the territory will inevitably breed grievances amongst minority groups.

The argument goes that secessionists should base their claims on territorial sovereignty rather than on unwinnable theories such as democratic governance which, in Brilmayer's view, do not provide the right for a segment of a population to leave the State in which they live. The current understanding of the right to self-determination does not provide any legal basis for a minority to secede, because it is the *peoples'* right. On the other hand, opting out of the State by a segment of a population is not a valid right in international law nor will it find any legality in terms of democratic government. The better position for secessionists, therefore, argues Brilmayer (1991:187), would be to claim that the State's powers over a part of the territory is illegitimate, because the territory in question belongs to the minority group which claims it. The territorial sovereignty of the disputed land in fact belongs to the minority rather than to the majority. The minority should also convince the international community that the current occupation of the land by a State is the result of an unjustifiable historical event (see further Buchanan, 1991:151-153). To have a better chance to success, secessionists should be able to link claims for territorial rights to claim for ethnic distinctiveness. Brilmayer (1991:189) further argues that "[s]ecessionists must somehow establish a claim to the territory on which they would found their new state. Such claims to territory do not flow automatically from ethnic distinctiveness. Groups that are ethnically distinct but possess no independent territorial claims have very poor chances of convincing anyone of their right to secede" (see also Heraclides, 1992:411-413).

It is frequently argued by some scholars that the right to secession is inherently a part of minorities' rights. According to this view, the right to opt out of the State is an entitlement which oppressed groups can exercise in certain situations. Benyamin Neuberger argues (1986:71, cited in Hannum, 1993):

> The right of secession is seen as a variant of the right of self-defence- you defend yourself by seceding from an oppressive system... There can be compelling reasons for secession such as if the physical survival or the cultural autonomy of a nation is threatened, or if a population would feel economically excluded and permanently deprived.

According to Robert McCorquodale (1992:593) groups such as minorities can exercise self-determination beyond the colonial context. The territorial integrity should not, in his view, obstruct the peoples' choice in determining their political future. "If the desire of the peoples is for independence then they should probably have the potential to satisfy some criteria of Statehood" (at 595). Referring to the Baltic States' independence from the former USSR, and the seceding of Croatia, Slovenia and Bosnia-Herzegovina from the former Yugoslavia, McCorquodale argues that in all these instances, none of which represented a colonial situation, independence was achieved by a segment of 'peoples'. With the adoption of the Covenants on human rights (ICCPR and ICESCR), the right of self-determination was widened, so that it can be exercised even against independent States (McCorquodale, 1992:603). His arguments are based on the assumption that both the Baltic and the former Republics of the Yugoslavia achieved independence by secession. If the State does not treat its population equally without distinction as to race, creed or colour, then the State cannot reject secessionist claims by any dissatisfied group on the ground that such claims violate its territorial integrity. Secessionist claims, in his view, can only be constrained "where objective threats to international peace and security are involved" (at 605). McCorquodale (1992:608) further argues, "While the exercise of this right may be different according to the circumstances, it can be applied to any situation where there is subjugation, domination and exploitation of peoples by a government, wherever located". This proposition will allow minorities, appearing as 'peoples', to secede by exercising the external right to self-determination. Thus, secession is, in his view, a part of an external self-determination.

Professor Ved P. Nanda (1972:321- 336) in his famous writing on the secession of East Pakistan in 1971, supports the theory that peoples under certain circumstances, even in a non-colonial setting, can exercise the right to self-determination. However, he admits that there is still a problem in harmonising 'territorial integrity', 'self-determination' and 'non-intervention'. If a region of the State "approaches the parameters of a colonial situation", argues Nanda (at 336), "a case can perhaps be made for the application of self-determination on that basis". If a given region is, as in the case of East Pakistan, physically separated from the other constituent part of the State, then it is not difficult to convince the international community of the practicability of secession for the region even though it violates international norms. And it is even easier for the secessionists to justify their claims if their peoples have continually been subjected to gross violations of human rights. In such a case territorial integrity and non-intervention cannot be used by the recalcitrant State to deny the legal justification of secession (Nanda, 1972: 336).

In his subsequent writing Professor Nanda came to a more radical conclusion that "On balance, however, severe deprivations of human rights often leave no alternative to territorial separation. The world community must respond efficiently and effectively to the consequences of such separation. There is a growing recognition of the close link between human rights and international peace and security. It is not premature to accord recognition to the right to secession in an effort to promote these goods" (Nanda, 1981:280).

Buchheit goes further than anyone mentioned above in providing legitimacy to the right to secession when he asserts that there is now a recognised rule of customary international law termed as *remedial secession*. He argues (1978:222):

> 'Remedial secession' seems to occupy a status as the *lex lata*... Remedial secession envisions a scheme by which, corresponding to the varying degrees of oppression inflicted upon a particular group by its governing State, international law recognizes a continuum of remedies ranging from protection of individual rights, to minority rights, and ending with secession as the *ultimate remedy*. At a certain point, the severity of a State's treatment of its minorities becomes a matter

of international concern. This concern may be evidenced by an international demand for guarantees of minority rights (which is as far as the League was willing to go) or suggestions of regional autonomy, economic independence and so on; or it may finally involve an international legitimation of a right to secessionist self-determination as a self-help remedy by the aggrieved group.

Buchheit (1978:475) however, admits that the ultimate success of secession depends on whether secessionists have "a political strength, which may well mean military force, to validate such claims".

Klabbers and Lefeber (1993:37-76) present another argument in favour of secession. If a minority or a sub-group:

a) is denied internal self-determination, in particular the right to take part in decision- making processes,
b) has been subjected to persistent gross violation of human rights, and
c) has exhausted all local and international remedies,

then such a group can form a new State by exercising the right of external self-determination, provided that the new State meets the traditional criteria of statehood and new criteria for the recognition of States. The international community, under such circumstances, has no alternative other than to recognise the new State. The principle of territorial integrity will, in such a situation, become non-operative (Klabbers and Lefeber, 1993:53-54). If a parent State tries to resist the secession by military force, they further argue, it will become an aggressor.

9.4 *Qualified or Limited Right to Secession?*

Professor Alan Buchanan (1991) is in favour of a limited right to secession on moral grounds under 'extreme conditions' (at 151 and 153). The following conditions should be prevalent before secession can be justified:

a) discrimination against a minority group on ethnic, racial, religious or cultural grounds, in particular in re-distribution of resources;
b) there is a serious threat to the survival and the culture of the minority group concerned;
c) the State's reluctance to protect the minority from a third party aggressor when there is an actual threat to its members;

d) where the State's title to the territory in question is dubious or the territory was in fact possessed by the secessionist group in the recent past; and

e) secessionists must also establish that they have a valid claim to the territorial unit in dispute.

In addition, nullification of the rights of minority groups such as the right to veto and the right to represent their group in the political process also increases the case for secession on moral grounds (Buchanan, 1991:153). In respect of culture, in Buchanan's view (153), "at the very least its prospects of demise in the near future must be significantly greater than the risks that all cultures face". However, this right is available only to those cultures which meet a decency test. Cultures such as those that flourished under the Nazi and Pol Pot regimes are not entitled to have the right to secession because they are repugnant to human civilization.

Past injustices committed against a minority may also, in Buchanan's view, (1991:40 and 151-153) help secessionists' claims. When there is a weighty case in favour of secession, "others have a weighty obligation not to interfere" with it (Buchanan, 1991:151). If secession succeeds the new State should "compensate innocent third parties that suffered" (at 152). Nonetheless, the right to secession will be invalid if secessionists try to establish an 'illiberal State'.

More cautious approaches are also presented in favour of a 'qualified right' to secession by Kamanu (1974:355-376), Heraclides (1992), and Nanda (1981:257-280). Absolute prohibition of secession, states Heraclides (1992: 408), would not help solve the problems in contemporary multi-ethnic polities. If each and every secessionist claim is suppressed, argues Kamanu (1974:360-361), oppressed minorities will be condemned "to physical liquidation by ruthless majorities". Kamanu (1974:361) also admits the possibility of chaotic and destructive effects if the demands of minority groups are allowed to lead to the disintegration of States. Merely racial or ethnic differences from the rest of the population of the parent State are, in his view, not enough to justify secessionist claims. 'Genuine, definite and substantial grievances' are the criteria which have to be met by secessionist groups (Kamanu, 1974:361).

Whilst discouraging weak cases of secession, argues Heraclides (1992: 403:420), reasonable solutions involving independence should be found for 'very good cases'. Others, (such as the Southern Sudanese between 1972 and 1982, the Nagas in India) would be required to prove that they can adhere to human rights standards, including, in particular, "the protection of new minorities in their midst". In other cases, suitable solutions involving autonomy may be considered (1992:410; see also Kamanu, 1974:361). In the view of Heraclide, a minority living compactly in a distinct territory having the support of the majority of the population of that territory have a good chance of meeting the criteria for a very good case. In addition, there should also be evidence that there has been deliberate and systematic exploitation or discrimination against them. Kamanu (1974:361) adds another important requirement for any consideration of secession, that is, "a measure of self-determination short of secession" should have been exhausted by the group which claim secession and there should be strong evidence that the dominant majority group has rejected it. In such a situation, outright independence, argues Kamanu (1974:362), may be the only viable means for a secessionist group, "where intense communal cleavage and violence have left a legacy of fear and mistrust that would rule out mutual co-operation except by the use of force".

To monitor the activities of secessionist movements and to address issues arising out of such movements, Heraclides (1992) thinks, similar to Professor Nanda (1972), that there should be a 'convincing filter' to act as an effective self-regulation mechanism.

9.5 *Secession by Consensus?*

New States can still emerge peacefully by consent of the contending parties. This is now theorised as "consensus secession" by some scholars (see Marchildon and Maxwell, 1992). Consensus secession may operate in a colonial as well as in a non-colonial context. In the latter case, it is argued that if consensus cannot be found between the metropolitan State and the peoples in the colony, the colonials can secede. This is a misinterpretation of the Colonial Declaration and GA Res. 1541 (1960), as will be shown below. The right to self-government and/ or independence provided in the Colonial Declaration has been misunderstood with regard to secession.

"Changes arising from peaceful negotiations, free of acts of aggression or external intervention", as stated by Eide, "are obviously in conformity with international law".[17] Examples abound. Panama's secession from Colombia, Venezuela's secession from Colombia in 1830, Senegal from the Mali Federation in 1960, Syria from the United Arab Republic in 1961, Singapore from the Malaysian Federation in 1965, and the emergence of Norway and Sweden as two separate independent States in 1905 are some of them (Shiels, 1984: chapter I). Both the Slovak and Czech Republics emerged as separate independent States on 1 January 1993 by mutual consent, the existing administrative borders becoming each country's external boundaries (Shaw, 1997:478-507). Secession by consensus may be implemented by both constitutional changes and international treaties. Thus, when a part of the peoples of a territory is granted the right to secede by constitutional arrangement and if secession occurs in a democratic way with the blessing of the popular will, the question of legitimacy will not be an issue at all.

9.6 *"Recognition of Secession Will Inaugurate Anarchy in International Life"?*

The right to secession, as a legal principle in international law, has not been accepted by most international jurists (see Mullerson, 1994; Frank, 1992 and 1993; Higgins, 1994; Cassese, 1995; Hannum, 1993). The theory that secession is an inherent part of self-determination is rejected by most of them. Self-determination is a radical principle that had revolutionary effects in former colonies and empires. It also has the potential for the creation of problems for independent nation-States. It is therefore admitted by many States and publicists that some limitations to it are "necessary to maintain international peace and stability of the nation-State (Schoenberg, 1976:94).

Refuting the notion that through self-determination a minority can secede from the State of which they form a part, Professor Rosalyn Higgins in her famous work 'The Development of International Law through the Political Organs of the United Nations' (1963:105) concludes:

> If, then, the right of self-determination is the right of the majority within an accepted political unit to exercise power, there can be no such thing as self-determination for Nagas". The Nagas live within the political unit of India, and do not constitute the majority therein. Their interests are to be safeguarded by Indian obligations on human rights and the protection of minorities.

In her recent work she concludes (1994: 124):

> Minorities *as such* do not have a right of self-determination. That means, in effect, that they have no right to secession, to independence, or to join with comparable groups in other States.

This should not be interpreted as the denial of the benefits of self-determination, in particular internal self-determination for minority groups. She challenges only the misinterpretation of the so-called secessionist self-determination, the myth which for many years has propagated the view that secession is an inherent part of self-determination. The evolving norm of self-determination, argues Higgins (1994:121), should not be used as an enemy of territorial integrity. This rational and correct position is reflected in many other scholars' works. In his classic analysis on the developments in 'Eastern Europe and the CIS', Professor Rein Mullerson writes (1994:71):

> One can say that in democratic countries different ethnic groups have more opportunities to gain independence but they have less incentive to do so. This does not mean that ethnically distinct and relatively large groups in non-democratic countries have an unconditional right to secession under international law. Contemporary international law simply does not contain such a right. This is the conclusion of states and of most experts. Nguyen Quoc Dinh, Patrick Daillier and Allain Pellet, for example, write that 'it is useless to try to find in positive international law texts or practice anything which would permit us to conclude that the right to the self-determination of peoples means the right to secession.

Such claims are seen as "an offensive exercise of self-determination", because they involve dismemberment of the State, thereby becoming a threat to international peace (see details Simma ed. 1994:65; Moynihan, 1994). Moreover other concerns are also voiced against secession. These include the impact on international peace and security and the non-viability of the rump State in terms of both its ability to protect itself against others and its economic viability. Also, the fear of indefinite conflicts between the rump and parent State, and the possibility of widespread anarchic situations in adjacent States are often mentioned (Heraclides, 1992:408). There is no doubt that the dismemberment of the State may create micro-States which may then become failed States. Heraclides writes (at 410): "Even more worrisome is the fact that if national self-determination- the pure nationalist approach- is to be condoned, it would imply that we would be endorsing, in our new post-bipolar world, an ideology of exclusivity, ethnic isolation and ethno-centrism. This is precisely the opposite of what we have been striving to achieve".

Secession is, in the view of Crawford (1979:247-70), neither legal nor illegal, but its effects may have legal consequences. Even though secession appears to be a justifiable option for minority groups living in oppressive regimes, argues Hannum (1993:44-45), the subsequent regime might be as bad as the previous one. He argues at 45:

> If a minority's physical existence is threatened, or if there is intense discrimination against a particular segment of society, some reaction against oppression is undoubtedly justified; even the Universal Declaration of Human Rights refers to

'rebellion against tyranny and oppression' as the last resort. However, secession may not be the most appropriate remedy. Overthrowing the oppressive government and restoring human rights would be as philosophically and politically sound as secession. And while secession may end the oppression, the norms of national unity and territorial integrity suggest that a less drastic alternative would be preferable. Finally, as demonstrated in some of the former republics of the Soviet Union and Yugoslavia, there is no guarantee that new states will be any more protective of human rights than those they replace.

Hannum, therefore, rightly argues that secession should not be applied as a solution to minorities' grievances. The better practices such as improving human rights and introducing internal self-determination are the practical and logical solutions, which the international community should adopt. If secession is a justifiable alternative that minority groups can use by reasons of their ethnic or racial origin, Hannum questions why secession is bad for other sub-groups such as political parties, which oppose the governing party in the territory. Furthermore, he warns that dubious rights such as secession should not be allowed to gain legitimacy on ethnic or racial grounds. "The mere desire to insulate one's group from ill-defined pressures from a dominant society cannot suffice to engage international law and obligate the international community either to support the secession or to oppose forceful opposition to the secession... International law should recognize a right to secession only in the rare circumstances when the physical existence of a territorially concentrated group is threatened by gross violations of fundamental human rights" (Hannum, 1993:46-47).

However, there appears to be a consensus amongst most jurists that in certain circumstances secession may be found justifiable as a final remedy. Daes argues (1993:8):

Self-determination has consequently taken on a new meaning in the post-colonial era. Ordinarily it is the right of the citizens of an existing independent State to share power democratically. However, a State may sometimes abuse this right of its citizens so grievously and irreparably that the situation is tantamount to classic colonialism, and may have the same legal consequences. The international community discourages secession as a remedy for the abuse of fundamental rights, but as recent events around the world demonstrate, does not rule out this remedy completely in all cases.

Conclusions

If secession is justified as a remedy for an oppressed group, or accepted as a legal right in terms of self-determination, the very foundation of human rights may become fragile and uncertain. Such a solution will no doubt encourage people to seek shelter in ethnic enclaves. Such a policy also has some similarities with the modern practice of ethnic cleansing, the aim of which is also to create ethnically pure tribal States. Solutions to the human tragedy of ethnic conflicts should not be found by giving way to ethnic, racial, religious or linguistic differences. The lessons of the world wars were instrumental in the promotion of human rights and representative democracy in the inter-State system built up in the post-war world. If a State lacks democracy or does not possess representative government the best solution would be for the international community to influence the State in question. Imposition of sanctions, both economic and political, against recalcitrant States has in certain cases proved successful in recent years. The mere threat of sanctions against Indonesia influenced the Generals to withdraw their armies and paramilitaries from East Timor. Croatia's aggression against Bosnia-Herzegovina also ceased after the UN and EU warned them not to continue their military activities or face economic sanctions.

The UN for its part has been consistent in its policy towards secession. The decision taken by the UN in the aftermath of the Kosovo conflict also suggests that the UN does not believe in secession even where a gross violation of human rights is committed by the dominant group against a minority and internal self-determination is alarmingly absent.

If secession is allowed as a solution to ethnic grievances/conflicts, will it create a peaceful society in which other subgroups will find protection? Unfortunately, recent examples such as Kosovo provide no positive answers. During NATO's bombing campaign and in the aftermath of the war between NATO and the Serbian regime, there were widespread violations of human rights by the Kosovar Albanians against Gypsies and minority Serbs in the province. Ethnic cleansing and genocide are being practised against both these ethnic groups. Even the UN has so far been unable to protect them as the Chief Administration Officer for the UN admitted on 24 October 1999 in his briefing to the press.[18] Simply, the oppressed became the oppressor of other smaller ethnic groups in the province. If we were to accept the theory that secession is warranted as a solution to persistent gross violation of human rights, then surely the Gypsies and Serbs should be allowed to secede from Kosovo! Rosalyin Higgins' famous statement (1994:123) that "virtually every minority has its own minority" should not be forgotten. Where should we draw the line if all minority groups inhabiting this globe begin to demand separate States by reason of their ethnicity or racial background? Are we not in danger of adopting a disastrous policy leading to the creation of thousands of Andorras and Micronesias? Do we want to live in a Tower of Babel where each ethnic group is at each other's throat?

Nanda's proposal that there should be an observer mission appointed, probably by the UN, to arbitrate secessionist claims is non-pragmatic and illogical. Such policies will, rather than discouraging secessionist groups, encourage minority groups to seek secession armed with the evidence required by the committee appointed to arbitrate such cases. There will be endless secessionist groups complaining of violation of democracy and human rights coming to the so-called arbitration commission to plead for secession. Equally, Buchheit's assertion that secession is a normative principle in customary international law is also a gross distortion of international law.

The theory that secession acquires its legality from the right to self-determination is also incorrect as will be shown in chapter 10. These arguments are not based on any substantial evidence. On the other hand, they fail to identify that self-determination and secession are diametrically different from each other. Whilst self-determination advocates human rights and greater democracy, secession incites hatred, violence and disorder in the State. Whilst the former advocates dialogue and better understanding amongst the various groups within a State, the latter self-centredly advocates separation from the rest of the population. In this respect, due to its unilateral nature, secession lacks legitimacy. As held in *Re Secession of Quebec* (1998) 2 SCR 217, secession is based on unilateral action on the part of a group within a State without prior negotiations with the other provinces and peoples of a territory. The most striking contradiction between these two principles is to be found in the approach taken towards democracy by each one. The promotion of self-government and the accommodation of different groups within a territory are the concerns of self-determination of which democracy is the main plank (see also see *R v Oakes* (1986) ISCR 103; *Re Provincial Electoral Boundaries (Sask)* (1991) 2 SCR 158. In *Re v Oaks* some of the qualities of democracy are emphasised as follows:

> To name but a few, respect for the inherent dignity of the human person, commitment to social justice and equality, accommodation of a wide variety of beliefs, respect for cultural and group identity, and faith in social and political institutions which enhance the participation of individuals and groups in society.

It was said in *re Quebec*:

Historically, this Court has interpreted democracy to mean the process of representative and responsible government and the right of citizens to participate in the political process as voters and as candidates. (see also *Harvey v New Brunswick (Attorney General)* (1996) 2 SCR 876.

Secession lacks most of the qualities mentioned above. The ultimate goal of secession appears to be the promotion of the values of one ethnic group (secessionist group) as opposed to others by creating 'uninational and unicultural tribal States' (Franck, 1993:4). Most importantly, secessionists try to achieve these goals by violent means. Democracy does not occupy a place in the vocabulary of most secessionists.

Moreover, some arguments presented to justify the legal basis of secession are not correct. For example, as has been seen earlier, Latvia, Lituania and Estonia, according to some scholars, achieved their independence by way of secession. This is clearly a wrong interpretation of both secession and self-determination. The Balkan countries' independence in 1991 was seen as a restoration of the sovereignty they lost in 1940 to the former USSR. In fact, the declarations of independence by the Baltic States were warmly welcomed on 27 August 1991 by the EC which immediately established diplomatic relations with them.[19] Before the conquest of these countries they were independent sovereign States. They were annexed by the Soviet Union by force without consulting the peoples concerned. Therefore the position was that until these three States gained independence they were colonies in terms of the Colonial Declaration.[20] The question of secession does not arise here at all, because, in the final analysis, it was their lost sovereignty which was restored in 1991.

Although Eritrea's independence is cited as a case of secession by some, it can be argued that Eritrea regained its lost sovereignty by exercising the right to self-determination within the meaning of both the Colonial Declaration and the ICCPR. Eritrea was a peripheral part of Ethiopia between the 11th and 19th centuries (see Sureda, 1973:133-139; Cassese, 1995:218-219). It then became a colony of Italy following the Treaty of Uccialli, 1889 between Ethiopia and Italy. Cassese argues that by this Treaty Ethiopia gave up all legal rights to Eritrea. Therefore any subsequent claim to Eritrea by Ethiopia does not have any legal foundation. This situation continued until Italy gave up its right to govern Eritrea in 1947. Eritrea then became a constituent part of the Ethiopian federation because the UN General Assembly decided by Res. 390-A (V) December 2, 1950 that "Eritrea shall constitute an autonomous unit federated with Ethiopia under the sovereignty of the Ethiopian Crown". This decision was taken, it should be remembered, without consulting the Eritrean people. Therefore, the subsequent independence of Eritrea, in 1993[21] cannot be considered a classic case of secession. It was rather also a case of question of regaining lost sovereignty.

Similarly, secessionist campaigners may find it difficult to prove that the dissolution of the former Socialist Federal Republic of Yugoslavia during 1991 was a case of secession. The Badinter Committee clearly indicated that when the EU was prepared to consider the independence of Croatia and Slovenia the Yugoslav Federation was "engaged in a process of dissolution".[22] The former Republics became sovereign States by recognition of the UN and others. The former boundaries of the Republics became the new boundaries of new nation-States. The Badinter Committee rejected the argument of the Republic of Serbia that the declarations of independence of Croatia and Slovenia should be considered as secession. It should not be forgotten that the Yugoslave Federation did not emerge as a nation-State by a process of organic development. It was an artificial entity cobbled together out of bits and pieces from the Balkans in the aftermath of the world wars. When the dissolution started it simply could not be stopped. There was not any parent State to secede. This is equally true of Bosnia-Herzegovina's independence in 1992.[23]

The case against secession presented by Higgins, Cassese, Mullerson, Franck and Hannum is in fact cautious and compatible with current understanding of international law and in conformity with UN practice. The possible chaotic effects on State structure and international peace if secession is granted a legal status, are amongst their concerns. A multiplicity of micro-States, and endless tribalization of the world will serve no one's interests except those who preach dismemberment of the State as a solution to ethnic grievances.

Notes

[1] For details see Cassese, A. (1995), *Self-Determination of Peoples: A Legal Reappraisal*, Cambridge University Press: Cambridge, p. 17, 20 and 23; see further Simma, B. ed. (1994), *The Charter of the United Nations: A Commentary*, Oxford University Press: Oxford, para. 9, p. 58. See Stalin, J. (1913), *Marxism and the National and Colonial Question, A Collection of Articles and Speeches*, London, re-published in 1941, pp.20-21. See also Lenin, V. I. (1969ed.), *Selected Works*, London, p. 159, cited in Cassese, *ibid*, p. 14. Kohn, H. (1958), 'The United Nations and National Self-Determination', 20 *Review of Politics*, p. 528.

[2] Both Covenants were adopted by the General Assembly Resolution 2200 A (XXI) 16, December 1966.

³ See also GA Res. 545 (vi) 357th plenary mtg. 5 February 1952, entitled 'Inclusion in the International Covenants on Human Rights of an Article Relating to the Right of Peoples to Self-Determination'.

⁴ A/C.3/50/SR. 7, 9 October 1995, para. 65, p. 15 (Pakistan).

⁵ See also Judge Weeramantry's dissenting opinion, *Case Concerning East Timor (Portugal v Australia)*, 90 *ICJ Reports*. [1995], para. 29, p. 102:

⁶ *Legal Consequences for Status of the Continued Presence of South Africa in Namibia (South West Africa) Notwithstanding Security Council Resolution 276/1970*, Advisory Opinion, *ICJ Reports* [1971], pp. 31-32.

⁷ See Advisory Opinion, *ICJ Reports* [1975], paras. 55- 59, pp. 31-33.

⁸ A/C.3/SR.449, 19 November 1952, para. 32, p.190 (Guatemala). See also the Bangkok NGO Declaration on Human Rights, UN Doc. A/CONF. 157/PC/83, printed in 18 (9/12) *HRLJ* 1997, pp. 478-479.

⁹ GA Res. 52/113, 12 December 1997, para.1, ('Universal Realization of the Right of Peoples to Self-Determination); A/C.3/51/SR.26, 18 September 1997, para.18, p.5 (Albania); A/C.3/52/SR.29, 1 December 1997, para.36, p.5 (Palestine); A/C.3/50 SR.4, 16 October 1995, para. 13, p. 4 (Syrian Arab Republic).

¹⁰ GA Res. 637 (viii), 16 December 1952, 403rd plenary mtg, preambular paragraph. See also the view of Cuba, A/C.3/50/SR. 4, 16 October 1995, para. 18, p. 5; see also UN Doc. 637 A (VII) 12 December 1952. The World Conference on Human Rights, 1993 also came to a similar conclusion, see UN Doc. A/Conf. 157/23, 12 July 1993, para. 2. See further A/C.3/50/SR. 4, 16 October 1995, para. 18, p. 5 (Cuba). See also GA Res. 637 A (VII) 12, December 1952; GA Res. 637 (viii) 16 December 1952, preambular paragraph (both resolutions are on the right to self-determination); A/C.3/SR.450, 28 November 1952, para. 46, p. 246 (Saudi Arabia); and A/C.3/L.296, 24 November 1952 which stated: "Whereas the right of peoples and nations to self-determination is a prerequisite to the enjoyment of all fundamental human rights", GAOR, 7th session, Annexes, Agenda Item 30, 1952-1953, p. 4.

¹¹ A/C.3/SR.397, 21 January 1952, para. 4, p.299 (Syria); A/C.3/SR. 460, 1 December 1952, para.19, p.259 (The Philippine); A/C.3/52/SR.29, 1 December 1997, para. 28, p. 4 (Pakistan).

¹² See UN Doc. A/5746, 16 November 1964, para. 111 (Ghana).

¹³ A/C.3/50/SR. 3, 11 October 1995, para. 23, p. 6. A/C.3/50/SR.3, 11 October 1995, para. 23, p. 6 (Algeria); A/C.3/SR.6, 14 October 1994, para. 48, p. 9 (Honduras); and A/C.3/49/SR.3, 17 October 1994, para. 24, p. 9 (Germany).

¹⁴ A/C.3/49/SR. 3/17 October 1994, para. 42, p. 9.

¹⁵ A/C.3/SR. 6/ 14 October 1994 (Honduras).

¹⁶A/C.3/SR. 366, 12 December 1951, para. 18, p. 115.

¹⁷ UN Doc. E/CN.4/Sub.2/1993/34, para. 86, p. 18.

¹⁸ See News Bulletin of the BBC 1, 24 October 1999.

¹⁹ The Declaration of European Community Foreign Ministers, Brussels, 28 August 1991, 24 (7/8) *Bull EC* 1991, p. 115.

[20] See the Declaration of European Community Foreign Ministers, Brussels, 28 August 1991, 24 (7/8) *Bull. EC.* 1991, p.115. See also Rich, R. (1993), 'Recognition of States: The Collapse of Yugoslavia and the Soviet Union', 4 *EJIL,* p. 38. Gazzini, T. (1996), 'Consideration on the Conflict in Chechnya', 17 (3-6) *HRLJ,* p. 96.

[21] In a referendum held in Eritrea from 23 to 25 of April 1993, registered voters "almost unanimously voted in favour of independence". 26 (4) *Bull. EC* 1993, point. 1.4.13, p. 81.

[22] Opinion, no. 1, Badinter Committee, 31 *ILM* 1488, 1992.

[23] See for a different view, Hannum, H. (1993), Self-Determination, Yugoslavaia, and Europe: Old Wine in New Bottles?', 3 *Transnational Law and Contemporary Problems*, pp. 58-69.

References

Alfredsson, G. (1996),'Different Forms of and Claims to the Right to Self-Determination', in D. Clark, and R. Williamson (eds), *Self-Determination: International Perspectives*, Macmillan Press: London, pp. 58-86.

Brilmayer, L. (1991), 'Secession and Self-Determination: A Territorial Interpretation', 16 *Yale J.Intl.L*, pp. 177-201.

Buchanan, A. (1991), *Secession: The Morality of Political Divorce from Fort Sumter to Lituania and Quebec*, Westview Press: Boulder/San Francisco/London.

Buchheit, A. (1978), *Secession: The Legitimacy of Self-Determination*, Yale University Press: New Haven, CT.

Cassese, A. (1995), *Self-Determination of Peoples: A Legal Reappraisal*, Cambridge UP: Cambridge.

Cobban, A. (1944), *The Nation States and National Self-Determination*, TY Crowell: New York.

Crawford, J. (1979), *The Creation of States in International Law*, Oxford UP: Oxford.

Daes, Erica-Irene. (1993), 'Some Considerations On the Rights of Peoples to Self-Determination', 3 (1) *Transnational Law and Contemporary Problems*, pp. 1-11.

Franck, T. M. (1992), 'The Emerging Right to Democratic Governance', 86 (1) *AJIL*, pp. 46-91.

Franck, T. M. (1993), 'Postmodern Tribalism and the Right to Secession', in C. Brolmann et al (eds), *Peoples and Minorities in International Law*, Martinus Nijhoff: Dordrecht/Boston/London, p. 3-27.

Hannum, H. (1993), 'Rethinking of Self-Determination', *Va. J.I.L*, pp. 1- 69.

Heraclides, A. (1991), *The Self-Determination of Minorities in International Politics*, Franck Cass: London.

Heraclides, A. (1992), 'Secession, Self-Determination and Non-intervention: In Quest of a Normative Symbiosis', *Journal of International Affairs*, pp. 403-420.

Higgins, R. (1963), *The Development of International Law Through the Political Organs of the United Nations*, Oxford UP: London.
Higgins, R. (1994), *Problems and Process: International Law and How We Use It*, Clarendon Press: Oxford.
Kamanu, O. (1974), 'Secession and the Right to Self-Determination: An OAU Dilemma', 12 (3) *The Journal of Modern African Studies*, pp. 355-376.
Klabbers, J. and Lefeber, R. (1993), 'Africa: Lost Between Self-Determination and Uti-Possidetis', in Brolmann et al (eds), *Peoples and Minorities in International Law*, as above, pp. 37-76.
Kohn, H. (1958), 'The United Nations and National Self-Determination', 20 *Review of Politics*, pp. 526-545.
Lansing, R. (1921), *The Peace Negotiations: A Personal Narrative*, New York and Boston.
Marchildon, G. and Maxwell, E. (1992), 'Quebec's Right of Secession Under Canadian and International Law', 32 (3) *Va. J.I.L*, pp. 583- 624.
McCorquodale, R. (1992), 'Self-Determination Beyond the Colonial Context and its Potential Impact on Africa', 4 *AJCIL*, pp. 592-608.
Moynihan, D. P. (1994ed.), *Pandaemonium: Ethnicity in International Politics*, Oxford UP: Oxford.
Mullerson, R. (1994), *International Law, Rights and Politics: Developments in Eastern Europe and the CIS*, LSE and Routledge.
Nanda, Ved. P. (1972), 'Self-Determination in International Law: The Tragic Tale of Two Cities, Islamabad (West Pakistan) and Dacca (East Pakistan)', 66 *AJIL*, pp. 321-336.
Nanda, Ved. P. (1981), 'Self-Determination Under International Law: Validity of Claims to Secede', 13 *Case W. Res. J.Intl. L*, pp. 257-280.
Nayar, K. M. G. (1975), 'Self-Determination Beyond the Colonial Context: Biafra in Retrospect', 10 *Texas International Law Journal*, pp. 321-345.
Nueberger, B. (1986), National Self-Determination in Postcolonial Africa, cited by Hannum (1993), as above.
Padover, S. K. ed. (1942), *Wilson's Ideals*, Washington DC, cited in Cassese (1995), as above.
Pomerance, M. (1982), *Self-determination in Law and Politics: The New Doctrine at the United Nations*, Martinus Nijhoff: The Hague/Boston/London.
Rigo-Sureda, A. (1973), *The Evolution of the Right of Self-Determination*, A.W.Sijthoff: Leiden.
Ronen, D. (1974), *The Quest for Self-Determination*, Yale UP: New Haven and London.
Schoenberg, H. O. (1976), 'Limits of Self-Determination', *IYHR*, pp. 91-103.
Shaw, M. N. (1997), 'Peoples, Territories and Boundaries', 3 *EJIL*, pp. 478- 507.
Shehadi, K. S. (1993), *Ethnic Self-Determination and the Break-up of States*, Adelphi Papers (283), Brassey's (UK): London.
Sheils, F. L. ed. (1984), *Ethnic Separatism and World Politics*, University Press of America: New York and London.

Simma, M. ed. (1994), *The Charter of the United Nations*, Oxford UP: Oxford.

Sinha, S. Prakash (1973), 'Is Self-Determination Passe?', *Colombia Journal of Transnational Law*, pp. 260-273.

Stalin, J. (1913), *Marxism and the National Question*, cited in Cassese, as above, p. 14.

Stavenhagen, R. (1996), *Ethnic Conflicts and the Nation-State*, UNRISD and Macmillan Press: London.

Temperley, H. M. V. (1969), *A History of the Peace Conference of Paris*, vol. VI, London, New York and Toronto.

Thornberry, P. (1989), 'Self-Determination, Minorities and Human Rights: A Review of International Instruments', 38 *ICLQ* 1989, pp. 867- 889.

White, R. C. A. (1981), 'Self-Determination: Time for a Re-Assessment?', *NILR*, pp. 147- 170.

10 The Right to Secession: International Law and UN Practice

Introduction

International law has been reluctant to validate secessionist claims (Tomuschat, 1993: 7). This position was reflected in the opinion delivered by the first Commission of Jurists appointed to inquire into the Aaland Islands question[1] (for details see Nanda, 1981:257; Sureda, 1973:32; Hannum, 1993a:8-10). It was held:

> Positive international law does not recognise the right of national groups, as such, to separate themselves from the State of which they form part by the simple expression of a wish, any more than it recognises the right of other States to claim such a separation. Generally speaking, the grant or refusal of the right to a portion of its population of determining its own political fate by plebiscite or by some other method, is, exclusively, an attribute of the sovereignty of every State which is definitively constituted.

The inquiry conducted by the jurists of the second Commission of Inquiry into the Aaland islands dispute also came to a similar conclusion. It was stated:

> Is it possible to admit as an absolute rule that a minority of the population of a State, which is definitely constituted and perfectly capable of fulfilling its duties as such, has the right of separating itself from her in order to be incorporated in another State or to declare its independence? The answer can only be in the negative. To concede to minorities, either of language or religion, or to any fractions of a population the right of withdrawing from the community to which they belong, because it is their wish or their good pleasure, would be to destroy order and stability within States and to inaugurate anarchy in international life; it would be to uphold a theory incompatible with the very idea of the State as a territorial and political unity.[2]

"One hundred years ago" writes Tomuschat (1993:8), "even to raise such a question would have been considered preposterous or nonsensical".

The United Nations also has not shown any interest in secession. It is alleged that the principle of territorial integrity has been favoured by the UN (see Nayar, 1975:333). Professor Van Dyke (1970:102) clarified, "The United Nations would be in an extremely difficult position if it were to interpret the right of self-determination in such a way as to invite or justify attacks on the territorial integrity of its own members" (cited in Nanda, 1972:327; see also Heraclides, 1992:405). The former UN Secretary-General U Thant clarifying the common position of the UN said at a press conference in Accra:

> As far as the question of secession of a particular section of a State is concerned, the United Nations' attitude is unequivocal. As an international organization, the UN has never accepted and does not accept and I do not believe it will ever accept the principle of secession of a part of its Member States.[3]

If not applied with care, U Thant pointed out, there would be endless claims for secession. He warned:

> Regarding the...question of self-determination, I think this concept is not properly understood in many parts of the world. Self-determination of the peoples does not imply self-determination of a section of population of a particular Member State. If the principle of self-determination is applied to ten different areas of a Member State, or five different areas of a Member State, or twenty different areas of a Member State, then I am afraid there will be no end to the problems.

Contemporary views on secession have not been different from the above opinions. Secession is seen as an illegal way of a creation of States by almost all States (see Crawford, 1979:120-128). Thus, the attainment of independent statehood by a minority group by virtue of the right to self-determination is not permitted by contemporary international law, nor will it have a great chance of getting any seal of approval even in the foreseeable future.

In *Re Secession of Quebec* [1998] 2 SCR 217,[4] the Canadian Supreme Court summarising the current position of international law held:

> The Court was also required to consider whether a right to unilateral secession exists under international law. Some supporting an affirmative answer did so on the basis of the recognized right to self-determination that belongs to all 'peoples'. Although much of the Quebec population certainly shares many of the characteristics of a people, it is not necessary to decide the 'people' issue because, whatever may be the correct determination of this issue in the context of Quebec,

a right to secession only arises under the principle of self-determination of people at international law where 'a people' is governed as part of a colonial empire; where a 'people' is subjected to alien subjugation, domination or exploitation; and possibly where 'a people' is denied any meaningful exercise of its right to self-determination within the state of which it forms a part. In other circumstances, peoples are expected to achieve self-determination within the framework of their existing state. A state whose government represents the whole of the people or peoples resident within its territory, on a basis of equality and without discrimination, and respect for the principles of self-determination in its internal arrangements, is entitled to maintain its territorial integrity under international law and to have the territorial integrity recognised by others.

Although international law does not proscribe secession it is equally correct that secession is not recognised as a valid right under international law. The Special Rapporteur Gross Espiell commented: [5]

The express acceptance of the principles of the national unity and the territorial integrity of the State implies non-recognition of the right to secession. The right of peoples to self-determination, as it emerges from the United Nations, exists for peoples under colonial and alien domination, that is to say, who are not living under the legal form of a State. The right to secession from an existing State Member of the United Nations does not exist as such in the instruments or in the practice followed by the Organisation, since to seek to invoke it in order to disrupt the national unity and the territorial integrity of a State would be a misapplication of the principle of self-determination contrary to the purposes of the United Nations Charter.

The subsequent discussion focuses on the main UN treaties, covenants and declarations to determine the exact current legal position with regard to minorities' claim to secession.

10.1 *There is no Right to Secession Explicitly or Implicitly in the UN Charter*

Self-determination was not included in the Charter as a legal principle (Higgins, 1994). This principle was mentioned, as among other things, *desideratum*. Nonetheless the Charter became the basis for subsequent development of self-determination from a political principle to a legal principle.

It is less controversial to say that the UN Charter did not legitimize secessionist rights. The principle enunciated in article 73 recognises that the *peoples* and *inhabitants* of Non-Self-Governing Territories and Trust territories have the right to 'self-government'. States are required to "take due account of the political aspirations of the peoples, and to assist them in the progressive development of their free political institutions, according to the particular circumstances of each territory and its peoples and their varying stages of advancement". But in general terms both articles 1 (2) and 55 recognise that one of the purposes of the United Nations is to develop friendly relations among nations based on respect for the principle of equal rights and self-determination of peoples. Does then the term *nation* indicate ethnic connotation? There is no documentary evidence to come to such a conclusion. Hannum (1993:11) correctly argues that: "The reference to friendly relations among 'nations' carried no connotation to ethnicity or culture; it merely reflected the name of an organization, the 'United Nations', composed of states". Travaux preparatoires reveal that any secessionist right was excluded when the draft of the UN Charter was finalised. The common understanding amongst member States on this was demonstrated by the delegate of Colombia:

> If it (self-determination) means self-government, the right of a country to provide its own government, yes, we would certainly like it to be included; but if it were to be interpreted, on the other hand, as connoting a withdrawal, the right of withdrawal or secession, then we should regard that as tantamount to international anarchy and we should not desire that it should be included in the text of the Charter.[6]

States have never been in doubt that groups of peoples living in the independent State would be the repository of secessionist rights. The UK representative's analysis of the *peoples* in the Charter (articles 1 (2) and 55) supports this proposition. He asserted that, "The United Kingdom delegation did not believe that the principle of self-determination had been intended to form a basis upon which provinces or other parts of independent States could claim a right to secession."[7] Charles De Visscher's (1957:128) statement that, "applied without discernment, self-determination would lead to anarchy", was quoted in support of his argument. The notion of self-determination was thus reformulated in a conservative State-oriented approach. It was not imagined by the founding States of the UN that by approving the peoples' right to self-determination there would be any threat to the territorial integrity of the nation-State which at that time was considered sacrosanct (Cassese, 1995:138). What the UN Charter provided for was self-government. Taking into account the concerns of most States, the drafting committee agreed that articles 1 (2), 55 and 73 would not confer secessionist rights on a section of the population of an independent State

(Cassese, 1995:40). This is also the view taken by the eminent commentator on nationalism and national self-determination, Hans Kohn (1958:536). Government based upon the consent of the governed and the respect for the equality of its peoples is what is enshrined in the Charter. Most importantly, any racial or ethnic connotation is absent in these Articles. Higgins (1995:467) rightly points out that "the Charter aims at bringing all human beings, irrespective of their origin or status, within the purview and range of human rights promotion".

10.2 *A Right to Secession is not in the Colonial Declaration: "If Care is not Taken, the Other Very Important Principle, the Territorial Integrity of the State Will be in Jeopardy"*

The Declaration on the Granting of Independence to Colonial Countries and Peoples (Colonial Declaration), GA Resolution 1514 (XV) 14 December 1960,[8] is considered by most States as the most authoritative pronouncement on the principle of self-determination since the adoption of the UN Charter.[9] It recognises that the peoples living in Non-Self-Governing Territories and all other territories which have not yet attained independence can achieve independence in accordance with their freely expressed will and desire. This is a further development of the principle of self-determination enshrined in the Charter. The Colonial Declaration covers territories which were not covered by the trusteeship system (see Franck and Hoffman, 1976:333). The Declaration recognised that the continued existence of colonialism prevents the development of international economic co-operation, impedes the social, cultural and economic development of dependent peoples and militates against the United Nations' ideal of universal peace. Thus, the main objective of the Declaration was to put an unconditional end to colonialism in all its forms and manifestations. As the basic rule the Declaration admitted, "all peoples have an inalienable right to complete freedom, the right to exercise their sovereignty and the integrity of their national territory". It was further emphasised that the denial of end to colonialism would constitute a serious threat to world peace.

However, the meaning of *peoples* in the Colonial Declaration has been subject to doubtful misinterpretation by some minority rights campaigners who assert that *minorities* are *peoples* who can decide their political future in whatever way they like. Paragraph 2 of the Colonial Declaration has often been cited to justify their argument. It states:

> All peoples have the right to self-determination; by virtue of that right they freely determine their political status and freely pursue their economic, social and cultural development.

A preambular paragraph also stresses that:

> Peoples may, for their own ends, freely dispose of their natural wealth and resources without prejudice to any obligations arising out of international economic co-operation, based upon the principle of natural benefit, and international law.

As has been seen in chapter 2, *all peoples* in paragraph 2 means the totality of the population of a given territory. Here the rights and benefits emanating from the Colonial Declaration are vested with the 'territory and its peoples' as was further elaborated by the GA Res. 1541, 1960.[10] Thus, the decolonisation should be achieved for the territory by the whole population. Once independence is achieved by peoples of non-self-governing or trust territory, the former boundaries of the territory become new boundaries of the new nation-State. During the debate on the Colonial Declaration this position never became a serious issue amongst State representatives. It is worth mentioning that paragraph 2 was being linked to paragraph 6 of the Colonial Declaration which states:

> Any attempt aimed at the partial or total disruption of the national unity and the territorial integrity of a country is incompatible with the purposes and principles of the Charter of the United Nations.

The emphasis was placed by paragraph 7 of the Declaration on 'the sovereign rights of all peoples and their territorial integrity'. The latter principle, territorial integrity, states Nanda (1981:264), lies at the heart of the contemporary inter-state system, any derogation of the principle is not warranted, nor will such an attempt be tolerated either by the UN or member States.

Independence for colonies and non-self-governing territories should not, as correctly argued by Professor Mullerson (1994:72), be interpreted as secession. As he points out, when Nigeria or Ghana gained independence they did not violate the territorial integrity of the UK. Neither did their acts affect the democratic rights of the peoples of the UK, because colonies and metropolitan States (colonial masters) have, in these instances, never been the same territory. By achieving independence the peoples of the former colonies do not violate the territorial integrity of and political unity of the State administering those colonies.

This was, according to the delegate of the Netherlands, the continuation of the principle enshrined in article 2 (4) of the UN Charter.[11] States expressed their concerns about the possible misuse of paragraph 2. For example, Guatemala wanted to be assured that "self-determination of peoples may in no case impair the right of territorial integrity of any states".[12] In fact, Guatemala presented a separate resolution emphasising that rights enshrined in paragraph 2 should in no case violate the Charter principle, "the other very important principle of a country's territorial integrity".[13] Sweden also wanted clarifications that paragraph 2 of the Declaration would not entitle "a segment of a population or region of a state" to secession. Otherwise, argued the delegate, secessionists in regions like Congo (Leopoldville) would be justified in continuing to pursue their secessionist agenda.[14] The Federation of Malaya[15] and Iran, both signatories to the forty-three-power resolution, assured countries like Guatemala and Sweden that the Forty-Three-Powers were in agreement with the rationale behind these two paragraphs - i.e., that the territorial integrity of a State would not be harmed by 'paragraph two rights'.[16] The 'Forty-Three-Power Resolution' (almost all of the signatories were from Latin America, Asia, the Middle East and Africa) was very carefully drafted to assure others that paragraph 2 did not interfere with or harm the territorial integrity of independent States. The common understanding appeared to be that any attempt by a segment of a population or a region of the State to exercise the right to self-determination by breaking away from the State would be nullified by the operation of paragraph 6. The rationale behind these two paragraphs is clear. Peoples' right to self-determination cannot be operated in conflict with another fundamental principle developed within the UN, the territorial integrity and sovereignty of a State. This is, as pointed out by Higgins (1994:122), very carefully thought out to balance the approach taken by the States' representatives who took part in the process of finalising the Colonial Declaration. Analysing paragraph 6 in particular and the Colonial Declaration in general, Buchheit (1978:87) commented, "both the context of the Colonial Declaration and the plain terms of paragraph 6 outweigh any speculation regarding a possible separatist interpretation of the right to self-determination." As viewed by some scholars paragraph 6 was meant to operate as a sort of "grandfather Clause" standing against any secessionist attempts (Clark, 1995:89).

10.3 *A Right to Secession is Not in the Declaration on Friendly Relations (GA Res. 2625, 24 October 1970)*[17]

The Declaration on Friendly Relations (see generally Rosenstock, 1971:713-735) is a further attempt to extend the scope and application of self-determination enshrined in the Charter and in both Covenants on human rights beyond colonial context. The universal character of the right to self-determination is re-affirmed. The Declaration has acquired a normative status in international law considering its elaboration of Charter principles (White, 1981: 147; see further Nayer, 1975:335-336; Rosenstock, 1971). However, it does not explicitly refer to the *self* which can exercise the rights emanating from the right to self-determination (see also Nanda, 1981:269). Does *self* mean the whole people in the State or does it cover ethnic, religious and linguistic minority groups?

Campaigners for secessionist rights have been trying to prove that *self* should be interpreted so as to include minority groups as well. They refer to Paragraph 2 in the Declaration on Friendly Relation, which states:

> By virtue of the principle of equal rights and self-determination of peoples enshrined in the Charter of the United Nations, all peoples have the right freely to determine, without external interference, their political status and to pursue their economic, social and cultural development, and every State has the duty to respect this right in accordance with the provisions of the Charter.

However, paragraph 2 should be read in conjunction with paragraph 7, which states:

> Nothing in the foregoing paragraphs shall be construed as authorizing or encouraging any action which would dismember or impair, totally or in part, the territorial integrity or political unity of sovereign or independent states conducting themselves in compliance with the principle of equal rights and self-determination of peoples as described above and thus possessed of a government representing the whole people belonging to the territory without distinction as to race, creed or colour. [18]

States are, thus, obliged to restrain from any action aimed at the partial or total disruption of the national unity and territorial integrity of other States.

As argued by Morocco in the *Western Sahara* case,[19] when these two paragraphs are read together two principles can be discerned:

a) self-determination of all peoples as indicated in paragraph 2 of the Resolution; and
b) the principle of national unity and the territorial integrity of nation-States as guaranteed in paragraph 7.

The effect of paragraph 2 is deliberately restricted by paragraph 7, which operates more or less as a subordinate clause to paragraph 2. More emphasis is thus placed on the territorial integrity of States "as a principle superior to that of self-determination" (Hannum, 1993a:16; Higgins, 1994:117-121; Thornberry, 1989:867- 889). This approach is a continuation of the earlier position taken in the UN Charter and the Colonial Declaration. Mauritania argued in the *Western Sahara* case that the principle of self-determination could not be disassociated from that of respect for national unity and territorial integrity. It also emphasised, as stated in the *Western Sahara* case,[20] that in certain cases priority should be given to territorial integrity. In fact, some States attempted during the debate on the Declaration on Friendly Relations to give priority to political unity over any other concerns. For example, the representative of Madagascar requested at the 871st meeting of the 6th committee that Madagascar's proposal emphasising five principles should be discussed. Amongst them, sovereignty of States, territorial integrity and the condemnation of subversive activities of an internal or external nature are prominent.[21] Morocco also voiced its concerns about seditious movements within the boundaries of independent States.[22] Czechoslovakia's opinion was that peoples' right to self-determination "connoted the right of a State freely to decide its destiny, including its form of statehood, and to choose the system and institutions which it deemed most appropriate".[23] Another representative stated that though peoples' right to self-determination meant their inalienable right freely to determine to chose the way of life they wanted, the principle should not be invoked by minorities within a State to cause its dismemberment.[24]

The Report of the Special Committee on the Declaration on Friendly Relations pointed to the fact that the overwhelming opinion of States was against any suggestion that *minorities* as *peoples* could exercise the peoples' right to self-determination or secede on that basis. The Committee reported:[25]

Certain representatives were of the opinion that the principle was a universal one and applied to all peoples and places. Other representatives, however, drew attention to the difficulties that would be involved with respect to the right of self-determination, should the expression be used without definition. It would, they pointed out, encourage secessionist movements within the territories of an independent State. As observed by one representative, every ethnic, cultural or geographical group within a sovereign state would consider it had the immediate and unqualified right to the establishment of its own states. This representative was of the view, therefore, that the right of self-determination should be regarded as referring to the right of a majority within a generally accepted political unit.

Referring to paragraph 7, The Committee on the Elimination of Racial Discrimination also held that paragraph 7 should not be interpreted as authorising or encouraging any form of secession or separatist movements.[26] Both paragraphs 2 and 7 should be read and construed in accordance with the broader principles of the UN Charter, which advocates territorial integrity, and the sovereignty of States. These two terms, territorial integrity and sovereignty are interrelated and voluminous UN documents repeatedly assert their significance as fundamental principles.[27]

It should be mentioned here that there is no expressed proscription of secession in this Declaration (see White, 1981:159), nor are there any guarantees that the oppressed minority groups may invoke the Declaration principles as a basis for dismembering the territorial integrity of sovereign states. It is quite clear that the Declaration on Friendly Relations does not allow peoples to secede or break away from the State of which they form a part by violating the territorial integrity of the State. As argued by Hannum (1993a:16), minorities therefore are not legally entitled to exercise the right to self-determination similar to that of the population as a whole. If we were to interpret the Declaration on Friendly Relations more generously so as to cover minorities' rights to self-determination, thereby conceding their right to secede, it could be like opening a Pandora's box. Indeed, there is a hidden danger that minorities might be used by ethno-politicians to pursue their aggressive agendas or subversive activities. Thus Eide argues that exaggerated and misconceived interpretations of the right to self-determination might encourage secessionist groups.[28] Moreover, as stated by the Committee on the Elimination of Racial Discrimination in its General Recommendation "a fragmentation of States may be detrimental to the protection of human rights, as well as to the preservation of peace and security".[29]

The position adopted in paragraph 7 has been reaffirmed by the Vienna Declaration, 1993 in its s. 2 (3), which states:

In accordance with the 1970 Declaration on Principles of International Law Concerning Friendly Relations and Coorperation Among States in Accordance with the Charter of the United Nations, this shall not be construed as authorizing or encouraging any action which would dismember or impair, totally or in part, the territorial integrity or political unity of sovereign and independent States conducting themselves in compliance with the principle of equal rights and self-determination of peoples and thus possessed of a government representing the whole people belonging to the territory without distinction of any kind.

The Declaration on Friendly Relations should also be seen as a continuation beyond the colonial principles enunciated in the Colonial Declaration. The interrelationship between these two documents cannot be ignored in interpreting and understanding the true legal structure of the phrase 'peoples' right to self determination'. Higgins (1994:121) states that "both GA. Res. 1514 (XV) and 2625 (XXV) - each of which emphasises self-determination - caution against anything being interpreted to violate territorial integrity...This is a standard formula, and is almost invariably to be found in instruments that affirmed the right of self-determination, as if to set the limits to that right or at least to provide a counterweight". These cautious and logical views were reflected in Cristescu's final report on the right to self-determination. He stated that *peoples* should not be interpreted so as to encourage secessionist or irredentist movements.[30]

The upshot is that the right enshrined in paragraph 2 is to be applied within existing boundaries. This conclusion is supported by some of the earlier UN General Assembly resolutions. For example, the resolution on Eritrea emphasised that the right to self-government (which was identified with the right to self-determination in the case of Non-Self-Governing Territories and Nations living in Colonies), should be enjoyed "while at the same time respecting the Constitution, institutions, traditions and international status and identity of others."[31] GA Res. 545 (vi) February 5, 1952 stated that it should be exercised in conformity with the purposes and principles of the United Nations. This operates reciprocally. States for their part, should show the fullest respect for the inhabitants of their territories, and are obliged to safeguard their institutions, traditions, religions and languages. Minorities, on the other hand, are expected to behave as loyal citizens.

10.4 *Can the Legitimacy of Secession be Discerned in Paragraph 7 of the Declaration on Friendly Relations?*

Paragraph 7 of the Declaration on Friendly Relations appeared to be an attempt to correct some injustices, which were neglected by earlier documents on self-determination. In particular paragraph 7 is a concession afforded to minority groups without seriously undermining the infra-structure of the nation-State system. Whilst discouraging secessionist attacks on most revered principles such as the territorial integrity and political unity of the State, the Declaration on Friendly Relations is trying to address certain concerns of minority groups living in an independent State. Paragraph 7 is the result of this carefully thought out scheme (see Schoenberg, 1976:94).

The second part of paragraph 7 of the Friendly Relations imposes some conditions upon States:

a) States should conduct their activities in compliance with the principle of self-determination;
b) States should possess a democratic government which represents the whole people; and
c) States should not discriminate against their subjects or persecute minority groups on the grounds of race, creed, colour etc.

Thus, it emphasises the necessity of having a democratic government representing the whole peoples in the territory conducting itself in compliance with the principle of equal rights and self-determination of peoples (see Rosenstock, 1971: Schoenberg, 1976). As far as minorities are concerned, States also have the responsibility to conduct domestic affairs without distinction as to race, creed or colour. States must afford them the rights recognised in international law.[32] If no such guarantees exist, and free and representative institutions are lacking in a given State, then the alleged State cannot claim the protection afforded by the first part of paragraph 7, which opposes "any action which would dismember or impair, totally or in part, the territorial integrity or political unity of sovereign or independent States". This is because the State in question loses any legal base since it is not a representative and democratic government conducting its affairs in compliance with the popular will. Nanda argues (1981:270; see further Nayer, 1975:338) in such a case self-determination acquires a priority over territorial integrity or political unity. Such an event, in his view, amounts to subjection of peoples to alien domination, which would in turn justify any secessionist claims by oppressed groups. It was also argued that the Declaration on Friendly Relations does admit secession as a valid means of achieving self-determination (see Nayer, 1975:337).

Cassese (1995:120) concludes that when it is absolutely apparent that internal self-determination is absent from the system and racial or religious groups are being subject to extreme and unremitting persecution, such an environment might make secession legitimate (see also Klabbers and Lefeber, 1993:45-46 and 53). In fact, as Cassese (1995:118 and 123) correctly points out, elements of secessionist rights can be discerned in paragraph 7 of the Declaration on Friendly Relations under certain very strict circumstances

Shaw (1986:483) also agrees that where human rights are grossly violated and internal self-determination is alarmingly absent, secession may, as a last resort, be recognised by the international community. Nonetheless, Shaw states that such a scenario is in practice unlikely. He emphasises that territorial integrity is given prominence over the right to internal self-determination in non-colonial settings. Shaw's arguments are in fact very persuasive. He does not think that paragraph 7 was under any circumstances intended to be used as a license to attack the territorial integrity of a given State. He argues at 483:

> The implication here is that, by reversing the proposition, States that do not so conduct themselves are not protected by the principle of territorial integrity. This, however, is hardly acceptable. Such a major change in legal principle cannot be introduced by way of an ambiguous subordinate clause, especially when the principle of territorial integrity has always been accepted and proclaimed as a core principle of international law, and is indeed placed before the qualifying clause in the provision in question...the inevitable and unavoidable starting point remains that of the primacy of the principle of territorial integrity.

Hannum's argument (1993a:17) is in agreement with the thesis that Declaration on Friendly Relations placed the importance of territorial integrity and political unity above that of other concerns, i.e. peoples' right to self-determination.

Capotorti's arguments are to a greater or lesser extent in agreement with Cassese rather than Shaw. While emphasising that minorities as such do not have a legal right to self-determination according to customary international law, Capotorti (1992:510) admitted, however, that when a particular minority group is subjected to persistent discrimination based on race, creed or colour they may have some reasonable claim to secession. Nanda (1981:270) argues that, "under specific circumstances, the principle of self-determination is to be accorded priority over the opposing principle of territorial integrity". He admits that paragraph 7 of the Declaration on Friendly Relations might open the door to secession under specific circumstances although there is no procedure to guarantee a smooth transition to statehood. Nonetheless, as he correctly points out, recognition of secessionist claims would not be easy. Nanda notes at 275:

> Even assuming the legitimacy and permissibility under international law of the right to secede, many difficult definitional hurdles remain before this right could

be applied and implemented. To establish the minimum standards of legitimacy, it is necessary to identify i) the group that is claiming the right of self-determination; ii) the nature and scope of their claim; iii) the underlying reasons for the claim; and iv) the degree of the deprivation of basic human rights.

Even in such a case, secession is considered to be the last resort. He notes (at 276) that there must be compelling evidence to prove that any action short of secession would not remedy the situation. However, he points out (at 277) that it would be dangerous and unworkable to accord legitimacy to secession based on ideological grounds.

According to the Secretariat of the International Commission of Jurists (1972) peoples' rights to have democratic governance are recognized by the right to self-determination. Analysing the events in East Pakistan in 1971, which ultimately led to the creation of Bangladesh, the Commission of Jurists was of the view (at 69):

> That the principle is subject to the requirement that the government does comply with the principle of equal rights and self-determination and does represent the whole principle without distinction. If one of the constituent peoples of a state is denied equal rights and is discriminated against, it is submitted that their full rights of self-determination will revive.

The Commission found (at 79) justification in the East Pakistan insurrection against West Pakistan's military aggression. The autocratic regime of West Pakistan was alleged to have discriminated against the East Pakistan peoples for a long time in almost all fields on the basis of ethnicity. Continuous economic exploitation and subjugation of East Pakistan by West Pakistan since the 1950s was identified by the Commission of Jurists in the context of neo-colonialism (Agrawala, 1978). Nanda (1981:336) argues that the prevailing situation in East Pakistan in 1971 and before warranted the resort to self-determination by East Pakistan.

10.5 *There is No Right to Secession Explicitly or Implicitly Provided For in Article 27 of the ICCPR*

For the first time, the universal character of self-determination was accepted by the UN in the ICCPR. Article 1 states:

> All peoples have the right of self-determination. By virtue of that right they freely determine their political status and freely pursue their economic, social and cultural development.

Article 1 (3) states:

> The State parties to the present Covenant, including those having responsibility for the administration of Non-Self-Governing and Trust Territories, shall promote the realization of the right of self-determination, and shall respect that right, in conformity with the provisions of the Charter of the United Nations.

Thus, rights enshrined in article 1 speak about the rights of 'all peoples' without, however, defining beneficiaries. As emphasised in article 1 (3), the State parties to the Covenant should undertake responsibility of promoting self-determination of peoples, in particular the right to democratic governance (Cassese, 1995:65-66).

It is often argued that when article 27 is read in conjunction with Article 1, minorities are entitled to self-determination appearing as *peoples*. Article 27 does confer some limited traditional civil and political rights upon persons belonging to ethnic, religious and linguistic minority groups. These rights have some resemblance to classical political and civil rights.

The wording of article 27 unequivocally suggests that it is only individuals belonging to minority groups who can claim benefit under it (see Sanders, 1991:376).[33] Nonetheless, article 27 has collective elements. The Human Rights Committee (HRC) stated in *Lubicon Lake Band*, "there is no objection to a group of individuals, who claimed to be similarly affected, collectively to submit a communication about alleged breaches of their rights."[34] It does not, however, guarantee any political rights under article 1 on a collective basis. Individuals or groups of individuals can complain about violation of rights contained in articles 6-27. Certainly, by invoking article 1 minorities cannot break-away from the State where they form a part. As Professor Rein Mullerson (1994:73-74) argues this does not mean that minorities cannot enjoy benefits guaranteed by article 1 of the ICCPR. "It would be more accurate to say that they can exercise the right of self-determination together with the rest of the population of a given state, as a part of this population" (Mullerson, 1994:73).

During the debate on article 25 of the proposed Covenants on Human Rights (article 25 became the present article 27 of the ICCPR), many States stressed that 'article 25 rights' should be a minimum right accommodating only for individuals belonging to minorities, not minorities as such.[35] Some States were of the view it should guarantee no more than the cultural, religious and linguistic practices of persons belonging to minorities.[36] Article 25 rights when exercised, argued Turkey, "must not conflict with public safety, public morality or national law".[37] Mali's representative stressed that "while enjoying the rights stated in article 25, minorities should not be given the rights which would permit them to gain national ascendancy".[38] Any "special political privileges", according to the delegate of Saudi Arabia, were not meant by article 25. He further stressed that minorities must remain loyal citizens.[39] Minorities, in the view of the Libyan delegate, could not within the ambit of article 25 enjoy rights in violation of the rights of majorities.[40] Nicaragua[41] and Australia[42] also entertained a similar view.

There is an unbridgeable difference between articles 1 and 27 of the ICCPR. Whilst peoples' right to self-determination is enshrined in article 1 (1), the rights of individuals belonging to minorities are included in article 27 (see further Higgins, 1994:127; Franck, 1992:58; Capotorti, 1976; Mullerson, 1994). Minorities as such have no right to self-determination based either on article 1 or 27 of the ICCPR. The Badinter Committee has given a wider interpretation to article 1. It concluded.

> Article 1 of both of the two 1966 International Covenants on Human Rights establishes that the principle of the right to self-determination serves to safeguard human rights. By virtue of that right *every individual* may choose to belong to whatever ethnic, religious or language community he or she wishes. [43]

Capotorti (1976:9) stated, "In the structure of the Covenants there is, undoubtedly, a clear distinction between the right conferred on all peoples in Article 1 and the rights of persons belonging to minorities in Article 27". He noted (at 21) that it is impossible to read article 1 as conferring any right of secession or special autonomy on minority groups living in States, which are well structured in democratic governance (see also Franck, 1992:58). One of the architects of the UDHR and the drafting of the Covenants on human rights, a former Director of the United Nations Division of Human Rights, Humphrey (1984:129) came to the conclusion that article 1 did not recognise secession except for colonies. The HRC's position is also that there is a distinction between article 1 and 27 of the ICCPR.[44] The HRC in its general comments stated that "the enjoyment of the right to which Article 27 relates does not prejudice the sovereignty and territorial integrity of a State party". However, it recognised that some of the rights relating to individuals belonging to minority groups have been "closely associated with territory and use of its resources".[45] The HRC commented:

> In some communications submitted to the Committee under the Optional Protocol, the right protected under Article 27 has been confused with the right of peoples to self-determination proclaimed in Article 1 of the Covenant...The Covenant draws a distinction between the right to self-determination and the rights protected under Article 27. The former is expressed to be a right belonging

to peoples and is dealt with in a separate part (part I) of the Covenant. Self-determination is not a right cognizable under the Optional Protocol. Article 27, on the other hand, relates to rights conferred on individuals as such and is included, like the Articles relating to other personal rights conferred on individuals, in part III of the Covenant and is cognizable under the Optional Protocol.[46]

Article 1 does confer a right of self-determination, in the view of the HRC, only upon *peoples* as such. The Band members' attempt in the case of *Lubicon Lake Band* to seek remedies under article 1 of the ICCPR on the basis that their right to self-determination was violated by misappropriation and destruction of their environmental and economic base, and by proposed developments by the Canadian government threatening their way of life and culture, was not successful. The HRC preferred to investigate the dispute under article 27.[47] The Committee held that individuals could not claim under the Optional Protocol alleging that they were victims of a violation of the right to self-determination under article 1. Confirming this position further in its final views of 26 March 1990, the HRC held that a group of people had no procedural rights provided under the Optional Protocol to pursue a case of alleged violation of self-determination against a State (see detail Nowak, 1993:16). An attempt by a group of residents of South Tyrol under article 1 in *A.B et al* v *Italy*[48] was rejected by the HRC. The Committee held in its views that an individual could not claim under the Optional Protocol alleging that he was a victim of a violation of the right to self-determination under article 1. In *San Andres* v *Colombia* the communication of a group of English-speaking Protestants on the island of San Andres claimed that their right to self-determination had been violated by the Colombian government by "systematic Colombianization of their island employing immigration policies, tourist industry, militarisation, employment discrimination, education policy etc".[49] Rejecting their communication, the HRC held that the individual communication procedure enshrined in the Optional Protocol does not apply to article 1 of the ICCPR. In the case of *Whispering Pines Indian Band*,[50] the Committee reaffirmed the position taken by earlier cases.

On the other hand, persons belonging to minorities cannot for all practical purposes seek secession under article 1 or 27 because without a collective basis secession is only a mirage (see Hannum, 1993a:11). Of course, individuals in minority communities can enjoy certain rights under article 27 in their personal capacity, but not minorities as such.

10.6 *The UN Declaration on Minorities Does Not Explicitly or Implicitly Provide for a Right to Secession*

The Declaration on the Right of Persons Belonging to National or Ethnic, Religious and Linguistic Minorities, 1992 recognises that the rights conferred by the Declaration would not allow the sanctity of territorial and political unity of States to be violated.[51] The travaux preparatoires reveal that many States reiterated their concerns about the possible effect on the territorial and political integrity of States unless safety measures were embodied in the Declaration. For example, Bulgaria and the USSR presenting an amendment[52] to the proposed article 5 urged: "In ensuring and promoting the rights of minorities, strict respect for the sovereignty, territorial integrity, political independence and non-interference in the internal affairs of those countries in which minorities live should be observed". The Representative of the Four Directions Council also placed emphasis on territorial integrity while arguing that minorities' rights be guaranteed. He proposed: "Nothing in the present Declaration shall be interpreted as permitting any activity which is contrary to the purposes and principles of the United Nations".[53] The representative of the Ukraine stressed that:

> Persons belonging to minorities shall respect the human rights and fundamental rights of others and refrain from activities which prejudice the promotion of mutual understanding, tolerance, good neighbourliness and friendship among nations and racial or ethnic groups in conformity with the principles enshrined in the United Nations Charter and with international instruments in the field of human rights.[54]

Although participatory rights of persons belonging to minorities at national and regional level in the areas of cultural, social, economic and public life have been recognised by article 2 (3) "within a democratic framework based on the rule of law",[55] they should exercise these rights in a manner not incompatible with national legislation. Commitments expected from States by articles. 4-7 is not obligatory. In fact they are very vague and imprecise. Terms contained in articles. 2-3 such as, 'encourage conditions', 'the State should consider appropriate measures', 'the State shall protect', 'the State shall fulfil in good faith', 'obligations and commitments that they have to assume', do not impose any binding obligations on States. Commitments and obligations rely on the goodwill of States. Should a State fail to take appropriate measures or fail to implement any of these obligations, can minorities opt for secessionist or irredentist paths? There is not even a glimpse of such a possibility to be discerned in the UN Declaration on Minorities, 1992.

Emphasis is placed by article 8 (2) on persons belonging to minorities so that the right set forth in the Declaration shall not prejudice enjoyment by all persons of universally recognized human rights and fundamental freedoms (see Alfredsson and Zayas, 1993:1-19; Omenga, 1991:33-41). Article 8 (4) states:

> Nothing in this Declaration may be construed as permitting any activity contrary to the purposes and principles of the United Nations, including sovereign equality, territorial integrity and political independence of States.

Therefore, any exercise of the rights recommended by the Declaration by a section of a population of a given territory will not be valid if such activities have a harmful effect on other communities.

The Chairman-Rapporteur Ms Zagroka Ilic of the Working Group on Minorities also reminded other members of the Working Group that their role mandated by the Commission's resolution 1995/24, was, while finding ways and means to implement the rights contained in the Declaration, to make sure that the territorial integrity and political independence of States were protected.[56] The position taken by the above UN treaties and resolutions was reaffirmed by the Vienna Declaration and Programme of Action, 1993. In its section 2 having affirmed that all peoples have a right to self-determination, it was emphasised that this right "should not be construed as authorising or encouraging any action which would dismember or impair, totally or in part, the territorial integrity or political unity of sovereign and independent States having democratic and representative government."

10.7 *"Frontiers Can Only be Changed by Peaceful Means and by Common Agreements"*

The legitimacy of existing boundaries (internationally recognised) of nation-States, as stated in *Burkina Faso* v *the Republic of Mali*,[57] and the Principle 3 of the Badinter Committee,[58] now come under *uti possidetis juris*. This principle, *uti possidetis*, is considered a general principle of international law (see Shaw, 1986, and 1996:76-154; Cassese, 1995:190-193 and Klabbers and Lefeber, 1993:37-76). Any violation of the boundaries of a State amounts to aggression against a State within the meaning of the GA Resolution 3314 (XXIX) on the Definition of Aggression (Shaw, 1986:77). Changes to boundaries can take place without involving aggression or the use of force, by peaceful means, and by common agreement. The static nature of this principle suggests that inter-State activities and the domestic functions of the nation-State are to operate within existing boundaries. *Uti possidetis juris* is concerned with territorial *status quo* or territorial sovereignty of States. Thus, *uti possidetis juris* provides legitimacy for both existing States and newly independent States, and "acts as a counter-weight to other legitimizing principles such as ethnic, religious or historic affinities" (Shaw, 1986:98). It was developed, as Judge Abi-Saab in his separate opinion in *Burkina Faso* v *Republic of Mali* held, as a means of "preventive conflicts."[59]

Although the origin of *uti possidetis juris* lies in Roman law, it was first applied in Latin America in the 19th century,[60] then in Africa it developed as an established principle. Similarly, Asia and Europe have adopted the principle of the sanctity of existing boundaries in their inter-State relations.

Indeed from the 1960s it was African States which further developed this principle. Considering that border problems constituted "a grave and permanent factor of dissension", the Assembly of Heads of State and Government at Cairo in 1964 pledged themselves to respect existing frontiers on their achievement of national independence (article 2 of the Cairo Resolution). This is the reaffirmation of Article III of the Charter of the OAU, 1963 (see Brownlie, 1971:1-17). The Cairo Declaration limits the operation of the right to self-determination in the post-colonial African States in order to guarantee the stability of territorial integrity and the political independence of newly independent African nation-States.[61] In 1967 a resolution adopted by the Assembly of Heads of State and Government of the OAU at its 4th ordinary session at Kinshasa deplored secessionist attempts against existing African States (see Brownlie, 1979: 115; Kamanu, 1974:370). The OAU resolution on the 'Situation in Nigeria', 1967, reaffirmed this position (Brownlie, 1990:364). The sanctity of boundaries was once again affirmed in the Cairo Declaration on Somalia, 1997.[62]

In *Burkina Faso* v *Mali* the request of both parties was that the frontier dispute be resolved, "based in particular on respect for the principle of the intangibility of frontiers inherited from colonization, and to effect the definitive delimitation and demarcation of their common frontiers".[63] It was held that the obvious purpose of the application of *uti possidetis* was "to prevent the independence and stability of new States being endangered by fratricidal struggles..."[64] The Chamber concluded that *uti possidetis juris* would be of value to the African peoples in preserving what has been achieved by them and "to avoid a disruption which would deprive the continent of the gains achieved by so much sacrifice."[65] A similar view was expressed in the *Guinea-Guinea Bissau Maritime Delimitation* case.[66]

This principle has also been applied in Asia. Although the ICJ did not mention the principle of *uti possidetis* as such in *Preah Vhear*,[67] the judgment delivered was in fact based on *status quo* boundaries between Thailand and Cambodia, thus admitting the principle in Asian countries (see European attitudes, 10.8.2, below).

10.8 *European Concerns: "Secessionist Activities Bring Shame, Bloodshed and Suffering to Our Continent"*

The opposition to any radical changes to existing internationally recognised boundaries and territorial sovereignty of States by aggression or use of force has been more prominent in the 1990s than at any other time in post-war Europe. The European position has been hardened by the unexpected surge of ethnic consciousness mixed with militant and anarchic tendencies since the Cold War ended (especially in Central and Eastern Europe), and by their effect on the "overall stability, the unification and democratisation of European States".[68] Most States were taken by surprise by the speed with which these new developments sprang up in the form of "a manifestation of aggressive nationalism".[69] The disintegration of the former USSR and the Socialist Federal Republic of Yugoslavia still rings alarm bells across the frontiers of the European continent. In addition to the human cost arising out of ethnic conflicts, Western Europe itself has to shoulder the consequences of these economic and social upheavals (Weller, 1992:580). For example, referring to the Balkan conflicts, the US delegate warned about their "dangerous impact on Yugoslavia's neighbours, who face refugee flows, energy shortfalls and the threat of a spillover of fighting".[70] Western Europe was deeply concerned about the fighting and indiscriminate bloodshed that took place in the heart of Europe.[71] Addressing the UN General Assembly on 24 September 1991, the President of the Council of European Communities, Mr. Hans van den Broek referred to the scenario of "uncontrolled and violent fragmentation" occurring in the heart of Europe due to extreme nationalism and ethno-centrism, which, in his view, did bring "shame, bloodshed and suffering to our continent".[72] The London Declaration on the Federal Republic of Yugoslavia, 1991,[73] admitted that military activities involving different ethnic groups caused serious concern among the members of the OSCE, the EU and the Heads of State or Government of the seven major industrial nations. The EU unashamedly admitted in public that its concern was not only for the peace and security of Yugoslavia itself and its constituent peoples, but for Europe as a whole.[74]

With this understanding, it was widely accepted by the European institutions (mainly, the Council of Europe, OSCE, EU) that there should be immediate action to secure the effective protection and promotion of ethnic, cultural, linguistic and religious identity[75] of persons belonging to national minorities within pluralist societies under the rule of law,[76] whilst respecting the territorial integrity and national sovereignty of States,[77] with a view to, a) achieving a lasting end to ethnic confrontations, and b) to preserving democracy, stability and peace within the continent.[78] A goodwill gesture was demonstrated by the decision to establish the post of High Commissioner on National Minorities by the CSCE in July 1992. However, European institutions were equally adamant that the solution should not be found by giving way to ethnic militarism thereby legitimizing secessionist and irredentist claims. This uncompromising position resulted in the proclamation of a chain of declarations and statements by intergovernmental organisations and Heads of States rejecting the legitimacy of secessionist and irredentist movements, in particular during the period 1989-1995, although there had been some initiatives from the 1970s to protect and promote the cultural dimension of minority rights. It seems that the broader liberal approach taken in paragraph 7 of the Declaration on Friendly Relations was followed in most of the resolutions, declarations and treaties adopted in Europe during this period. In particular, the phrase "States conducting themselves in compliance with the principle of self-determination and thus possessed of a government representing the whole people belonging to the territory without distinction as to race, creed or colour" was enshrined together with the human dimension. It was further emphasised that the active involvement of persons, groups, organisations and institutions would be essential to ensure continuing progress towards the achievement of a peaceful and stable Europe.[79] However, it was reiterated that minority rights should be exercised within existing boundaries in compliance with domestic and international law. The culmination of this process was reached with the pronouncements of a series of Opinions by the Badinter Committee, as will be shown in detail below.

10.9 *From the Helsinki Final Act to the Badinter Committee: "Any Right to Engage in Activity or Perform any Action in Contravention of the Purposes and Principles of..."*

The point of departure in the human dimension of the CSCE commenced with the Helsinki Final Act, 1975.[80] The main objective, as enshrined in the preamble, was to "promote better relations among signatory States and to ensure conditions in which their people can live in true and lasting peace free from any threat to or attempt against their security" (see also Hannum, 1993a). Even though certain human rights and fundamental freedoms and most importantly "equal rights and self-determination of peoples" (Principle VIII) were enshrined in the Final Act as some of its objectives, the emphasis was placed on the requirements that parties should refrain from the threat or use of force (Principle II); the inviolability of boundaries (Principle III) and the territorial integrity of the State (Principle IV). Principle I states that "they consider that their frontiers can be changed, in accordance with international law by peaceful means and by agreement". However, principle III operates as a subordinate clause to principle I. The former emphasised that the participating States should regard one another's boundaries as inviolable. Will this enable "peoples" (mentioned in Principle VIII) to pursue their political, economic, social and cultural development as they wish? It is worthy of mention that the rights recognised in Principle VIII are to be exercised in harmony with the ideals enshrined in Principle III. Campaigns for peoples' right to self-determination should be within the confines of the existing boundaries of European States. Any elements of secessionist rights are absent in the Helsinki Final Act.

The Ten Principles adopted by the Helsinki Final Act have been the foundation for subsequent European declarations and treaties. Having affirmed its commitment to the Principle VIII enunciated in the Final Act, the CSCE Concluding Document of the Vienna Meeting on the follow up to the Conference 1989 confirmed its "commitment strictly and effectively to observe the principle of the territorial integrity of States".[81] Principle V stressed that "no actions or situations in contravention of this principle will be recognized as legal by the participating States of the Conference on the Human Dimension of the CSCE". The Document of the Copenhagen Meeting, 1990 in its Principle IV (37) states:

> None of these commitments may be interpreted as implying any right to engage in activity or perform any action in contravention of the purposes and principles of

the Charter of the United Nations, other obligations under international law or the provisions of the Final Act, including the principle of territorial integrity of States.

This prohibition clause was to appear in almost all European declarations, resolutions or treaties which dealt with either the security of Europe or the human dimension of the issues concerning minorities' problems. In the *Charter of Paris for a New Europe,* 1990,[82] under the sub-title 'Security', it was stated that the Heads of State or Government of the States of the CSCE were "determined to co-operate in defending democratic institutions against activities which violate the independence, sovereign equality or territorial integrity of the participating States". These include illegal activities involving outside pressure, coercion and subversion. The *EC's Declaration on the Guidelines on the Recognition of New States in Eastern Europe and in the Soviet Union,* December 16, 1991, also confirmed the commitment to the "inviolability of all frontiers" stating unequivocally that frontiers could only be changed "by peaceful means and by common agreement".[83] This position has continually been applied in other declarations. The European Communities, for example, insisted that "any change of internal and international borders by force is not acceptable."[84] It was reiterated at a Ministerial Meeting of 8 November 1991 that the use of force and the policy of *fait accompli* to achieve changes of borders were illusory and would never be recognized by the Community and its Member States of the EC.[85] The *European Charter for Regional or Minority Languages* 1992,[86] which is in many ways constructive in its approach to the protection and promotion of "the cultural dimension of regional or minority languages",[87] nevertheless in its article 5 proscribes any secessionist activities within the national borders of nation-States. It states, "Nothing in this Charter may be interpreted as implying any right to engage in any activity or perform any action in contravention of the purposes of the Charter of the United Nations or other obligations under international law, including the principle of the sovereignty and territorial integrity of States."

This position was continued in article 1 (2) of the *Proposal for a European Convention for the Protection of Minorities,* 1991.[88] Any action contrary to the fundamental principles of international law and in particular of the sovereignty, territorial integrity and political independence of States is prohibited. Article 15 (I) requires that any member of a minority "shall loyally fulfil the obligations deriving from his status as a national of his State". Article 15 (2) states that when the rights set forth in this Convention are exercised by minorities, they "shall respect the national legislation, the right of others, in particular those of the members of the majority and of other minorities". This position is also maintained in the CSCE Document of the *Moscow Meeting of the Conference on the Human Dimension of the CSCE*, October 3, 1992.[89] This hard-line, yet cautious and pragmatic position was re-affirmed by article 21 of *the Council of Europe Framework Convention for the Protection of National Minorities,* 1994. This article reaffirmed both Principle IV of the Document of the Copenhagen Meeting and article 5 of the European Charter for Regional or Minority Language. It says, "Nothing in the present framework Convention shall be interpreted as implying any right to engage in any activity or perform any act contrary to the fundamental principles of international law and in particular of the sovereign equality, territorial integrity and political independence of States".[90] It is worthy of note that especial measures were introduced in many of these documents to suspend any rights and freedoms guaranteed for minorities in case of such rights being violated to the detriment of the State and the rights of others. Article 14 of the *Recommendation* 1201 (1993) of the Council of Europe's Parliamentary Assembly on an Additional Protocol on the Rights of National Minorities to the European Convention on Human Rights provides that the rights and freedoms in this protocol can be restricted in the interest of national security, territorial integrity or public safety, for the prevention of disorder or crime, for the protection of health or morals or for the protection of the rights and freedom of others".[91] The General Framework Agreement for Peace in Bosnia and Herzegovina, 1995 in its article 1 stated that no one should be allowed to use "threat or use of force against the territorial integrity or political independence of independent countries.[92] The Cannes European Council in 1995[93] and the European Council meeting in Luxembourg on 12-13 December 1997 reaffirmed this long-standing commitment to the integrity and inviolability of external borders and the sovereignty of States.[94] This position acquired legitimacy by the Badinter Committee's decision that existing boundaries cannot be legally changed except where the States concerned agree. As Opinion no. 3 (4) of the Badinter Committee states, the alteration of existing frontiers or boundaries by force is not capable of producing any legal effect.[95]

Can the break up of Yugoslavia be recognised as a case of secession? Some scholars argue that Slovenia, Bosnia and Herzegovina and Croatia seceded (Blum, 1992:830-833; Hannum, 1993b:58-69). It is noteworthy that the Conference on Yugoslavia's Arbitration Committee (Badinter Committee) came to its decisions by assuming that the Republic of Yugoslavia was then irreversibly in the "process of dissolution." [96] The former boundaries of the republics of the federation, it was held in Opinion no. 3, would acquire the character of borders protected by international law.[97] The Badinter Committee rejected the position taken by Serbia that "those Republics, which have declared or would declare themselves independent or sovereign, have seceded or would secede from the SFRY."[98] Any suggestion that Slovenia and Croatia emerged by exercising the right to self-determination was also rejected. The emergence of Slovenia, Croatia and Bosnia-Herzegovina as new States was identified by the Badinter Committee in terms of doctrine of the succession of States.[99] Opinion 2 (1) states:[100]

> However, it is well established that whatever the circumstances, the right to self-determination must not involve changes to existing frontiers at the time of independence (*uti possidetis juris*) except where the States concerned agree otherwise.

Respect for territorial integrity and the acceptance of existing boundaries of independent States have now become the standard formula in inter-State relations. Articles 4 and 15 (12) of the Hungary-Romania Treaty on Understanding, Co-operation and Good Neighbourliness of 1996[101] and the Agreement Establishing the Commonwealth of Independent States (between Belarus, the Russian Federation and the Ukraine),[102] and the subsequent Alma Ata Declaration on 21 December 1991,[103] and the Border Agreement between Lithuania and the Russian Federation on 24 October 1997 (between Azerbaijan, Armenia, Kazakhastan, Kyrgystan, Moldava, Tajikistan, Turkmenistan and Uzbekistan) reiterated the inviolability of existing boundaries and the territorial integrity of their respective States. Shaw (1997:499) states, "Although these instruments refer essentially to the principle of territorial integrity protecting international boundaries, it is clear that the intention was to assert and reinforce the *uti possidetis* doctrine."

Conclusions

Neither UN practice, nor the conclusions of other arbitration committees recognise the right to secession as a legal principle. It is not a legal right, which can be exercised by minorities as of right by attacking the territorial integrity and political unity of the State. The current jurisprudence on the *peoples' right to self-determination* does not support the theory that minorities can secede by invocation of the right to self-determination. Most importantly there is no interrelationship between the right to self-determination and secession. Self-determination is a collection of human rights, which has to be exercised in conformity with the territorial integrity of the State. As an alternative to breaking existing States, self-determination is intended to promote peace and prosperity and to guarantee the universal human rights of individuals as well as groups. It is not a destructive force or a tool, which can legitimately be used to dismantle the State. However, international law does not refuse to accept political realities in each case. The emergence of new States or the dissolution and disappearance of existing states are not a new phenomenon. If a State emerges as a consequence of secession having fulfilled the criteria within the meaning of the Montevideo Convention and the guidelines issued by the EC, then international law will eventually recognise such a State. However, this should not be taken as endorsing any right to secession on the basis of self-determination.

Notes

[1] See the Report of the International Committee of Jurists Entrusted by the Council of the League of Nations with the Task of Giving an Advisory Opinion Upon the Legal Aspects of the Aaland Islands Question, *LNOJ*, Special Supl. 1, 1920, p. 5.

[2] The report submitted to the Council of the League of Nations by the Commission of Rapporteurs, *LNOJ*, Doc. B7.21/68/106, 1921, p. 27.

[3] 7 *UN Monthly Chronicle*, p. 40, February 1970.

[4] See the full text, Http://www.mbnet.mb.ca/psim/can-law.html.

[5] Gross Espiell, H. (1980), *The Right to Self-Determination, Implementation of United Nations Resolutions*, E/CN.4/Sub.2/405/Rev.1, para. 90. See also Cristescue, A. (1981), *The Right to Self-Determination, Historical and Current Development on the Basis of United Nations Instruments*, E/CN.4/ Sub.2/ 404, Rev. 1, para.136, and para. 279.

[6] Unpublished microfilmed minutes of the debate of the First Committee of the First Commission of the San Francisco Conference, quoted as note. 2, meeting of 14 and 15 May 1945, cited in Cassese, A. (1979), 'Political Self-Determination-Old Concepts and New Developments', in A. Cassese (ed), *UN Law / Fundamental Rights: Two Topics in International Law*, Sijthoff and Noordhoff: Alphen and den Rijn, footnote, 3, pp. 162 and p. 138. See also Cassese, A. (1995), *Self-Determination: A Legal Reappraisal*, Cambridge UP: Cambridge, pp.38-49.

[7] A/C.3/SR.890, 3 December 1965, paras. 18-19, p. 303.

[8] 15 UN GAOR Supp. 16, pp. 66-67, UN Doc. A/L.323 and Add. 1-6, 1960.

[9] See GAOR, Agenda Item, 87, Annexes (xxii), 22nd session, 1967, para.184.

[10] UN Doc. A/4651, 1960.

[11] A/PV. 947, 14 December 1960, para. 62, p.1276.

[12] *Ibid.* para. 63, p.1276.

[13] A / L. 325, *ibid.* para. 63, p. 1276.

[14] A/PV. 946, 14 December 1961, para.14, p. 1266.

[15] *Ibid.* para. 39, p. 1268.

[16] *Ibid.* para. 54, p. 1269 (Iran).

[17] UN Doc. A/8028, 1970. This resolution was adopted by the General Assembly by a vote of 89 to 0 with 9 abstentions.

[18] See further GA Res. 1654/16, 1961. *The Situation with Regard to the Implementation of the Declaration on the Granting of Independence to Colonial Countries and People.* In the preambular paragraph, emphasis was placed on the national unity and territorial integrity.

[19] *Western Sahara* (Advisory Opinion) Order of 3 January 1975 *ICJ Reports*, para. 49, p. 29.

[20] *Western Sahara, ibid.* para. 50, p. 29.

[21] For details see A/C.6/SR.871, 8 November 1965, para. 12, p. 188. See Madagascar's resolution, A/5757, Add. 1.

[22] A/C.6/SR. 883, 26 November 1965, para. 31, p. 257.

[23] A/C.6/SR. 886, 1 December 1965, para. 54, p. 279.

[24] Ecuador's statement, A/C.6/SR. 891, 6 December 1965, para. 54, p. 316. See also GAOR, Agenda Item 87, Annexes (xxii) 1967 (on Friendly Relations), para. 68, p. 81.

[25] *Ibid.* para. 63, p. 80.

[26] The Committee on the Elimination of Racial Discrimination, General Recommendation, XXI, UN Doc. A/51/18, 1996, para. 11, 5 (1) *IHRR* 1998, pp. 19-20.

[27] See the following UN Documents, the Art 2 (4) of the UN Charter; Article 111 (3) of the Charter of the Organisation of African Unity 1963; See also the following case laws, *Frontier Dispute Case (Burkina Faso v Republic of Mali)* [1986] *ICJ Reports*, 554. Military and Paramilitary Activities in and against Nicaragua, *Nicaragua case* [1986] *ICJ Reports*. 14. See also the judgment of the Russian Constitutional Court, 31 July 1995 on the unilateral declaration of secession by Chechnya, reprinted in the European Commission for Democracy through Law of the Council of Europe, CDL-INF (96) 1, cited in Gaeta, P. (1996), 'The Armed Conflict in Chechnya before the Russian Constitutional Court, 7 (4) *EJIL*, p. 565.

[28] UN Doc. E/CN.4/Sub.2/1993/34, para. 79, p. 17.

[29] The General Recommendation of the Committee on the Elimination of Racial Discrimination, above. 1996, para. 11.

[30] UN Doc. E/CN.4/Sub.2/404, Rev. 1, 1981, para. 268, p. 39.

[31] GA Res. 390 (v) 14 December 1950, Preambular paragraph C.

[32] The Committee on the Elimination of Racial Discrimination, General Recommendation XXI, 1996, UN Doc. A/51/18, PARA.11, 5 (1) *IHRR* 1998, p. 20. See also ss. 25, 26 and 27 of the *Vienna Declaration and Programme of Action* 1993, 32 *ILM* 1661 [1993], pp.1663-1687. This aspect of States' obligations and requirements of representative government was emphasised by western powers, notably by the UK. See GAOR, Agenda Item. 87, Annexes (xxii) 22nd session, 1967, para. 176, p. 29. See also the decision of the Special Arbitration Committee on

Yugoslavia (Badinter Committee), Opinion no. 1, 31 *ILM* 1494 [1992], para. 3, p. 1497 and Opinion no. 2, 31 *ILM* 1497 [1991], para. 2, p. 1498.

[33] See also the following decisions of the Human Rights Committee: *Chief Ominayak and the Lubicon Lake Band* v *Canada*, communication no. 167/1984 in 11 *HRLJ* 1990, p. 305; *Ivon Kitok* v *Sweden*, Communication no 197/1985; *Sandra Lovelace* v *Canada*, communication no. 24/1977, 2 *HRLJ* 1981, p.158: *Mikmaq Tribal Society*, communication no. 205/1986, in 5 *HRLJ* 1984, p. 194.

[34] See *Lubicon Lake Band, ibid.* p. 311. See also The General Comment no. 23/50 on Article 27 of the ICCPR/ minority rights, under Article 40, para. 4 of the ICCPR, para. 3.2, 4 and 5.3. See the full text, 15 (4/6) *HRLJ* 1994, pp. 234-236.

[35] See A/C.3/SR.1103, 14 November 1961, para. 39, p. 222 (Australia).

[36] A/C.3/SR. 1004, 14 November 1961, para. 16, p. 220 (Pakistan).

[37] *Ibid.* para. 20, p. 220 (Turkey).

[38] *Ibid.*para. 21, p. 220.

[39] *Ibid.* para. 32, p. 221.

[40] *Ibid.* para. 38, p. 222.

[41] *Ibid.* paras. 36-37, p. 222.

[42] *Ibid.* para. 39, p. 222.

[43] Emphasis added. The Badinter Committee, opinion, no.2, 31 *ILM* 1497, 1992, para. 3. p. 1498.

[44] Human Rights Committee, General Comment on Article 27 of the ICCPR, no. 23/50, UN Doc. CCPR/C/21/Rev. 1/ Add. 5 (1994). See the full text, 15 (3/4) *HRLJ* 1994, pp.234-236.

[45] *Ibid.* para. 3.2.

[46] *Ibid*, see paras. 1 and 8. See also GAOR, 39th session, supl. no. 40, A/39/40, Annex VI, General Comment on Article 1, no. 12/21, 95th session, supl. 40, A/45/40, Vol. II, Annex IV, Sect. A.

[47] No. 167/1984, 11 *HRLJ* 1990, p. 311.

[48] Communication no. 413/1990, Decision of 2 November 1990, 12 *HRLJ* 1991 p. 25.

[49] Communication no. 318/1988. Decision of 25 July 1990, *ibid.* p. 14.

[50] Communication no. 358/1989, Decision of 5 November 1991, *ibid.* p. 16.

[51] See preambular paragraph, 14 *HRLJ* 1993, p. 54.

[52] UN Docs. E/CN.4/Sub.2/L.734, see E/CN.4/1989/36, Annex III, included in UN Doc. E/CN. 4/1989/38/ 7 March 1989, p. 14.

[53] UN Doc. E/CN.4/1989/WG. 5/WP. 2, recorded in UN Doc. E/CN.4/1989/38, 7 March 1989, para. 38, p. 9.

[54] UN Doc. E/CN.4/1989/WG.5/WP.3, included in UN Doc. E/CN.4/1989/38, para. 4. p. 9.

[55] See the Preamble of the UN declaration on the Rights of Persons Belonging to National or Ethnic, Religious and Linguistic Minorities, 1992.

[56] The Report of the Working Group on the Rights of Persons Belonging to National or Ethnic, Religious and Linguistic Minorities, UN Doc. E/CN.4/ Sub.2/ 1996/2 30 November 1995, para. 27, p. 8.

[57] *Burkina Faso v Republic of Mali,* as above, p. 554. See also Naldi, G. J. (1987), 'The Case Concerning the Frontier Dispute (Burkina Faso v Republic of Mali): Uti Possidatis in an African Perspective', 36 *ICLQ,* pp. 893-903; Oellers-Frahm, K. (1990), 'Frontier Dispute Case (Burkina Faso v Mali)', in 12 *Encyclopaedia of Public International Law,* 1990, pp. 122-126.

[58] 31 *ILM* 1488 [1992], pp. 1499- 1500. See also Pellet, A. (1992), 'The Opinions of the Badinter Committee: A Second Breath for the Self-Determination of Peoples', 3 *EJIL,* pp. 178-181.

[59] *Burkina Faso* case, as above, p. 661.

[60] The starting point of this principle in Latin America is considered to be the adoption of the Treaty of Confederation signed by the Congress of Lima in 1847. See Brownlie, I. (1998), *Principles of Public International Law,* Clarendon Press: Oxford, pp. 132-133.

[61] See OAU Resolution on Border Disputes, 1964, OAU Doc. AHG/Res. 16 (1), pp. 360-361. It is worth noting that Somalia and Morocco did not ratify this resolution. For details see Brownlie, I. (1979), *African Boundaries: A Legal and Diplomatic Encyclopaedia,* Hurst and Comp: London, pp. 9-11. See further Touval, S. (1967), 'The Organization of African Unity and African Borders', 21 *International Organization,* pp. 102-127. See also Articles 2 (1) and 3 (3) of the Charter of the Organisation of African Unity 1963 which placed emphasis on the territorial integrity of African States and stability of existing boundaries inherited from the colonial empires.

[62] SC Res. 1000, 29 December 1997, Annex, see the full text in 37 *ILM* 780 [1998], pp. 781-787.

[63] *Burkina Faso,* as above. p. 557.

[64] *Ibid.* p. 565.

[65] *Ibid.* pp. 566-67.

[66] 77 *Iinternational Law Report* [1988], pp. 636-692.

[67] *Case Concerning the Temple of Preah Vihear, Cambodia v Thailand* (Merits) *ICJ* Reports 1962, p. 34. See also *Rann of Kutch case,* award, 7 *ILM* 633 [1968].

[68] Council of Europe (1995), *Human Rights: A Continuing Challenge for the Council of Europe,* Strasbourg, p. 45.

[69] CSCE Budapest Document of 6 December 1994, see the full text, 15 (11/12) *HRLJ* 1994, pp. 449-458.

[70] SC Res. 23067, 25 September 1991.

[71] The joint statement by the Community and its Member States on 6 November 1991, 24 (11) *Bull. EC* 1991, p. 91.

[72] Statement made by Mr. Hans van den Broek, the President of the Council of the European Communities to the UN, on 24 September 1991, 24 (9) *Bull. EC* 1991, p. 87. See also the statement made by Presidential Meeting between Mr. Delors, Mr. Lubbers and Mr. Bush (EC-US), 24 (11) *Bull. EC* 1991, p. 93.

[73] The London Declaration by the Community and its Member States on Yugoslavia was adopted on 17 July 1991. See 24 (7/8) *Bull. EC* 1991, pp. 140-144.

[74] See the Joint statement of the Community and its Member States on Yugoslavia, 2 August 1991, 24 (7/8) *Bull EC.* 1991, p. 112.

[75] See for example Principle 4, para. 32 of the Document of the Copenhagen Meeting of the Conference on the Human Dimension of the CSCE, 29 June 1990, in *Human Rights in International Law, Basic Texts,* Council of Europe: Strasbourg, 1992, p. 444. See further *The Charter of Paris for a New Europe,* 21 November 1990, *ibid.* p. 450. See also the Recommendation No. R (92) on the Implementation of Rights of Persons Belonging to National Minorities, in *European Convention on Human Rights: Collected Texts*, Council of Europe: Strasbourg, 1994, pp. 340-341.

[76] CFSP Presidency statement, Cannes European Council, 26 and 27 June 1995, Presidency Conclusions (SN 211/95), p. 7.

[77] See the Preamble in the Framework Convention for the Protection of National Minorities 1995, 16 (1/3) *HRLJ* 1995, p. 98. Parliamentary Assembly of the Council of Europe, Strasbourg, Recommendations 1134/1990; 1177/1992, and 1201 /1993.

[78] See preamble in the Proposal for an Additional Protocol to the ECHR concerning Persons Belonging to National Minorities, 14 *HRLJ* 1993, p. 145.

[79] The Document of the Copenhagen Meeting of the Conference on the Human Dimension of the CSCE, 1990, above, Preamble, p. 426.

[80] See the full text in *Human Rights in International Law, Basic Rights*, Council of Europe: Strasbourg, 1992, pp. 363-402.

[81] See Principle V, 10 *HRLJ* 1989, p. 273.

[82] 11 (4/3) *HRLJ* 1990, pp. 381-384. See on this Roth, A. J. (1990), 'The CSCE Charter of Paris for a New Europe: A new Chapter in the Helsinki Process', 11 (3/4) *HRLJ* 1990, pp. 373-379.

[83] See the full text, 4 *EJIL* 1993, p. 72.

[84] See the joint statement of the Member States of the EC published in the Hague and Brussels on Yugoslavia, 2 August 199, 124 (7/8) *Bull. EC* 1991, p. 112.

[85] 24 (11) *Bull. EC* 1991, p. 91. A similar statement was made at the UN General Assembly debate on 24 September 1991, see details 24 (9) *Bull. EC* 1991, p. 87.

[86] See the full text in 14 (3/4) *HRLJ*, 1993, pp.148-152.

[87] See further the *European Charter for Regional or Minority Language*, Explanatory Report, Council of Europe Press: Strasbourg, p. 5.

[88] See 12 (6/7) *HRLJ* 1991, p. 270.

[89] See the full text, 12 (11/12) *HRLJ* 1991, pp. 471-478.

[90] 16 (1/3) *HRLJ* 1995, pp. 98-101. This was opened for signature on 1 February 1995.

[91] See 14 (3/4) *HRLJ* 1993, pp. 145-146.

[92] See the full text in 18 *HRLJ* 1997, pp. 309-310.

[93] See the Conclusions of Presidency of the Cannes European Council (SN 211/95), p. 5, entitled, 'Stability, Security and Good-neighbourliness', points 1-5, 26 and 27 June 1995

[94] Conclusion of the Presidency, 12 *Bull. EC* 1997, point 1.4.4, p. 9.

[95] Opinion no. 3 of the Badinter Committee, 31 *ILM* 1488 [1992], para. 2, p. 1500. See also Opinion no. 2 of the Badinter Committee, 31 *ILM* 1488 [1992], para. 1, pp. 1497-1498.

[96] Opinion no.1 of the Badinter Committee, 31 *ILM* 1488 [1992], para. 3, p. 1497 and Opinion no. 8 of the Badinter Committee, 31 *ILM* 1521, [1992], para. 1, p. 1522.

[97] Opinion no. 3 of the Badinter Committee, 31 *ILM* 1488 [1992], para. 2, p. 1500.

[98] See Opinion no. 1 of the Badinter Committee, 31 *ILM* 1488 [1992], p. 1494. See also Opinion no. 8 of the Badinter Committee, 31 *ILM* 1494 [1992], p. 1522.

[99] *Ibid.* p. 1494.

[100] Opinion no. 2 of the Badinter Committee, 31 *ILM* 1488 [1992], para. 1, p. 1498.

[101] See the full text, 36 *ILM* 340 [1997], ("Parties shall respect the inviolability of their common borders and the territorial integrity of other party").

[102] See the full text, 31 *ILM* 138 [1992] ("High Contracting Parties acknowledge and respect each other's territorial integrity and the inviolability of existing borders within the Commonwealth").

[103] See the full text, 31 *ILM* 138 [1992], p. 148 ("Recognising and respecting each other's territorial integrity and the inviolability of existing borders").

References

Agrawala, S. K. (1978), 'New Norm-Creating Potentialities of Bangladesh Tragedy in the Area of Human Rights', in R. P. Dhokalia (ed), *Essays on Human Rights in India*, B. H. Univ: Varanasi, pp. 140- 146.

Alfresson, G. and Zayas, A. de. (1993), 'Minority Rights: Protection by the United Nations', 14 (1/2) *HRLJ*, pp. 1- 19.

Blum, Y. Z. (1992), 'UN Membership of the 'New' Yugoslavia: Continuity or Break?', 86 (4) *AJIL*, pp. 830- 833.

Brownlie, I. (1971), *Basic Documents on African Affairs*, Clarendon Press: Oxford.

Brownlie, I. (1979), *African Boundaries: A Legal and Diplomatic Encyclopaedia*, Hurst and Comp: London.

Brownlie, I. (1990), *Principles of Public International Law*, 4th ed. Clarendon Press: Oxford.

Buchheit, L. C. (1978), *Secession: The Legitimacy of Self-Determination*, Yale University Press: New Haven, C. T.

Capotorti, F. (1976), 'The Protection of Minorities Under Multilateral Agreements on Human Rights', 1 (2) *IYIL*, pp. 4- 32.

Capotorti, F. (1992), 'Are Minorities Entitled to Collective International Rights', in Y. Dinstein and M. Tabory (eds), *The Protection of Minorities and Human Rights*, Kluwer Academic: Dordrecht, pp. 505- 511.

Cassese, A. (1995), *Self-Determination of Peoples: A Legal Reappraisal*, Cambridge UP: Cambridge.

Clark, R. S. (1995), 'The Decolonisation of East Timor and the United Nations Norms on Self-determination and Aggression', in Catholic Institute for International Relations (ed), *International Law and the Question of East Timor*, London, pp. 65- 102.

Crawford, J. (1979), *The Creation of States in International Law*, Oxford UP: Oxford.

Dyke (1970), *Human Rights: The United States and the World Community*, p. 102, cited in Nanda (1972), as below, p. 327.

Franck, T. M. and Hoffman, P. (1973), 'The Right to Self-Determination in Very Small Places', 8 *International Law and Politics*, pp. 331- 386.

Franck, T. M. (1992), 'The Emerging Right to Democratic Governance', 86 (1) *AJIL*, pp. 46- 91.

Hannum H. (1993a), 'Rethinking Self-Determination', 34 (1) *Va. JIL*, pp. 1-69.

Hannum, H. (1993b), 'Self-Determination, Yugoslavia and Europe: Old Wine in New Bottles?', 3 *Transnational Law and Contemporary Problems*, pp. 57- 69.

Heraclides, A. (1992), 'Secession, Self-Determination and Non-Intervention: In Quest of a Normative Symbiosis', 45 *Journal of International Affairs*, pp. 403-420.

Higgins, R, (1994), *Problems and Process: International Law and How We Use It*, Clarendon Press: Oxford..

Higgins, R. (1995), 'Peace and Security: Achievements and Failure', 6 (3) *EJIL* pp. 445- 460.

Kamanu, O. (1974), 'Secession and the Right to Self-Determination: An OAU Dilemma', 12 (3) *The Journal of Modern African Studies*, pp. 355- 376.

Klabbers, J. and Lefeber, R. (1993), 'Africa: Lost Between Self-Determination and Uti Possidetis', in C. Brolmann et al (eds), *Peoples and Minorities in International Law*, Martinus Nijhoff: Dordrecht/Boston/London, pp. 37-76.

Kohn, H. (1958), 'The United Nations and National Self-Determination', 20 *Review of Politics*, pp. 526-545.

Mullerson, R. (1994), *International Law, Rights and Politics: Developments in Eastern Europe and the CIS*, LSE and Routledge: London.

Nanda, Ved. P. (1972), 'Self-Determination in International Law: The Tragic Tale of Two Cities- Islamabad (West Pakistan) and Dacca (East Pakistan)', 66 *AJIL*, pp. 321-336.

Nanda, Ved. P. (1981), 'Self-Determination Under International Law: Validity of Claims to Secede', 13 *Case W. Res. J.Int.lL*, pp. 257-280.

Nayer, K. M. G. (1975), 'Self-Determination Beyond Colonial Context: Biafra in Retrospect', 10 *Texas International Law Journal*, pp. 321- 345.

Nowak, M. (1993), 'The Activities of the Human Rights Committee: Developments From 1 August 1989 Through 31 July 1992', 14 *HRLJ*, pp. 9-19.

Omenga, B. I. (1991), 'The Draft Declaration of the United Nations on the Rights of Persons Belonging to National Ethnic, Religious and Linguistic Minorities', *The Review* of the International Commission of Jurists, pp. 33- 41.

Rigo-Sureda, A. (1973), *The Evolution of the Right to Self-Determination*, A. W. Sihthoff: Leiden.

Rosenstock, R. (1971), 'The Declaration of Principles of International Law Concerning Friendly Relations', 65 *AJIL* pp. 713- 735.

Sanders, D. (1991), 'Collective Rights', 13 *HRQ*, pp. 369- 386.

Schoenberg, H. O. (1976), 'Limits of Self-Determination', *IYHR*, pp. 91- 103.

Shaw, M. N. (1986), *Title to Territory in Africa: International Legal Issues*, Clarendon Press: Oxford.

Shaw, M. N. (1986), 'Peoples, Territorialism and Boundaries', 3 *EJIL*, pp. 478- 507.

Shaw, M. N. (1996), 'The Heritage of States: The Principle of Uti possidetis Juris Today', 67 *BYIL*, pp. 76- 154.

Shaw, M. N. (1997), 'Peoples, Territorialism and Boundaries', 3 *EJIL*, pp. 487- 505.

The Secretariat of the International Commission of Jurists (1972), *The Events in East Pakistan*, H. Studer: Geneva.

Thornberry, P. (1989), 'Self-Determination, Minorities and Human Rights: A Review of International Instruments', 38 *ICLQ*, pp. 867- 889.

Tomuschat, C. ed. (1993), *Modern Law of Self-Determination*, Martinus Nijhoff: Dordrecht/Boston/London.

Visscher, C. De. (1957), *Theory and Reality in Public International Law*, Princeton UP: Princeton.

Weller, M. (1992), 'The International Response to the Dissolution of the Socialist Federal Republic of Yugoslavia', 86 *AJIL*, pp. 569- 607.

White, R. C. A. (1981), 'Self-Determination: Time for a Re-Assesment?', *NILR*, pp. 147- 170.

11 Secessionist Attempts: Case Studies

Introduction

Secession is strongly opposed by the UN and other regional bodies who fear that any recognition of it will set "dangerous precedents that would undermine the legitimacy of multi-national states" (Kamanu, 1974:360). In Africa, Asia and Europe secessionists' struggles for the creation of new nation-States have, with few exceptions, failed. The most difficult task for secessionists is to justify the break-up of a State as a radical solution to the political problems arising from ethnic and other diversities. World opinion seems to have taken the view that the demands for secession are a kind of "virus of tribalism" (*The Economist*, 29 June 1991). This chapter examines selected samples of secessionist attempts and analyses how the UN and other international and regional institutions respond to such actions.

11.1 *Katanga 1960-1963: "The UN's First Face-to-Face Confrontation with the Spectre of Secession"?*

Katanga is a province in the Republic of Congo, the former Belgian colony which achieved independence in 1960. Katanga's proclamation of independence of 11 July 1961 and its request for recognition were refused by the UN Security Council.[1] Moise Tshombe's declaration that "Katanga will appeal to the entire free world, and ask all nations to recognise our right, like that of every other nation, to self-determination" was not successful (see Dugard, 1987:87; Higgins, 1963:228-234). The Secretary-General decided to intervene in the Congo crisis at the request (telegram dated 12 July 1960) of the President and the Prime Minister of the Republic of Congo.[2] The Security Council did everything to prevent secessionists' armed struggle even by employing soldiers against the secessionist fighters.[3] The Katangan insurrection was seen by the UN Secretary General Dag Hammarskjold as a "question between the provincial government and the Central Government".[4] He refused to entertain the idea that the conflict was between Katanga and

289

the Congo. The Security Council and the General Assembly had continually maintained that the issue was an "internal political problem", or a problem of the Congolese authorities,[5] which was "threatening international peace".[6] The Security Council had repeatedly emphasised the importance and necessity of preserving "the territorial integrity and the political independence of the Republic of Congo".[7] The secessionist leaders were urged not to do anything "which might undermine the unity, territorial integrity and the political independence of the Republic of Congo".[8] Demanding that the parties to the dispute should take recourse to "constitutional solutions",[9] the Security Council without dissension (two members abstaining, France and the United Kingdom of Great Britain and Northern Ireland) urged and authorised the Secretary-General to take "vigorous action, including the use of the requisite measures of force, if necessary" to halt the violence and if necessary to deter any unruly mobs.[10] The Katangan secession was seen by the UN (both in the Security Council and the General Assembly) as a rebellion against the legitimate State.[11]

This was the first time that the UN had to confront the issue of recognition in the context of the right to secession. Consequently, Katanga abandoned its secessionist struggle in January 1963. The UN's organised opposition was seen by some academics as "face-to-face confrontation with the spectre of secession" (Buchheit, 1978:141; Nanda, 1972).

11.2 *Biafra 1967-1970*

Biafra, the eastern region of Nigeria, proclaimed its independence, seceding from the Republic of Nigeria,[12] on 30 May 1967 (Nixon, 1972:412-436; Heraclides, 1991:97-106: Jorre, 1972). Immediately, the federal government of Nigeria sent in the army to crush the uprising, rejecting the claim that Biafra as a separate territorial unit could secede by virtue of the right to self-determination. Biafra was recognised by only four African States, Gabon, Ivory Coast, Tanzania, and Zambia. However, issuing a statement on 13 April 1968, Tanzania said that the recognition of Biafra would be "a setback to our goal of unity" (see Kamanu, 1974:362). A delegation of the OAU headed by Emperor Haile Selassie condemned all secessionist activities in Africa in a statement on 22 Nov 1967, stressing that the conflicts should only be solved by preserving the unity and territorial integrity of Nigeria (Okoye, 1972:172). At the Summit Meeting of the OAU in Algeria on 14 September 1968, the Assembly of Heads of States urged the secessionist Biafrans to co-operate with the federal authorities of Nigeria in order to restore the peace, unity and territorial integrity of the Republic of

Nigeria (see Brownlie, 1971:364). Preferring a different approach to that of Katanga, the UN avoided any direct involvement in the dispute, allowing and encouraging the OAU to find a peaceful solution. The Biafran uprising was considered by the UN as "purely an internal problem".[13] Moreover, clarifying the UN's position, the Secretary-General U Thant stated that it has never accepted and would not accept secession as a principle of the United Nation system: [14]

Two and a half-years later, on 12 Jan 1970, the secessionist leaders surrendered to the Nigerian Federal government (see details in Ijalye, 1971:551). The Biafran conflict resulted in an unprecedented catastrophe in Biafra's post-colonial history. It was widely reported that at least one million people died due to military oppression, starvation and diseases (Nixon, 1972).

11.3 *Bangladesh, 1971: Self-determination through Gun-Barrels?*

East Pakistan had been a constituent part of the Republic of Pakistan since 1947. Pakistan itself emerged by seceding from India in 1947. In March 1971 Sheikh Mujibur Rahman proclaimed the birth of the Republic of Bangladesh. This was immediately branded as a "treasonous act" by the President of Pakistan Yahya Khan (Nanda, 1972; Nawaz, 1971:251-266). On 10th of April 1971 the Provincial Government of Bangladesh reaffirmed Mujibur Rahman's declaration of independence as being "in due fulfilment of the legitimate right of self-determination of the Peoples of Bangladesh" (see details in Buchheit, 1978:207).

The UN did not come forward to recognise Bangladesh. However, it was "deeply concerned at the magnitude of the human suffering", at the "crisis in East Pakistan", and at "the disturbing influence of the general situation on the process of economic and social development in the area".[15] The UN urged the parties to the disputes (India, West Pakistan and East Pakistan) to settle this 'tragedy' by respecting the principles of the Charter of the United Nations,[16] whilst recognising the territorial integrity of the Republic of Pakistan. The Secretary-General's report to the Security Council on 20 July 1971 acknowledged that the issue "falls within the competence of the judicial system of a member State - in this case, Pakistan".[17] Secretary-General U Thant expressed his concerns about the potential threat to peace and security, and about "unprecedented problems confronting the international community".[18]

In fact, during the General Assembly debate on the conflicts in Bangladesh, the President of the Security Council stated that recognition of Bangladesh could not arise since the necessary criteria were lacking.[19] Twenty-two non-governmental organisations, which had consultative status with the UN Economic and Social Council, made a request from the Security Council to intervene immediately or take other suitable steps to stop human rights violations.[20] However, even the International Commission of Jurists' request went unheeded.[21] The Security Council's decision not to become involved in the civil war was due to its fear that such actions would not only "inflame the situation" but could also become a precedent (Nanda, 1972:335). None of the members, as pointed out by Shiels (1984:250), "was prepared to place the United Nation's seal of approval on a secessionist movement". It was only the sheer scale of the war, which compelled both the Security Council and the General Assembly to take the matter seriously.[22]

By February 1972 Bangladesh was recognised by 47 States. In 1972 the application to the UN was refused due to China's veto. Subsequently, in 1974 the UN General Assembly decided without dissent to admit the People's Republic of Bangladesh to membership of the United Nations.[23]

Was the emergence of Bangladesh as a new nation-State a case of secession or was it a classic case in which Bangladesh exercised its right to self-determination within the meaning of the Colonial Declaration? Some scholars' analyses support the view that the Bangladeshi people simply exercised a legal right, that is the right to secession (Dinstein, 1976:108). Buchheit (1978:198) also argued that it was an example of secession. Nonetheless, it is, in the view of Heraclides (1992:406), highly unlikely to be followed as a precedent.

Nanda argues that the oppressive situation prevalent in Bangladesh before the insurrection justified the proclamation of independence by Bangladeshi people. "Since East Pakistan approaches the parameters of a colonial situation, a case can perhaps be made for the application of self-determination on that basis" (Nanda, 1972:336). He correctly identifies the Bangladesh insurrection as different to those of Katanga and Biafra. The oppressive regime prevalent in East Pakistan was similar to that of a colony. East Pakistan was exploited and its peoples' human rights were grossly violated by the West Pakistan regime. On top of all this, the genocide committed against the civilian population of East Pakistan and the grave violation of human rights by the West Pakistan military junta justified the insurrection of the East Pakistani peoples against the military regime of West Pakistan. Even though the emergence of Bangladesh possessed all the ingredients of secession, it can be argued that they achieved independence by virtue of the right to self-determination. Their independence struggle was in compliance with both the Colonial Declaration and article 1 of both human rights Covenants. Thus, the situation prevalent prior to the rebellion justifies the argument that the peoples of East Pakistan qualified as *peoples* within the meaning of the Colonial Declaration and the human rights Covenants. As Thornberry (1989:875) correctly argues, the international community did not find great difficulty in adjusting to the situation through recognition of the new State" rather than admitting the right to secession of the Bangladeshi peoples.

11.4 *The Republic of Kosovo?*

Since 1913 Kosovo has been a province of Serbia. The province of Kosovo was recognised in 1974 by the Constitution of the Socialist Federal Republic of Yugoslavia as a socialist autonomous region, in addition to Yugoslavia's six provincial republics. Kosovo was given extensive power (Varady. 1997:23). Its demand for Republic status was rejected by the Federal Government. The majority population, the Kosovar Albanians were considered *narodnosti* (nationalities). Only *narodi* (nations) were granted Republics (Caplan, 1998:748). Even though the Kosovo region was not a Republic, as pointed out by Caplan (at 748), Kosovo enjoyed "all the prerogatives of a Republic, including its own constitution, government, and national bank, and an equal voice within the collective federal presidency". However, as stated in detail in *Prosecutor* v *Dusko Tadic* a/k/a[24] autonomous status was abrogated during the period 1989-1991 by various constitutional and legislative means, that is, by the suspension of Parliament, Executive Council and the Presidium on the pretext that the Albanians in Kosovo had manipulated the existing system to their advantage. However, these allegations are refuted by many. The International Criminal Tribunal for the former Yugoslavia (ICTY) found that these allegations were used as a smoke-screen by the Serbian leaders to annex the Vojvodina and Kosovo autonomous regions to the Serbian Republic. The Tribunal found that:[25]

> Some Serbs had long dreamed of a Great Serbia, a nation which would include within its borders all ethnic Serbs. The effective extension of Belgrade's direct rule over the two provinces was a step in this direction and one that was implemented despite the fact that in Kosovo ethnic Albanians had come to far outnumber Serbs. Kosovo is the part of the homeland of the Serbs of past centuries, the battle of Kosovo was fought there, and the province has particular significance for present day Serbs who regarded its autonomy as a province as

specifically hurtful, depriving Serbia of coherent statehood and of control over what is considered to by ancestral Serbian territory.

Not surprisingly, Kosovar Albanians' response has been to resort to armed struggle to achieve independence or join Albania. The slogan of the Albanian liberation fighters is "Kosovo will fight to the death"[26] until the Serbs leave the region.[27] A key commander of the KLA, Remi, dismissed any proposal of dismantling the rebel forces as part of any negotiated settlement that stopped sort of giving full independence to the Kosovo region. Commander Remi is quoted as saying, "We obey our orders, but the General Staff is fighting for the freedom of Kosovo, so we don't expect orders to disarm or disband. We'll put our weapons in warehouses only when we have liberated Kosovo". Remi expressed his doubt about any solution of the Contact Group's meeting at Rambouillet, saying:

> I am hoping that we will be accepted by the international community just as our representatives have been accepted at Rambouillet. Freedom means not only the withdrawal of police and military forces from Yugoslavia, but also the constitution of a new state with a new system as Albanians wish. And as far as unification with Albania? It's an on-going process, but a slow one.[28]

At the beginning of the conflict (from February 1998), the response of the European Communities to the demand for independence for the province of Kosovo was not so hostile. It stressed that "the constituent republics and autonomous provinces must have the right freely to determine their own political future in a peaceful and democratic manner and on the basis of recognized international and internal borders".[29] The subsequent policies adopted until March 24, 1999 by the European institutions, mainly the EU and its allies NATO represent a significant change in the thinking on secessionist rights, perhaps after realizing the dangerous consequences for multiethnic polities in the European continent if Kosovar Albanians' secessionist demands were accepted.

Kosovar Albanians proclaimed Kosovo as an independent State in December 1991 (Caplan, 1998:748). However, both the Badinter Committee and the EC have continually refused to recognise its independence. In the referendum held from 26-30 September 1991, it was reported that 99.87% voted for independence out of 87% of the Kosovo population who took part in the voting (Rich, 1993:61). The elected leaders of the Kosovo independence movement promised that they would abide by the guidelines set by the EC. Only Albania recognised Kosovo as an independent State (Mullerson, 1994). Refusing to accept the Kosovar Albanians' constant request for the recognition of 'the Republic of Kosovo', the EC issued a statement stressing that:

> Frontiers can only be changed by peaceful means and the EC and its Member States reminded the inhabitants of Kosovo that their legitimate quest for autonomy should be dealt with within the framework of the EC Peace Conference.[30]

The Cardiff (European Council) Declaration of 1998 is more explicit:

> A solution to the problem of Kosovo's status can only be found through a vigorous political process. The European Council calls urgently on both sides to return to the negotiating table, with international involvement to agree confidence-building measures and to define a new status for Kosovo. *The European Union remains firmly opposed to independence.* It continues to support a special status, including a large degree of autonomy for Kosovo, within the Federal Republic of Yugoslavia.[31]

The proposed Kosovo Interim Agreement presented by the Six-Nations Contact Group also emphasises that any solution should be found within the existing boundaries of the FRY and should include mechanisms for serving a high degree of self-governance for Kosovo, e.g. with its own Parliament, President and Judiciary.[32] The European diplomats in the Contact Group at Rambouillet insisted that Kosovo secessionist forces should drop their claim to independence if they wanted peace talks to succeed. The Contact Group delivered an ultimatum to the KLA emphasising that "if the KLA does not renounce independence, then there will be no Nato troops in Kosovo".[33]

But this position later changed dramatically with the bombing campaign against FRY, commenced on 24th of March 1999 by the NATO forces. As bombing on FRY has intensified some European politicians have begun to advocate that Kosovo should be granted international 'protectorate status', whilst others supported a partition. The former Dutch Foreign Minister and Secretary-General of the Western European Union (WEU) from 1989-1994 was in favour of independent Kosovo. He argued, "of course, the proliferation of small, perhaps unviable States is not an attractive prospect... But why make a difference in principle between, say, Slovenia and Kosovo when fundamental rights are being crushed".[34] Other European leaders have promoted this position during the NATO's bombing campaign. At the height of the conflict, the President of France, Jacques Chirac, stressed that the EU should take over the administration of post-war Kosovo as a protectorate under a legal mandate from the UN.[35]

The former leader of the United Kingdom Liberal Democrats, Paddy Ashdown, argued: [36]

> There are three things that can clear [sic]about the future of Kosovo. It cannot remain under Serb control. By their action the Serbs have forfeited the right to govern the province on the basis of only five percent (sic) of the population. But neither in the short term at least, can Kosovo become independent; that would destabilise Macedonia, undermine Albania and severely damage the fragile peace in Bosnia. And Kosovo certainly cannot remain at war which leaves only one realistic option - an international protectorate, if not *de jure* then *de facto*!

This may be a new beginning where solutions to minorities' problems are found by super-powers bypassing the authority of the UN. The consequences of such a practice may, as South Asian countries recently alleged, create more unstable regions in multiethnic polities, thereby encouraging secessionist and separatist groups.

Before NATO's military action, the UN General Assembly (GA) wanted the FRY to establish genuine democratic institutions in Kosovo, including the parliament and the judiciary, thereby respecting the "will of the inhabitants as the best means of preventing the escalation of the conflict".[37] The UN Security Council (SC) has emphasised repeatedly that the warring parties in Kosovo should seek "meaningful dialogue" with a view to resolving existing problems by political means on the basis of equality for all citizens and ethnic communities in Kosovo.[38] The SC reassured the commitment of all its Member States to the sovereignty and territorial integrity of the FRY.[39] The KLA's military campaign has not been seen as a liberation struggle. Instead, the military activities of the KLA have been identified with "terrorism in pursuit of political goals". All external support for the KLA's armed struggle in Kosovo, including the supply of arms and training for terrorist activities in Kosovo, has been condemned. Rejecting the request by the Kosovar Albanians for independence, the SC reiterated that it was prepared only to consider "enhanced status for Kosovo, a substantially greater degree of autonomy, and meaningful self-administration".[40] The Security Council reaffirmed this position on 24 October 1998.[41] In the view of both the SC and the GA ethnic violence and military activities in Kosovo were a "human catastrophe", which constitutes a continuing threat to peace and security in the region.[42] The SC urged the FRY and the Kosovar Albanian leadership "to enter immediately into a meaningful dialogue without preconditions and with international involvement, leading to an end of the crisis and to a negotiated political solution to the issue of Kosovo".[43] Rejecting the KLA's demand for independence, as recently as October 1999 the Secretary General Kofi Anan stressed that any solution to ethnic conflicts in Kosovo should not involve breaking up the Republic of Yugoslavia (FRY). Many States are still are of the view that any solution should be found without disrupting the existing boundaries of the FRY. For example, during the GA debate China stated that "Kosovo is part of the Federal Republic of Yugoslavia, which is a sovereign country whose sovereignty and territorial integrity should be respected".[44]

11.5 *An Independent Republika Srpska Krajina and Republika Srpska of Bosnian Serbs*

The Krajina Serbs in Croatia declared an independent Republika Srpska Krajina on 19 December 1991. Later they rejected the autonomous status offered by Croatia in the belief that they would be able to set-up their own Serb-dominated State.[45] The so-called Republika was composed of West Slavinia, East Slavinia, and Krajina (Bowker, 1998:1247). The request made by the Assembly of Serbian People in Bosnia and Herzegovina for an independent Republika Srpska on 7 April 1992 was also rejected by the EC (Rich, 1993:61-62; Mullerson, 1994:132-135). In condemning the proposal of the Serbian parliaments in Knin and Pale to merge with the self-proclaimed Serb Republika Srspka of Krajina, the EU stressed that any such illegal acts would be contrary to the framework established by UN Security Council Resolutions 981 of 31 March 1995 and 990 of 27 April 1995. Emphasising its commitment to the territorial integrity of Croatia and Bosnia-Herzegovina, the EU stated that any activities of the Serbs violating the boundaries of those two States "would be null and void".[46] The Badinter Committee was also of the view that enhanced minority protective measures and greater autonomous powers to the regions of the former Yugoslavia would prevent further escalation of ethnic conflicts. It further held that "the Serbian population in Bosnia-Herzegovina and Croatia must therefore be afforded every right accorded to minorities under international conventions as well as national and international guarantees consistent with the principles of international law".[47]

Having deplored the Bosnian Serbs' military attempt to establish an independent Republika Srpska, the EC warned that those trying to change boundaries would never achieve recognition. It stressed that "territorial conquests, not recognized by the international community will never produce the kind of legitimate protection sought by all in the new Yugoslavia...the Community and its Member States will never accept a policy of *fait accompli*. They are determined not to recognize changes of borders by force and will encourage others not to do so either".[48] Condemning the Bosnian Serbs' secessionist attempt to dismember Bosnia-Herzegovina, the EC issued a statement on 11 April 1992 affirming that "they strongly uphold the principle of the territorial integrity of the Republic of Bosnia-Herzegovina as the unquestionable foundation of any constitutional order. They wish to make clear that violations of this principle will not be tolerated and will certainly affect the future relations of those responsible with the Community".[49] The EC and its Member States in its Paris Declaration on 13 January 1993 again emphasised their previous position and demanded unequivocally that the Bosnian Serbs accept the proposed constitutional framework for Bosnia-Herzegovina "without any conditions whatsoever within the next six days". The EC stressed that the Serbs in Bosnia-Herzegovina should fulfil their commitment to the Vance-Owen Peace Plan and insisted that all groups should respect the sovereignty of the Republic of Bosnia-Herzegovina and the inviolability of its territorial integrity.[50]

The UN's response has been similar to that of the European Union. The Serbs' attack on Bosnia- Herzegovina were seen as 'aggressive acts', 'ethnic cleansing', and 'terrorist activities' to acquire territory by forceful means. Strongly condemning separatist acts of violence against the sovereignty, territorial integrity and political independence of Bosnia-Herzegovina, the General Assembly warned the separatists that their violence should be halted immediately.[51] In fact, the GA regarded the Bosnian government and its peoples' defensive acts as a 'just struggle' to safeguard their sovereignty, political independence and territorial integrity.[52] In a resolution on Yugoslavia, the GA declared that all the acts of the "self-proclaimed Serbian authorities" and their followers' to be invalid.[53] The efforts of the Serbs and Croats to partition Bosnia-Herzegovina along ethnic lines have continually been condemned by the Security Council.[54]

As Rich (1993:62) points out, "the issue of whether any of these entities meet the traditional criteria of statehood is not being addressed because they have not passed the EC threshold test. Any acceptance of such entities would be seen as a green light for minorities throughout Europe to assert their independence". However, some critics point out that European institutions including the Badinter Committee have failed to apply a coherent policy in the recognition of new States on the territory of the former Yugoslavia (Mullerson, 1994: 54-75 and, 125-135; Hannum, 1993:58-69).

11.6 *Nagorny Karabakh*

The Nagorny Karabakh region is an integral part of the Republic of Azerbaijan (Mooradian, 1998:5-17). The Karabakh Armenians consider their armed struggle against Azerbaijan as a liberation struggle against colonialism. In fact, they have already set-up their own institutions to deal with every aspect of their lives. On the other hand, they are branded as irredentists whose only purpose is to annex the Karabakh region to Armenia (for further details see Mooradian, 1985:6). The proposed plan for maximum autonomy for Karabakh within Azerbaijan has already been rejected by secessionist leader and self-proclaimed President Arkady Gukasian (Bloed, 1998: 238). The declaration of independence by the Armenian ethnic groups in Nagorny Karabakh in September 1992 was equally rejected by the EC. The Russian Federation and the EC on 10 March 1992 expressed their profound concerns "about the continuing conflicts over Nagorny Karabakh, which threatens to grow into a protracted and bloody war". They stated that such a development would be tragic for the Armenian and Azeri peoples and would threaten regional peace.[55] In fact, issuing a statement on 22 May 1992, the EC condemned any attempts upon the territorial integrity of existing States (see detail Rich, 1993:62). The EC on 1 September 1993 condemned the military incursion of Armenians into Nagorny Karabakh reaffirming the territorial integrity and sovereignty of the States in the region.[56] Any political solution, in the view of the EU, "should lead to a settlement respecting the dignity and interests of the parties to the conflicts in Nagorny Karabakh".[57]

11.7 *Abkhazian Secession: "Secessionist Goals Through Sophistries and the Rape of International Law"?*

The separatist struggle of the Abkhazia to secede from Georgia has resulted in one of the worst humanitarian disasters in the Caucasus. It is estimated that more than 300,000 people in Abkhazia were displaced due to ethnic cleansing and the policy of genocide adopted by the Abkazian secessionist fighters.[58] The separatists' demands from the outset have been that the political status of Abkhazia should be defined by the recognition of their right to determine their political future without interference from Georgia. The Abkhazian secessionist forces have continually rejected the proposal for greater autonomy within a federative framework. Instead, they have stressed that any solutions to the dispute between Georgia and themselves should be as between "two subjects of international law". The Georgian leaders described this situation as "secessionist goals through sophistries and the rape of international law".[59] Rejecting any claims for independence by Abkhazians the UN emphasised that the sovereignty and territorial integrity of Georgia was inviolable.[60] The Security Council when referring to Abkhazian separatist claims further emphasised that the borders of a State could not be changed by violence and by force.[61] Both parties were urged to "resolve their differences" "through dialogue and mutual accommodation".[62] The Abkhazian secessionists' policy of changing demographic structure by ethnic cleansing was condemned and declared unacceptable.[63] Any political status for Abkhazia should be within the State of Georgia and should fully respect the sovereignty and territorial integrity of Georgia.[64] The increasing subversive activities of the secessionists, including kidnapping, murder and other criminal activities, have caused grave concern to the UN because they have the potential for impeding any political settlement to the dispute. The Security Council especially expressed its concerns about the continued failure of the parties to resolve their differences, in particular about the uncompromising position taken by the Abkhazian side. The constantly deteriorating safety and security situations of the local population, refugees, and displaced persons have become the priority of the UN.[65] A similar position was adopted by the EU.[66]

11.8 *Secessionist Struggles in Chechnya, Tartastan, Tajikistan and Cyprus*

Previously, Chechnya was an autonomous region under the federal structure of the former USSR. It was then called Chechen-Ingushetia (Tskhovrebov, 1995: 304-307). Chechnya's declaration of independence on 1 November 1991 was not accepted either by the EU[67] or the UN. The Russian Federation immediately declared Chechnya as a part of the Russian Federation. Rejecting any compromise on their stance on independence the separatist leader General Djokhae Dudgev stressed that "Chechnya is a sovereign State and will enter into negotiations with Russia as equal partners" (Tskhovrebov, 1995:307). The reaction of the Russian Federation was to send in the army on 11 December 1991 to defeat secessionist insurrection. The first major armed conflict between secessionists and the Russian army lasted until August 1996. This war is considered as the most severe and destructive in the Caucasus since 1981 (Bovay, 1995:34; Gall and Waal, 1997). The Chechens' secession was found illegal and in violation of the Constitution of the Russian Federation (1993), by the Constitutional Court. The Court held that the Constitution of the Russian Federation, like the previous constitutions of the USSR, did not permit a unilateral declaration of secession by a component part of the Federation. Justifying its position the Constitutional Court said, "The constitutional goal of preserving the integrity of the Russian State accords with the universally recognised principles concerning the right of nations to self-determination".[68] The reaction of the international community by and large has been that the crisis in Chechnya is an internal affairs of the Russian Federation (Cornell, 1996:91). The Western powers do not want to create a diplomatic crisis with "emerging democratic Russia" (Cornell, 1996:91). Some American politicians, notably the former US Secretary of State Warren Christopher compared the situation of Chechnya with the American civil war (Cornell, 1996:91).

The OSCE emphasised that the crisis in Chechnya could not be resolved by separatism but only by peaceful negotiation respecting the territorial integrity of the Russian Federation and its constitution.[69] While deploring the grave violation of human rights by both parties to the conflict, the UN Commission on Human Rights urged the parties on February 27, 1995 to show respect for the territorial integrity and constitution of the Russian Federation.[70]

The Chechen crisis broke-out again in earnest in October 1999. This time it is the Russian Federation, which has declared war against the so-called terrorist Chechen warlords. Hundreds of thousands of Chechen refugees are fleeing for their lives. The Defence Minister of the Russian Federation was quoted as saying that Chechnya would be captured by the Russian army. He was later obliged to retract this (*Financial Times*, November 6-7, 1999). But the Russian Government's desire to keep Chechnya under the sovereignty of the Russian Federation was not hidden from the world community.

Tartastan's declaration of independence against the Russian Federation on 21 March 1992, and the Crimean independence declaration of 5 May 1995 were also not recognised. Equally, the Islamic Revival Movement's attempt to secede from Tajikistan was rejected by the UN reaffirming its commitment to the sovereignty and territorial integrity of the Republic of Tajikistan and to the inviolability of its borders. The parties were urged to undertake vigorous efforts to find a political solution that preserved the sovereignty and territorial integrity of Tajikistan in accordance with the General Agreement on the Establishment of Peace and National Accord in Tajikistan.[71]

The UN's disapproval of the secession of the Turkish Cypriots has been prominent in recent years. The solution, it argued, should be based on a State of Cyprus with a single sovereignty and international personality and a single citizenship, with its independence and territorial integrity safeguarded, constituting two politically equal communities in a bicameral and bi-zonal federation.[72]

Conclusion

As these cases demonstrate, the UN or regional organisations dealing with human rights, security and peace have never encouraged or given the seal of approval to secessionist movements. The approach adopted by these institutions has varied from outright hostility (as in the case of Biafra) to a lukewarm and negative response (as in the case of Bangladesh). The international community has been following a cautious and, perhaps, pragmatic approach to secession. Parties to secessionist conflicts are encouraged to find peaceful and democratic solutions within existing nation-State structures. Alternative models in the form of greater autonomy for regions or for ethnic groups are the preferred solution encouraged by the UN and others, as in the case of Kosovo and Nagorny Karabakh. It seems that security concerns, in addition to other spill-over effects such as refugee problems and scarcity of resources, have become some of the most prominent factors in discouraging secession.

It should also be mentioned that if a secessionist group succeeds in achieving a separate State, the UN ultimately does not stand in their way if it is clear that the seceding territory can defend itself, command the loyalty of its citizens, and respect the human rights of other ethnic groups living in the new State. In re *Secession of Quebec* (1998) 2 SCR 217, the Supreme Court of Canada held, "The ultimate success of secession would be dependent on recognition by the international community". This position undoubtedly provides encouragement to secessionist groups.

Notes

[1] SC Res. 5002, 24 November 1961.
[2] SC Res. 4382, 13 July 1960.
[3] SC Res. 143, 14 July 1960; SC Res. 145, 22 July 1960; SC Res. 146, 9 August 1960; SC Res. 161, 21 February 1961.
[4] SC Res. 4417, 6 August 1960.
[5] SC Res. 4417, 6 August 1960.
[6] GA Res. 1474 (ES-IV), 20 September 1960, para. 3. See also SC Res. 4405, 22 July 1960; SC Res. 474, 21 February 1961.
[7] SC Res. 4741, 21 February 1961; SC Res. 5002, 24 November 1961.

[8] GA Res. 1474 (ES-IV) 20 September 1960, para. 5 (a). See also SC Res. 4741, 21 February 1961.

[9] GA Res. 1600 (xv) 15 April 1961 (entitled "The Situation in the Republic of Congo"). See SC Res. 5002, 24 November 1961, para. 4.

[10] SC Res. 5002, 24 November 1961, para. 4. SC Res. 4741, 21 February 1961, and the Secretary-General's report to the SC, SC Res. 4398, 18 July 1960 and Add. 1.6.

[11] SC Res. 4405, 22 July 1960; SC Res. 5002, 24 November 1961, and GA. Res. 1474, Rev. 1 (ES- IV).

[12] See its declaration of independence, 6 *ILM* 665 [1967], pp. 679-680.

[13] Statement issued by the Secretary-General, UN press release, SG/SM/1062, 29 January 1969.

[14] 7 (2) *UN Monthly Chronicle*, 1970, February p:36.

[15] GA Res. 2790 (xxvi) 6 December 1971. para. 1.

[16] GA Res. 2790 (xxvi) B, 6 December 1971, para. C.

[17] SC Res. 10410, 3 December 1971, para. 3.

[18] See GA Res. 2790 (xxv) 6 December 1971, B, preambular paragraph.

[19] SCOR, 1613th Mtg. 13 December 1971, paras. 92-93, p. 9.

[20] UN Doc. E/CN.4/Sub.2/NGA/46, 23 July 1971.

[21] Press Release of the International Commission of Jurists, 16 August 1971.

[22] GA Res. 2793 (xxvi) 7 December 1971; SC Res. 307 (1971) 21 December 1971.

[23] GA Res. 3203 (xxix) 17 September 1974, and 2937 (xxvii) 29 November 1972.

[24] See *Prosecutor* v *Dusko Tadic a/k/a,* case no. IT/94/1/T, 7 May 1997, the judgment of the International Criminal Tribunal for the Prosecution of Persons Responsible for Serious Violations of International Humanitarian Law Committed in the Territory of Former Yugoslavia Since 1991, 4 (3) *IHRR* 1997, para. 65, p. 660.

[25] *Ibid.* para. 69, p. 661. See also Denitch, B. (1994), *Ethnic Nationalism: The Tragic Death of Yugoslavia*, University of Minnesota Press: Minneapolis/London, chapter 4. Human Rights Watch (1992), *Human Rights Abuse in Kosovo*, 1990- New York, 1992.

[26] Walker, T. 'Kosovo Will Fight to the Death', *The Times*, 23 March 1999.

[27] Loyd, A. 'Serbs Must Go or We Fight on, Says Rebel Chief', *The Times*, 17 February 1999. See also Bloed, A. (1998), 'The Kosovo Crisis', 16 (4) *NQHR*, pp. 528-530.

[28] Loyd, *ibid.* p. 12.

[29] EU Parliament's resolution on the Situation in Yugoslavia, 15 March 1991, 24 (3) *Bull.EC* 1991, p. 70.

[30] 25 (6) *Bull.EC* 1992, p. 108. Kosovo was recognised as an independent State, but only by Albania, see Mullerson, R. (1994), *International Law, Rights and Politics, Developments in Eastern Europe and the CIS*, LSE and Routledge, p. 133.

[31] See the Cardiff European Council's Declaration on Kosovo, CFSP Presidency statement, Cardiff, 15 June 1998, Nr. 09553/98 (Presse 209), CFSP: 062/98, p. 1.

See also CFSP Presidency statement, 20. July 1998, Nr. 10397/98 (Presse 256), CFSP 77/98, and The Declaration by the European Union on a Comprehensive Approach to Kosovo, CFSP Presidency statement, Brussels, 27 October 1997.

[32] See part I-III of the *Draft Kosovo Interim Agreement,* 27 January 1999, http://www. balkanaction.org /pubs/ dkia.html.

[33] Walker, T. 'US Stance on Kosovo Talks and 'Secret Flight' Infuriate Diplomats', *The Times*, 18 February 1999.

[34] 'Recognize Kosovo', *International Herald Tribune,* 19 June 1998, cited in Caplan (1998), below, p. 761.

[35] See Walker, M. Black, I. and Traynor, I. 'Britain and US Shun New Peace Plan', *The Gardian*, 15 April 1999.

[36] Ashdown, P. 'We Must Aim for a Kosovon Protectorate', *The Observer*, 28 March 1999. The term *international protectorate* is not a clear concept in international law. As far as a territory remains as an 'international protectorate' it does not possess international personality. See Jennings, R. Y. and Watts, A. (1992) 9th ed. *Oppenheim's International Law*, Vol. 1, *PEACE*, para. 81, pp. 268-271.

[37] GA Res. 52/139, 12 December 1997, para. 2 (d).

[38] SC Res. 1199, 23 September 1998. See also GA Res. 52/139, 12 December 1997, para. 3.

[39] SC Res. 1199, 24 September 1998.

[40] SC Res. 1199, 23 September 1998.

[41] SC Res. 1203, 24 October 1998.

[42] *Ibid*. See also GA Res. C.3/52/L.61, the Draft Resolution on the Human Rights Situation in Kosovo.

[43] SC Res. 1203, 24 October 1994.

[44] A/52/PV.70, 12 December 1997, p. 33.

[45] *Yearbook*, published by the UN and International Tribunal for the former Yugoslavia, p. 141. See also Varady, (1997), below, p. 49.

[46] CFSP Presidency statement on Krajina and Bosnia-Herzegovina and alleged merging of the self-proclaimed Serbian Republics, 2 June 1995 Nr. 7570/95 (Presse 164) CFSP, 54/95.

[47] See paragraph 2 of the Opinion no. 2 of the Badinter Committee, 31 (6) *ILM* [1992], p. 1498. See further Hille, S. (1995), 'Mutual Recognition of Crotia and Serbia (+Montenegro)', 6 *EJIL*, p. 604.

[48] The statement by the EC and its Member States, 24 (7/8) *Bull.EC* 1991, pp. 115-116.

[49] 25 (4) *Bull.EC* 1992, p. 83.

[50] 26 (6) *Bull.EC* 1993, p. 122.

[51] GA Res. 47/121, 91st plen. mtg. 18 December 1992, para. 2.

[52] *Ibid*. para. 1.

[53] GA Res. 47/147, plen. mtg. 18 December 1992, para. 19.

[54] See for example, SCOR, 3647th mtg. S/PV.3647, 4 Apara. 1996, p. 4.

[55] 25 (3) *Bull.EC* 1992, p.100, point. 1.4.4.

[56] 26 (9) *Bull.EC* 1993, p. 77, point. 1.4.5.

[57] Luxembourg's statement on behalf of the EU during the debate on the Co-operation between the UN and the OSCE. See A/52/PV.55, 25 November 1997, p. 4.

[58] See for details S/PV.3535, 12 May 1995, Agenda Item, The Situation in Georgia, p. 3.

[59] *Ibid.* p. 3.

[60] SC Res. 1124, 31 July 1997. See further SC Res. 1096, 30 January 1997; SC Res. 876, 19 October 1993; SC Res. 896, 13 January 1994; SC Res. 906, 25 March 1994; SC Res. 937, 21 July 1994; SC Res. 971, 12 January 1995; SC Res. 993, 12 March 1995; SC Res. 1036, 12 January 1996; SC Res. 1065, 12 July 1996.

[61] SC Res. 688, 5 April 1991.

[62] SC Res. 1124, 31 July 1997.

[63] SC Res. 1187, 30 July 1998. See further SC Res. 1150, 30 January 1998.

[64] SC Res. 1150, 30 January 1998. See also SC Res. 1124, 31 July 1997.

[65] SC Res. 1096, 30 January 1997.

[66] CFSP Presidency statement, Brussels 2 June 1998, Nr. 9033/98 (Presse 177) CFSP 49/98.

[67] The statement issued by the EU Presidency, CFSP/2/95, 17 January 1995. See also the CFSP Presidency statement, Brussels, 23 January 1995, Nr. 4385/95 (Presse 24) CFSP, 7/95 on Chechnya.

[68] This judgment was delivered on 31 July 1995. It was published by the European Commission for Democracy through Law of the Council of Europe, CDL-INF (96) 1, cited in Gaeta, P. (1996), 'The Armed Conflict in Chechnya before the Russian Constitutional Court', 7 (4) *EJIL,* p. 564.

[69] OSCE Permanent Council, Journal no. 6, 2 February 1995, cited in Gazzini, T. (1996), 'Consideration on the Conflict in Chechnya', 17 (3/6) *HRLJ,* p. 101.

[70] UN Doc. E/CN.4/1995/SR. 44, 3 March 1995, p. 18.

[71] SC Res. 1167, 14 May 1998. See further SC Res. 1113, 12 June 1997; S/PV.3544, 16 June. 1995, p. 3. See further CFSP presidency statement, 8 June 1998, Nr. 9244/98 (Presse 191) CFSP, 53/98.

[72] SC Res. 1179, 29 June 1998, para. 2. See further SC Res. 1146, 23 December 1997; SC Res. 1178, 29 June 1998; SC Res. 186, 4 March 1964; SC Res. 367/, 12 March 1975; SC Res. 939, 29 July 1994; and SC Res. 1117. 27 June 1997.

References

Bloed, A. (1998), 'The Kosovo Crisis', 16 (4) *NQHR*, pp. 528-530.

Bloed, A. (1998), 'Conflict in and Around Nagorno-Karabakh', 16 (2) *NQHR*, pp. 329-342.

Bovay, M. L. (1995), 'The Russian Armed Intervention in Chechnya and its Human Rights Implications', in 54 *The Review* of International Commission of Jurists, p. 34.

Bowker, M. (1998), 'The Wars in Yugoslavia: Russia and the International Community', 50 (7) *Europe-Asia Studies*, pp. 1245- 1261.

Brownlie, I. (1971), *Basic Documents on African Affairs*, Clarendon Press: Oxford.

Buchheit, L. C. (1978), *Secession, The Legitimacy of Self-Determination*, Yale University Press: New Haven and London.

Caplan, R. (1998), 'International Diplomacy and the Crisis in Kosovo', 74 (4) *International Affairs*, pp. 745- 761.

Cornell, S. E. (1996), 'Intentional Reactions to Massive Human Rights Violations: The Case of Chechnya', 51 (1) *Europe- Asia Studies*, p. 91.

Dinstein, Y. (1976), 'Collective Human Rights of Peoples and Minorities', 25 *ICLQ*, pp. 102- 120.

Duggard, J. (1987), *Recognition and the United Nations*, Grotius Publications Ltd: Cambridge.

Gall, C. and Waal, T. de. (1997), *Chechnya: A Small Victorious War*, Bashingtoke: Ban Bocks.

Hannum, H. (1993), 'Self-Determination, Yugoslavia, and Europe: Old Wine in New Bottles?' 3 *Transnational Law and Contemporary Problems*, pp. 58- 69.

Heraclides, A. (1991), *The Self-Determination of Minorities in International Politics*, Frank Cass: London.

Heraclides, A. (1992), 'Secession, Self-Determination and Non-Intervention: In Quest of a Normative Symbiosis', 45 *Journal of International Affairs*, pp.403-420.

Higgins, R. (1963), *The Development of International Law Through the Political Organs of the United Nations*, Oxford UP: London/New York/Toronto.

Ijalye, D. J. (1971), 'Was Biafra at Any Time a State in International Law', 65 *AJIL*, pp. 551- 559.

Jorre, J. D. St. (1972), *The Nigerian Civil War*, Hodder and Stougton: London.

Kamanu, O. S. (1974), 'Secession and the Right to Self-Determination: An OAU Dilemma', 12 (3) *The Journal of Modern African Studies*, pp. 355- 376.

Mooradian, M. (1998), 'The OSCE: Neutral and Impartial in the Karabakh', 9 (2) *Helsinki Monitor*, pp. 5- 17.

Mullerson, R. (1994), *International Law, Rights and Politics: Developments in Eastern Europe and the CIS*, LES and Routledge: London.

Nanda, Ved. P. (1972), 'Self-determination in International Law: The Tale of Two Cities, Islamabad (West Pakistan) and Dacca (East Pakistan)', 66 *AJIL*, pp. 321- 336.

Nawaz, M. K. (1971), Editorial Comment, 'Bangladesh and International Law', 11 *IJIL*, pp. 251- 266.

Nixon, C. R. (1972), 'Self-Determination: The Nigeria / Biafra Case', 24 *World Politics*, pp. 412- 436.

Okoye, F. C. (1972), *International Law and the New African States*, Sweet and Maxwell: London.

Rich, R. (1993), 'Recognition of States: The Collapse of Yugoslavia and the Soviet Union', 4 *EJIL*, pp. 36- 65.

Shiels, F. L. ed. (1984), *Ethnic Separatism and World Politics*, University Press of America: Lanham/New York and London.

Thornberry, P. (1989), 'Self-Determination, Minorities and Human Rights: A Review of International Instruments', 38 *ICLQ*, pp. 867- 889.

Tskhovrebov, Z. (1995), 'An Unfolding Case of a Genocide: Chechnya, World Order and the Right to be Left Alone', 64 (3) *Nord.Jint.L*, pp. 304- 307.

Varady, T. (1997), 'Minorities, Majorities, Law and Ethnicity: Reflections of the Yugoslav Case', 19 (1) *HRQ*, pp. 9- 54.

12 The Right to Secession Through the Right to Self-determination? Attitudes of States

Introduction

States are adamant that the right to self-determination should not be interpreted in the sense of entailing secessionist elements which allow groups of people to secede from the State in which they live. Any suggestion that minorities can create States by virtue of the right to self-determination is vehemently opposed by most nation-States. Secession, as will be shown below, is an extremist political concept tinged with tribalism. The views of States seems to be that "the slogan of self-determination was increasingly being used by political elites and clans in order to seize and maintain power".[1] They do not have any desire for an experiment of self-determination beyond the colonial context, because the secessionists' ultimate aim is to assail the sanctity of the State system (White, 1981:160 and 162; see also Nanda, 1981:263 and 270; Buchheit, 1978:105; Nayar, 1975:321-345). Therefore it is not surprising that the inter-State system has intentionally set limits to the application of self-determination beyond the colonial context (Schoenberg, 1976:63).

Nevertheless, in this hostile environment, some radical ideas are emerging which give a new interpretation to the right to self-determination and are supportive of minorities' claims for greater political power beyond autonomy. In particular this is so in cases where ethnic conflicts are so deep that no other alternative is possible and or where grave human rights violations taking place oppressing minority groups (Simpson, 1996:54-60). The purpose of this chapter is to examine these trends.

Misunderstanding and confusion on the right to self-determination have resulted, in the view of many States, in numerous regional conflicts since the end of the Cold War.[2] Members are urged to place specific limitations on it to avoid claims for an "unlimited right of secession".[3] States have generally been opposed to any kind of measures which would weaken their structure, because States are "the fundamental units of the international community and the United Nations could not support proposals tending to weaken that basic concept".[4] Nor do they approve a right to secession for a certain segment of the population in a State.[5] Most States are likely to resist, as Liechtenstein observes, any secessionist activities "by force of arms, if necessary".[6] Changes within the 'national boundaries' of States are expected to be in accordance with democratic means.[7] Minorities living in multi-ethnic polities are expected to enjoy rights accorded to them whilst respecting human rights and the fundamental freedoms of others. It is also expected that minorities should refrain from any activities, which might harm the territorial integrity or political unity of sovereign and independent States.[8] Neither concession beyond autonomy nor any element of secession is tolerated, as stated by the first Premier of India, Jawaharlal Nehru, half a century ago. Clarifying unequivocally the position of the post-independence Indian Republic, Nehru emphasised this hard line policy on the eve of Indian independence in response to the declaration of independence made by Dr Zapu Angami Phizo, the leader of the Nagas:

> We can give you complete autonomy but never independence. You can never hope to be independent. No state, big or small, in India will be allowed to remain independent. We will use all our influence and power to suppress such tendencies (see Maxwell, 1980 cited in Ali, 1993:31).

Some States even take the extreme position that the creation of a State by exercising the right to self-determination can be achieved by the people of a territorial unit only once in a life-time, and that this right remains valid until freely exercised.[9] During the debate on the right to self-determination it was argued:

> Nations were created by the exercise of self-determination. But once they had been so created, the right had been exercised and the resulting entity possessed an inviolable and indivisible personality with its own constitution and institutions. It was a principle of international law that States must be taken as they were; self-determination, once exercised, had to be respected.[10]

States' practice in post-world-war II suggests that the Nehruvian approach has been followed by many in response to secessionist claims. Their utmost concern has been about the danger of fragmentation of States due to secession.

However, only a few States ever supported the right to secession. During the debate on the proposed article 1 (ICCPR) on the right of self-determination, Saudi Arabia advanced the theory that by exercising the right to self-determination minorities could secede when their interests so required. It argued:

> Secession need not be a tragedy; Ireland had at long last severed the ties binding it into the United Kingdom, but the two countries continued to live side by side in perfect amity. When their interests so required, minorities should be allowed to secede; a number of Member States of the United Nations have come into being through the exercise by minorities of their right to self-determination....when their interests were fully safeguarded minorities had no reason and no desire to set up separate States.[11]

Although it is not exactly clear, the current Saudi Arabian position seems to support the above position. It stated that the international community should admit the fact that "peoples who are still subject to injustice, repression and racism" could exercise the right of self-determination.[12] The USSR repeatedly (1917, 1924, 1936 and 1978) stated that the right to secession was compatible with the right to self-determination. Article 72 of the 1978 Soviet Constitution reads: "Each Union Republic shall retain the right freely to secede from the USSR" (Dixon and McCorquodale, 1991:256). But these constitutional guarantees were in fact fake promises only (Hannikainen, 1998:85). In practice the Soviet leaders did everything to prevent provinces breaking away. Secessionist tendencies were condemned by the Communist leadership as "fundamentally opposed to the interests of the mass of the peoples both of the centre and of the border regions" (Gazzini, 1996:94; Gaeta, 1996:564; Mullerson, 1994:58-91). The USSR Law on Procedure for Deciding the Secession of a Union Republic 1990 and the Russian Constitution 1993 in its article 66 (5) made a secessionist attempt virtually impossible by constitutional manoeuvring, that is, Republics should get the consent of the USSR Supreme Soviet before seceding (Dixon and McCorquodale, 1991:256-258). In 1992, the Constitutional Court of the Russian Federation in the *Tartastan*[13] case stated that self-determination has to be exercised in accordance with the principle of the territorial integrity of States. Referring to the 1978 Constitution, the Court held that both Tartastan's declaration of independence and its proposed referendum was unconstitutional (Gazzini, 1996:94). The Court found that Tartastan could change its internal political structure by virtue of the right to self-determination by staying within a State thereby respecting its territorial integrity and the human rights of others. At the same time, it emphasised that the right to self-determination did not provide any legal base for secession (Danilenko, 1994: 463). Another State which recognised secession as a constitutional right was the former Socialist Federal Republic of Yugoslavia (SFRY). Article 1 of SFRY's Constitution 1974 recognised the right of every nation to self-determination, including the right to secession. Yet most importantly, there was not any mechanism in the Constitution to implement such a right in the event of a nation wanting to secede (Hille, 1995:598). Nonetheless, in practice secession was never considered a justifiable option. The Danish constitution also provides that Greenland and the Faeroe Islands can secede if they want (see details Hannikainen, 1998:85). The South African constitution 1996, provides some encouragement to secessionists. Section 235 states:

> The right of the South African people as a whole to self-determination, as manifested in the constitution, does not preclude, within the framework of this right, recognition of the notion of self-determination of any community sharing a common cultural and language heritage, within a territorial entity in the Republic or *in any other way*, determined by national legislation (emphasis added).

There is a possibility that the phrase, "or in any other way", argued Dugard (1997:89-90), might be used by secessionists to justify their separatist claims

Currently, the right to self-determination is going through a revolutionary stage different to that from the 1950s to 1980s. Some States have begun to consider that a) there is a link between "the situation of minorities and self-determination",[14] b) there may be cases in which minorities could exercise certain rights in the context of internal self-determination, provided that they are prepared to uphold the national sovereignty and territorial integrity of States in which they live, [15] and c) the scope of the right to self-determination should be expanded in both its internal and external aspects to encompass "the right of distinct peoples within a State, particularly indigenous peoples and national minorities to make decisions on their own affairs".[16] However, any such rights should be confined to internal self-determination.[17]

Liechtenstein argued that a new approach was needed to finding solutions to minorities' grievances.[18] By finding new meanings to the right to self-determination beyond its traditional context, and by enabling a segment of a population living within nation-States to exercise the right to self-determination, most of these conflicts could be solved.[19] In suitable cases, argued the Liechtenstein delegate, secession should be considered as a pragmatic solution. He stated:

> The inherent right of communities having territorial and social unity to self-determination must be recognized. That involved the free choice by each community of its political, social, economic and cultural diversity in accordance with the interests of its members.[20]

A few States supported the initiative of Liechtenstein arguing that any programme which aimed at promoting the "debate on the right to self-determination" would be helpful,[21] and a step forward.[22] The meaning of self-determination, argued Uganda, should move beyond the colonial situation.[23] However, the strongest support for Liechtenstein's proposal has so far come from Albania which supported the view that the right to secession is included in the right to self-determination. It stated:

> The relationship between the right to self-determination, territorial integrity of States and the rights of minorities must be addressed... Denial of the rights of peoples to self-determination on the pretext of preserving the territorial integrity of States and the treatment of those peoples as minorities had led to tragic conflicts. No nation in a multinational State could be treated as a minority.[24]

Turning to secession, it stated:

> Secession was one way in which the right of peoples to self-determination was exercised... The recent experience of the former Soviet Union and the former Yugoslavia showed that peoples should be allowed to exercise their right of self-determination even if it jeopardized territorial integrity... Independent States were reluctant to accommodate separatist claims for fear that they would threaten internal order and the stability of the international system. However, developments in international law and General Assembly resolutions recognizing the right of self-determination would seem to allow the principle of self-determination to be invoked, under certain circumstances, as the basis for legitimate secession.[25]

However, these views represent only a minority. The majority of States do not welcome any such accommodations. Moreover, many States have been cautious not to promote secession as a right in international law. Such moves, in their views, "would undermine the modern concept of the nation-State".[26] For example, the Acehnese peoples' claims for independence is not only resisted by Indonesia for fear that it would lead to the break up of Indonesia, but also its neighbouring country, the Philippines fears that it would encourage separatist movements on the Island of Mindanao. Domingo Saizon, the Foreign Secretary of the Philippines, was quoted as saying:

Aceh has always been an integral part of Indonesia like Mindanao, which has always been an integral part of the Philippines. When a vote for independence is made, that could become a serious issue, particularly to national integrity and security". [27]

12.1 *The Right to Self-determination Does not Entail a Right to Secession*

Peoples or *all peoples* have the right to determine the form of States "by the democratic means of a majority decision".[28] However, the common understanding of States appears to be that minorities' problems should not be raised in connection with the right to self-determination or implementation of that right. They are completely different issues. Partial views and misconception of the right to self-determination "could encourage separatism based on ethnic consideration".[29] Many emphasised that secession should not be considered as a component part of the right to self-determination,[30] because fragmentation of States conflicts with the right to self-determination. By referring to the final outcome of the San Francisco Conference and the Atlantic Charter, the Netherlands's delegate categorically rejected the notion that secession was implicitly or explicitly approved by the States which took part in the proceedings. "The fear of claims for secession based on self-determination for minority and other groups remains an overriding concern for many States" (McGoldrick, 1991:257).

Many considered that secession or separatism could not be equated with self-determination.[31] If the right to self-determination be given new meanings beyond the current understanding, argued the delegate of the Russian Federation, "the noble objectives of protection of the right of the peoples could be reduced to the level of primitive separatism" eventually constituting a threat for both international stability and security. It was further argued:[32]

> At the current time extremists were increasingly using the slogan of self-determination, which in practice led to its confusion with aggressive separatism. The right of self-determination was a right of the peoples, and no clan or group could be allowed to usurp it.

Those destructive groups and movements that have emerged in the name of the right to self-determination should, urge some States, be contained by Governments[33] because in the interest of peace, security and economic well-being under no circumstances should fragmentation of multi-ethnic States be tolerated. It was further suggested that self-determination could not be interpreted as a pretext for any cultural, religious or ethnic minority to demand its own State.[34] The Ethiopian delegation explained:

> There was a tendency to confuse peoples with national minorities in interpreting the principle of self-determination. That interpretation was illogical since the benefits arising out of the right to self-determination could not be conferred on minorities which already had that right on an equal footing with other component groups of sovereign States. Moreover, the right of self-determination, which was an essential condition for the preservation of peace, could not be applied in such a destructive way as to become a possible source of disruption and conflict.[35]

There is another dimension to the differences between secession and self-determination. Self-determination is closely bound up with international peace and security. Yet, secession often creates problems for the harmony of international relations and obstructs the peace, law and order of multiethnic polities. It can be argued that juxtaposition of these diametrically opposed principles does not help minorities' claim to secession.

The view that a region or a regionally based group of States has no right to secession by virtue of the right to self-determination has gained popularity amongst many States.[36] A slightly modified view is also evident. If ethnic groups formed neither a compact community nor a majority in a specific territory, they could not, according to the Ukraine, claim the right to secession.[37] The Ukraine stated:

> Certain States considered that the right to self-determination of peoples was applicable to the claims of national and even regional minorities but in the opinion of her delegation that is unjustified... Her delegation considered that the right to self-determination could not entail territorial separation for an ethnic group if that group was not in a majority in the territory concerned and if the other group living there objected to the separation.[38]

12.2 *Secession is Illegal, and it is Not a Positive Rule in International Law*

Current States' attitudes seem to be that the method of creating States should not involve force or secession.[39] If secession involves violence and non-democratic methods, States are reluctant to grant any legal recognition, except in the case of national-liberation movements which are fighting for independence. In fact, liberation struggles against alien and colonial domination are encouraged. A violation of the right of peoples, who are struggling to achieve independence, is considered "an international crime and contrary to the purpose of the United Nations". Therefore, use of force by liberation forces could, in Tunisia's view, be permitted and even encouraged in the exercise of the right to self-determination. [40] However, international law, according to some States, has not recognized the position that a segment of a population can unilaterally declare secession from the State of which it forms a part.[41] This proposition found many supporters, because the contrary position would obstruct any attempt to maintain the unity of the State.[42] There are many examples. The unilateral declaration of independence by the Republic of Northern Cyprus has continually been condemned as illegal. The secessions of Katanga from the Congo, Southern Rhodesia from the UK, Biafra from Nigeria, the Comorian Island of Mayotte from the Lomoro Archipelago were condemned as illegal or unacceptable in international relations (Klabbers and Lefeber, 1993:46).

Generally, States considers secession as high treason, and a violation of established norms of international law (Crawford, 1979:120-128). As stated by Roberts (1978:354), ethnic divisions or ethnic claims for separate States were considered "divisive, barbarous and vile". For example, movements fighting for secession, in the view of Turkey, are terrorist groups. In fact, Turkey has been adamant that it will not tolerate terrorist acts against its territory. The separatist leader of the Kurdish Workers Party was condemned to death recently for high treason (see also *Yasa* v *Turkey* and *Tekin* v *Turkey*).[43] Minorities living within the borders of Turkey, "should fully participate in any local administrative arrangements".[44] India considered secessionists in Kashmir and Jammu as terrorist movements which should be severely dealt with.[45]

12.3 *Secession is Valid only if it is Achieved through Peaceful and Democratic Means*

The majority of States are of the view that the creation of a State or the achievement of independence is legally valid only if it is achieved by "democratic means".[46] By peaceful and democratic means peoples could determine their political future "whether it led to independence or to the establishment of rights within the community".[47] This should be accomplished through the wishes of the people, expressed through democratic means such as plebiscites or referenda held under the auspices of the UN,[48] or "other regionalized democratic means".[49] "Recognized democratic means", as explained by the Indian delegate, "should not be divorced from the conventions of the United Nations".[50] On the other hand, if secession can be achieved with the consent of the parties concerned, it is then in compliance with international law and acceptable to the international community.[51]

12.4 *The Right to Create an Independent State Applies Only to Peoples under Colonialism or Other Form of Foreign Domination?*

When a country achieves its independence does a segment of people living in the independent State possess any residual power to secede? In a non-colonial setting, minorities' claims to secession in terms of the right to self-determination have been disputed by a majority of States. There are a significant number of States who maintain the position that it is only peoples under colonialism or other forms of alien domination who can claim independence by forming their own form of government by virtue of the right to self-determination. The practice of the Latin American and Afro-Asian countries on this score appears to be largely unanimous.

The Indian delegate said as early as the 1950s that the right to create an independent State as guaranteed in common Article I of both Covenants could apply only to peoples who were under the authority of other nations, i.e., to peoples living in the Non-Self-Governing Territories and the Trust Territories,[52] a position later approved by other Asian countries.[53] Replying to the US delegate Mrs. Roosevelt's criticism, the Indian delegate told the Third Committee that the application of the right to self-determination in the post-colonial setting was "fraught with dangerous consequences".[54] This apparently extreme and negative position has since then been continually followed by India and many other States.

Most States are adamant that that the right to create States cannot be validated in terms of the right to self-determination.[55] Any attempt to universalise the right, in the view of Lebanon, would not be satisfactory, "because it would imply intervention in matters which were essentially within the domestic jurisdiction of any State".[56] The approach taken by the Northern African States,[57] was similar to that of Asian countries, i.e., that the right to self-determination meant the right of peoples to free themselves from colonialist oppression or foreign occupation.[58] It could therefore not be invoked as an argument in favour of the disintegration or dismemberment of sovereign States.[59]

The position of the Latin American countries on this issue demonstrates a remarkable understanding with their Asian and African counterparts. Minorities, in the view of many Latin American countries, should not be allowed to exercise the right to secession by abusing the right to self-determination.[60] For example, Brazil argued: "It should be clearly stated that self-determination was a fundamental human rights of those who suffered under colonialism and other forms of foreign domination."[61]

12.5 *An Acknowledgement of Secession Will Entail a Danger of Anarchy and Untold Human Suffering?*

The argument that the misuse of the right to self-determination could lead to anarchy and chaos had been advanced by the Western powers and their allies in the formative stage of the UN. The distinguished jurists Cassin, the delegate of France, told the Third Committee during the debate on the right to self-determination that such an undefined Article on the right to self-determination "would allow certain powerful nations to try to disintegrate other nations by instigating artificial separatist movements within peoples united by mutual consent".[62] A similar view was expressed by the Australian delegate.[63] They were concerned that the exercise of the right of self-determination without any limitations or safeguards might be a cause of friction and it would disturb friendly relations between nations. Such a policy might lead to anarchy. The delegate of the Netherlands cautioned that those countries which try to undermine the State by expanding the principle of self-determination were at the same time undermining the whole world order. States were the principal subjects of existing international law; therefore it was everyone's responsibility to protect them from secessionist movements:

> The question then was when such a right of secession should be acknowledged. Should it be acknowledged even if the seceding part could neither support itself economically nor defend itself? Would acknowledgement of the right not entail the danger of anarchy? Was there no fear that hostile interests would try to incite to and promote secession?[64]

Commenting on a proposed Resolution on the right to self-determination, the New Zealand delegate stated:[65]

> If the Committee affirmed the right to self-determination without defining the circumstances in which the members of a group might exercise it, the right would be exploited and used as a propaganda weapon to foment unrest and to divide loyalties. The granting of the right would not produce any beneficial results, but would help those who wished to undermine the stability of a democratic State.

At present, most States in Africa, Asia and some in Latin America have been concerned about the possible consequences for the nation-State of "mindless advocacy of the doctrine of the right to self-determination".[66] However justifiable the demands of a separatist group may be, States are unlikely to encourage secessionist groups for fear of opening a Pandora's box. Most States in the African continent are concerned about the possible balkanization effect such secessionist claims might bring into the African continent given ethnic and tribal diversities in the continent.[67] It is often the case, for example, that every African nation has its own Katanga. Once the logic of secession is admitted, there is no end other than anarchy. Such movements, if encouraged, said the former Emperor Haile Selassie, would harm the "larger and greater objective of African unity" (Ijalye, 1971:551-556). Ghana's representative argued that "sacrificing the principle of self-determination, or on the other hand, encouraging the dismemberment of States, could not be seen as a meaningful response to the resurgence of nationalism."[68] The danger of supporting secessionist movements in independent countries, in the view of Ceylon, is enormous. It would create "a deadly precedent if we regard it as such".[69] Cyprus concluded that if the application of that principle is interpreted as a right which minorities could use to establish sovereign entities then it could "create chaos and cause untold human suffering".[70]

New attempts to enhance the scope of the right to self-determination have been identified as a conspiracy to destabilise the political structure, in particular, of developing countries by Western powers. This consideration made the importance of defending "that principle more necessary than ever before".[71] Some States seem to suspect "powerful States" of exerting external pressures or coercive measures "to effect policy changes" in the developing countries.[72] It was, in Iraq's view, western imperialism which made "erroneous attempts to reinterpret the principle of the right to self-determination as the right of all ethnic, linguistic and religious groups to rebel or secede from the States".[73] In condemning the "repeated attempts" or inappropriate approaches of powerful countries "to modify the concept of the right to self-determination,[74] it was argued that such attempts a) are in violation of the principles of the Charter, and the "basic principles of international law,[75] b) will promote secession and give rise to the eventual breakdown of a sovereign State",[76] c) destroy the political structure of countries they do not like,[77] d) can turn the right of peoples to self-determination into a weapon to be used against the political unity of States,[78] and e) can be used by 'interested parties' to encourage secession by undermining multiethnic polities.[79] Azerbaijan's delegate summarised the concerns of many States:

> Self-determination was sometimes used with pernicious effect to justify territorial expansion under the pretext of protecting ethnic groups in other States. A glaring example was the use of that principle to cover military aggression against an independent State aimed at annexing its territory.[80]

India, most appropriately, suggested that "if every ethnic, religious or linguistic group claimed statehood, there would be no limit to the fragmentation of States, and the peace, security and economic well-being of peoples.[81] States are therefore determined that they will not allow "subversive elements to undermine established political entities" by abusing the right to self-determination.[82]

12.6 *Frontiers Inherited From the Colonial Era Should be Maintained: "Even the Slightest Recognition Would be Unwise"?*

It is evident from current practice that the right of self-determination has invariably been linked with national sovereignty and the territorial integrity of sovereign States.[83] Changes to boundaries, from States' perspectives, will result in a disastrous reassertion of ancient tribal, linguistic or religious divisions. The argument goes that "even the slightest recognition of secession by states would be unwise as showing blood in the lion cage" (Buchheit, 1978:103). African States are adamant that *status quo* boundaries should be preserved. In particular, the common consensus of African States appears to be that the colonial borders of African States should be "left unaltered" to avoid the risk of disintegration of the States concerned [84] and no one should be allowed to undermine the territorial integrity of sovereign and independent States[85] in the pursuit of their own narrow interests.[86] This uncompromising stance is reflected in the statement made by the Sudan:

> The Sudan agreed with the position of the African countries which had decided, as early as the 1960s and within the framework of the Organisation of African Unity, that the frontiers inherited from the colonialist era should be maintained since to do so otherwise should have meant destroying African unity and would therefore have constituted a threat to international peace and security.[87]

The Ghanaian representative to the UN, during the debate on the Bangladeshi secessionist struggle, argued:

> We have to respect the sovereignty and the territorial integrity of every State member of this organization. This is one of the most fundamental principles which has been accepted by the organization of African Unity. The Organization of African Unity knows that once intervention in the domestic affairs of a member State is permitted, once one permits oneself the higher wisdom of telling another member State what it should do with regard to arranging its own political affairs, one opens a Pandora's box. And no continent can suffer more than Africa when the principle of non-intervention is flouted.[88]

Chad' delegate stated during the debate on East Pakistan's secessionist war:

> Knowing what the consequences of blind and unreasonable application of the principle of self-determination may be, my Government, which has said 'No' to Katanga and 'No' to Biafra, cannot say 'Yes' to what is now being asked of Pakistan, namely the disintegration of the territorial and national unity of that country.[89]

That the right to self-determination should not be construed as authorizing or encouraging any action which would dismember or impair, totally or in part, the territorial integrity or political unity of sovereign or independent States has become the standard formula amongst the nation-States of the post-war nation-States.[90] This position was reaffirmed in the 'Declaration on Human Rights and Terrorism'.[91] Any fragmentation of States would be harmful.[92] The Ukraine therefore argued that the right to self-determination should be used "in order to prevent new conflicts, in strict accordance with constitutional procedures and the internal legislation of the State concerned".[93] The European Union's position is also that any political conflicts between the rights of self-determination and the territorial integrity of sovereign States should be avoided.[94]

12.7 *Future Directions?*

Only a few States still argue that the concept of self-determination is no longer helpful in resolving the minority problems of multi-ethnic societies.[95] However, more and more States are now of the view that a new approach is needed to find flexible solutions to problems arising from the exercise of the right to self-determination. Various proposals have been presented: a) that a broader approach aimed at meeting the aspirations of the numerous national and ethnic groups in order to create a pluralist and multiparty democracy might be a solution,[96] b) that measures should be taken to improve solidarity amongst peoples and individuals,[97] c) that tolerance and peaceful coexistence should be the foundation of stable multiethnic polities,[98] and d) that diversity should be viewed as "a source of creativity and productivity".[99]

It is still possible, as correctly pointed out by the Russian Federation, that without impairing the principle of territorial integrity, the right of ethnic and national minorities to self-determination can be guaranteed. Autonomy may be the best formula.[100] Any solution, argued the Russian Federation, should be consistent with the principle of the territorial integrity and sovereignty of States.[101] The granting of independence to minority groups is not usually "the ideal solution and could not be applied in all cases".[102]

The argument that the right to self-determination cannot be meaningfully enjoyed when minorities are neglected is gaining ground.[103] Many States now emphasise that by accommodating human rights, minorities' concerns can be addressed. In this context, what are these human rights which have been emphasised by many States? According to Turkey they are a Government representing "the entire population" whilst simultaneously respecting the rights of each and every group.[104] The importance of the conditions favourable to the free and overall political, economic, social and cultural developments of nations" was emphasised by some.[105] Representation of minorities in the power structure was emphasised by others.[106] The representative of Germany stated that States should operate within a "democratic and representative political structures, including special sensitivity to the rights of minorities".[107] In the view of Germany, a long list of such rights is necessary to maintain a representative democracy which respects the rights of peoples. Amongst them, the right to freedom of expression, freedom of peaceful assembly and association, opportunities for every one to take part in the conduct of public affairs, the right of access to public service and to vote in periodic elections based on universal and equal suffrage.[108] On behalf of the EU, Spain added a few more rights to the above list, that is the rule of law and the existence of democratic institutions. Democratic and responsive political structures could be of paramount importance in averting any potential conflicts between the right of self-determination and the territorial integrity of sovereign States.[109] 'Distinct peoples and indigenous peoples' should have the right, as pointed out by the Australian delegate to the UN, to make decisions on their own affairs. He particularly mentioned the obligation of national Governments to accommodate the demands of peoples for internal self-determination.[110] In the absence of the above rights, in particular of participatory and representative democracy, is there a case for secession? Even in the absence of these rights there is not, in the view of most States, a case for secession.

In conclusion, the current State practice suggests that almost all States refuse to recognise any claims of minorities' right to secession based on the doctrine of self-determination. Territorial integrity and the sanctity of the boundaries of independent sovereign States are given priority over claims of the right to secession.

Notes

[1] A/C.3/49/SR.8, 25 October 1994, para. 9, p. 4 (the Russian Federation).

[2] A/C.3/48/SR.21, 26 November 1993, para. 14, p. 4 (the Philippine).

[3] A/C.3/SR.460, 1 December 1952, para. 24, p. 260 (New Zealand); A/C.6/SR.893, 8 December 1965, para. 28, p. 331(the Republic of Mali).

[4] See for example A/C.3/SR.459, 29 November 1952, para. 26, p. 253 (Argentina).

[5] A/C.6/SR.893, 8 December 1965, para. 28, p. 331 (Mali).

[6] See A/C.3/51/SR.27, 13 August 1997, para. 5, p. 2 (Liechtenstein).

[7] A/C.3/52/SR.29, 1 December 1997, para. 22, p. 3 (India). A similar view was expressed by the Ukraine, A/C.3/51/SR.28, 9 September 1997, para. 12, p. 4.

[8] A/C.3/51/SR.26, 18 September 1997, para. 62, p. 13 (Brazil). See also UN Doc. E/CN.4/1989/WG.5/WP.3, Drafting Proposal Concerning Article 5 of the Declaration on Minorities, Annex III, UN Doc. E/CN.4/1989/38, 7 March 1989, p. 16 (the Ukrainian Soviet Socialist Republic).

[9] A/C.3/51/SR.28, 19 September 1967, para. 39, p. 9 (Pakistan).

[10] E. 2256, Annex V, Res. A and B. A/C.3/SR. 457, 28 November 1952, para. 28, p. 239 (Peru).

[11] A/C.3/SR. 446, 17 November 1952, para. 37, p. 168 (Saudi Arabia).

[12] A/C.3/47/SR. 9, 27 October 1992, para. 71, p. 15.

[13] Vedomosty RF, Issue, no.13, Han no.71 (1992) 1 VKS (1993), cited in Danilenko, G. M. (1994), 'The New Russian Constitution and International Law', 88 *AJIL*, p.463.

[14] A/C.3/47/SR.7, 5 October 1992, para. 57, pp. 12-13 (Brazil).

[15] A/C.3/48/SR. 21, 26 November 1993, para.13, p. 4 (The Philippine).

[16] A/C.3/49/SR.6, 31 October 1994, para. 24, p. 6 (Australia).

[17] *Ibid.* para. 25, p. 6.

[18] See its original proposal UN Doc. A/48/147, 1992, Add.1.

[19] A/51/PV.11, 26 September 1996, p. 11 (Liechtenstein).

[20] A/C.3/47/SR.5, 13 October 1992, para. 35, p. 8 (Liechtenstein).

[21] A/C.3/51/SR.28, 19 September 1997, para. 55, p.12 (Andorra).

[22] A/C.3/48/SR.22, 30 November 1993, para. 9, p. 3 (Estonia).

[23] A/C.3/47/SR.9, 27 October 1992, para. 18, p. 6 (Uganda).

[24] A/C.3/47/SR. 8, 14 October 1992, para. 36, p. 10.

[25] *Ibid.* para. 47, pp.12-13.

[26] A/C.3/48/SR.22, 30 October 1994, para. 22, p. 5 (Malaya).

[27] See Mackay, A. 'Indonesia's Next Tinderbox', *Sunday Business*, 14 November 1999.

[28] A/C.6/SR. 892, 7 December 1965, para. 320 (Cyprus).

[29] A/C.3/50/SR.5, 27 October 1995, para. 7, p. 4 (Brazil). See also A/C.3/50/SR.8, 12 October 1995, para. 8, p. 4 (Cyprus) and A/C.3/48/SR.9, 16 November 1993, para. 12, p. 4 (the Russian Federation).

[30] A/C.3/SR. 447, paras. 26 and 27, 18 November 1952, p. 175 (US delegate Mrs. Roosevelt).

[31] A/C.3/51/SR.28, 19 September 1997, para.13, p.4 (the Ukraine); A/C.3/47/SR.8, 19 October 1992, para. 36, p. 10 (Australia); A/C.3/48/SR.9, 16 November 1993, para. 12, p. 4 ("self-determination does not automatically mean separatism", Russian Federation).

[32] A/C.3/51/SR.26, 18 September 1997, respectively, para. 66, p.14, para. 69, p. 15 (the Russian Federation).

[33] A/C.3/49/SR. 8, 25 October 1994, para. 46, p. 11 (India).

[34] A/C.3/47/SR.9, 27 October 1992, para. 96, p.20 (Equador); and. A/C.3/50/SR.4, 16 October 1995, para. 29, p. 7 (Republic of China).

[35] A/C.3/SR. 453, 24 November 1952, para. 14, p. 214.

[36] A/C.3/SR. 451, 21 November 1952, para. 31-32, p. 204 (Venezuela).

[37] A/C.3/51/SR.28, 19 September 1996, para.13, p. 4, and E/CN.4/1996/SR.7, para. 31 (the Ukraine).

[38] A/C.3/51/SR. 28, 19 September 1996, para. 14, p.5.

[39] A/C.3/SR. 457, 28 November 1952, para. 27, p. 239 (Peru).

[40] GAOR, Agenda item 87, Annexes (xxii) 22 session, 1967, para. 186, p. 3. See A/C.6/SR.887, 1 December 1965, para. 26, p. 284 (Tunisia). A/C.6/51/SR.30, 12 August 1997, para. 71, p. 13 (Pakistan). See Ceylonese representative's statement, A/PV. 947, 14 December 1960, para. 73, p. 1277. A similar statement made by Ecuador approving the "legitimacy of national-liberation movements struggling for their independence", A/C.3/47/SR. 9, 14. October 1992, para. 96, p. 20. See further Articles 20 (2) and 20 (3) of the African Charter on Human and Peoples' Right 1981. Article 20 (3) says: "Colonial or oppressed peoples shall have the right to free themselves from the bonds of domination by resorting to any recognized means by the international community". Article 20 (3) states: "All peoples shall have the right to the assistance of the state parties to the present Charter in their liberation struggle against foreign domination, be it political, economic or culture". See also GA Res. 47/82, 16 December 1992, para. 2, which reaffirms the legitimacy of the struggle of peoples for independence, territorial integrity, national unity and liberation from colonial domination in all its forms and by all available means. See also GA Res. 3314 of 14, December 1974. Further see Small, K. (1983), 'The Legal Status of National Liberation Movements with Particular Reference to South Africa', 15 *Zambia Law Journal*, pp. 37-59.

[41] A/C.3/52/SR. 29, 1 December 1997, para. 22, p. 4 (India).

[42] For example see A/C.3/SR. 450, 20 November 1952, para. 3, p. 195 (New Zealand).

[43] See also *Yasa* v *Turkey*, 9 June 1998 (Eur. Ct. HR), 16 (4) *NQHR* 1998, pp.509-510; *Tekin* v *Turkey*, 9 June 1998 (Eur. Ct. HR), *ibid.* pp. 510-511.

[44] A/51/PV.15, 30 September 1996, p. 6 (Turkey).

[45] A/C.3/47, SR. 10, 19 October 1992, para. 7, p. 3.

[46] See for example GAOR, 7th session, Annexes, Agenda Item 30, 1952-1953, p. 7, A/C.3/L. 305, 28 November 1952 (Lebanon).

[47] A/C.3/SR. 459, 29 November 1952, para. 21, p. 253 (Denmark).

[48] GAOR, 7th session, Annexes, Agenda Item 30, 1952-1953, p. 3, A/C.3/L.294, 18 November 1952 (US).

[49] GAOR, 7th session, Annexes, Agenda Item 30, 1952-1953, p. 4 (India), A/C.3 L.297/Rev.1, 25 November 1952 (on the proposed provision on self-determination). A similar view of Ethiopia, GAOR 7th session, Annexes, Agenda Item 30, 1952-1953, p. 6, A/C.3/L.301, 28 November 1952.

[50] A/C.3/SR.459, 29 November 1952, para. 58, pp. 255-256.

[51] A/C.3/47/SR.4, 19 October 1992, para. 43, p. 11 (Czechoslovakia).

[52] A/C.3/SR. 447, 18 November 1952, para. 43, p. 177; see further A/C.3/SR. 399, 23 January 1952, para. 2, p. 311, and GAOR, 7th session, Agenda Item 30, Annexes, 1952-1953, p. 15, UN Doc. A/L.3/L.297, para. 2. See also A/C.3/50/SR.18, 2 November 1995, para. 44, p. 9.

[53] A/C.3/48/SR.22, 3 November 1993, para.24, p.6 (Indonesia); A/C.3/50/SR.56, 14 February 1996, para.15, p. 4 (Pakistan); A/C.3/50/SR.4, 16 October 1995, para. 29, p. 7 (China).

[54] A/C.3/SR. 447, 18 November 1952, para. 43. p. 177 (India). See also A/C.3/48/SR.22, 30 November 1993, paras. 18-20, p. 5 (Sri Lanka).

[55] A/C.3/48/SR.22, 30 November 1993, para. 54, p. 12 (Hungary); A/C.3/SR.447, 18 November 1952, para. 43, p.177 (India).

[56] A/C.3/SR. 459, 29 November 1952, para. 43, p. 254.

[57] A/C.3/50/SR. 3, 9 October 1995, para. 23, p. 6 (Algeria): A/C.3/50/SR.8, 30 October 1995, para. 10, p. 4 (Libya).

[58] A/C.3/51/SR.26, 18 September 1997, para. 26, p. 7 (Sudan).

[59] A/C.3/SR. 8, 30 October 1995, para. 13, p. 5 (Sudan).

[60] A/C.3/SR.449, 19 November 1952, para. 21, p. 189 (Argentina), para. 39, p.191 (Guatemala) and, A/C.3/49/SR.6, 31 October 1994, para. 48, p. 9 (Honduras).

[61] A/C.3/50/SR. 5, 27 October 1995, para. 7, p. 4, and A/C.3/51/SR.26, 18 September 1997, para. 61, p. 13.

[62] A/C.3/SR. 399, 23 January 1952, para. 30, p. 314.

[63] A/C.3/SR.44, 14 November 1952, para. 40, p. 163.

[64] A/C.3/SR. 447, 18 November 1952, para. 8, p. 172 (the Netherlands).

[65] E.2256, Annex V, A/C.3/SR. 450, 20 November 1952, para. 5, p. 196.

[66] A/C.3/49/SR.8, 25 October 1994, para. 47, p. 11(India).

[67] A/PV. 976, para. 135, 4 Apara. 1961, p. 187 (Upper Volta).

[68] A/C.3/48/SR.22, 30 November 1993, para. 5, p. 3.

[69] A/PV. 2003, 7 December 1971, para. 34, p. 3. See also Indonesia's view, A/PV.2002, 7 December 1971, para. 82, p. 7.

[70] A/C.3/47/SR.9, 14 October 1992, para. 88, p. 18.

[71] A/C.3/47/SR.9, 27 October 1992, para. 69, p.15 (Cuba).

[72] A/C.3/49/SR.6, 31 October 1994, para. 22, p. 5 (Malaysia).

[73] A/C.3/48/SR.21, 26 November 1993, para. 25, p. 7.

[74] A/C.3/52/SR.29, I December 1997, para. 47-48, p. 6 (Cuba).

[75] A/C.3/50/SR. 4, 16 October 1995, para. 16, p. 5 (Cuba).

[76] A/C.3/47/SR.9, 27 October 1992, para. 88, p.18 (Cyprus).

[77] *Ibid*, para. 87, p.18.

[78] *Ibid.* para. 88, p.18.

[79] A/C.3/50/SR.7, 30 October 1995, para. 74, p. 17 (India).

[80] A/C.3/49/SR.8, 25 October 1994, para. 6, p. 3.

[81] AC.3/51/SR.28, 19 September 1997, para. 8, p. 3 (India).

[82] A/C.3/48/SR. 22, 3 November 1993, para. 4, p. 2 (Nepal).

[83] For example see GA Res. 47/82/, 89th Ple.mtg. 16 December 1992. GA Res. 49/151, 7 February 1995, para. 2 (on the right to self-determination).

[84] A/C.3/51/SR.26, 18 September 1997, para. 26, p. 7 (Sudan).

[85] A/C.3/48/SR.22, 30 November 1993, para. 38, p. 9 (Kenya); A/C.3/50/SR.7, 30 October 1995, para. 6, p. 3, (Nigeria), A/C.3/50/SR.56, 14 February 1995, para. 59, p. 13 (Egypt).

[86] A/C.3/48/SR.21, 26 November 1993, para. 25, p. 7 (Iraq).

[87] A/C.3/50/SR.8, 30 October 1995, para. 13, p. 5. See also A/C.3/51/SR. 26, 18 September 1997, para. 26, p. 7.

[88] A/PV. 2002, 7 December 1971, para. 68, p. 6. See also the statement made by the former President of Ghana, Mr.Nkrumah, in the event of the Congo crisis, A/PV.869, 23 September 1960, para. 26, p. 63.

[89] A/PV. 2003, 7 December 1971, para. 295, p. 27.

[90] A/C.3/49/SR.6, 31 October 1994, para. 66, p. 12 (Turkey), A/C.3/51/SR.28, 19 September 1997, para.13, p. 4 (the Ukraine), A/C.3/51/SR.26, 18 September 1997, para. 26, p. 7 (Sudan), A/C.3/51/SR.26, 18 September 1997, para.70, p.15 (Russian Federation), A/C.3/50/SR.4, 16 October 1995, para. 29, p. 7 (China), A/C.3/51/SR.28, 19 September 1997, para. 78, p. 16 (Myanmar), A/C.3/48/SR.9, 16 November 1993, para. 29, p. 7 (Trinidad and Tobago on behalf of the CARICOM); A/C.3/52/L.58 submitted by the Republic of Korea, the Sudan, Tajikistan, Macedonia and Turkey entitled 'the Draft Resolution on Human Rights and Terrorism' (this proposal was adopted by 97 votes to 0 with 57 abstentions), see A/C.3/48/SR.22, 30 November 1993, para. 24, p. 6 (Indonesia), and A/C.3/47/SR.4, 19 October 1992, para. 25, p. 7 (Australia).

[91] A/C.3/52/L.58, see A/C.3/52/SR.49, 9 December 1997, para. 32, p. 5.

[92] A/51/PV.18, p. 21 and A/C.3/47/SR.9, 27 October 1992, para. 96, p. 20 (Ecuador).

[93] A/C.3/50/SR.7, 11 October 1995, para. 43, p. 11.

[94] A/C.3/50/SR.4, 16 October 1995, para. 5, p. 3 (Spain on behalf of the EU).

[95] A/C.3/49/SR.8, 25 October 1994, para. 46, p. 11 (India).

[96] A/C.3/51/SR.28, 19 September 1997, para. 79, p. 16 (Myanmar).

[97] A/C.3/50/SR.5, 27 October 1995, para. 10, pp. 4-5 (Mauritania).

[98] A/C.3/51/SR.28, 19 September 1997, para. 2, p. 2 (Slovenia).

[99] A/C.3/50/SR.5, 27 October 1995, para. 13, p. 5 (Australia).

[100] A/C.3/48/SR.9, 16 November 1993, para. 13, p. 4 (the Russian Federation).

[101] A/C.3/48/SR.9, 16 November 1993, para. 12, p. 4. See further A/C.3/50/SR.4, 16 October 1995, para. 17, p. 5 (Cuba).

[102] A/C.3/51/SR.28, 19 September 1997, para. 15, p. 5 (the Ukraine).

[103] A/C.3/49/SR.6, 31 October 1994, para. 24, pp. 5-6 (Australia).

[104] A/C.3/51/SR.26, 18 September 1997, para.13, p. 4, and A/C.3/49/SR.6, 31 October 1994, para. 66, p.12.

[105] A.C.3/49/SR.8, 25 October 1994, para. 4, p. 3 (Czech Republic).

[106] A/C.3/49/SR.8, 25 October 1994, para. 10, p. 4 (Russian Federation).

[107] A/C.3/SR, 3, 17 October 1994. para. 42, p. 9.

[108] A/C.3/49/SR.3, 17 October 1994, para. 42, p. 9.

[109] A/C.3/50/SR.4, 16 October 1995, para. 5, p. 3.

[110] A/C.3/49/SR.6, 31 October 1994, para.24, pp. 6-6.

References

Ali, S. M. (1993), *The Federal States: Power, People and International War in South Asia*, Zed Books: London and New Jersey.

Buchheit, L. C. (1978), *Secession: The Legitimacy of Self-Determination*, Yale University Press: New Haven and London.

Crawford, J. (1997), *The Creation of States in International Law*, Oxford UP: Oxford.

Danilenko, G. M. (1994), 'The New Russian Constitution and International Law', 88 *AJIL*, pp. 451-470.

Dixon, M. and McCorquodale, D. (1991), *Cases and Materials in International Law*, Blackstone: London.

Duggard, J. (1997), 'International Law and the South African Constitution', 8 (1) *EJIL*, pp. 77-92.

Gaeta, P. (1996), 'The Armed Conflict in Chechnya before the Russian Constitutional Court', 7 (4) *EJIL*, pp. 563-570.

Gazzini, T. (1996), 'Consideration of the Conflict in Chechnya', 17 (3/4) *HRLJ*, pp. 93-105.

Hannikainen, L. (1998), 'Self-Determination and Autonomy in International Law', in M. Suksi (ed), *Autonomy: Applications and Implications*, Kluwer Law International: The Hague/London/Boston, pp. 79-95.

Hille, S. (1995), 'Mutual Recognition of Croatia and Serbia (+ Montenegro)', 6 (4) *EJIL*, pp. 598-611.

Ijalye, D. A. (1971), 'Was Biafra at Any Time a State in International Law', 65 *AJIL*, pp. 551-556.

Klabbers, J. and Lefeber, R. (1993), 'Africa: Lost Between Self-Determination and Uti Possidetis', in C. Brolmann, R. Lefeber, and M, Zieck (eds), *Peoples and Minorities in International Law*, Kluwer Law: Dordrecht Boston/ London, pp. 37-76.

McGoldrick, D. (1991), *The Human Rights Committee, Its Role in the Development of the International Covenant on Civil and Political Rights*, Clarendon Press: Oxford.

Maxwell, N. (1980), *India, the Nagas and the North-East*, cited in Ali, as above.

Mullerson, R. (1994), *International Law, Rights and Politics: Developments in Eastern Europe and the CIS, LSE* and Routledge, London and New York, pp. 58-91.

Nanda, Wed. P. (1981), 'Self-determination In International Law: The Tragic Tale of Two Cities- Islamabad (West Pakistan) and Dacca (East Pakistan)' 66 *AJIL*, pp. 321- 336.

Nayer, K. M. G. (1975), 'Self-determination Under International Law: Validity of Claims to Secede', 13 *Case W. Res. Jintl.L*, pp. 257- 280.

Roberts, M. (1978), 'Ethnic Conflict in Sri Lanka and Sinhalese Perspectives: Barriers to Accommodation', 12 (3) *MAS*, pp. 353- 375.

Schoenberg, H. O. (1976), 'Limits of Self-Determination', *IYHR*, pp. 91- 103.

Simpson, G. J. (1996), 'The Defusion of Sovereignty: Self-Determination in the Post-Colonial Age', in M. Sellers (ed), *The New World Order: The Sovereignty, Human Rights and the Self-Determination of Peoples*, BERG: Oxford Washington, DC, pp. 54-60.

White, R. C. A (1981), 'Self-determination: The Time for a Re-Assessment'? *NILR*, pp. 147- 170.

Conclusions

Both autonomy and secession, as has been seen, are controversial concepts. Although autonomy is increasingly being considered as a pragmatic political solution to ethnic conflicts and minorities' grievances, secession is not favourably seen either by the UN or other international organisations or by nation-States. Instead, protection of minorities and less controversial rights such as religious, cultural and linguistic rights are recommended as means of addressing issues relating to minorities.

In fact, the protection of minorities and promotion of their ethnic, cultural, religious and linguistic identities have become an integral part of the international protection of human rights.[1] Contemporary pluralist societies are required in good faith,[2] and "to ensure respect for the rights of minorities"[3] to take steps to ensure "the survival and continued development of the cultural, religious and social identity of the national minorities concerned"[4] by creating appropriate and favourable conditions,[5] if necessary, through legislative, judicial or administrative authorities.[6] In respect of indigenous groups, their traditional ways of life associated with the use of land resources, including such traditional activities as fishing or hunting and the right to live on reserves or native lands are now recognised,[7] as explained in chapter 5. Moreover their claim to participate, if they so choose, "at all levels of decision-making in matters which affect their rights, lives and destinies" is recognised as a legitimate right.[8]

As has been seen, minorities' rights moved beyond article 27 of the ICCPR as significant progress has been made in extending the scope of minority rights.[9] In Europe, specially, much progress has been achieved.[10] However, some academics and most minority groups, as examined in chapter 6, are of the view that the rights mentioned above are not sufficient to prevent ethnic conflicts in pluralist societies, nor do they meet the aspirations of minority groups. Most minority groups believe, as has been seen in chapter 8, that the ultimate solution to their problems is to have their own States.

At present, autonomy within existing nation-State structures is the maximum which international organisations and most States are prepared to allow. Even military action may not suffice to compel reluctant States to compromise their territorial integrity in favour of greater autonomy for minority groups as in the case of the present Balkan conflict (see chapter 11). But how far can a greater autonomy be used as a solution to minorities' problems? In cases where there is a danger to minorities' existence or minorities are not sufficiently represented in decision making and the political process, constitutional arrangements and international treaties involving autonomy may be an option that can be employed. Van Dyke, a prominent collectivist, sees autonomy as the "most prominent and widespread political arrangement" employed to provide a solution to ethnic conflicts in modern plural societies (Dyke,1980:5; Varady, 1997:49). According to Suksi (1997:99), a model similar to that of the Aaland autonomy could be used as a solution. A prominent federalist Elazar (1991: 34; see also Sohn, 1980:190; Brownlie, 1992:1-16) and the Special Rapporteur Eide[11] also agree that territorial subdivisions through federalism can be used to defuse ethnic tensions and to accommodate the genuine concerns and grievances of ethnic groups (see chapter 4.6). However, Eide argues that any autonomy model involving territorial subdivision has to be implemented carefully since such arrangements may endanger the State structure.[12]

Special Rapporteur Eide concludes that any decentralization of power in territorial terms should be "coupled with genuine pluralist democratic governance in each territorial unit".[13] As set out in chapters 7 and 12, from the States' point of view, the importance of internal and external territorial integrity is however a *sine qua non* in any territorial realignment in plural societies.[14] Territorial subdivisions, as Eide correctly points out, should not be designed merely on ethnocratic lines because they might be used by ethnocratic politicians for their own political ends as explained in chapters 6 and 8.[15] There are other valid reasons: a), autonomy based on ethnicity may be abused by minority groups to discriminate against other ethnic communities, b) it may also encourage segregation and exclusion rather than diversity, c) and this might give rise to more ethnic rivalries and polarization of ethnocratic movements (Stavenhagen, 1996:263), as in the case of Sri Lanka. Thus, autonomy may indirectly institutionalise separatism, creating ethnic enclaves in which the dominant ethnic group does not usually welcome outsiders or aliens and though the latter resides in the same territory. Steiner (1991:1551) says such models "resemble more a museum of social and cultural antiquities than any human rights ideals". Steiner (at 1557) therefore argues that autonomy is the least bad solution for preventing minority groups from seeking separation.

It is difficult to determine whether autonomous arrangements can be used as a panacea for modern ethnic conflicts. Although in some countries, for instance, South Tyrol in Italy and the Basque and the Catalan provinces in Spain,[16] a decentralization of power to the regions or provinces has been able to defuse ethnic tensions to a certain extent, it is too early to say that they can be seen as examples which can be experimented with elsewhere. On the other hand, autonomy may not be able to appease certain minority groups, as is evident from the Kosovo disputes and secessionist movements in Quebec. The behaviour of the latter is a classic case in point. Extensive autonomous power for the Provincial government in Quebec has been significantly enhanced in recent times. Yet, as set out in brief, a significant proportion of Quebecois is still not satisfied with this. Their perception is that only independence will provide an environment within which they can flourish as a new nation.

The success of autonomous models hinges upon the willingness of the parties to back them fully. "Even when autonomy appears to function satisfactorily for some time, a cleavage may occur when suddenly - due to a change in the psychological climate - the impulse for independence becomes prevalent" (Dinstein, 1992:295). When autonomous regions spin out of control of the federal or central government it is not easy to bring them within the ambit of the centre again, as was the case with the Republics of the former USSR (see chapter 7.1). Where autonomous arrangements have been imposed upon the parties by force or without the consent of the parties involved, such arrangements may not work in the long run. The classic example is that of the Eritrean autonomy during 1952-62 which at the time was hailed as a "Swiss federation adapted to an African absolute monarchy". The experiment failed miserably, creating "one of Africa's longest wars, which killed tens of thousands of combatants and civilians and created several hundreds of thousands of refugees".[17] The only outcome of this experiment was that the autonomous model awakened new ethnic particularism which later resulted in a long drawn-out-war ultimately breaking up Ethiopia (see chapter 7.1).[18]

Autonomy may not work where an effective alliance between democracy and national feelings cannot be found. In such cases different ethnic groups may try to achieve their aspirations by moving in different directions at the expense of national unity. Centuries old rivalries and competing cultures may also undermine any political rearrangements involving autonomy as in the case of in Kosovo, Chechnya and Sri Lanka. It is well known how autonomy models have failed tragically in Lebanon and Cyprus to meet the needs of different minority groups (Steiner,

1991:1542). The strong presence of centrifugal forces is not fertile ground for any experiment using autonomy as a device to defuse ethnic tensions.

Another solution often mentioned is that of secession. However, as explained in chapter 10, secession is not a recognised legal concept in international law. It is not considered as a practical and logical solution to contemporary ethnic conflicts. In general, States try to preserve the *status quo* at whatever cost, as is evident in the current crisis in the Balkan and the Caucasus and in many other similar conflicts in Asia, Africa and Latin America. Continued Indo-Pakistan border clashes and the armed conflicts between Eritrea and Ethiopia (see chapter 1.6) demonstrate that secession rather than solving ethnic conflicts may be a trigger for persistent clashes between the parties where secession is accompanied by acrimony. It seems that the majority of Ethiopians are not prepared to forget the fact that it was Eritrea that broke up Greater Ethiopia. On the other hand, Eritreans are resentful of Ethiopia for having held Eritrea in a colonial situation for decades. Thus, instead of good-will, lingering bitterness and a sense of betrayal may continue to produce resentments. It is not surprising therefore that the majority opinion, both amongst States and scholars, as has been seen in chapters 12 and 9 respectively, is that secession should not be applied as a solution to modern ethnic conflicts. Otherwise, "the result would be the fragmenting of states and the multiplication of frontiers and barriers among nations" (Cassese, 1981:93). Cristescu warns that no State, whether new or old, can consider itself free from this danger if secession is recognised as a legal right.[19] He stresses that "even those states, which are ethnically the most homogeneous, may find themselves the object of covetousness or of designs to dismember them".[20] Moreover, if secession is legally recognised as a solution to ethnic conflict, it may encourage disharmony and mistrust amongst ethnic groups. From the standpoint of States, the outcome of such a scenario could be disastrous for the stability of modern plural societies. As argued by many States (see chapters 12.5 and 12.6), no one can turn a blind eye to a possible scenario of total chaos and absolute anarchy. Any attempt to legitimize these tendencies, wrote Higgins, by the misapplication of legal terms runs the risk of harming the very values that international law is meant to promote (Higgins, 1992).

Some critics also point to the social and economic cost arising from such movements. Cobban (1944) noted that any attempt to divide the world into micro-States would result only in chaos. Consequently, in his view, it would increase internal and international tensions. He stated (at 259) that the adoption of a policy that all nations and ethnic groups shall have their own States would create the maddest balkanisation of the whole world. Such illogical and dangerous endeavours, in the view of former Secretary-General Ghali, would be an obstacle to peace, security and economic well-being for all.[21] Solutions can only be found within democratic institutions that respect the diversities of sub-groups, in particular, ethnic, religious and linguistic minorities.

However, we should not forget the fact that solutions to human frailties are difficult to find. Having divided into groups, human beings fight for land, resources, and power. In the process enormous barriers have been erected between *them and us*. Don't we all have our own heroes and martyrs who laid down their lives for the cause? Isn't it our historic obligation to carry on what our forefathers started with so much sacrifice and bloodshed? These are the prejudices that are woven into us from birth. These are the fundamentals that are working against any sensible solution to ethnic conflicts. Can we disassociate ourselves from such prejudices? Unfortunately it is not so easy. These prejudices are transferred from generation to generation.

Any solutions to these conflicts can only be temporary. Parties to the conflicts, exploring all the avenues ultimately come to the same differences and prejudices. Capitalism, Marxism, socialism and liberal democracy each using its different methods have tried and still try to find solutions to ethnic conflicts. Have they yet succeeded or will they ever succeed? Can international and human rights jurists find any long-term pragmatic solutions where others have so far failed? Only subjective answers can be given. It is submitted that reasonable short-term solutions can be found within advanced human rights mechanisms. Better understanding between groups and willingness to live in a pluralist structure respecting each other's culture and diversity might be ideal means of overcoming prejudices. Until we are prepared to accept the most basic principle that every individual shall have an indisputable right to live as he or she likes without harming the society that they form a part of, tribal conflicts will not cease or disappear. Until we accept the fact that diversity is the most beautiful part of the mosaic of contemporary plural societies, there will be no harmony or peace, only conflicts.

Notes

[1] See for example, The Framework Convention for the Protection of National Minorities, 1995; the preamble of the UN Declaration on Minorities, 1992.
[2] Article 2, the Framework Convention, *ibid.* 1995.

[3] The Badinter Committee, Opinion no.2, 30 *ILM* 1494 [1992] p. 1498.

[4] General Comment on Article 27 of the ICCPR/ minority rights, no. 23/50, adopted by the Human Rights Committee under article 40, para. 4 of the ICCPARA. See the full text, 15 (4-6) *HRLJ* 1994, pp. 234-236. See Article 2 of the UN Declaration on Minorities 1992.

[5] Article 4 (2) of the Framework Convention 1995, as above; Articles 4 (1) (2), 16, 28 and 37 of the Draft UN Declaration on Indigenous Peoples 1994.

[6] Article 1 (2) of the UN Declaration on Minorities 1992.

[7] See Articles 12, 13 and 14 of the Draft UN Declaration on Indigenous Peoples 1994. See Daes, Erica-Irene (1997), *Protection of the Heritage of Indigenous People*, UN: New York and Geneva.

[8] Articles 20 and 21, *ibid.*

[9] Rights promoted by Article 27 of the ICCPR have appeared in many other subsequent declarations or conventions. See Articles 11 (1) (2) (3), 12 (1) (2), 14 (1) (2) of the Framework Convention for the Protection of National Minorities 1995; Articles 2, 4 (2) (4) of the UN Declaration on Minorities 1992; the European Charter for Regional or Minority Languages 1992; see also Articles 12 (culture), 13 (religious rights), 14 (language) of the Declaration of Indigenous Peoples 1994, and Principle 67 of the Declaration on the Principles of International Cultural Corporation (UNESCO), 1966, reprinted in *Erica-Irene Daes*, above, pp. 28-29.

[10] See the Charter for Regional or Minority languages 1992 and the Framework Convention for the Protection of National Minorities 1995.

[11] *Possible Ways and Means of Facilitating the Peaceful and Constructive Solution of Problems involving Minorities*, UN Doc. E/CN.4/Sub.2/1993 34, 10 August 1993, para. 247, p. 54.

[12] *Ibid.* para. 247. p. 54.

[13] *Ibid.* para. 253, p. 54.

[14] *Ibid.* para. 246, p. 53.

[15] *Ibid.* para. 251, p. 54.

[16] Spanish autonomous arrangements are seen as an example of 'extraordinary success' by some. See Elazar, D. (1991), *Federal Systems of the World: A Handbook of Federal, Confederal and Autonomy Arrangements*, Longman: Essex, p. viii.

[17] Department of Public Information (1996), *The United Nations and the Independence of Eritrea*, UN: New York, p. 3.

[18] The Organization of African Unity Observer Mission on 26 of April 1993 gave its approval for the independent Eritrea. See details *ibid.* p. 295.

[19] The Right to Self-Determination: Historical and Current Development on the Basis of the United Nations Instruments, UN Doc. E/CN.4/Sub.2/204/Rev.1, para. 275, p. 40.

[20] *Ibid.* p.31.

[21] Agenda for Peace, GA Sec Re, A/47/277, para. 11; S/24111, 17 June 1992.

References

Brownlie, I. (1992), 'The Rights of Peoples in Modern International Law', in J. Crawford (ed), *The Rights of Peoples,* Clarendon Press: Oxford, pp. 1-16.

Cassese, A. (1981), 'The Self-Determination of Peoples', in L. Henkin (ed), *The International Bill of Rights*, Colombia UP: New York, p. 93.

Cobban, A. (1944), *The Nation State and National Self-Determination*, Oxford UP: London/New York.

Dinstein, Y. (1992), 'Autonomy', in Y. Dinstein, and M. Tabory (eds), *The Protection of Minorities and Human Rights*, Kluwer Academic: Dordrecht, pp. 291- 303.

Dyke, V. V. (1980), 'The Cultural Rights of Peoples', 2 *Universal Human Rights*, p. 5.

Elazar, D. (1991), *Federal Systems of the World: A Handbook of Federal, Confederal and Autonomy Arrangements*, Longman Group: London.

Higgins, R. (1992, Autumn), 'Minorities, Secession and Self-Determination', *Justice*, pp. 1-3.

Sohn, L. B. (1980), 'The Concept of Autonomy in International Law and the Practice of the United Nations', 15 (2*) ILR*, pp. 180-190.

Stavenhagen, R. (1996), *Ethnic Conflicts and the Nation State*, Macmillan Press in Association with UNRISD: London.

Steiner, J. C. (1991), 'Ideals and Counter-Ideals in the Struggle Over Autonomy Regimes for Minorities', 66 *Notre Dame LR*, pp. 1539-1559.

Suksi, M. (1997), 'The Constitutional Setting of the Island Islands Compared', in L. Hannikainen, and F. Horn (eds), *Autonomy and Demilitarisation in International Law: The Aaland Islands in a Changing Europe*, Kluwer Law International: The Hague/London/Boston, pp. 99- 129

Varady, T. (1997), 'Minorities, Majorities, Law and Ethnicity: Reflections on the Yugoslav Case', 19 (1) *HRQ*, pp. 9-54.

Index

Aaland Islands, 97, 115, 185, 255
Abkhazia, 30, 182, 183, 299
Aboriginal peoples, 135
Aboriginal rights, 135
Aceh region, 26, 168, 210
Affirmative action, 162
African Charter on Human and
Peoples Rights, 79, 86
Afrikaaner Peoples' State, 164
Aggression, 273
Alaskan secessionists, 222
Albania, 31, 181, 213, 312
Alfredsson, 48, 49, 77, 88, 101, 138,
141, 145, 232, 273
All peoples, 79, 81, 84, 260, 313
Anarchy, 320, 334
Angola, 220
Arab Charter on Human Rights, 79
Armenians, 222, 299
Article 1 of the ICCPR, 146, 148, 268,
316
Article 27 of the ICCPR, 2, 23, 24, 50,
54, 66, 88, 96, 136, 145, 269, 328
Asam, 183, 184
Asheville Declaration, 211
Assimilation, 160
Atlantic Charter, 11
Autonomous arrangements, 106
Autonomous enclaves, 159
Azcarate, 5, 7, 9, 18, 21
Azerbaijan, 210, 213, 299
Azeri peoples, 299

Badinter Committee, 273, 276,
Balkanization, 28, 191
Balkan conflicts, 275
Baltic States, 239, 249
Bangladesh, 161, 215, 223, 268,
Barcelona Summit (1992), 194

Basque Country, 166, 181, 223,
333
Belgrade, 211
Bengali Hindus, 184
Biafra, 2, 215, 290, 302, 315
Blood tribe, 139
Bodoland, 184
Bodoland Liberation Tigers, 184
Bosnia-Herzegovina, 32, 33, 77,
161, 170, 183, 210, 213, 220,
247, 250, 279, 297
Bosnian Serbs, 162
Brazil, 89, 196, 197, 317
Brownlie, 131, 274, 329
Buchheit, 208, 232, 248, 290
Bulgaria, 33, 62
Burundi, 220

Cairo Declaration, 274
Capotorti Report, 5, 13, 18, 24,
46, 48, 58, 60, 63
Cardiff Declaration, 295
Cassese, 77, 87, 88, 131, 216,
266, 273, 331
Catalans, 104, 168, 171, 212
Caucasus, 2, 25, 211, 299
Cayuga case, 136
Ceylon, 318
Charter of Paris, 278
Chechnya, 32, 213, 300, 330
Chittagong Hill Tracks, 161
Citizen Band Potawatomi tribe,
140
Cobban, 104, 166, 216, 232, 331
Colonial Declaration, 147, 292
Commission on Human Rights, 48,
52, 53, 54, 55, 79, 82, 301
Congo, 289
Congress of minorities, 9

Consociational democracy, 130, 144
Council of Europe, 21, 57, 61, 62, 66, 276
Crawford, 77, 106, 245, 256, 315
Crimean Tartars, 165
Croatia, 33, 162, 168, 182, 212, 239, 247, 279
CSCE, 62, 66, 102, 127, 192, 276,
Cultural autonomy, 103, 104, 135 146, 190, 197
Cultural groups, 103
Cultural home rule, 106
Cultural rights, 96, 163, 191, 331
Cyprus, 301, 315, 318, 330

Dagestan, 213
Darjeeling Gurkha Hill Council, 224
Dayton Peace Accord, 185
Declaration on Friendly Relations, 80, 86, 262, 267
Democracy, 249
Democratic governance, 127, 233
Deschenes, 55, 56
Dinstein, 24, 98, 100, 104, 292
Discrimination, 21, 22, 31, 134, 142, 165
Divided sovereignty, 108, 110
Draft UN Declaration on Indigenous Peoples, 100, 142
Dravidastan, 213
Dumbarton Oaks proposal, 12, 81
Dyke, 50, 219, 256, 329

East Pakistan, 292, 320
East Timor, 30, 105, 107, 210, 235, 247
East Timor case, 235
Economic and Social Council, 17, 18, 51, 53, 54, 59, 83, 147, 292
ECHR, 21, 61, 66, 192
Eide, 19, 24, 46, 50, 85, 88, 98, 103, 105, 143, 216, 243, 264
EPRLF, 183
Eritrea, 78, 171, 210, 249, 331
Eritrean autonomy, 97, 182

Ermacora, 24, 46, 49, 50, 53, 65
Estonia, 186, 189
ETA, 181, 212, 218, 221
Ethiopia, 180, 210, 220, 249
Ethnicity, 3, 27, 64, 185, 188
Ethnic cleansing, 31, 34
Ethnic conflicts, 7, 25, 30, 133, 188, 215
Ethnic groups, 66, 163, 209, 232
Ethnic minorities, 2, 23, 57, 63, 66, 79, 96
Ethnic violence, 1, 29, 296
Ethnocentrism, 31, 32, 245
Ethnonaionalism, 34
Every people, 76
External self-determination, 31, 240

Faeroe Islands, 97, 106, 311
Federalism, 96, 112, 113, 330
Federal government, 99
Fifteen Powers' Resolution, 84
Forty-Three-Power Resolution, 263

Genocide, 34
Ghali, 25, 26, 29, 96, 213, 332
Good Friday Agreement, 105
Greater autonomy, 165, 180, 210
Greater Serbia, 161
Greco-Bulgarian communities, 63
Greenland, 98, 106, 169, 311
Gunasekara, 161
Gurkhaland, 227
Gypsies, 247

Hannum, 48, 65, 87, 97, 105, 137, 159, 162, 239, 244, 258, 267, 298
Harris Batasuna, 181
Helsinki Final Act, 79, 86, 87, 89, 126, 130, 277
Heyking, 6, 9, 97, 125
Higgins, 77, 250, 244, 289
Hindus, 184
Home rule, 100
HRC, 24, 145, 148, 269

Humphrey, 2, 18, 128, 270
Hungary, 189

ICTY, 33, 34, 162
ILO Convention (no. 169), 140, 145
India, 59, 84, 169, 183, 223, 316
Indian sub-continent, 189
Indian Tamils, 184
Indigenous peoples, 96, 100, 136, 139, 141, 145, 195
Indonesia, 190, 210
Indo-Pakistan borders, 331
Indo-Sri Lanka Accord, 183, 223
Inhabitants, 16, 78, 187
Internal self-determination, 31, 145
IRA, 218
Irian Jaya, 211
Irredentism, 212
Irredentists, 84

Jennings, 78
Jewish minorities, 6

Karelia, 182
Kasai and Shaba, 167
Katanga, 289, 315, 318
Kenya, 181, 192, 199
Khalistan, 165
Kitok, 136, 149
KLA, 161, 217, 294
Kofi Anan, 297
Komarno proposal, 163
Kosovar Albanians, 29, 89, 161, 181, 247, 293
Kosovo, 26, 30, 71, 89, 107, 211, 217, 247, 293
Krajina, 297
Kurds, 6, 32, 166, 206
Kurdistan, 98, 191
Kurdish Workers Party, 218, 315
Kwazulu Kingdom, 161

Lapidoth, 98, 100, 103, 107, 170
League Covenant, 5

League of Nations, 5, 7, 10, 13, 19, 21, 32, 63, 97
Lebanon, 330
Liechtenstein, 24, 186, 189, 309
Liberation movements, 215, 317
Light Houses Case, 108
Lijphart, 3, 130
Local autonomy, 101
Lozi homeland, 217
LTTE, 161, 183, 215, 217
162, 170, 184, 218, 219
Lubicon Lake Band, 136, 137, 147, 148, 269, 271

Macedonia, 163, 180, 213
Macedonian Albanians, 165
Malaysia, 190
Maoris, 137
Marshall Islands, 166
McGoldrick, 28, 61, 77, 88, 313
Mello-Franco Thesis, 7
Memel territory, 97, 108, 185
Micro-States, 250
Mikmaq Tribal Society, 146, 147
Millets, 3, 104
Minority rights, 99, 129, 159, 212
Minority rights campaigners, 161
Minority Schools in Albania, 104
Minorities treaties, 97
MISURASTA, 137
Mizoram, 223
Moynihan, 225, 247
Mullerson, 26, 27, 162, 180, 182, 206, 211, 244, 294, 310
Multiculturalism, 127
Multiethnic polities, 159, 209
Myanmar, 225

Nagaland, 183, 226
Nagas, 223, 242, 309
Nagorny Karabakh, 26, 116, 211, 221, 299
Nanda, 240, 242, 248, 260, 266, 290

Nationalism, 4, 166
National minorities, 4, 49, 56, 66, 193
National self-determination, 233
Nations, 76, 77, 81, 85, 258
Nation-States, 66, 82, 108, 134, 150, 159, 210, 220, 231
Nation-State system, 167, 186
NATO, 294
Nepal, 186, 190, 199
Nicaragua, 196, 270
Nigeria, 27, 189, 192, 207, 260, 274, 290
Non-discrimination, 21, 64, 187
Non-self-governing territories, 78, 81, 83, 257, 265, 316
Northern Ireland, 218
Nowak, 2, 24, 47, 50, 54, 64

OAU, 179, 274
OAS, 179
Oblast, 106, 187
Ogoni peoples, 169
Okruga, 106
Ominayak, 136, 147
Oppenheim, 108, 109, 179
Oppressed peoples, 79, 86
OSCE, 19, 49, 66, 192, 199, 275

Pakistan, 188, 207, 223
Pandora's box, 188, 318
Pathans, 225
Peoples, 15, 76, 85, 136, 231, 238, 240, 259, 265, 293, 313
Peoples' rights, 238
Plural societies, 1, 3, 29, 97
Post-modern tribal-State, 208
Preah Vhear, 275
Prior sovereignty, 112
Protectorate, 295, 298
Punjab, 165, 206

Quebec, 139, 222, 330
Queer nation, 2

Race, 64
Racial groups, 30, 85, 161
Racial minorities, 63, 66
Refugees, 29
Re Secession of Quebec, 256
Remedial secession, 240
Representative democracy, 319
Republika Srpska, 220, 297
Right to secession, 241
Russian Federation, 300
Romania, 33
Rwanda, 29, 30, 220

San Francisco Conference, 82, 313
Sandra Lovelace, 136
Saudi Arabia, 270, 310
Secession, 78, 206
Secessionist movements, 17, 211, 221
Self-determination, 76, 81, 138, 190
Self-government, 78, 97, 100, 129, 115, 138, 140, 186, 234
Senegal, 180, 243
Separatism, 192, 212
Separatist movements, 209
Serbs, 32, 182
Serbia, 108, 250, 280
Shared-sovereignty, 96, 117, 125,
Sikhs, 32
Sinhalese, 28, 180
Six-Nations Contact Group, 106, 295
Slovakia, 136, 187
Slovenia, 182, 187, 191, 199, 239, 279, 295
Sohn, 18, 24, 49, 50, 97,
Somalia, 213
Somaliland, 221
Sovereignty, 19, 108, 110
South Tyrol, 11, 98, 165, 181, 271
Soyinka, 29, 110, 162, 207
Sparrow case, 136

Sri Lanka, 32, 107, 116, 137, 161, 165, 215, 223
Sub-Commission on Minorities, 53
Sudan, 30, 181, 221
Susksi, 98, 102, 105, 115, 129, 132, 329

Tajikistan, 280, 301
Tamils, 28, 168, 212, 223
Tamil Eelam, 183, 185
Tanzania, 290
Tartastan, 188, 221, 301, 310
Territorial autonomy, 160
Territorial integrity, 31, 111, 147, 191, 237, 240, 245, 256, 261
Thornberry, 2, 26, 47, 54, 86, 96, 128, 216, 232, 263
Tomuschat, 126, 144, 255
Tribal groups, 101, 135, 183
Tribalism, 308
Tribal-State, 206, 220, 247, 249
Tribal-wars, 29
Tunesia, 315

Udayachat, 184
UDHR, 16, 19, 23, 126, 270
Uganda, 312
UN Charter, 15, 19, 76, 79, 80, 82, 191, 236, 257
UN Declaration on minorities, 96, 133, 145
UNESCO, 20
Upper Silesia, 164, 165, 197
USSR, 163, 209, 232, 272
U Thant, 11, 256, 291
Uti possidetis juris, 273, 274

Vance-Owen Peace Plan, 298
Veddhas, 137
Venezuela, 196
Vienna World Conference on Human Rights (1993), 264
Vojvodina, 293

Western Sahara, 235, 279
Whispering Pines Indian Band, 271

Yugoslavia, 30, 239, 275, 297